YOUR
MAGIC POWER
TO BE RICH!

Jeremy P. Tarcher/Penguin

a member of

Penguin Group (USA) Inc.

New York

YOUR MAGIC POWER TO BE RICH!

FEATURING

THINK AND GROW RICH
Revised and Updated by Arthur R. Pell, Ph.D.

THE MAGIC LADDER TO SUCCESS
Revised and Updated by Patricia G. Horan

THE MASTER-KEY TO RICHES
Revised and Updated by Patricia G. Horan

NAPOLEON HILL

Jeremy P. Tarcher/Penguin
Published by the Penguin Group
Penguin Group (USA) Inc., 375 Hudson Street, New York, NY 10014, USA
Penguin Group (Canada), 90 Eglinton Avenue East, Suite 700, Toronto, Ontario M4P 2Y3, Canada
(a division of Pearson Penguin Canada Inc.)
Penguin Books Ltd, 80 Strand, London WC2R 0RL, England
Penguin Ireland, 25 St Stephen's Green, Dublin 2, Ireland (a division of Penguin Books Ltd)
Penguin Group (Australia), 250 Camberwell Road, Camberwell, Victoria 3124, Australia (a division of Pearson Australia Group Pty Ltd)
Penguin Books India Pvt Ltd, 11 Community Centre, Panchsheel Park, New Delhi–110 017, India
Penguin Group (NZ), 67 Apollo Drive, Rosedale, North Shore 0745, Auckland, New Zealand (a division of Pearson New Zealand Ltd)
Penguin Books (South Africa) (Pty) Ltd, 24 Sturdee Avenue, Rosebank, Johannesburg 2196, South Africa

Penguin Books Ltd, Registered Offices: 80 Strand, London WC2R 0RL, England

Think and Grow Rich originally published in 1937; revised edition first published in the United Kingdom in 2004 by Vermillion;
first Tarcher edition published 2005
The Magic Ladder to Success originally published in 1930; revised Tarcher edition published 2007
The Master-Key to Riches originally published in 1945; revised Tarcher edition published 2007

Think and Grow Rich © 2003, 2005 by JMW Group, Inc. First published in 1937.
The Master-Key to Riches © 2007 by JMW Group, Inc. First published in 1945.
The Magic Ladder to Success © 2007 by JMW Group, Inc. First published in 1930.

Most Tarcher/Penguin books are available at special quantity discounts for bulk purchase for sales promotions, premiums, fund-raising, and
educational needs. Special books or book excerpts also can be created to fit specific needs.
For details, write Penguin Group (USA) Inc. Special Markets, 375 Hudson Street, New York, NY 10014.

Library of Congress Control Number: 2007925842
ISBN 978-1-58542-555-6

Printed in the United States of America
1 3 5 7 9 10 8 6 4 2

While the authors have made every effort to provide accurate telephone numbers and Internet addresses at the time of publication, neither the
publisher nor the authors assume any responsibility for errors, or for changes that occur after publication. Further, the publisher does not have
any control over and does not assume any responsibility for author or third-party websites or their content.

CONTENTS

THINK AND GROW RICH

THE MAGIC LADDER TO SUCCESS

THE MASTER-KEY TO RICHES

THINK AND
GROW RICH

Revised and Updated by
Arthur R. Pell, Ph.D.

AUTHOR'S PREFACE
TO THE ORIGINAL EDITION

Every chapter of this book mentions the moneymaking secret that has made fortunes for more than 500 exceedingly wealthy people whom I have carefully analyzed over a long period of years.

The secret was brought to my attention more than a quarter of a century ago by Andrew Carnegie. The canny, lovable old Scotsman carelessly tossed it into my mind when I was but a boy. Then he sat back in his chair, with a merry twinkle in his eye, and watched carefully to see if I had brains enough to understand the full significance of what he had said to me.

When he saw that I had grasped the idea, he asked if I would be willing to spend twenty years or more preparing myself to take it to the world, to men and women who, without the secret, might go through life as failures. I said I would, and with Mr. Carnegie's cooperation, I have kept my promise.

This book contains the secret, which has been put to a practical test by thousands of people from almost every walk of life. It was Mr. Carnegie's idea that the magic formula, which gave him a stupendous fortune, ought to be placed within reach of people who do not have time to investigate how people make money. He hoped that I might test and demonstrate the soundness of the formula through the experience of men and women in every calling. He believed the formula should be taught in all schools and colleges, and expressed the opinion that if it was properly taught it would so revolutionize the entire educational system that the time spent in school could be reduced to less than half.

His experience with Charles M. Schwab (see page 48), and other young men of Mr. Schwab's type, convinced Mr. Carnegie that much of what is taught in schools is of no value whatsoever in connection with the business of earning a living or accumulating riches. He arrived at this decision having taken into his business one young man after another, many with little schooling, and developed in them rare leadership by coaching them in the use of this formula. Moreover, his coaching made fortunes for every one of them who followed his instructions.

In the chapter on Faith, you will read the astounding story of how the formula was applied to the organization of the giant United States Steel Corporation. It was conceived and carried out by one of the young men through whom Mr. Carnegie proved that his formula will work for all who are ready for it. This single application of the secret by that young man—Charles M. Schwab—made him a huge fortune in both money and *opportunity*. Roughly speaking, this particular application of the formula was worth $600 million.

These facts—and they are facts well known to almost everyone who knew Mr. Carnegie—give you a fair idea of what the reading of this book may bring to you, provided you *know what you want.*

Even before it had undergone twenty years of practical testing, the secret was passed on to more than 100,000 men and women who have used it for their personal benefit, as Mr. Carnegie planned that they should. Some have made fortunes with it. Others have used it successfully in creating harmony in their homes.

The secret to which I refer has been mentioned no fewer than a hundred times throughout this book. It has not been directly named, for it seems to work more successfully when it is merely uncovered and left in sight, where *those who are ready* and *searching for it* may pick it up. That is why Mr. Carnegie tossed it to me so quietly, without giving me its specific name.

If you are *ready* to put it to use, you will recognize this secret at least once in every chapter. I wish I could tell you how you will know if you are ready, but that would deprive you of much of the benefit you will receive when you make the discovery in your own way.

While this book was being written, my own son, who was then finishing the last year of his college work, picked up the manuscript of Chapter 2, read it, and discovered the secret for himself. He used the information so effectively that he went directly into a responsible position at a starting salary greater than the average man ever earns. His story has been briefly described in Chapter 2. When you read it, perhaps you will dismiss any feeling you may have had at the beginning of the book that it promised too much. And, too, if you have ever been discouraged, if you have had difficulties to surmount which took the very soul out of you, if you have tried and failed, if you were ever handicapped by illness or physical affliction, this story of my son's discovery and use of the Carnegie formula may prove to be the oasis in the Desert of Lost Hope for which you have been searching.

This secret was extensively used by President Woodrow Wilson, during World War I. It was passed on to every soldier who fought in the war, carefully wrapped in the training received before going to the front. President Wilson told me it was a strong factor in raising the funds needed for the war.

Early in the twentieth century, Manuel L. Quezon (then resident commissioner of the

Philippines) was inspired by the secret to gain freedom for his people, and went on to lead them as its first president.

A peculiar thing about this secret is that those who acquire it and use it find themselves literally swept on to success with but little effort, and they never again submit to failure! If you doubt this, study the names and records of those who have used it, wherever they have been mentioned, and be convinced.

There is no such thing as SOMETHING FOR NOTHING!

The secret to which I refer cannot be had without a price, although the price is far less than its value. Those who are not intentionally searching for it cannot have it at any price. It cannot be given away; it cannot be purchased for money, because it comes in two parts. One part is already in possession of those who are ready for it.

The secret serves equally well all who are ready for it. Education has nothing to do with it. Long before I was born, the secret had found its way into the possession of Thomas A. Edison, and he used it so intelligently that he became the world's leading inventor, although he had but three months of schooling.

The secret was passed on to a business associate of Mr. Edison's. He used it so effectively that although he was then making only $12,000 a year, he accumulated a great fortune, and retired from active business while still a young man. You will find his story at the beginning of the first chapter. It should convince you that riches are not beyond your reach, that you can still be what you wish to be, that money, fame, recognition, and happiness can be had by all who are ready and determined to have these blessings.

How do I know these things? You should have the answer before you finish this book. You may find it in the very first chapter, or on the last page.

While I was performing the twenty-year task of research, which I had undertaken at Mr. Carnegie's request, I analyzed hundreds of well-known men, many of whom admitted that they had accumulated their vast fortunes through the aid of the Carnegie secret. Among these men were:

Henry Ford
Theodore Roosevelt
William Wrigley Jr.
John Wanamaker
James J. Hill
Wilbur Wright

William Jennings Bryan
Woodrow Wilson
William Howard Taft
Elbert H. Gary
King Gillette
Alexander Graham Bell
John D. Rockefeller
Thomas A. Edison
F. W. Woolworth
Clarence Darrow

These names represent but a small fraction of the hundreds of well-known Americans whose achievements, financially and otherwise, prove that those who understand and apply the Carnegie secret reach high stations in life. All the people I have known who have been inspired to use the secret have achieved noteworthy success in their chosen calling. I have never known any person to distinguish himself, or to accumulate riches of any consequence, without possession of the secret. From these two facts I draw the conclusion that the secret is more important, as a part of the knowledge essential for self-determination, than anything one receives through what is popularly known as "education."

What is *education,* anyway? As far as schooling is concerned, many of these men had very little. John Wanamaker once told me that what little schooling he had he acquired in very much the same manner as a locomotive takes on water, by "scooping it up as it runs." Henry Ford never reached high school, let alone college. I am not attempting to minimize the value of schooling, but I am trying to express my earnest belief that those who master and apply the secret will reach high stations, accumulate riches, and bargain with life on their own terms, even if their schooling has been meager.

Somewhere, as you read, the secret to which I refer will jump from the page and stand boldly before you, *if you are ready for it!* When it appears, you will recognize it. Whether you receive the sign in the first or the last chapter, stop for a moment when it presents itself and raise your glass to toast your epiphany.

Chapter 1 tells the story of my very dear friend who has generously acknowledged having seen the mystic sign, and whose business achievements are evidence enough that he turned down a glass. As you read his story, and the others, remember that they deal with the important problems of life, such as all people experience, the problems arising from one's endeavor to earn a living; to find hope, courage, contentment, and peace of mind; to accumulate riches and to enjoy freedom of body and spirit.

Remember, too, as you go through the book that it deals with facts and not with fiction. Its purpose is to convey a great universal truth through which all who are *ready* may learn, not only *what to do* but also *how to do it*, and receive *the needed stimulus to make a start*.

As a final word of preparation, may I offer one brief suggestion that may provide a clue to recognizing the Carnegie secret. It is this: *All achievement, all earned riches have their beginning in an idea!* If you are ready for the secret, you already possess one half of it; therefore you will readily recognize the other half the moment it reaches your mind.

—NAPOLEON HILL
1937

PREFACE TO THE CURRENT EDITION

When *Think and Grow Rich* was published in 1937, it was acclaimed as one of the great inspirational books of its time. Together with Dale Carnegie's *How to Win Friends and Influence People* and Norman Vincent Peale's *The Power of Positive Thinking,* it became essential reading for men and women who pursued success in their lives and careers.

Over 15 million copies of this book have been sold. It became a road map for many millions of people to escape the poverty of the Depression era and gain prosperity for themselves, their families, and in many cases, their employees.

Who was Napoleon Hill and what was the source of his philosophy? Napoleon Hill was born into a poor family in 1883 in a one-room cabin in rural Virginia. He was orphaned at the age of twelve and brought up by relatives. Overcoming poverty and his rebellious nature, he struggled to obtain an education and developed into one of the pragmatic geniuses of his time.

At age thirteen, he started his writing career as a stringer for small-town newspapers—a reporter who wrote items and stories about happenings in his area for pennies a line. Perhaps because of his own struggle to overcome poverty, he became obsessed with why people fail to achieve true financial success and happiness in their lives.

To earn a living he chose to pursue careers in both law and journalism. His early career as a reporter helped finance his way through law school. His big break came when he was given an assignment to write a series of success stories of famous men.

One of the men he interviewed for this series was Andrew Carnegie, the world-renowned steel magnate. Mr. Carnegie was so impressed by the young journalist that he gave him a commission that would dominate the next twenty-five years of Hill's life. The project was to interview over 500 millionaires to find a success formula that could be used by the average person.

The interviewees included the greatest and wealthiest men of the era. Among them were Thomas Edison, Alexander Graham Bell, Henry Ford, Charles M. Schwab, Theodore Roosevelt, William Wrigley Jr., John Wanamaker, William Jennings Bryan, George Eastman, Woodrow Wilson, William H. Taft, John D. Rockefeller, F. W. Woolworth, and many others who are not as well-known today. During this period Andrew Carnegie became Hill's mentor, helping Hill formulate a philosophy of success, drawing on the thoughts and experience of the people who were interviewed.

The success of *Think and Grow Rich* led to a long career as consultant to business leaders, a lecturer, and a writer of several more books, and made Hill a millionaire in his own right.

Napoleon Hill died in November 1970 after a long and successful career. His work stands as a guidepost to individual achievement and has influenced readers for almost seventy years.

Updating a classic work is a monumental task. The basic philosophy of the writer cannot be changed. It must always be Napoleon Hill's book, not mine. I approached it in the same way an art restorer looks at a classic painting that is being refurbished. I carefully studied the text and deleted stories and anecdotes that, although meaningful to the reader of the 1930s, have little significance to the reader of the twenty-first century. I replaced them with examples and illustrations of men and women who, in their careers in recent times, exemplify the principles Napoleon Hill promulgated.

In the following chapters you will learn these principles. In addition to reading the success stories of the people Hill studied for the original book, you will meet some of the top achievers of our time, such as Bill Gates, Mary Kay Ash, Arnold Schwarzenegger, Ray Kroc, Michael Jordan, and others.

Napoleon Hill's proven steps to riches are as valid for today's reader as they were for his contemporaries. All who read, understand, and apply this philosophy will be better prepared to attract and enjoy these higher standards of living that always have been and always will be denied to all except those who are ready for them.

Be prepared, therefore, when you actively follow Napoleon Hill's precepts to make major changes in your approach to life. It will pay off in enabling you to enjoy a life of harmony and understanding, as well as setting the stage for you to join the ranks of wealthy people.

—DR. ARTHUR R. PELL
2004

CHAPTER 1

THE POWER
OF THOUGHT

The Man Who "Thought" His Way into
Partnership with Thomas A. Edison

Truly, "thoughts are things," and powerful things at that, when mixed with purpose, persistence, and a *burning desire* for their translation into riches or other material objects.

Edwin C. Barnes discovered how true it is that men really do *think and grow rich*. His discovery did not come about at one sitting. It came little by little, beginning with a *burning desire* to become a business associate of the great Thomas Edison.

One of the chief characteristics of Barnes's desire was that it was definite. He wanted to work *with* Edison, not *for* him. Observe, carefully, the description of how he went about translating his *desire* into reality, and you will have a better understanding of the 13 principles which lead to riches.

When this desire, or impulse of thought, first flashed into his mind, he was in no position to act upon it. Two difficulties stood in his way: He did not know Mr. Edison, and he did not have enough money to pay his rail fare to Orange, New Jersey. These difficulties were sufficient to have discouraged the majority of people from making any attempt to carry out the desire. But his was no ordinary desire! He was so determined to find a way to carry out his desire that he finally decided to travel by "blind baggage" rather than be defeated. (To the uninitiated, this means that he went to East Orange on a freight train.)

He presented himself at Mr. Edison's laboratory, and announced he had come to go into business with the inventor. In speaking of the first meeting between them, years later, Mr. Edison said, "He stood there before me, looking like an ordinary tramp, but there was something in the expression of his face which conveyed the impression that he was determined to get what he had come after. I had learned, from years of experience with men, that when a man really *desires* a thing so deeply that he is willing to stake his entire future on a single turn of the wheel in order to get it, he is sure to win. I gave him the opportunity he asked for, because I saw he had made up his mind to stand by until he succeeded. Subsequent events proved that no mistake was made."

Just what young Barnes said to Mr. Edison on that occasion was far less important than what he thought. Edison himself said so! It could not have been the young man's appearance that got him his start in the Edison office, for that was definitely against him. It was what he *thought* that counted.

If the significance of this statement could be conveyed to every person who reads it, there would be no need for the remainder of this book.

Barnes did not get his partnership with Edison on his first interview. He did get a chance to work in the Edison offices, at a very nominal wage, doing work that was unimportant to Edison but most important to Barnes. It gave him an opportunity to display his "merchandise" where his intended "partner" could see it.

Months went by. Apparently nothing happened to bring the coveted goal, which Barnes had set up in his mind as his *definite major purpose.* But something important was happening in Barnes' mind. He was constantly intensifying his desire to become the business associate of Edison.

Psychologists have correctly said, "When one is truly ready for a thing, it puts in its appearance." Barnes was ready for a business association with Edison; moreover, he was determined to remain ready until he got that which he was seeking.

He did not say to himself, "Ah well, what's the use? I guess I'll change my mind and try for a salesman's job." But he did say, "I came here to go into business with Edison, and I'll accomplish this end if it takes the remainder of my life." He meant it! What a different story people would have to tell if only they would adopt a *definite purpose,* and stand by that purpose until it had time to become an all-consuming obsession!

Maybe young Barnes did not know it at the time, but his bulldog determination, his persistence with a single *desire,* was destined to mow down all opposition and bring him the opportunity he was seeking.

When the opportunity came, it appeared in a different form, and from a different direction than Barnes had expected. That is one of the tricks of opportunity. It has a sly habit of slipping in by the back door, and often comes disguised in the form of misfortune or temporary defeat. Perhaps this is why so many fail to recognize opportunity.

Mr. Edison had just perfected a new office device, known at that time as the Edison Dictating Machine (later called the Ediphone). His salesmen were not enthusiastic over the machine. They did not believe it could be sold without great effort. Barnes saw his opportunity. It had crawled in quietly, hidden in a queer-looking machine that interested no one but Barnes and the inventor.

Barnes knew he could sell the Edison Dictating Machine. He suggested this to Edison and promptly got his chance. He did sell the machine. In fact, he sold it so successfully that Edison gave him a contract to distribute and market it all over the nation. Out of that business association grew the slogan "Made by Edison and installed by Barnes." This business alliance made Barnes rich in money, but he accomplished something infinitely greater: he proved that one really may "Think and Grow Rich."

How much actual cash that original *desire* of Barnes was worth to him, I have no way of knowing. Perhaps it brought him $2 million or $3 million. Whatever the amount, it becomes insignificant when compared with the greater asset he acquired: the definite knowledge that an intangible impulse of thought can be transmuted into its physical counterpart by the application of known principles.

Barnes literally thought himself into a partnership with the great Edison! He thought himself into a fortune. He had nothing to start with, except the capacity to know what he wanted and the determination to stand by that desire until he realized it.

He had no money to begin with. He had but little education. He had no influence. But he did have initiative, faith, and the will to win. With these intangible forces he made himself number one man with the greatest inventor who ever lived.

Now let us look at a different situation, and study a man who had plenty of tangible evidence of riches, but lost it because he stopped three feet short of the goal he was seeking.

Three Feet from Gold

One of the most common causes of failure is the habit of quitting when one is overtaken by temporary defeat. Every person is guilty of this mistake at one time or another.

R. U. Darby, who later became one of the most successful insurance salesmen in the country, tells the story of his uncle, who was caught by the "gold fever" in the gold-rush days, and went West to dig and grow rich. He had never heard the saying that more gold has been mined from the brains of men than has ever been taken from the earth. He staked a claim and went to work with pick and shovel. The going was hard, but his lust for gold was definite.

After weeks of labor, he was rewarded by the discovery of the shining ore. He needed machinery to bring the ore to the surface. Quietly, he covered up the mine, retraced his footsteps to his home in Williamsburg, Maryland, and told his relatives and a few neighbors of the "strike." They got together money for the needed machinery and had it shipped. The uncle and Darby went back to work the mine.

The first car of ore was mined and shipped to a smelter. The returns proved they had one of the richest mines in Colorado! A few more cars of that ore would clear the debts. Then would come the big killing in profits.

Down went the drills! Up went the hopes of Darby and Uncle! Then something happened—the vein of gold ore disappeared. They had come to the end of the rainbow, and the pot of gold was no longer there. They drilled on, desperately trying to pick up the vein again, all to no avail.

Finally, they decided to quit. They sold the machinery to a junk man for a few hundred dollars, and took the train back home. Some "junk" men are dumb, but not this one! He called in a mining engineer to look at the mine and do a little calculating. The engineer advised that the project had failed because the owners were not familiar with "fault lines." His calculations showed that the vein would be found *just three feet from where the Darbys had stopped drilling*! That is exactly where it was found.

The junk man took millions of dollars in ore from the mine because he knew enough to seek expert counsel before giving up. Most of the money which went into the machinery was procured through the efforts of R. U. Darby, who was then a very young man. The money came from his relatives and neighbors, because of their faith in him. He paid back every dollar of it, although he was years in doing so.

Long afterward, Mr. Darby recouped his loss many times over when he made the discovery that desire can be transmuted into gold. The discovery came after he went into the business of selling life insurance.

Remembering that he lost a huge fortune because he stopped three feet from gold, Darby profited by the experience in his chosen work. His simple method was to say to himself, "I stopped three feet from gold, but I will never stop because men say 'no' when I ask them to buy insurance." He owes his "stickability" to the lesson he learned from his "quitability" in the gold-mining business.

Before success comes to most people, they are sure to meet with much temporary defeat, and perhaps some failure. When faced with defeat the easiest and most logical thing to do is to *quit*. That is exactly what the majority of people do.

More than 500 of the most successful people America has ever known told the author their greatest success came just one step beyond the point at which defeat had overtaken them. Failure is a trickster with a keen sense of irony and cunning. It takes great delight in tripping one up when success is almost within reach.

A Fifty-Cent Lesson in Persistence

Shortly after Mr. Darby received his degree from the "University of Hard Knocks," and had decided to profit by his experience in the gold-mining business, he had the good fortune to be present on an occasion that proved to him that *no* does not necessarily mean *no*.

One afternoon he was helping his uncle grind wheat in an old-fashioned mill. The uncle operated a large farm on which a number of sharecrop farmers lived. Quietly, the door was opened, and a small child, the daughter of a tenant, walked in and took her place near the door.

The uncle looked up, saw the child, and barked at her roughly, "What do you want?"

Meekly, the child replied, "My mammy says send her fifty cents."

"I'll not do it," the uncle retorted. "Now, you run on home."

"Yes, sir," the child replied. But she did not move.

The uncle went ahead with his work, so busily engaged he did not notice that the child had not left. When he looked up and saw her still standing there, he yelled at her, "I told you to go on home! Now, go, or I'll take a switch to you."

The little girl said, "Yes, sir," but she did not budge an inch.

The uncle dropped a sack of grain he was about to pour into the mill hopper, picked up a barrel stave, and started toward the child with an expression on his face that indicated trouble.

Darby held his breath. He was certain he was about to witness a murder. He knew his uncle had a fierce temper. When the uncle reached the spot where the child was standing, she quickly stepped forward one step, looked up into his eyes, and screamed at the top of her shrill voice, "MY MAMMY'S GOTTA HAVE THAT FIFTY CENTS!"

The uncle stopped, looked at her for a minute, then slowly laid the barrel stave on the floor, put his hand in his pocket, took out half a dollar, and gave it to her.

The child took the money and slowly backed toward the door, never taking her eyes off the man whom she had just conquered. After she had gone, the uncle sat down on a box and looked out the window into space for more than ten minutes. He was pondering, with awe, on the whipping he had just taken.

Mr. Darby, too, was doing some thinking. That was the first time in all his experience that he had seen the child of a sharecropper deliberately master an adult authority figure. How did she do it? What happened to his uncle that caused him to lose his fierceness and become as docile as a lamb? What strange power did this child use that made her master over her superior? These and other similar questions flashed into Darby's mind, but he did not find the answer until years later, when he told me the story.

Strangely, the story of this unusual experience was told to the author in the old mill, on the very spot where the uncle took his whipping. As we stood there in that musty old mill, Mr. Darby repeated the story of the unusual conquest, and finished by asking, "What can you make of it? What strange power did that child use that so completely whipped my uncle?"

The answer to his question will be found in the principles described in this book. The answer is full and complete. It contains details and instructions sufficient to enable anyone to understand and apply the same force that the little child accidentally stumbled upon.

Keep your mind alert and you will observe exactly what strange power came to the rescue of the child. You will catch a glimpse of this power in the next chapter. Somewhere in the book you will find an idea that will quicken your receptive powers and place at your command, for your own benefit, this same irresistible power. The awareness of this power may come to you in the first chapter, or it may flash into your mind in some subsequent chapter. It may come in the form of a single idea. Or it may come in the nature of a plan, or a purpose. Again, it may cause you to go back into your past experiences of failure or defeat, and bring to the surface some lesson by which you can regain all that you lost through defeat.

After I had described to Mr. Darby the power unwittingly used by the little child, he quickly retraced his thirty years of experience as a life insurance salesman. He frankly acknowledged that his success in that field was due, in no small degree, to the lesson he had learned from the child.

Mr. Darby pointed out, "Every time a prospect tried to bow me out, without buying, I saw that child standing there in the old mill, her big eyes glaring in defiance, and I said to myself, 'I've gotta make this sale.' The better portion of all sales I have made were made after people had said no."

He recalled, too, his mistake in having stopped only three feet from gold. "But," he said, "that experience was a blessing in disguise. It taught me to keep on keeping on, no matter how hard the going may be, a lesson I needed to learn before I could succeed in anything."

This story of Mr. Darby and his uncle, the sharecropper's child, and the gold mine will doubtless be read by hundreds of people who make their living by selling life insurance. To all of these, the author wishes to offer the suggestion that Darby owes to these two experiences his ability to sell more than a million dollars of life insurance every year.

Life is strange, and often imponderable! Both the successes and the failures have their roots in simple experiences. Mr. Darby's experiences were commonplace and simple enough, yet as they held the answer to his destiny in life, they were as important (to him) as life itself. He profited by these two dramatic experiences because he analyzed them and found the lesson they taught. But what of the person who has neither the time nor the inclination to study failure in search of knowledge that may lead to success? Where and how are they to learn the art of converting defeat into stepping stones to opportunity?

In answer to these questions, this book was written.

The answer called for a description of 13 principles. However, remember as you read that the answer you may be seeking to the questions which have caused you to ponder over the strangeness of life may be found in your own mind. Some idea, plan, or purpose may spring into your mind as you read.

One sound idea is all you need to achieve success. The principles described in this book contain the best and most practical ways and means of creating useful ideas.

Before we go any further in our approach to the description of these principles, we believe you are entitled to receive this important suggestion: WHEN RICHES BEGIN TO COME, THEY COME SO QUICKLY, IN SUCH GREAT ABUNDANCE, THAT ONE WONDERS WHERE THEY HAVE BEEN HIDING DURING ALL THOSE LEAN YEARS. This is an astounding statement, and all the more so when we take into consideration the popular belief that riches come only to those who work hard and long.

When you begin to think and grow rich, you will observe that riches begin with a state of mind, with definiteness of purpose, with little or no hard work. You, and every other person, ought to be interested in knowing how to acquire a state of mind that will attract riches. I spent twenty-five years in research, analyzing more than 25,000 people, because I, too, wanted to know "how wealthy men become that way."

Without that research, this book could not have been written.

Here take notice of a very significant truth: The business Depression started in 1929, and continued on an all-time record of destruction until sometime after President Roosevelt entered office. Then the Depression began to fade into nothingness. Just as an electrician in a theater raises the lights so gradually that darkness is transmuted into light before you realize it, so did the spell of fear in the minds of the people gradually fade away and become faith.

As soon as you master the principles of this philosophy and begin to follow the instructions for applying those principles, your financial status will begin to improve. Everything you touch will begin to transmute itself into an asset for your benefit. Impossible? Not at all!

One of the main weaknesses of mankind is the average person's familiarity with the word "impossible." He knows all the rules that will *not* work. He knows all the things that *cannot* be done. This book was written for those who seek the rules that have made others successful, and are willing to stake everything on those rules.

A great many years ago I purchased a fine dictionary. The first thing I did was turn to the word "impossible," and neatly clip it out of the book. That would not be an unwise thing for you to do.

Success comes to those who become *success conscious*.

Failure comes to those who indifferently allow themselves to become *failure conscious*.

The object of this book is to help all who seek it learn the art of changing their minds from *failure consciousness* to *success consciousness*.

Another weakness found in altogether too many people is the habit of measuring everything, and everyone, by their own impressions and beliefs. Some who read this will believe that no one can think and grow rich. They cannot think in terms of riches, because their thought habits have been steeped in poverty, want, misery, failure, and defeat.

Millions of people look at the achievements of Henry Ford and envy him his good fortune, or luck, or genius, or whatever it is they credit for Ford's fortune. Perhaps one person in every hundred thousand knows the secret of Ford's success, and those who do know are too modest, or too reluctant, to speak of it, because of its simplicity. A single transaction will illustrate the "secret" perfectly.

When Ford decided to produce his now famous V-8 motor, he chose to build an engine with the entire eight cylinders cast in one block, and instructed his engineers to produce a design for the engine. The design was placed on paper, but the engineers believed it was simply impossible to cast an eight-cylinder gas engine block in one piece.

Ford said, "Produce it anyway."

"But," they replied, "it's impossible!"

"Go ahead," Ford commanded, "and stay on the job until you succeed, no matter how much time is required."

The engineers went ahead. There was no other option if they were to remain on the Ford staff. Six months went by and nothing happened. Another six months passed, and still nothing happened. The engineers tried every conceivable plan to carry out the orders, but the thing seemed out of the question: "Impossible!"

At the end of the year Ford checked with his engineers, and again they informed him they had found no way to carry out his orders.

"Go right ahead," said Ford. "I want it, and I'll have it."

They went ahead, and then, as if by a stroke of magic, the secret was discovered. The Ford *determination* had won once more!

This story may not be described with minute accuracy, but the sum and substance of it is correct. Deduce from it, you who wish to think and grow rich, the secret of the Ford millions, if you can. You'll not have to look very far.

Henry Ford is a success because he understands and applies the principles of success. One of these is desire: knowing what one wants. Remember this Ford story as you read, and pick out the lines in which the secret of his stupendous achievement has been described. If you can do this, if you can lay your finger on the particular group of principles that made Henry Ford rich, you can equal his achievements in almost any calling for which you are suited.

The Henry Ford of the late twentieth century was Bill Gates. Just as Ford revolutionized the transportation industry by creating a car that almost anyone could afford and drive, Bill Gates transformed the computer industry by designing software that enabled everybody—not just the specialized technocrats—to be able to use computers, and later making the personal computer a virtual necessity in every office, school, and home. This resulted in Bill Gates's accruing billions of dollars and becoming the richest man in America.

He first became entranced with computers and began programming them at the age of thirteen. In 1973, he entered Harvard University, where he lived down the hall from Steve Ballmer, now Microsoft's chief executive officer. While at Harvard, Gates developed a version of the programming language BASIC for the first microcomputer.

Gates was so absorbed in his dream of building a software company that he left Harvard to devote his energies to fulfilling it. A few years earlier, he and his childhood friend Paul Allen had formed a company, Microsoft, as the vehicle for this endeavor. Guided by a belief that the computer would be a valu-

able tool on every office desktop and in every home, they began developing software for personal computers. Gates's foresight and his vision for personal computing have been central to the success of Microsoft and the software industry.

Having achieved his major goal, Bill Gates continues to pursue new goals both in the business of creating ever-improving computer programs and in his philanthropic work, having founded with his wife, Melinda, the largest charitable foundation in the world.

You are "the Master of your Fate, the Captain of your Soul"

When the English poet W. E. Henley wrote the prophetic lines "I am the Master of my Fate, I am the Captain of my Soul," he should have informed us that the reason we are the masters of our fate, the captains of our souls is because we have the power to control our thoughts.

He should have told us that the ether in which this little planet floats, in which we move and have our being, is a form of energy moving at an inconceivably high rate of vibration, and that the ether is filled with a form of universal power which *adapts* itself to the nature of the thoughts we hold in our minds, and *influences* us, in natural ways, to transmute our thoughts into their physical equivalent.

If the poet had told us of this great truth, we would know why it is that we are the masters of our fate, the captains of our souls. He should have told us, with great emphasis, that this power makes no attempt to discriminate between destructive and constructive thoughts, that it will urge us to translate into physical reality thoughts of poverty just as quickly as it will influence us to act upon thoughts of riches.

He should have told us, too, that our brains become magnetized with the dominating thoughts we hold in our minds. By means with which no one is familiar, these "magnets" attract to us the forces, the people, the circumstances of life which harmonize with the nature of our dominating thoughts.

He should have told us that before we can accumulate riches in great abundance, we must magnetize our minds with intense desire for riches, that we must become money conscious until the desire for money drives us to create definite plans for acquiring it.

But being a poet, and not a philosopher, Henley contented himself by stating a great truth in poetic form, leaving those who followed him to interpret the philosophical meaning of his lines. Little by little, the truth has unfolded itself, until it now appears certain that the principles described in this book hold the secret of mastery over our economic fate.

Another man who exemplifies being master of his fate is Steven Spielberg, one of the all-time great motion picture directors. He dreamed of being a movie director from childhood. He began making amateur films with a primitive camera when he was still a child, and the dream never subsided.

How Spielberg broke into Universal Studios is a legend in the movie industry. He took the Universal Studios Tour, an attraction that enables visitors to get an inside look at the movie business. Visitors ride around the studio lots on a tram. Steven sneaked off the tram and hid between two sound stages until the tour ended. When he left at the end of the day, he made a point of saying a few words to the gate guard.

Day after day, he went back to the studio for three months. He walked past the guard, waved at him, and he waved back. He always wore a suit and carried a briefcase, letting the guard assume he was one of the students with a summer job in the studio. He made a point of speaking to and befriending directors, writers, and editors. He even found a vacant office, took it over, and listed his name in the building directory.

He made it his business to get to know Sid Sheinberg, then head of production for the studio's television arm. He showed him his college film project, which so impressed Sheinberg that he put the young man under contract with the studio.

His first full-length film, The Sugarland Express, *received critical acclaim and won a best screenplay award at the 1974 Cannes Film Festival. Unfortunately, it did not do very well at the box office.*

His big break came a year later, when he discovered the book Jaws. *The studio had already decided to produce* Jaws *and had chosen a well-known director to film it.*

Spielberg desperately wanted to make this movie. Despite the financial failure of The Sugarland Express, *his self-confidence had not diminished, and he persuaded the producers to dismiss the chosen director and give the film to him.*

It was not an easy assignment. From the beginning trouble beset the production. It ran into technical and budget problems. However, when Jaws *was released in June 1975, it enjoyed twofold success: it broke box-office records, and the critics loved it. Within a month of its release, the film had taken in $60 million at the box office, an unheard-of amount at the time.*

Over the next few years Spielberg directed several movies, including the popular Indiana Jones *series, the award-winning* The Color Purple, Empire of the Sun, *and* E.T.

He later directed Jurassic Park, *which would also become—at its time—the most successful movie in history, the third Spielberg film to break the record. It also brought in over $1 billion in gross receipts, toys, and other merchandise.*

Spielberg continues to pursue his dreams. When he and two other Hollywood moguls created their own production company, they called it "DreamWorks."

We are now ready to examine the first of these principles. Maintain a spirit of open-mindedness. Remember as you read that they are the invention of no single person. The principles were gathered from the life experiences of more than 500 men who actually accumulated riches in huge amounts; men who began in poverty, with little education or influence. The principles worked for these men. You can put them to work for your own enduring benefit.

You will find it easy, not hard, to do.

Before you read the next chapter, I want you to know that it conveys factual information that might easily change your entire financial destiny, as it has so definitely brought changes of stupendous proportions to two people described.

I want you to know, also, that the relationship between these two men and myself is such that I could have taken no liberties with the facts, even if I had wished to do so. One of them has been my closest personal friend for almost twenty-five years; the other is my own son. The unusual success of these two men, success that they generously accredit to the principle described in the next chapter, more than justifies this personal reference as a means of emphasizing the far-flung power of this principle.

CHAPTER 2

DESIRE:
The Starting Point
of All Achievement

(The First Step to Riches)

When Edwin C. Barnes climbed down from the freight train in Orange, New Jersey, he may have resembled a tramp, but his thoughts were those of a king! As he made his way to Thomas A. Edison's office, his mind was at work. He saw himself *standing in Edison's presence.* He heard himself asking Mr. Edison for an opportunity to carry out the one *consuming obsession of his life,* a *burning desire* to become the business associate of the great inventor.

Barnes's desire was not a hope. It was not a wish. It was a keen, pulsating *desire,* which transcended everything else. It was *definite.*

The desire was not new when he approached Edison. It had been Barnes's dominating desire for a long time. In the beginning, when the desire first appeared in his mind, it may have been—probably was—only a wish, but it was no mere wish when he appeared before Edison with it.

A few years later, Edwin C. Barnes again stood before Edison, in the same office where he first met the inventor. This time his desire had been translated into reality. He was in business with Edison. The dominating dream of his life had become a reality. Today, people who know Barnes envy him because of the "break" life yielded him. They see him in the days of his triumph, without taking the trouble to investigate the cause of his success.

Barnes succeeded because he chose a definite goal, and placed all his energy, all his willpower, and all his effort into achieving that goal. He did not become the partner of Edison the day he arrived. He was content to start in the most menial work, as long as it provided an opportunity to take even one step toward his cherished goal.

Five years passed before the chance he had been seeking made its appearance. During all those years not one ray of hope, not one promise of attainment of his desire had been held out to him. To everyone, except himself, he appeared only another cog in the Edison business wheel, but in his own mind *he was the partner of Edison every minute of the time,* from the very day he first went to work there.

It is a remarkable illustration of the power of a definite desire. Barnes won his goal because he wanted to be a business associate of Mr. Edison's more than he wanted anything else. He created a plan by which to attain that purpose. But he burned all bridges behind him. He stood by his desire until it became the dominating obsession of his life and, finally, a fact.

When he went to Orange, he did not say to himself, "I will try to induce Edison to give me a job of some sort." He said, "I will see Edison and put him on notice that I have come to go into business with him."

He did not say, "I will work there for a few months, and if I get no encouragement, I will quit and get a job somewhere else." He did say, "I will start anywhere. I will do anything Edison tells me to do, but before I am through, I will be his associate." He did not say, "I will keep my eyes open for another opportunity, in case I fail to get what I want in the Edison organization." He said, "There is but *one* thing in this world I am determined to have, and that is a business association with Thomas A. Edison. I will burn all bridges behind me, and stake my *entire future* on my ability to get what I want."

He left himself no possible way of retreat. He had to win or perish! That is all there is to the Barnes story of success.

A long while ago, a great warrior had to make a decision which ensured his success on the battlefield. He was about to send his armies against a powerful foe, whose men outnumbered his own. He loaded his soldiers into boats, sailed to the enemy's country, unloaded soldiers and equipment, then gave the order to burn the ships that had carried them. Addressing his men before the first battle, he said, "You see the boats going up in smoke. That means that we cannot leave these shores alive unless we win! We now have no choice—we win or we perish!" They won. Every person who wins in any undertaking must be willing to burn his ships and cut all sources of retreat. Only by so doing can one be sure of maintaining that state of mind known as a *burning desire to win,* essential to success.

The morning after the great Chicago fire, a group of merchants stood on State Street, looking at the smoking remains of what had been their stores. They went into a conference to decide if they would try to rebuild, or leave Chicago and start over in a more promising part of the country. They reached a decision—all except one—to leave Chicago.

The merchant who decided to stay and rebuild pointed a finger at the remains of his store, and said, "Gentlemen, on that very spot I will build the world's greatest store, no matter how many times it may burn down." The store was built. It stands there today, a towering monument to the power of that state of mind known as a *burning desire.* The easy thing for Marshall Field to have done would have been exactly what his fellow merchants did. When the going was hard and the future looked dismal, they pulled up and went where the going seemed easier.

Mark well this difference between Marshall Field and the other merchants, because it is the same difference that distinguishes Edwin C. Barnes from thousands of other young men who have worked in the Edison organization. It is the same difference that distinguishes practically all who succeed from those who fail.

Every human being who understands the purpose of money wishes for it. Wishing will not bring riches. But desiring riches with a state of mind that becomes an obsession, then planning definite ways and means to acquire riches, and backing those plans with persistence which does not recognize failure, will bring riches.

The method by which *desire* for riches can be transmuted into its financial equivalent consists of six definite, practical steps:

1. Fix in your mind the exact amount of money you desire. It is not sufficient merely to say, "I want plenty of money." Be definite as to the amount. (There is a psychological reason for definiteness which will be described in a subsequent chapter.)

2. Determine exactly what you intend to give in return for the money you desire. (There is no such reality as "something for nothing.")

3. Establish a definite date when you intend to possess the money you desire.

4. Create a definite plan for carrying out your desire, and begin at once, whether you are ready or not, to put this plan into action.

5. Write out a clear, concise statement of the amount of money you intend to acquire. Name the time limit for its acquisition. State what you intend to give in return for the money, and describe clearly the plan through which you intend to accumulate it.

6. Read your written statement aloud, twice daily, once just before retiring at night, and once after rising in the morning. AS YOU READ, SEE AND FEEL AND BELIEVE YOURSELF ALREADY IN POSSESSION OF THE MONEY.

It is important that you follow the instructions described in these six steps. It is especially important that you observe and follow the instructions in the sixth paragraph.

You may complain that it is impossible for you to see yourself in possession of money before you actually have it. Here is where a *burning desire* will come to your aid. If you truly *desire* money so keenly that your desire is an obsession, you will have no difficulty in convincing yourself that you will acquire it. The object is to want money, and to become so determined to have it that you *convince* yourself you will have it.

Only those who become money conscious ever accumulate great riches. Money consciousness means that the mind has become so thoroughly saturated with the desire for money that one can see oneself already in possession of it.

To those who have not been schooled in the working principles of the human mind, these instructions may appear impractical. It may be helpful, to all who fail to recognize the soundness of the six steps, to know that the information they convey was received from Andrew Carnegie, who began as an ordinary laborer in the steel mills. Despite his humble beginning, Carnegie managed to make these principles yield him a fortune of considerably more than $100 million.

It may be of further help to know that the six steps recommended here were carefully scrutinized by Thomas A. Edison. He placed his stamp of approval upon them as being not only the steps essential for the accumulation of money but also for the attainment of any definite goal. The steps call for no "hard labor." They call for no sacrifice. They do not require one to become ridiculous, or credulous. To apply them calls for no great amount of education. But the successful application of these six steps does call for sufficient imagination to enable one to see, and to understand, that accumulation of money cannot be left to chance, good fortune, and luck. One must realize that all who have accumulated great fortunes first did a certain amount of dreaming, hoping, wishing, *desiring,* and *planning* before they acquired money.

You may as well know, also, that every great leader, from the dawn of civilization down to the present, was a dreamer. If you do not see great riches in your imagination, you will never see them in your bank balance. Never has there been so great an opportunity for practical dreamers as now exists. We who are in this race for riches should be encouraged to know that this dynamic world in which we live is demanding new ideas, new ways of doing things, new leaders, new inventions, new methods of teaching, new methods of marketing, new books, new literature, new applications for computers, new cures for diseases, and new approaches to every aspect of business and life. Behind this demand for new and better things there is one quality one must possess to win, and that is *definiteness of purpose,* the knowledge of what one wants, and a burning *desire* to possess it. To accomplish this requires practical dreamers who can, and will, put their dreams into action. The practical dreamers have always been, and always will be, the pattern-makers of civilization. We who desire to accumulate riches should remember that the real leaders of the world have always been people who harnessed, and put into practical use, the intangible, unseen forces of unborn opportunity. They have converted those forces (or impulses of thought) into skyscrapers, cities, factories, aeroplanes, cars, better health care, and every form of convenience that makes life more pleasant.

Tolerance and an open mind are practical necessities for the dreamer of today. Those who are afraid of new ideas are doomed before they start. Never has there been a time more favorable to pioneers than the present. There is a vast business, financial, and industrial world to be remolded and redirected along new and better lines.

In planning to acquire your share of the riches, let no one influence you to scorn the dreamer. To win the big stakes in this ever-changing world, you must catch the spirit of the great pioneers of the past, whose dreams have given to civilization all that it has of value, the spirit which serves as the lifeblood of our society—your opportunity, and mine, to develop and market our talents. Let us not forget, Columbus dreamed of an unknown world, staked his life on the existence of such a world, and discovered it! Copernicus, the great astronomer, dreamed of a multiplicity of worlds, and revealed them! No one denounced him as "impractical" after he had triumphed. Instead, the world worshipped at his shrine, thus proving once more that *success requires no apologies, failure permits no alibis.*

If the thing you wish to do is right, and you believe in it, go ahead and do it! Put your dream across, and never mind what "they" say if you meet with temporary defeat, for "they," perhaps, do not know that *every failure brings with it the seed of an equivalent success.*

Henry Ford, poor and uneducated, dreamed of a horseless carriage. He went to work with what tools he possessed, without waiting for opportunity to favor him, and now evidence of his dream belts the entire earth. He has put more wheels into operation than any man who ever lived, because he was not afraid to back his dreams.

Thomas Edison dreamed of a lamp that could be operated by electricity. Despite more than 10,000 failures, he stood by that dream until he made it a physical reality. Practical dreamers *do not quit*!

Lincoln dreamed of freedom for the black slaves, put his dream into action, and barely missed living to see a united North and South translate his dream into reality. The Wright brothers dreamed of a machine that would fly through the air. Now one may see evidence all over the world that they dreamed soundly. Marconi dreamed of a system for harnessing the intangible forces of the ether. Evidence that he did not dream in vain may be found in every radio, TV, and cell phone in the world. Moreover, Marconi's dream brought the humblest cabin and the most stately manor house side by side. It made the people of every nation on earth next-door neighbors by creating a medium where news, information, and entertainment could instantly be disseminated throughout the world. It may interest you to know that Marconi's "friends" had him taken into custody and examined in a psychiatric hospital when he announced he had discovered a principle by which he could send messages through the air, without the aid of wires or other direct physical means of communication.

The dreamers of today fare better. The world has become accustomed to new discoveries. Indeed, it has shown a willingness to reward the dreamer who gives the world a new idea.

Ray Kroc is another good example of someone who made his dream come true. Kroc was a salesman of milkshake mixers. Most of his customers—restaurants and diners—purchased one or two units. When he received an order for eight mixers from a small food outlet in San Bernardino, California, he decided to visit them and see how they could sell so many shakes. It was the busiest restaurant he had ever seen. The owners—the McDonald brothers—offered a very limited menu: hamburgers, cheeseburgers, French fries, shakes, and soft drinks—all at the lowest prices in the area.

Kroc saw an opportunity. If he could open a chain of these restaurants, each as productive and profitable as this, money would flow in. He proposed the idea to the McDonald brothers and agreed to implement it. Within a few years, McDonald's not only became the top-selling food outlet in the country but also created the fast-food industry. Kroc later bought out the McDonald brothers and expanded the business into an international phenomenon, making him one of the richest men of his time.

The world is filled with an abundance of *opportunity* which the dreamers of the past never knew. *A burning desire to be and to do* is the starting point from which the dreamer must take off. Dreams are not born of indifference, laziness, or lack of ambition. The world no longer scoffs at dreamers or calls them impractical. Remember, too, that all who succeed in life get off to a bad start, and pass through many heartbreaking struggles before they arrive. The turning point in the lives of those who succeed usually comes at the moment of some crisis, through which they are introduced to their "other selves." John Bunyan wrote *The Pilgrim's Progress* after he had been confined in prison and sorely punished because of his religious views.

O. Henry discovered the genius that slept within his brain after he had met with great misfortune and was confined in a prison cell in Columbus, Ohio. Being *forced,* through misfortune, to become acquainted with his "other self" and to use his *imagination,* he discovered himself to be a great author instead of a miserable criminal and outcast. Strange and varied are the ways of life, and stranger still are the ways of Infinite Intelligence, through which people are sometimes forced to undergo all sorts of punishment before discovering their own brains, and their own capacity to create useful ideas through imagination.

Edison, the world's greatest inventor and scientist, was a part-time telegraph operator. He failed innumerable times before he was driven, finally, to the discovery of the genius that slept within his brain. Charles Dickens began by pasting labels on blacking pots. The tragedy of his first love penetrated the depths of his soul and converted him into one of the world's truly great authors.

Disappointment over love affairs generally has the effect of driving people to drink and ruin. This is because most people never learn the art of transmuting their strongest emotions into dreams of a constructive nature.

Helen Keller became deaf, dumb, and blind shortly after birth. Despite her great misfortune, her name is written indelibly in the pages of the history of the great. Her entire life served as evidence that no one is ever defeated until defeat has been accepted as a reality. Robert Burns was an illiterate country lad. He was cursed by poverty and grew up to be a drunkard. The world was made better for his having lived because he clothed beautiful thoughts in poetry, thereby plucking a thorn and planting a rose in its place.

Booker T. Washington was born in slavery, handicapped by race and color. Because he was tolerant, had an open mind at all times, on all subjects, and was a *dreamer,* he left his impress for good on an entire race. Beethoven was deaf, Milton was blind, but their names will last as long as time endures, because they dreamed and translated their dreams into organized thought.

Arnold Schwarzenegger is another person who converted his desire into action and achievement. He first came into the public eye as "Mr. Universe," a glorified weight lifter.

But Schwarzenegger was not a typical "muscle man." He was a man with dreams and goals. He achieved them by becoming a wealthy businessman, one of the highest-paid movie stars, and eventually governor of California.

Born and raised in Austria, as a child he began training as a weight lifter. At eighteen, he won his first bodybuilding contest and the first of five consecutive Mr. Universe titles. He emigrated to the United States and continued winning similar contests.

He eventually accomplished more than any other person in the art of bodybuilding, and it was no longer a challenge, so he sought other areas where he could use his talents. His training in physical development taught him that there was a need for knowledge about physical fitness. He had that knowledge and wanted to share it.

He wrote an autobiography, Arnold: The Education of a Bodybuilder, *which became a bestseller. He followed it with a book on bodybuilding for women, showing female readers how to use weight training to get in shape. This led to the creation of a mail-order exercise business, and a company to produce bodybuilding events. These businesses started him on the road to business success.*

His next goal was to become a movie star. Even before he had secured his first movie role, he set himself a goal to be as big in movies as he was in bodybuilding. After he turned down minor roles, his persistence paid off when he was cast as the lead in Conan the Barbarian. *This led to a series of action films that made him one of the highest-paid actors in Hollywood.*

Success in the movies did not make Schwarzenegger complacent. He set new goals for himself, this time in the world of business. He invested in real estate, created a restaurant chain, and became actively involved in other enterprises—and became a multimillionaire.

As his successes mounted, however, he added what became his dream goal—to serve the community. He traveled around the country to promote health and fitness for youth. He went into the inner cities and inspired the kids to eschew violence and crime, to say no to drugs, guns, and gangs and yes to education. He has taken an active leadership role in several organizations dedicated to physical fitness and health.

In 2003, Schwarzenegger threw his hat into the ring and was overwhelmingly elected as the new governor of California.

You can learn much from this man. In setting goals you are not limited to any one area. Schwarzenegger could have limited his future to bodybuilding and become quite successful, but he dreamed of much more, set higher goals, and strove to reach them. He learned from his successes and adapted this knowledge in other aspects of his life.

Like Schwarzenegger, do not be discouraged by criticism. Critics belittled his acting ability in his first films, but he was not dissuaded and pursued his goal to become one of the highest-paid actors in Hollywood.

Before passing to the next chapter, kindle anew in your mind the fire of hope, faith, courage, and tolerance. If you have these states of mind, and a working knowledge of the principles described, all else that you need will come to you when you are *ready* for it. Let Emerson state the thought in these words: "Every proverb, every book, every byword that belongs to thee for aid and comfort shall surely come home through open or winding passages. Every friend whom not thy fantastic will, but the great and tender soul in thee craveth, shall lock thee in his embrace."

There is a difference between *wishing* for a thing and being *ready* to receive it. No one is ready for a thing until he believes he can acquire it. The state of mind must be *belief,* not mere hope or wish. Open-mindedness is essential for belief. Closed minds do not inspire faith, courage, or belief.

Remember, no more effort is required to aim high in life, to demand abundance and prosperity, than is required to accept misery and poverty. A great poet has correctly stated this universal truth through these lines:

> I bargained with Life for a penny
>   And Life would pay no more,
> However I begged at evening
>   When I counted my scanty store.
>
> For Life is a just employer,
>   He gives you what you ask,
> But once you have set the wages,
>   Why, you must bear the task.
>
> I worked for a menial's hire,
>   Only to learn, dismayed,
> That any wage I had asked of Life,
>   Life would have willingly paid.

Mary Kay Ash, the founder of Mary Kay Cosmetics, attributed her success to the development of self-confidence and faith in herself, and in all the people in her vast organization, which now consists of more than 250,000 independent beauty consultants worldwide.

Her sales career began twenty-five years earlier when she joined Stanley Home Products. She often commented that she was not at all successful during her first year and was ready to give up. This changed when she attended her first Stanley sales seminar.

She reported: "There I saw this tall, svelte, pretty, successful woman crowned queen as a reward for being the best in a company contest. I determined to be that queen the following year, which seemed impossible. However, I decided to go up and talk to the president and tell him that I intended to be queen next year.

"Mr. Beveridge didn't laugh at me, but looked me in the eye, held my hand, and said, 'Somehow I think you will.' Those five words drove me and the next year I was queen."

Mary Kay preached and practiced that the first step in achieving success is to firmly believe that you are an excellent person who deserves success. In an article in Personal Excellence, she suggested some exercises to help create your image of excellence and begin to establish an atmosphere of success in your life. Here are some of her suggestions:

IMAGINE YOURSELF SUCCESSFUL. *Always picture yourself successful. Visualize the person you desire to become. Set aside time each day to be alone and undisturbed. Get comfortable and relax. Close your eyes and concentrate on your desires and goals. See yourself in this new environment, capable and self-confident.*

REFLECT ON YOUR PAST SUCCESSES. *Every success, be it large or small, is proof that you are capable of achieving more successes. Celebrate each success. You can recall it when you begin to lose faith in yourself.*

SET DEFINITE GOALS. *Have a clear direction of where you want to go. Be aware when you begin to deviate from these goals and take immediate corrective action.*

RESPOND POSITIVELY TO LIFE. *Develop a positive self-image. Your image, your reactions to life, and your decisions are completely within your control.*

Desire Outwits Mother Nature

As a fitting climax to this chapter, I wish to introduce one of the most unusual people I have ever known. I first saw him a few minutes after he was born. He came into the world without any physical sign of ears, and the doctor admitted, when pressed for an opinion, that the child might be deaf and mute for life.

I challenged the doctor's opinion. I had the right to do so; I was the child's father. I, too, reached a decision and rendered an opinion, but I expressed the opinion silently, in the secrecy of my own heart. I decided that my son would hear and speak. Nature could send me a child without ears, but Nature could not induce me to accept the reality of the affliction. In my own mind I knew that my son would hear and speak. How? I was sure there must be a way, and I knew I would find it. I thought of the words of the immortal Emerson: "The whole course of things goes to teach us faith. We need only obey. There is guidance for each of us, and by lowly listening, we shall hear the right word."

The right word? DESIRE! More than anything else, I *desired* that my son should not be a deaf-mute. From that desire I never receded, not for a second. Many years previously, I had written, "Our only limitations are those we set up in our own minds." For the first time, I wondered if that statement was true. Lying on the bed in front of me was a newborn child without the visible natural equipment of hearing. Even though he might hear and speak, he was obviously disfigured for life. Surely, this was a limitation that this child had not set up in his own mind. What could I do about it? Somehow I would find a way to transplant into that child's mind my own *burning desire* for ways and means of conveying sound to his brain without the aid of ears.

As soon as the child was old enough to cooperate, I would fill his mind so completely with a *burning desire* to hear that Nature would, by methods of her own, translate it into physical reality. All this thinking took place in my own mind, and I spoke of it to no one. Every day I renewed the pledge I had made to myself not to accept a deaf-mute for a son.

As he grew older, and began to take notice of things around him, we observed that he had a slight degree of hearing. When he reached the age when children usually begin talking, he made no attempt to speak, but we could tell by his actions that he could hear certain sounds slightly. That was all I wanted to know! I was convinced that if he could hear, even slightly, he might develop still greater hearing capacity.

Then something happened which gave me hope. It came from an entirely unexpected source—we bought a record player. When the child heard the music for the first time, he went into ecstasies, and promptly appropriated the machine. He soon showed a preference for certain records, among them "It's a Long Way to Tipperary." On one occasion, he played that piece over and over for almost two hours, standing in front of the record player with his teeth clamped on the edge of the case. The significance of this self-formed habit of his did not become clear to us until years later, for we had never heard of the principle of "bone conduction" of sound at that time.

Shortly after he appropriated the record player, I discovered that he could hear me quite clearly when I spoke with my lips touching his mastoid bone behind the ear, or at the base of the brain. These discoveries placed in my possession the necessary media by which I began to translate into reality my burning desire to help my son develop hearing and speech. By that time he was making stabs at speaking certain words. The outlook was far from encouraging, but *desire backed by faith* knows no such word as "impossible."

Having determined that he could hear the sound of my voice plainly, I began, immediately, to transfer to his mind the desire to hear and speak. I soon discovered that the child enjoyed bedtime stories, so I went to work creating stories designed to develop in him self-reliance, imagination, and a keen desire to hear and to be normal.

There was one story in particular that was designed to plant in his mind the thought that his affliction was not a liability, but an asset of great value. I emphasized the point by giving the story some new and dramatic coloring each time it was told.

Despite the fact that all the philosophy I had examined clearly indicated that *every adversity brings with it the seed of an equivalent advantage,* I must confess that I had not the slightest idea how this affliction could ever become an asset. However, I continued my practice of wrapping that philosophy in bedtime stories, hoping the time would come when he would find some plan by which his handicap could be made to serve some useful purpose.

Reason told me plainly that there was no adequate compensation for the lack of ears and natural hearing equipment. *Desire* backed by *faith* pushed reason aside and inspired me to carry on.

As I analyze the experience in retrospect, I can see now that my son's faith in me had much to do with the astounding results. He did not question anything I told him. I sold him the idea that he had a distinct advantage over his older brother, and that this advantage would reflect itself in many ways. For example, the teachers in school would observe that he had no ears, and because of this, they would show him special attention and treat him with extraordinary kindness. They always did. His mother saw to that by visiting the teachers and arranging with them to give the child the extra attention necessary. I sold him the idea, too, that when he became old enough to sell newspapers (his older brother had already become a newspaper merchant), he would have a big advantage over his brother, as people would pay him extra money for his wares because they could see he was a bright, industrious boy despite the fact he had no ears.

We noticed that, gradually, the child's hearing was improving. Moreover, he had not the slightest tendency to be self-conscious because of his affliction. When he was about seven, he showed the first evidence that our method of servicing his mind was bearing fruit. For several months he begged for the privilege of selling newspapers, but his mother would not give her consent. She was afraid that his deafness made it unsafe for him to go on the street alone. Finally, he took matters in his own hands. One afternoon, when he was left at home with the servants, he climbed through the kitchen window, shinned to the ground, and set out on his own. He borrowed 6 cents in capital from the neighborhood shoemaker, invested it in papers, sold out, reinvested, and kept repeating until late in the evening. After balancing his accounts, and paying back the 6 cents he had borrowed from his banker, he had a net profit of 42 cents. When we got home that night, we found him in bed asleep, with the money tightly clenched in his hand. His mother opened his hand, removed the coins, and cried. Of all things! Crying over her son's first victory seemed so inappropriate. My reaction was the reverse. I laughed heartily, for I knew that my endeavor to plant in the child's mind an attitude of faith in himself had been successful. His mother saw, in his first business venture, a little deaf boy who had gone out in the streets and risked his life to earn money. I saw a brave, ambitious, self-reliant little businessman whose stock in himself had increased 100 percent because he had gone into business on his own initiative, and had won. The transaction pleased me, because I knew he had given evidence of a trait of resourcefulness that would go with him all through life.

Later events proved this to be true. When his older brother wanted something, he would lie down on the floor, kick his feet in the air, cry for it—and get it. When the "little deaf boy" wanted something, he would plan a way to earn the money, then buy it for himself. He still follows that plan! Truly, my own son has taught me that handicaps can be converted into stepping stones on which one may climb toward some worthy goal, unless they are accepted as obstacles and used as alibis.

The little deaf boy went through grade school, high school, and college without being able to hear his teachers, except when they shouted loudly at close range. He did not go to a school for the deaf. We would not permit him to learn sign language. We were determined that he should live a normal life and associate with normal children, and we stood by that decision, although it cost us many heated debates with school officials.

While he was in high school, he tried an electrical hearing aid, but it was of no value to him. We believed this was due to a condition that was disclosed when the child was six. Dr. J. Gordon Wilson of Chicago operated on one side of the boy's head and discovered that there was no sign of natural hearing equipment.

During his last week in college (eighteen years after the operation), something happened which marked the most important turning point of his life. Through what seemed to be mere chance, he came into possession of another electrical hearing device, which was sent to him on trial. He was slow about testing it, due to his disappointment with a similar device. Finally he picked the instrument up, and more or less carelessly placed it on his head and hooked up the battery, and lo! as if by a stroke of magic, his lifelong DESIRE FOR NORMAL HEARING BECAME A REALITY! For the first time in his life he heard practically as well as any person with normal hearing.

"God moves in mysterious ways, His wonders to perform." Overjoyed because of the changed world that had been brought to him through his hearing device, he rushed to the telephone, called his mother, and heard her voice perfectly. The next day he plainly heard the voices of his professors in class for the first time in his life! He heard the radio. He heard the cinema. For the first time in his life, he could converse freely with other people without their having to speak loudly. Truly, he had come into possession of a changed world. We had refused to accept Nature's error, and by *persistent desire,* we had induced Nature to correct that error, through the only practical means available.

Desire had commenced to pay dividends, but the victory was not yet complete. The boy still had to find a definite and practical way to convert his handicap into an equivalent asset.

Hardly realizing the significance of what had already been accomplished, but intoxicated with the joy of his newly discovered world of sound, he wrote a letter to the manufacturer of the hearing aid, enthusiastically describing his experience. Something in his letter—something, perhaps, which was not written on the lines but between them—caused the company to invite him to New York. When he arrived, he was escorted through the factory. While talking with the chief engineer, telling him about his changed world, a hunch, an idea, or an inspiration—call it what you wish—flashed into his mind. It was this impulse of thought which converted his affliction into an asset destined to pay dividends in both money and happiness to thousands for all time to come.

The sum and substance of that impulse of thought was this: It occurred to him that he might be of help to the millions of deaf people who go through life without the benefit of hearing devices if he could find a way to tell them the story of his changed world. Then and there, he reached a decision to devote the remainder of his life to providing a useful service to the hard of hearing. For an entire month, he carried out intensive research. He analyzed the entire marketing system of the manufacturer of the hearing device, and created ways and means of communicating with the hard of hearing all over the world for the purpose of sharing with them his newly discovered changed world. When this was done, he wrote a two-year plan based upon his findings. On presenting the plan to the company, he was instantly given a position for the purpose of carrying out his ambition. Little did he dream, when he went to work, that he was destined to bring hope and practical relief to thousands of deaf people who, without his help, would have been doomed forever to deaf-mutism.

Shortly after he became associated with the manufacturer of his hearing aid, he invited me to attend a class conducted by his company for the purpose of teaching deaf-mutes to hear and speak. I had never heard of such a form of education, therefore I visited the class skeptical but hopeful that my time would not be entirely wasted. Here I saw a demonstration that gave me a greatly enlarged vision of what I had done to arouse and keep alive in my son's mind the *desire* for normal hearing. I saw deaf-mutes actually being taught to hear and speak through application of the selfsame principle I had used, more than twenty years previously, in saving my son from deaf-mutism.

Thus, through some strange turn of the wheel of fate, my son Blair and I were destined to aid in correcting deaf-mutism for those as yet unborn. There is no doubt in my mind that Blair would have been a deaf-mute all his life if his mother and I had not managed to shape his mind as we did.

When Blair was an adult, Dr. Irving Voorhees, a noted specialist in such cases, examined him thoroughly. He was astounded when he learned how well my son hears and speaks, and said his examination indicated that "theoretically, the boy should not be able to hear at all." But the lad does hear, despite the fact that X-ray pictures show there is no opening in the skull, whatsoever, from where his ears should be to the brain.

When I planted in his mind the *desire* to hear and talk, and live as a normal person, there went with that impulse some strange influence which caused Nature to become bridge-builder, and span the gulf of silence between his brain and the outer world by some means which the keenest medical specialists have not been able to interpret. It would be sacrilege for me to even conjecture as to how Nature performed this miracle. It would be unforgivable if I neglected to tell the world as much as I know of the humble part I assumed in the strange experience. It is my duty and a privilege to say I believe, and not without reason, that nothing is impossible to the person who backs *desire* with enduring *faith*.

I have no doubt that a *burning desire* has devious ways of transmuting itself into its physical equivalent. Blair *desired* normal hearing; now he has it! He was born with a handicap, which might easily have sent one with a less defined *desire* to the street with a bundle of pencils and a tin cup. That handicap now promises to serve as the medium by which he will render useful service to many millions of hard of hearing, as well as to give him useful employment at adequate financial compensation for the remainder of his life. The little "white lies" I planted in his mind when he was a child, leading him to *believe* his affliction would become a great asset on which he could capitalize, have been justified. There is nothing, right or wrong, which *belief* plus *burning desire* cannot make real. These qualities are free to everyone.

In all my experience in dealing with men and women who had personal problems, I never handled a single case which more definitely demonstrates the power of *desire*. Authors sometimes make the mistake of writing of subjects of which they have but superficial, or very elementary, knowledge. It has been my good fortune to have had the privilege of testing the soundness of the *power of desire* through the affliction of my own son. Perhaps it was providential that the experience came as it did, for surely no one is better prepared than he to serve as an example of what happens when desire is put to the test. If Mother Nature bends to the will of desire, is it logical that mere men can defeat a burning desire? Strange and imponderable is the power of the human mind! We do not understand the method by which it uses every circumstance, every individual, every physical thing within its reach as a means of transmuting desire into its physical counterpart. Perhaps science will uncover this secret. I planted in my son's mind the desire to hear and to speak as any normal person hears and speaks. That desire has now become a reality. I planted in his mind the desire to convert his greatest handicap into his greatest asset. That desire has been realized.

The modus operandi by which this astounding result was achieved is not hard to describe. It consisted of three very definite facts. First, I MIXED FAITH with the DESIRE for normal hearing, which I passed on to my son. Second, I communicated my desire to him in every conceivable way available, through persistent, continuous effort, over a period of years. Third, HE BELIEVED ME!

Several years ago, one of my business associates became ill. He became worse as time went on, and finally was taken to the hospital for an operation. Just before he was wheeled into the operating room, I took a look at him and wondered how anyone as thin and emaciated as he could possibly go through a major operation successfully. The doctor warned me that there was little, if any, chance of my ever seeing him alive again. But that was the *doctor's opinion*. It was not the opinion of the patient. Just before he was wheeled away, he whispered feebly, "Do not be disturbed, chief. I will be out of here in a few days."

The attending nurse looked at me with pity. But the patient did come through safely. After it was all over, his physician said, "Nothing but his own desire to live saved him. He never would have pulled through if he had not refused to accept the possibility of death." I believe in the power of *desire* backed by *faith* because I have seen this power lift people from lowly beginnings to places of power and wealth; I have seen it rob the grave of its victims; I have seen it serve as the medium by which people staged a comeback after having been defeated in a hundred different ways; I have seen it provide my own son with a normal, happy, successful life, despite Nature having sent him into the world without ears.

How can one harness and use the power of *desire*? This has been answered through this chapter, and the subsequent chapters of this book.

I wish to convey the thought that all achievement, no matter what its nature or purpose, must begin with an intense, *burning desire* for something definite. Through some strange and powerful principle of "mental chemistry," Nature wraps up in the impulse of *strong desire* "that something" which recognizes no such word as "impossible" and accepts no such reality as failure.

CHAPTER 3

FAITH:
Visualizing and Believing in the Attainment of Desire

(The Second Step to Riches)

FAITH is the head chemist of the mind. When *faith* is blended with the vibration of thought, the subconscious mind instantly picks up the vibration, translates it into its spiritual equivalent, and transmits it to Infinite Intelligence, as in the case of prayer.

Faith, love, and *sex* are the most powerful of all the major positive emotions. When the three are blended, they have the effect of "coloring" the vibration of thought in such a way that it instantly reaches the subconscious mind, where it is changed into its spiritual equivalent, the only form that induces a response from Infinite Intelligence.

Love and faith are psychic, related to our spiritual side. Sex is purely biological, and related only to the physical. The mixing, or blending, of these three emotions has the effect of opening a direct line of communication between the finite, thinking mind and Infinite Intelligence.

How to Develop Faith

FAITH is a state of mind that may be induced, or created, by affirmation or repeated instructions to the subconscious mind, through the principle of autosuggestion. As an illustration, consider the purpose for which you are, presumably, reading this book. The object is, naturally, to acquire the ability to transmute the intangible thought impulse of *desire* into its physical counterpart, *money.* By following the instructions laid down in Chapter 3, on autosuggestion, and Chapter 11, on the subconscious mind, you may *convince* the subconscious mind that you believe you will receive what you ask for. It will act upon that belief, passing back to you in the form of *faith,* followed by definite plans for procuring your goal.

The method by which one develops *faith,* where it does not already exist, is extremely difficult to describe. Almost as difficult, in fact, as it would be to describe the color of red to a blind man. Faith is a state of mind that you may develop at will, after you have mastered the 13 steps to riches in this book.

Making repeated affirmations to your subconscious mind is the only known method of developing the emotion of faith voluntarily. Perhaps the meaning may be made clearer through the following explanation as to the way people sometimes become criminals. Stated in the words of a famous criminologist, "When people first come into contact with crime, they abhor it. If they remain in contact with crime for a time, they become accustomed to it, and endure it. If they remain in contact with it long enough, they finally embrace it, and become influenced by it."

This is the equivalent of saying that any impulse of thought which is repeatedly passed on to the subconscious mind is finally accepted and acted upon. The subconscious mind proceeds to translate that impulse into its physical equivalent by the most practical procedure available. In connection with this, consider again the statement "ALL THOUGHTS WHICH HAVE BEEN EMOTIONALIZED (given feeling) AND MIXED WITH FAITH begin immediately to translate themselves into their physical equivalent or counterpart."

The emotions, or the "feeling" portion of thoughts, are the factors that give thoughts vitality, life, and action. The emotions of faith, love, and sex, when mixed with any thought impulse, give it greater action than any of these emotions can do singly. Not only thought impulses which have been mixed with *faith* but also those that have been mixed with any of the positive emotions—or any of the negative emotions—may reach and influence the subconscious mind.

From this statement you will understand that the subconscious mind will translate a thought impulse of a negative or destructive nature into its physical equivalent, just as readily as it will act upon thought impulses of a positive or constructive nature. This accounts for the strange phenomenon so many millions of people experience, referred to as "misfortune" or "bad luck."

Millions of people *believe* themselves "doomed" to poverty and failure because of some strange force over which they *believe* they have no control. They are the creators of their own "misfortunes" because of this negative *belief,* which is picked up by the subconscious mind and translated into its physical equivalent.

This is an appropriate place at which to suggest again that you may benefit by passing on to your subconscious mind any *desire* that you wish translated into its physical or monetary equivalent, in a state of expectancy or *belief* that the transmutation will actually take place. Your *belief* or *faith* is the element that determines the action of your subconscious mind. There is nothing to hinder you from "deceiving" your subconscious mind when giving it instructions through autosuggestion, as I deceived my son's subconscious mind. To make this "deceit" more realistic, conduct yourself just as you would if you were ALREADY IN POSSESSION OF THE MATERIAL THING WHICH YOU ARE DEMANDING when you call upon your subconscious mind. The subconscious mind will transmute into its physical equivalent, by the most direct and practical media available, any order given to it in a state of *belief* or *faith* that the order will be carried out.

Surely enough has been stated to give a starting point from which one may, through experiment and practice, acquire the ability to mix *faith* with any order given to the subconscious mind. Perfection will come through practice. It cannot come by merely reading instructions.

If it is true that one may become a criminal by association with crime (and this is a known fact), it is equally true that one may develop faith by voluntarily suggesting to the subconscious mind that one has faith. The mind comes, finally, to take on the nature of the influences that dominate it. Understand this truth and you will know why it is essential for you to encourage the positive emotions as dominating forces of your mind, and discourage—and eliminate—negative emotions.

A mind dominated by positive emotions becomes a favorable abode for the state of mind known as faith. A mind so dominated may, at will, give the subconscious mind instructions, which it will accept and act upon immediately.

Faith Is a State of Mind Which May Be Induced by Autosuggestion

All through the ages, religious leaders have admonished struggling humanity to "have faith" in this, that, and the other dogma or creed, but they have failed to tell people *how* to have faith. They have not stated that faith is a state of mind, and that it may be induced by self-suggestion.

In language any normal human being can understand, I will describe all that is known about the principle through which *faith* may be developed, where it does not already exist.

Have faith in yourself, faith in the Infinite.

Before we begin, you should be reminded again that:

FAITH is the "eternal elixir" which gives life, power, and action to the impulse of thought!

The foregoing sentence is worth reading a second time, and a third, and a fourth. It is worth reading aloud!

FAITH is the starting point of all accumulation of riches!

FAITH is the basis of all "miracles" and mysteries that cannot be analyzed by the rules of science!

FAITH is the only known antidote to FAILURE!

FAITH is the element, the "chemical" which, when mixed with prayer, gives one direct communication with Infinite Intelligence.

FAITH is the element that transforms the ordinary vibration of thought, created by the finite mind of man, into the spiritual equivalent.

FAITH is the only agency through which the cosmic force of Infinite Intelligence can be harnessed and used.

EVERY ONE OF THE FOREGOING STATEMENTS IS CAPABLE OF PROOF!

The proof is simple and easily demonstrated. It is wrapped up in the principle of auto-suggestion. Let us center our attention, therefore, upon the subject of self-suggestion, and find out what it is capable of achieving.

It is a well-known fact that one comes, finally, to *believe* whatever one repeats to oneself, whether the statement be true or false. If a person repeats a lie over and over, the lie will eventually be accepted as truth. Moreover, it will be *believed* to be the truth. Each of us is what we are because of the *dominating thoughts* we permit to occupy our minds. Thoughts which are deliberately placed in our own mind, and encouraged with sympathy, and with which are mixed any one or more of the emotions, constitute the motivating forces. These forces direct and control our every movement, act, and deed!

THOUGHTS WHICH ARE MIXED WITH ANY OF THE FEELINGS OR EMO-

TIONS CONSTITUTE A "MAGNETIC" FORCE WHICH ATTRACTS, FROM THE VIBRATIONS OF THE ETHER, OTHER SIMILAR OR RELATED THOUGHTS.

A thought thus "magnetized" with emotion may be compared to a seed that, when planted in fertile soil, germinates, grows, and multiplies itself over and over again, until that one small seed becomes countless millions of seeds of the *same brand*!

The ether is a great cosmic mass of eternal forces of vibration. It is made up of both destructive vibrations and constructive vibrations. It carries, at all times, vibrations of fear, poverty, disease, failure, misery; and vibrations of prosperity, health, success, and happiness. It does this just as surely as it carries the sound of hundreds of orchestrations of music and hundreds of human voices, all of which maintain their individuality and means of identification, through the medium of radio.

From the great storehouse of the ether, the human mind is constantly attracting vibrations that harmonize with that which *dominates* the mind. Any thought, idea, plan, or purpose which one holds in one's mind attracts, from the vibrations of the ether, a host of its relatives. It adds these "relatives" to its own force, and grows until it becomes the dominating *motivating master* of the individual in whose mind it has been housed.

Now let us go back to the starting point, and find out how the original seed of an idea, plan, or purpose may be planted in the mind. The information is easily conveyed: any idea, plan, or purpose may be placed in the mind through repetition of thought. This is why you are asked to write out a statement of your major purpose, or Definite Chief Aim, commit it to memory, and repeat it—in audible words, day after day—until these vibrations of sound have reached your subconscious mind.

We are what we are because of the vibrations of thought that we pick up and register through the stimuli of our daily environment.

Resolve to throw off the influences of any unfortunate environment and to build your own life to *order*. Taking an inventory of mental assets and liabilities, you will discover that your greatest weakness is lack of self-confidence. This handicap can be surmounted—and timidity translated into courage—through the aid of the principle of autosuggestion. The application of this principle may be made through a simple arrangement of positive thought impulses stated in writing, memorized, and repeated, until they become a part of the working equipment of the subconscious faculty of your mind.

Self-Confidence Formula

1. I know that I have the ability to achieve the object of my *Definite Purpose* in life. Therefore I *demand* of myself persistent, continuous action toward its attainment, and I here and now promise to take such action.

2. I realize the dominating thoughts of my mind will eventually reproduce themselves in outward, physical action and gradually transform themselves into physical reality. Therefore I will concentrate my thoughts for 30 minutes daily upon the task of thinking of the person I intend to become, thereby creating in my mind a clear mental picture of that person.

3. I know through the principle of autosuggestion that any desire I persistently hold in my mind will eventually seek expression through some practical means of attaining the object. Therefore I will devote 10 minutes daily to demanding of myself the development of *self-confidence*.

4. I have clearly written down a description of my Definite Chief Aim in life. I will never stop trying until I have developed sufficient self-confidence for its attainment.

5. I fully realize that no wealth or position can long endure unless built upon truth and justice. Therefore I will engage in no transaction that does not benefit all whom it affects. I will succeed by attracting to myself the forces I wish to use, and the co-operation of other people. I will induce others to serve me because of my willingness to serve others. I will eliminate hatred, envy, jealousy, selfishness, and cynicism by developing love for all humanity, because I know that a negative attitude toward others can never bring me success. I will cause others to believe in me, because I will believe in them, and in myself. I will sign my name to this formula, commit it to memory, and repeat it aloud once a day, with full *faith* that it will gradually influence my *thoughts* and *actions* so that I will become a self-reliant and successful person.

Underpinning this formula is a law of Nature that no one has yet been able to explain. It has baffled the scientists of all ages. Psychologists have named this law "autosuggestion" and let it go at that. The name by which one calls this law is of little importance. The important fact about it is it *works* for the glory and success of humankind *if* it is used constructively. If used destructively, on the other hand, it will destroy just as readily. In this statement may be found a significant truth: those who go down in defeat and end their lives in poverty, misery, and distress do so because of negative application of the principle of autosuggestion.

The cause may be found in the fact that ALL IMPULSES OF THOUGHT HAVE A TENDENCY TO CLOTHE THEMSELVES IN THEIR PHYSICAL EQUIVALENT.

The subconscious mind (the chemical laboratory in which all thought impulses are combined and made ready for translation into physical reality) makes no distinction between constructive and destructive thought impulses. It works with the material we feed it through our thought impulses. The subconscious mind will translate into reality a thought driven by *fear* just as readily as it will translate into reality a thought driven by *courage* or *faith*.

The pages of medical history are rich with illustrations of cases of "suggestive suicide." A person may commit suicide through negative suggestion just as effectively as by any other means. In a Midwestern city, a bank official named Joseph Grant borrowed a large sum of the bank's money without the consent of the directors. He lost the money through gambling. One afternoon, the bank examiner came and began to check the accounts. Grant left the bank and took a room in a local hotel. When they found him, three days later, he was lying in bed, wailing and moaning, repeating over and over these words, "My God, this will kill me! I cannot stand the disgrace." In a short time he was dead. The doctors pronounced the case one of "mental suicide."

Just as electricity will turn the wheels of industry and provide useful service if used constructively, or snuff out life if wrongly used, so will the law of autosuggestion lead you to peace and prosperity or down into the valley of misery, failure, and death. It all depends on your degree of understanding and application of it.

If you fill your mind with *fear,* doubt, and disbelief in your ability to connect with and use the forces of Infinite Intelligence, the law of autosuggestion will take this spirit of unbelief and use it as a pattern which your subconscious mind will translate into its physical equivalent.

THIS STATEMENT IS AS TRUE AS THE STATEMENT THAT TWO AND TWO ARE FOUR!

Like the wind that carries one ship east and another west, the law of autosuggestion will lift you up or pull you down, according to the way you set your sails of *thought*.

The law of autosuggestion, through which any person may rise to altitudes of achievement that stagger the imagination, is well described in the following verse:

> If you *think* you are beaten, you are,
> If you *think* you dare not, you don't.
> If you like to win, but you *think* you can't,
> It is almost certain you won't.

If you *think* you'll lose, you're lost,
For out of the world we find,
Success begins with a person's will—
It's all in the *state of mind*.

If you *think* you are outclassed, you are,
You've got to *think* high to rise.
You've got to be *sure of yourself* before
You can ever win a prize.

Life's battles don't always go
To the stronger or faster man
But soon or late the one who wins
Is the one WHO THINKS HE CAN!

Observe the words which have been emphasized and you will catch the deep meaning the poet had in mind.

Somewhere in your makeup (perhaps in the cells of your brain) lies sleeping the seed of achievement. If aroused and put into action, this would carry you to heights such as you may never have hoped to attain.

Just as a master musician may cause the most beautiful strains of music to pour forth from the strings of a violin, so may you arouse the genius which lies asleep in your brain, and cause it to drive you upward to whatever goal you may wish to achieve.

Abraham Lincoln was a failure at everything he tried until he was well past the age of forty. He was a Mr. Nobody from Nowhere until a great experience came into his life, aroused the sleeping genius within his heart and brain, and gave the world one of its really great men. That "experience" was mixed with the emotions of sorrow and *love*. It came to him through Ann Rutledge, the only woman he ever truly loved.

It is a known fact that the emotion of *love* is closely akin to the state of mind known as *faith*. Love comes very near to translating one's thought impulses into their spiritual equivalent. During his research, the author discovered, from the analysis of the work and achievements of hundreds of men of outstanding accomplishment, that there was the influence of a woman's love behind nearly *every one of them*.

The emotion of love, in the human heart and brain, creates a favorable field of magnetic attraction, This causes an influx of the higher and finer vibrations that are afloat in the ether.

Let us consider the power of *faith* as it was demonstrated by a man well known to all of civilization, Mahatma Gandhi of India. In this man the world experienced one of the most astounding examples of the possibilities of FAITH. Gandhi wielded more potential power than any man living in his time, and this despite the fact that he had none of the orthodox tools of power, such as money, battleships, soldiers, and materials of warfare. Gandhi had no money. He had no home. He didn't even own a suit of clothes but *he did have power.* How did he come by that power?

HE CREATED IT OUT OF HIS UNDERSTANDING OF THE PRINCIPLE OF FAITH. AND THROUGH HIS ABILITY TO TRANSPLANT THAT FAITH INTO THE MINDS OF 200 MILLION PEOPLE.

Gandhi accomplished, through the influence of *faith,* something that the strongest military power on earth could not, and never will, achieve through soldiers and military equipment. He accomplished the astounding feat of *influencing* 200 million minds to *coalesce and move in unison, as a single mind.* What other force on earth, except *faith,* could do as much?

In the mid-twentieth century, Martin Luther King, Jr., through his deep faith in his belief in human rights and dignity for all people, led men and women of all races, religions, and beliefs to join in his struggle for civil rights. His dream that people will not be judged by the color of their skin but the content of their character has not been fully realized, but his work and his death have led to significant improvements in civil rights and an impetus to keep fighting for their achievement.

The watchword of the future will be *human happiness and contentment.* When this state of mind has been attained, the production will take care of itself more effectively than anything ever accomplished where people did not, and could not, mix *faith* and individual interest with their labor.

Because of the need for faith and cooperation in business and industry, it will be both interesting and profitable to analyze a particular event. This provides an excellent understanding of the method by which industrialists and leaders of business accumulate great fortunes, by giving before they try to get.

The event chosen for this illustration dates back to 1900, when the United States Steel Corporation was being formed. As you read the story, keep in mind these fundamental facts and you will understand how *ideas* have been converted into huge fortunes.

First, the huge United States Steel Corporation was born in the mind of Charles M. Schwab, in the form of an *idea* he created through his *imagination.* Second, he mixed *faith* with his idea. Third, he formulated a *plan* for the transformation of his idea into physical and financial reality. Fourth, he put his plan into action with his famous speech at the University Club. Fifth, he applied and followed through on his plan with *persistence,* and backed it with firm *decision* until it had been fully carried out. Sixth, he prepared the way for success by a *burning desire* for success.

If you have often wondered how great fortunes are accumulated, this story of the creation of the United States Steel Corporation will be enlightening. If you have any doubt that people can *think and grow rich,* this story should dispel that doubt, because in it you can plainly see the application of a major portion of the 13 principles described in this book.

John Lowell, in the *New York World-Telegram,* with whose courtesy it is here reprinted, dramatically told this astounding story of the power of an *idea.*

A Pretty After-Dinner Speech for $1 Billion

"When, on the evening of December 12, 1900, some eighty of the nation's financial nobility gathered in the banquet hall of the University Club on Fifth Avenue to do honor to a young man from out of the West, not half a dozen of the guests realized they were to witness the most significant episode in American industrial history.

"J. Edward Simmons and Charles Stewart Smith, their hearts full of gratitude for the lavish hospitality bestowed on them by Charles M. Schwab during a recent visit to Pittsburgh, had arranged the dinner to introduce the thirty-eight-year-old steel man to Eastern banking society. But they didn't expect him to stampede the convention. They warned him, in fact, that the bosoms within New York's stuffed shirts would not be responsive to oratory, and that, if he didn't want to bore the Stilimans and Harrimans and Vanderbilts, he had better limit himself to fifteen or twenty minutes of polite vaporings and let it go at that.

"Even John Pierpont Morgan, sitting on the right hand of Schwab as became his imperial dignity, intended to grace the banquet table with his presence only briefly. And so far as the press and public were concerned, the whole affair was of so little moment that no mention of it found its way into print the next day.

"So the two hosts and their distinguished guests ate their way through the usual seven or eight courses. There was little conversation, and what there was of it was restrained. Few of the bankers and brokers had met Schwab, whose career had flowered along the banks of the Monongahela, and none knew him well. But before the evening was over, they—and with them Money Master Morgan—were to be swept off their feet, and a billion-dollar baby, the United States Steel Corporation, was to be conceived.

"It is perhaps unfortunate, for the sake of history, that no record of Charlie Schwab's speech at the dinner ever was made. He repeated some parts of it at a later date during a similar meeting of Chicago bankers. And still later, when the government brought suit to dissolve the Steel Trust, he gave his own version, from the witness stand, of the remarks that stimulated Morgan into a frenzy of financial activity.

"It is probable, however, that it was a 'homely' speech, somewhat ungrammatical (for the niceties of language never bothered Schwab), full of epigrams and threaded with wit. But aside from that it had a galvanic force and effect upon the five billion of estimated capital that was represented by the diners. After it was over and the gathering was still under its spell, although Schwab had talked for ninety minutes, Morgan led the orator to a recessed window where, dangling their legs from the high, uncomfortable seat, they talked for an hour more.

"The magic of the Schwab personality had been turned on, full force, but what was more important and lasting was the full-fledged, clear-cut program he laid down for the aggrandizement of Steel. Many other men had tried to interest Morgan in slapping together a steel trust after the pattern of the biscuit, wire and hoop, sugar, rubber, whiskey, oil, or chewing gum combinations. John W. Gates, the gambler, had urged it, but Morgan distrusted him. The Moore boys, Bill and Jim, Chicago stockbrokers who had glued together a match trust and a cracker corporation, had urged it and failed. Elbert H. Gary, the sanctimonious country lawyer, wanted to foster it, but he wasn't big enough to be impressive. Until Schwab's eloquence took J. P. Morgan to the heights from which he could visualize the solid results of the most daring financial undertaking ever conceived, the project was regarded as a delirious dream of easy-money crackpots.

"The financial magnetism that began, a generation ago, to attract thousands of small and sometimes inefficiently managed companies into large and competition-crushing combinations had become operative in the steel world through the devices of that jovial business pirate John W. Gates. Gates already had formed the American Steel and Wire Company out of a chain of small concerns, and together with Morgan had created the Federal Steel Company. The National Tube and American Bridge companies were two more Morgan concerns, and the Moore Brothers had forsaken the match and cookie business to form the 'American' group: Tin Plate, Steel Hoop, Sheet Steel—and the National Steel Company.

"But by the side of Andrew Carnegie's gigantic vertical trust, a trust owned and operated

FAITH

by fifty-three partners, those other combinations were picayune. They might combine to their heart's content but the whole lot of them couldn't make a dent in the Carnegie organization, and Morgan knew it.

"The eccentric old Scot knew it, too. From the magnificent heights of Skibo Castle he had viewed, first with amusement and then with resentment, the attempts of Morgan's smaller companies to cut into his business. When the attempts became too bold, Carnegie's temper was translated into anger and retaliation. He decided to duplicate every mill owned by his rivals. Hitherto, he hadn't been interested in wire, pipe, hoops, or sheet. Instead, he was content to sell such companies the raw steel and let them work it into whatever shape they wanted. Now, with Schwab as his chief and able lieutenant, he planned to drive his enemies to the wall.

"So it was that in the speech of Charles M. Schwab, Morgan saw the answer to his problem of combination. A trust without Carnegie—giant of them all—would be no trust at all, a plum pudding without the plums, as one writer said. Schwab's speech on the night of December 12, 1900, undoubtedly carried the inference, though not the pledge, that the vast Carnegie enterprise could be brought under the Morgan tent. He talked of the world future for steel, of reorganization for efficiency, of specialization, of the scrapping of unsuccessful mills and concentration of effort on the flourishing properties, of economies in the ore traffic, of economies in overhead and administrative departments, of capturing foreign markets.

"More than that, he told the buccaneers among them wherein lay the errors of their customary piracy. Their purposes, he inferred, had been to create monopolies, raise prices, and pay themselves fat dividends out of privilege. Schwab condemned the system in his heartiest manner. The shortsightedness of such a policy, he told his hearers, lay in the fact that it restricted the market in an era when everything cried for expansion. By cheapening the cost of steel, he argued, an ever-expanding market would be created, more uses for steel would be devised, and a goodly portion of the world trade could be captured. Actually, though he did not know it, Schwab was an apostle of modern mass production.

"So the dinner at the University Club came to an end. Morgan went home to think about Schwab's rosy predictions. Schwab went back to Pittsburgh to run the steel business for Andrew Carnegie, while Gary and the rest went back to their stock tickers, to fiddle around in anticipation of the next move.

"It was not long coming. It took Morgan about one week to digest the feast of reason Schwab had placed before him. When he had assured himself that no financial indigestion

51

was to result, he sent for Schwab—and found that young man rather coy. Mr. Carnegie, Schwab indicated, might not like it if he found his trusted company president had been flirting with the Emperor of Wall Street, the street upon which Carnegie was resolved never to tread. Then it was suggested by John W. Gates, the go-between, that if Schwab 'happened' to be in the Bellevue Hotel in Philadelphia, J. P. Morgan might also 'happen' to be there. When Schwab arrived, however, Morgan was inconveniently ill at his New York home, and so, on the elder man's pressing invitation, Schwab went to New York and presented himself at the door of the financier's library.

"Now, certain economic historians have professed the belief that from the beginning to the end of the drama, the stage was set by Andrew Carnegie—that the dinner, the famous speech, the Sunday-night conference between Schwab and the Money King were events arranged by the canny Scot. The truth is exactly the opposite. When Schwab was called in to consummate the deal, he didn't even know whether "the little boss," as Andrew was called, would so much as listen to an offer to sell, particularly to a group of men whom Andrew regarded as being endowed with something less than holiness. But Schwab did take into the conference with him, in his own handwriting, six sheets of copperplate figures, representing to his mind the physical worth and the potential earning capacity of every steel company he regarded as an essential star in the new metal firmament.

"Four men pondered over these figures all night. The chief, of course, was Morgan, steadfast in his belief in the Divine Right of Money. With him was his aristocratic partner, Robert Bacon, a scholar and a gentleman. The third was John W. Gates, whom Morgan scorned as a gambler and used as a tool. The fourth was Schwab, who knew more about the processes of making and selling steel than any whole group of men then living. Throughout that conference, the Pittsburgher's figures were never questioned. If he said a company was worth so much, then it was worth that much and no more. He was insistent, too, upon including in the combination only those concerns he nominated. He had conceived a corporation in which there would be no duplication, not even to satisfy the greed of friends who wanted to unload their companies onto the broad Morgan shoulders. Thus he left out, by design, a number of the larger concerns upon which the Walruses and Carpenters of Wall Street had cast hungry eyes.

"When dawn came, Morgan rose and straightened his back. Only one question remained.

"'Do you think you can persuade Andrew Carnegie to sell?' he asked.

"'I can try,' said Schwab.

"'If you can get him to sell, I will undertake the matter,' said Morgan.

"So far so good. But would Carnegie sell? How much would he demand? (Schwab thought about $320 million.) What would he take payment in? Common or preferred stocks? Bonds? Cash? Nobody could raise a third of a billion dollars in cash.

"There was a golf game in January on the frost-cracking heath of the St. Andrews links in Westchester, with Andrew bundled up in sweaters against the cold, and Charlie talking volubly, as usual, to keep his spirits up. But no word of business was mentioned until the pair sat down in the cozy warmth of the Carnegie cottage nearby. Then, with the same persuasiveness that had hypnotized eighty millionaires at the University Club, Schwab poured out the glittering promises of retirement in comfort, of untold millions to satisfy the old man's social caprices. Carnegie capitulated, wrote a figure on a slip of paper, handed it to Schwab, and said, 'All right, that's what we'll sell for.'

"The figure was approximately $400 million, and was reached by taking the $320 million mentioned by Schwab as a basic figure and adding to it $80 million to represent the increased capital value over the previous two years.

"Later, on the deck of a transatlantic liner, the Scotsman said ruefully to Morgan, 'I wish I had asked you for $100 million more.'

"'If you had asked for it, you'd have gotten it,' Morgan told him cheerfully.

"The thirty-eight-year-old Schwab had his reward. He was made president of the new corporation and remained in control until 1930."

This dramatic story of big business was included in this book because it is a perfect illustration of the method by which *desire can be transmuted into its physical equivalent.* I imagine some readers will question the statement that a mere intangible *desire* can be converted into its physical equivalent. Doubtless some will say, "You cannot convert *nothing* into *something!*" The answer is in the story of United States Steel. That giant organization was created in the mind of one man. The plan by which the organization was provided with the steel mills that gave it financial stability was created in the mind of the same man. His *faith,* his *desire,* his *imagination,* his *persistence* were the real ingredients that went into United States Steel. The steel mills and mechanical equipment acquired by the corporation *after it had been brought into legal existence* were incidental, but careful analysis will disclose the fact that the appraised value of the properties acquired by the corporation increased in value by an estimated *$600 million* by the mere transaction that consolidated them under one management.

In other words, Charles M. Schwab's *idea,* plus the *faith* with which he conveyed it to the minds of J. P. Morgan and the others, was marketed for a profit of approximately $600 million. Not an insignificant sum for a single idea!

What happened to some of the people who took their share of the millions of dollars of profit made by this transaction is a matter with which we are not now concerned. The important feature of the astounding achievement is that it serves as unquestionable evidence of the soundness of the philosophy described in this book. Moreover, the practicality of the philosophy has been established by the fact that the United States Steel Corporation prospered. It became one of the richest and most powerful corporations in America, employing thousands of people, developing new uses for steel, and opening new markets; thus proving that the $600 million in profit which the Schwab *idea* produced was earned.

Riches begin in the form of *thought.* The amount is limited only by the person in whose mind the thought is put into motion. *Faith* removes limitation. Remember this when you are ready to bargain with life for whatever it is that you ask as your price for having passed this way. Remember, also, that the man who created the United States Steel Corporation was practically unknown at the time. He was merely Andrew Carnegie's "Man Friday" until he gave birth to his famous idea. After that, he quickly rose to a position of power, fame, and riches.

Now for another example of how faith *in an idea made millions for one man and through it helped countless others increase their wealth. Sir John Templeton is a man with great faith in his talent to make sound and profitable investments.*

Templeton was better than most people at investing money because people often made investments based on emotion and ignorance and not common sense. He felt that by using his skill in investing, he could not only provide a needed service to the small investor, but make a good deal of money for himself as well.

To accomplish this he started a group of mutual funds to manage other people's money. This was a pioneering project, as mutual funds were a relatively new concept at the time. Templeton honed that concept into what it is today.

He reminisced that at the Templeton Growth Fund's first annual meeting the participants consisted of John Templeton, one part-time employee, and one shareholder. "We held the meeting in the dining room of a retired General Foods executive, to save money."

The Templeton funds now have more than 6,000 employees worldwide and $36 billion in assets.

Driving that growth is the Templeton Group's well-earned reputation as the premier fund group for investing. A $10,000 investment in the Templeton Growth Fund 40 years ago is worth $3 million today.

By the time he retired and sold his Templeton Group fund interests in 1992 (estimated at $400 million), John Templeton estimated that he had helped a million people make money, in addition to his own success.

THERE ARE NO LIMITATIONS
TO THE MIND EXCEPT THOSE
WE ACKNOWLEDGE.

BOTH POVERTY AND RICHES
ARE THE OFFSPRING OF
THOUGHT.

CHAPTER 4

AUTOSUGGESTION:

The Medium for Influencing the Subconscious Mind

(The Third Step to Riches)

Autosuggestion" is a term that applies to all suggestions and all self-administered stimuli that reach one's mind through the five senses. Stated in another way, auto-suggestion is self-suggestion. It is the agency of communication between that part of the mind where conscious thought takes place and that which serves as the seat of action for the subconscious mind. Through the dominating thoughts one permits to remain in the conscious mind (whether these thoughts be negative or positive is immaterial), the principle of autosuggestion voluntarily reaches the subconscious mind and influences it with these thoughts.

NO THOUGHT, whether it is negative or positive, CAN ENTER THE SUBCONSCIOUS MIND WITHOUT THE AID OF THE PRINCIPLE OF AUTOSUGGESTION, with the exception of thoughts picked up from the ether. Stated differently, all sense impressions which are perceived through the five senses are stopped by the *conscious* thinking mind, and may be either passed on to the subconscious mind or rejected at will. The conscious faculty serves, therefore, as an outer guard to the approach of the subconscious.

Nature has so built us that we have *absolute control* over the material which reaches our subconscious mind through our five senses, although this is not meant to be construed as a statement that we always *exercise* this control. In the great majority of instances, we do *not* exercise it, which explains why so many people go through life in poverty.

Recall what has been said about the subconscious mind resembling a fertile garden spot in which weeds will grow in abundance if the seeds of more desirable crops are not sown there. Autosuggestion is the agency of control through which an individual may voluntarily feed the subconscious mind thoughts of a creative nature or, by neglect, permit thoughts of a destructive nature to find their way into this rich garden of the mind.

You were instructed, in the last of the six steps described in Chapter 2, to read aloud twice daily the written statement of your desire for money, and to see and feel yourself already in possession of the money, By following these instructions, you communicate the object of your *desire* directly to your *subconscious* mind in a spirit of absolute *faith*. Through repetition of this procedure, you voluntarily create thought habits favorable to your efforts to transmute desire into its monetary equivalent.

Go back to these six steps described in Chapter 2 and read them again, very carefully, before you proceed further. Then (when you come to it) read very carefully the four instructions for the organization of your "Master Mind" group, described in Chapter 7. By comparing these two sets of instructions with that which has been stated on autosuggestion, you will see that the instructions involve the application of the principle of autosuggestion.

Remember, therefore, when reading aloud the statement of your desire (through which you are endeavoring to develop a money consciousness), that the mere reading of the words is of no consequence unless you mix emotion, or feeling, with your words. If you repeat a million times the famous Émile Coué formula, "Day by day, in every way, I am getting better and better," without mixing emotion and *faith* with your words, you will experience no desirable results. Your subconscious mind recognizes and acts *only* upon thoughts that have been well mixed with emotion or feeling.

This is a fact of such importance as to warrant repetition in practically every chapter. The lack of understanding of this is the main reason the majority of people who try to apply the principle of autosuggestion get no desirable results.

Plain, unemotional words do not influence the subconscious mind. You will get no appreciable results until you learn to reach your subconscious mind with thoughts or spoken words that have been well emotionalized with *belief*. Do not become discouraged if you cannot control and direct your emotions the first time you try to do so. Remember, there is no such possibility as *something for nothing*. Ability to reach and influence your subconscious mind has its price, and you *must pay that price*. You cannot cheat, even if you desire to do so. The price of ability to influence your subconscious mind is everlasting *persistence* in applying the principles described here. You cannot develop the desired ability for a lower price. You, and *you alone,* must decide whether or not the reward for which you are striving (the money consciousness) is worth the price you must pay for it in effort.

Wisdom and cleverness alone will not attract and retain money except in a few very rare instances where the law of averages favors the attraction of money through these sources. The method of attracting money described here does not depend upon the law of averages. Moreover, the method plays no favorites. It will work for one person as effectively as it will for another. Where failure is experienced, it is the individual, not the method, which has failed. If you try and fail, make another effort, and still another, until you succeed.

Your ability to use the principle of autosuggestion will depend, very largely, upon your capacity to *concentrate* upon a given *desire* until that desire becomes a *burning obsession*.

When you begin to carry out the instructions in connection with the six steps described in the second chapter, it will be necessary for you to make use of the principle of *concentration*.

Let us here offer suggestions for the effective use of concentration. When you begin to carry out the first of the six steps, which instructs you to "fix in your own mind the *exact* amount of money you desire," hold your thoughts on that amount of money by *concentration,* or fixation of attention, with your eyes closed, until you can *actually see* the physical appearance of the money. Do this at least once each day. As you go through these exercises, follow the instructions given in the chapter on *faith,* and see yourself actually *in possession of the money.*

Here is a most significant fact: The subconscious mind takes any orders given it in a spirit of absolute *faith* and acts upon those orders, although the orders often have to be presented over and over again, through repetition, before they are interpreted by the subconscious mind. Consider the possibility of playing a perfectly legitimate "trick" on your subconscious mind by making it believe—because you believe it—that you must have the amount of money you are visualizing, that this money is already awaiting your claim, that the subconscious mind *must* hand over to you practical plans for acquiring the money which is yours. Hand over this thought to your *imagination,* and see what your imagination can, or will, do to create practical plans for the accumulation of money through transmutation of your desire.

Do not wait for a definite plan through which you intend to exchange services or merchandise in return for the money you are visualizing. Begin at once to see yourself in possession of the money, *demanding* and *expecting* meanwhile that your subconscious mind will hand over the plan, or plans, you need. Be on the alert for these plans, and when they appear, put them into action immediately. They will probably "flash" into your mind through the sixth sense, in the form of an "inspiration." This inspiration may be considered a direct message from Infinite Intelligence. Treat it with respect, and act upon it as soon as you receive it. Failure to do this will be *fatal* to your success.

In the fourth of the six steps, you were instructed to "Create a definite plan for carrying out your desire, and begin at once to put this plan into action." You should follow this instruction in the manner described in the preceding paragraph. Do not trust to your "reason" when creating your plan. Your reason is faulty. Moreover, your reasoning faculty may be lazy, and if you depend entirely upon it to serve you, it may disappoint you.

When visualizing the money you intend to accumulate (with closed eyes), see yourself rendering the service, or delivering the merchandise you intend to give in return for this money. This is important!

Summary of Instructions

The fact that you are reading this book is an indication that you earnestly seek knowledge. It is also an indication that you are a student of this subject. If you are only a student, there is a chance you may learn much, but you will learn only by assuming an attitude of humility. If you choose to follow some of the instructions but neglect or refuse to follow others, you will fail! To get satisfactory results, you must follow *all* instructions in a spirit of *faith*.

The instructions given in connection with the six steps in Chapter 2 will now be summarized and blended with the principles covered by this chapter:

1. Go into some quiet spot (preferably in bed at night) where you will not be disturbed or interrupted. Close your eyes and repeat aloud (so you may hear your own words) the written statement of the amount of money you intend to accumulate, the time limit for its accumulation, and a description of the service or merchandise you intend to give in return for the money. As you carry out these instructions, *see yourself already in possession of the money*. For example: suppose you intend to accumulate $100,000 by the first of January, five years hence, and that you intend to give personal services in return for the money in the capacity of a sales representative. Your written statement of your purpose should be similar to the following:

   "By the first day of January 2———, I will have in my possession $100,000, which will come to me in various amounts from time to time during the interim.

   "In return for this money I will give the most efficient service of which I am capable, rendering the fullest possible quantity and the best possible quality of service as a sales representative of [describe the service or merchandise you intend to sell].

"I believe I will have this money in my possession. My faith is so strong that I can now see this money before my eyes. I can touch it with my hands. It is now awaiting transfer to me in the proportion that I deliver the service I intend to render in return for it. I am awaiting a plan by which to accumulate this money, and I will follow that plan when it is received."

2. Repeat this program night and morning until you can see (in your imagination) the money you intend to accumulate.
3. Place a written copy of your statement where you can see it night and morning. Read it just before retiring and upon rising until it has been memorized.

As you carry out these instructions, remember that you are applying the principle of autosuggestion for the purpose of giving orders to your subconscious mind. Remember, also, that your subconscious mind will act *only* upon instructions that are emotionalized and handed over to it with "feeling." *Faith* is the strongest and most productive of the emotions. Follow the instructions given in Chapter 3.

These instructions may, at first, seem abstract. Do not let this disturb you. Follow them anyway. The time will soon come, if you do as you have been instructed in spirit as well as in action, when a whole new universe of power will unfold to you. Skepticism, in connection with *all* new ideas, is characteristic of all human beings. But if you follow the instructions outlined, your skepticism will soon be replaced by belief, and this in turn will soon become crystallized into *absolute faith*. Then you will have arrived at the point where you may truly say, "I am the master of my fate, I am the captain of my soul!"

Many philosophers have made the statement that people have control over their own earthly destinies, but most of them have failed to say why this is. The reason why one may control one's own earthly status, and especially one's financial status, is thoroughly explained in this chapter. People may gain control of themselves and their environment because they have the *power to influence their own subconscious minds,* and through it gain the cooperation of Infinite Intelligence.

You are now reading the chapter that represents the keystone to the arch of this philosophy. The instructions contained in this chapter must be understood and *applied with persistence* if you are to succeed in transmuting desire into money.

The actual performance of transmuting *desire* into money involves the use of autosuggestion as an agency by which one may reach, and influence, the subconscious mind. The other principles are simply tools with which to apply autosuggestion. Keep this thought in mind, and you will, at all times, be conscious of the important part the principle of autosuggestion is to play in your efforts to accumulate money through the methods described in this book.

Carry out these instructions as though you were a small child. Inject into your efforts something of the *faith* of a child. The author has been most careful to see that no impractical instructions have been included, because of his sincere desire to be helpful.

After you have read the entire book, come back to this chapter, and follow in spirit, and in action, this instruction:

READ THE ENTIRE CHAPTER ALOUD ONCE EVERY NIGHT, UNTIL YOU BECOME THOROUGHLY CONVINCED THAT THE PRINCIPLE OF AUTO-SUGGESTION IS SOUND, THAT IT WILL ACCOMPLISH FOR YOU ALL THAT HAS BEEN CLAIMED FOR IT. AS YOU READ, UNDERSCORE WITH A PENCIL EVERY SENTENCE THAT IMPRESSES YOU FAVORABLY.

Follow this instruction to the letter and it will open the way for a complete understanding and mastery of the principles of success.

CHAPTER 5

SPECIALIZED KNOWLEDGE:

Personal Experiences or Observations

(The Fourth Step to Riches)

There are two kinds of knowledge. One is general, the other is specialized. General knowledge, no matter how great in quantity or variety it may be, is of but little use in the accumulation of money. The faculties of the great universities possess, in the aggregate, practically every form of general knowledge known to civilization. They specialize in teaching knowledge, but they do not specialize in the organization, or the use, of knowledge.

Knowledge will not attract money unless it is organized and intelligently directed through practical *plans of action* to the *definite end* of accumulation of money. Lack of understanding of this fact has been the source of confusion to millions of people who falsely believe that "knowledge is power." It is nothing of the sort! Knowledge is only potential power. It becomes power only when, and if, it is organized into definite plans of action and directed to a definite end.

This "missing link" in all systems of education known to civilization today may be found in the failure of educational institutions to teach their students HOW TO ORGANIZE AND USE KNOWLEDGE AFTER THEY ACQUIRE IT.

Many people make the mistake of assuming that because Henry Ford had but little "schooling," he is not a man of "education." Those who make this mistake do not know Henry Ford, nor do they understand the real meaning of the word "educate." That word is derived from the Latin "*educo*," meaning "to educe, to draw out, to *develop from within*."

An educated person is not necessarily one who has an abundance of general or specialized knowledge. Educated people have developed the faculties of their minds so that they may acquire anything they want, or its equivalent, without violating the rights of others. Henry Ford comes well within the meaning of this definition.

During World War I, a Chicago newspaper published certain editorials in which, among other statements, Henry Ford was called "an ignorant pacifist." Mr. Ford objected to the statements, and brought a suit against the paper for libeling him. When the suit was tried in the courts, the attorneys for the paper pleaded justification, and placed Mr. Ford himself on the witness stand for the purpose of proving to the jury that he was ignorant. The attorneys asked Mr. Ford a great variety of questions, all of them intended to prove, by his own evidence, that while he might possess considerable specialized knowledge pertaining to the manufacture of cars, he was, in the main, ignorant.

Mr. Ford was plied with such questions as the following:

"Who was Benedict Arnold?" and "How many soldiers did the British send over to America to put down the Rebellion of 1776?" In answer to the last question, Mr. Ford replied, "I do not know the exact number of soldiers the British sent over, but I have heard that it was a considerably larger number than ever went back."

Finally, Mr. Ford became tired of this line of questioning. In reply to a particularly offensive question, he leaned over, pointed his finger at the lawyer who had asked the question, and said, "If I should really *want* to answer the foolish question you have just asked, or any of the other questions you have been asking me, let me remind you that I have a row of electric push buttons on my desk, and by pushing the right button, I can summon to my aid people who can answer *any* question I desire to ask concerning the business to which I am devoting most of my efforts. Now, will you kindly tell me *why* I should clutter up my mind with general knowledge, for the purpose of being able to answer questions, when I have people around me who can supply any knowledge I require?"

There certainly was good logic to that reply.

That answer floored the lawyer. Every person in the courtroom realized it was the answer not of an ignorant man but of a man of *education.* Any person is educated who knows where to get knowledge when needed, and how to organize that knowledge into definite plans of action. Through the assistance of his Master Mind group, Henry Ford had at his command all the specialized knowledge he needed to enable him to become one of the wealthiest men in America. It was not essential that he have this knowledge in his own mind. Surely no person who has sufficient inclination and intelligence to read a book of this nature can possibly miss the significance of this illustration.

Before you can be sure of your ability to transmute *desire* into its monetary equivalent, you will require *specialized knowledge* of the service, merchandise, or profession you intend to offer in return for fortune. Perhaps you may need much more specialized knowledge than you have the ability or the inclination to acquire, and if this should be true, you may bridge your weakness through the aid of your Master Mind group.

Andrew Carnegie stated that he, personally, knew nothing about the technical end of the steel business; moreover, he did not particularly care to know anything about it. The specialized knowledge he required for the manufacture and marketing of steel he found available through the individual units of his MASTER MIND GROUP.

The accumulation of great fortunes calls for *power,* and power is acquired through highly organized and intelligently directed specialized knowledge, but that knowledge does not necessarily have to be in the possession of the person who accumulates the fortune.

The preceding paragraph should give hope and encouragement to individuals with ambition to accumulate a fortune who have not acquired the necessary "education" to supply such specialized knowledge as may be needed. People sometimes go through life suffering from inferiority complexes because they do not have formal education. The person who can organize and direct a Master Mind group of people who possess knowledge useful in the accumulation of money is just as much an educated person as anyone in the group. Remember this if you suffer from a feeling of inferiority because your schooling has been limited.

Thomas A. Edison had only three months of schooling during his entire life. He did not lack education; neither did he die poor. Henry Ford had limited schooling but he managed to do pretty well by himself financially. The fact that Ford and Edison did not have much formal schooling does not give today's young people an excuse to drop out of school. Today a minimum standard of formal education is necessary to get a good start in the world of business.

Of course, there are exceptions. Dave Thomas, who founded the Wendy's restaurant chain, was a dropout. But after he achieved success, he encouraged youngsters to continue their schooling. He backed this up by choosing to be an example to dropouts by working to get his own high school diploma forty-five years after he left school.

He took, and passed, his General Educational Development (GED) exam—the equivalent of a high school diploma. He was awarded the diploma during a special ceremony at a school in the community in which he resides in Florida. Thomas addressed more than 500 students from the school, as well as GED candidates from across the state. "Being a high school dropout has always bothered me, but I guess I always thought it was too late to get my diploma," said an enthusiastic Thomas. "Now I know it's never too late, and maybe this will inspire others to do the same."

The inspiration to get his diploma came to Thomas during a cross-country book tour promoting his autobiography, Dave's Way. *In many cities, Thomas met with high school journalists, answering their questions, offering advice, and encouraging students to stay in school and succeed. "These high school journalists were very sharp," said Thomas. "They kept asking me why I say education is so important, yet I never finished school—why didn't I practice what I preached? I didn't have a good answer, so I decided to get my high school diploma."*

His goal now is to publicize to school dropouts—whether they've recently dropped out or whether it's been years since they've been in school—that it's never too late to graduate.

"I tell people to get all the education they possibly can. The fact that I got my diploma forty-five years after dropping out shows that it's never too late," said Thomas. "Even with everything that's happened in my life, getting this diploma is one of my most important accomplishments."

It Pays to Know How to Purchase Knowledge

First of all, decide on the sort of specialized knowledge you require, and the purpose for which it is needed. To a large extent your major purpose in life, the goal toward which you are working, will help determine what knowledge you need. With this question settled, your next move requires that you have accurate information concerning dependable sources of knowledge. The more important of these are:

  a. One's own experience and education
  b. Experience and education available through cooperation of others
  c. Colleges and universities
  d. Public libraries (through books and periodicals, in which may be found all the knowledge organized by civilization)
  e. Special training courses (through evening classes and distance-learning courses in particular).

As knowledge is acquired it must be organized and put into use, for a definite purpose, through practical plans. Knowledge has no value except that which can be gained from its application toward some worthy end. This is one reason why university degrees are not guarantees of successful careers. If you contemplate taking additional schooling, first determine the purpose for which you want the knowledge you are seeking, then learn where this particular sort of knowledge can be obtained from reliable sources.

Successful people, in all callings, never stop acquiring specialized knowledge related to their major purpose, business, or profession. Those who are not successful usually make the mistake of believing that the knowledge-acquiring period ends when they finish school. The truth is that schooling does little more than point one in the direction of how to acquire practical knowledge.

Year after year, university career advisers report that recruiters who come to their campuses are chiefly interested in hiring students who have studied in a specialized field such as business management, computer science, mathematics, chemistry, and other areas that prepare them to move rapidly into productive jobs, rather than the liberal arts students, who have broader but unspecialized schooling.

However, there are many students with great potential who did not choose a specialization because they were not sure at age eighteen to twenty in what areas they wanted to make their careers. Many of these men and women have a diversified education as undergraduates but choose a career-oriented postgraduate qualification. Young readers of this book should not rush into choosing a specialty until they learn enough about what the field entails, its opportunities, and its disadvantages.

Most universities and colleges provide information and guidance to students to help them make this key decision. Whether or not such guidance is available, students should explore a variety of fields, read as much as possible about that field, and talk with people who currently are engaged in that work.

Not all careers require university degrees. Other types of training are available. Most universities have continuing education programs for people who want specialized knowledge. Some offer certificate programs in which people desirous of either learning a new field or honing their skills in that field can take a series of carefully designed courses to obtain the necessary knowledge. These courses are given in the evening or at weekends and are usually attended by adults rather than college-age students.

Home study programs—often referred to as "distance learning"—are available by correspondence or through the Internet. One advantage of home study is the flexibility of the program that permits one to study during spare time. Another stupendous advantage (if the provider is carefully chosen) is the fact that most courses offered provide opportunity for students to obtain clarification or additional information by mail or e-mail, which can be of priceless value to those needing specialized knowledge. No matter where you live, you can share the benefits.

The *self-discipline* one receives from a definite program of specialized study makes up to some extent for the wasted opportunity when knowledge was available without cost. The home study method of training is especially suited to the needs of employed people who find, after leaving school, that they must acquire additional specialized knowledge but cannot spare the time to go back to school. The continuously changing economic conditions in our society have made it necessary for thousands of people to find additional, or new, sources of income. For the majority, the solution to their problem may be found only by acquiring specialized knowledge. Many will be forced to change their occupations entirely. When a merchant finds that a certain line of merchandise is not selling, he usually supplants it with another that is in demand. People whose business is that of marketing their services must also be efficient merchants. If their services do not bring adequate returns in one occupation, they must change to another where broader opportunities are available.

People who stop studying merely because they have finished school are forever hopelessly doomed to mediocrity, no matter what their calling. The way of success is the way of continuous pursuit of knowledge. Let us consider a specific instance:

During an economic downturn, a salesman in a grocery store was made redundant. Rather than seek a job in an economy where jobs were scarce, he chose to create a business of his own. He had some bookkeeping experience, so he took a special course in accounting, familiarizing himself with the latest bookkeeping techniques and office equipment.

Starting with the grocer for whom he had formerly worked, he made contracts with more than a hundred small merchants to keep their books, at a very nominal monthly fee. His idea was so practical that he soon found it necessary to set up a portable office in a light delivery truck, which he equipped with modern office equipment. He now has a fleet of these bookkeeping offices "on wheels" and employs a large staff of assistants, thus providing small merchants with accounting service equal to the best money can buy, at very nominal cost.

Specialized knowledge, plus imagination, were the ingredients that went into this unique and successful business. Last year the owner of that business paid income tax almost ten times as much as he was paid by the merchant for whom he once worked. The loss of his job forced upon him a temporary adversity that proved to be a blessing in disguise.

The beginning of this successful business was an *idea*. Inasmuch as I had the privilege of supplying the unemployed salesman with that idea, I now assume the further privilege of suggesting another idea that has within it the possibility of even greater income, plus the possibility of rendering useful service to thousands of people who badly need that service.

The idea was suggested to the salesman who gave up selling and went into the business of keeping books on a wholesale basis. When the plan was suggested as a solution to his unemployment problem, he quickly exclaimed, "I like the idea, but I would not know how to turn it into cash." In other words, he complained he would not know how to market his bookkeeping knowledge after he acquired it.

So that brought up another problem to be solved. With the aid of a young woman clever at hand-lettering, and who could put the story together, a very attractive book was prepared, describing the advantages of the new system of bookkeeping. The pages were neatly typed and pasted in an ordinary scrapbook, which was used as a sales tool. The story of this new business was so effectively told that its owner soon had more accounts than he could handle.

Thousands of people need the services of a merchandising specialist capable of preparing an attractive brief for use in marketing their services. The aggregate annual income from such a service might easily exceed that received by the largest employment agency, and the benefits of the service might be made far greater to the purchaser than any to be obtained from an employment agency.

The *idea* here described was born of necessity, to bridge an emergency that had to be covered, but it did not stop by merely serving one person. The woman who created the idea has a keen *imagination*. She saw in her newly born brainchild the making of a new profession, one destined to provide a valuable service to thousands of people who need practical guidance in marketing their services.

Spurred to action by the instantaneous success of her first "prepared plan to market services", this energetic woman turned next to the solution of a similar problem for her son, who had just finished college but had been totally unable to find a market for his services. The plan she originated for his use was the finest specimen of merchandising of services I have ever seen.

When the plan book had been completed, it contained nearly 50 pages of beautifully typed, properly organized information, telling the story of her son's natural ability, schooling, and personal experiences, and a great variety of other information too extensive for description. The plan book also contained a complete description of the position her son desired, together with a marvelous word picture of the exact plan he would use in filling the position.

The preparation of the plan book required several weeks' labor, during which time its creator sent her son to the public library almost daily to procure data needed in selling his services to best advantage. She also sent him to all the competitors of his prospective employer, and gathered from them vital information concerning their business methods which was of great value in the formation of the plan he intended to use in filling the position he sought. When the plan had been finished, it contained more than half a dozen very fine suggestions for the use and benefit of the prospective employer, which were put to use by the company after he was hired.

One may be inclined to ask, "Why go to all this trouble to secure a job?" The answer is straight to the point. It is also dramatic, because it deals with a subject which assumes the proportion of a tragedy with millions of men and women whose sole source of income is their services.

The answer is, DOING A THING WELL IS NEVER TROUBLE! THE PLAN PREPARED BY THIS WOMAN FOR THE BENEFIT OF HER SON HELPED HIM GET THE JOB FOR WHICH HE APPLIED, AT THE FIRST INTERVIEW, AT A SALARY FIXED BY HIMSELF.

Moreover—and this, too, is important—THE POSITION DID NOT REQUIRE THE YOUNG MAN TO START AT THE BOTTOM. HE BEGAN AS A JUNIOR EXECUTIVE, AT AN EXECUTIVE'S SALARY.

"Why go to all this trouble?" do you ask? Well, for one thing, the *planned presentation* of this young man's application for a position clipped off no less than ten years of time he would have required to get to where he began had he started at the bottom and worked his way up.

This idea of starting at the bottom and working one's way up may appear sound, but the major objection to it is this: too many of those who begin at the bottom never manage to lift their heads high enough to be seen by *opportunity,* so they remain at the bottom. It should be remembered, also, that the outlook from the bottom is not so very bright or encouraging. It has a tendency to kill off ambition. We call it "getting into a rut," which means we accept our fate because we form the *habit* of daily routine, a habit that finally becomes so strong we cease to try to throw it off. And that is another reason why it pays to start one or two steps above the bottom. By so doing one forms the *habit* of looking around, of observing how others get ahead, of seeing *opportunity,* and of embracing it without hesitation.

Dan Halpin is a splendid example of what I mean. During his college days, he was student-manager of the famous 1930 National Championship Notre Dame football team, when it was under the direction of the great football coach Knute Rockne. Perhaps he was inspired by Rockne to aim high and *not mistake temporary defeat for failure,* just as Andrew Carnegie, the great industrial leader, inspired his young business lieutenants to set high goals for themselves. At any rate, young Halpin finished college at a mighty unfavorable time, when the Depression had made jobs scarce, so, after a fling at investment banking and motion pictures, he took the first opening with a potential future he could find—selling electrical hearing aids on a commission basis. Anyone could start in that sort of job, and Halpin knew it, but it was enough to open the door of opportunity to him.

For almost two years, he continued in a job not to his liking, and he would never have risen above that job if he had not done something about his dissatisfaction. He aimed, first, at the job of assistant sales manager of his company, and got the job. That one step upward placed him high enough above the crowd to enable him to see still greater opportunity. In addition, it placed him where *opportunity could see him*.

He made such a fine record selling hearing aids that A.M. Andrews, chairman of the board of the Dictograph Products Company, a business competitor, took notice. He wanted to know something about that man Dan Halpin who was taking big sales away from the long-established Dictograph Company. He sent for Halpin. When the interview was over, Halpin was the new sales manager, in charge of Dictograph's Acousticon Division.

Then, to test young Halpin's mettle, Mr. Andrews went away to Florida for three months, leaving him to sink or swim in his new job. He did not sink! Knute Rockne's spirit of "All the world loves a winner and has no time for a loser" inspired him to put so much into his job that he was elected vice president of the company, and general manager of the Acousticon and Silent Radio Division, a job which most men would be proud to earn through ten years of loyal effort. Halpin turned the trick in little more than six months.

It is difficult to say whether Mr. Andrews or Mr. Halpin is more deserving of eulogy, as both showed evidence of having an abundance of that very rare quality known as *imagination*. Mr. Andrews deserves credit for seeing in young Halpin a go-getter of the highest order. Halpin deserves credit for refusing to compromise with life by accepting and keeping a job he did not want. That is one of the major points I am trying to emphasize through this entire philosophy—that we rise to high positions or remain at the bottom *because of conditions we can control if we desire to control them*.

I am also trying to emphasize another point—namely, that both success and failure are largely the results of *habit*! I have not the slightest doubt that Dan Halpin's close association with the greatest football coach America ever knew planted in his mind the same brand of *desire* to excel which made the Notre Dame football team world-famous. Truly, there is something to the idea that hero worship is helpful, provided one worships a *winner*. Halpin tells me that Rockne was one of the world's greatest leaders of men in all history.

My belief in the theory that business associations are vital factors both in failure and in success was demonstrated when my son Blair was negotiating with Dan Halpin for a position. Mr. Halpin offered him a starting salary of about one-half what he could have got from a rival company. I brought parental pressure to bear and induced him to accept the place with Mr. Halpin, because I believe that close association with one who refuses to compromise with circumstances he does not like is an asset that can never be measured in terms of money.

Honing one's skills to become top in one's field is not limited to people in business. Michael Jordan planned every step to becoming one of the greatest athletes of his generation.

He has always had the determination to win and the willpower to keep in shape and play his very best. He is committed to maintaining high standards and improving his own records.

Jordan learned this lesson early. In high school, he was dropped from the team, but his determination to be reinstated led to his starting a heavy practice regimen daily—which he still follows. He takes each doubt as a challenge, and each year he's had a new incentive.

When he returned to basketball after a few years away from the game, his critics said he was past his prime, that he was slower and couldn't win another championship. He took this as a challenge. It just honed his determination to show them they were wrong.

He worked harder than ever. He designed a year-round training program with his personal trainer and his own gym and weight room. He recognized that as one grows older, the body starts giving signals you must listen to, and that it is essential to do things correctly to stay in the best shape possible to consistently play at championship level.

The results were astounding. Jordan led his team to the championship in 1996 and 1997, and in both years was named the Most Valuable Player.

Michael Jordan's determination is a lesson to all of us that if we are determined to achieve our goals, neither our age nor the skepticism of others can deter us. But determination is only the first step. It must be followed by hard work, a regimen of physical and mental exercise, and whatever else it takes to bring us to peak performance.

The bottom is a monotonous, dreary, unprofitable place for any person. That is why I have taken the time to describe how proper planning may circumvent lowly beginnings. Also, that is why so much space has been devoted to a description of this new profession, created by a woman who was inspired to do a fine job of *planning* because she wanted her son to have a favorable "break."

When the economy slows down and jobs become scarce, a means of creating newer and better ways of marketing our services is needed. It is hard to determine why someone had not previously discovered this stupendous need, in view of the fact that more money changes hands in return for services than for any other purpose. The sum paid out monthly to people who work for wages and salaries is so huge that it runs into hundreds of millions, and the annual distribution amounts to billions.

Perhaps some will find, in the *idea* here briefly described, the nucleus of the riches they *desire*! Ideas with much less merit have been the seedlings from which great fortunes have grown. Woolworth's five-and-ten-cent store idea, for example, had far less merit, but it piled up a fortune for its creator.

Those seeing *opportunity* lurking in this suggestion will find valuable aid in the chapter "Organized Planning." Incidentally, an efficient marketer of services would find a growing demand for *his* services wherever there are men and women who seek better markets for *their* services. By applying the Master Mind principle (see page 139), a few people with suitable talent could form an alliance, and have a paying business very quickly. One would need to be a fair writer with a flair for advertising and selling, one should be handy at graphic design, and one should be a first-class business getter who would let the world know about the service. If one person possessed all these abilities, he or she might carry on the business alone until it became too big for one person to handle.

The woman who prepared the sales plan for her son received requests from all parts of the country for her cooperation in preparing similar plans for others who desired to market their services for more money. She eventually supervised a staff of expert typists, artists, and writers who had the ability to dramatize the case history so effectively that one's services could be marketed for much more money than the prevailing wages for similar services. She was so confident of her ability that she accepted, as the major portion of her fee, a percentage of the increased pay she helped her clients earn.

It must not be supposed that her plan merely consisted of clever salesmanship by which she helped men and women to demand and receive more money for the same services they formerly sold for less pay. She looked after the interests of the purchaser as well as the seller of services, and so prepared her plans that the employer would receive full value for the additional money paid. The method by which she accomplished this astonishing result is a professional secret that she disclosed to no one except her own clients.

If you have the *imagination* and seek a more profitable outlet for your services, this suggestion may be the stimulus for which you have been searching. The *idea* is capable of yielding an income far greater than that of the "average" doctor, lawyer, or engineer whose education required several years in college. The idea is salable to those seeking new positions in practically all positions calling for managerial or executive ability, and those desiring rearrangement of incomes in their present positions.

There is no fixed price for sound ideas! Underpinning all ideas is specialized knowledge. For those who do not find riches in abundance, specialized knowledge is more abundant and more easily acquired than ideas. Because of this very truth, there is a universal demand and an ever-increasing opportunity for the person capable of helping men and women sell their services advantageously. Capability means imagination, the one quality needed to combine specialized knowledge with ideas in the form of *organized plans* designed to yield riches.

If you have imagination, this chapter may present you with an idea sufficient to serve as the beginning of the riches you desire. Remember, the idea is the main thing. Specialized knowledge may be found just around the corner—any corner!

CHAPTER 6

IMAGINATION:
The Workshop of the Mind

(The Fifth Step to Riches)

The imagination is literally the workshop wherein are fashioned all plans created by people. The impulse, the *desire,* is given shape, form, and *action* through the aid of the imaginative faculty of the mind.

It has been said that we can create anything we can imagine. Of all the ages of civilization, this is the most favorable for the development of the imagination, because it is an age of rapid change. Everywhere we come into contact with stimuli that develop the imagination. Through the aid of the imaginative faculty, humankind has discovered, and harnessed, more of Nature's forces during the past fifty years than during the entire history of the human race previous to that time. We have conquered the air so completely that the birds are a poor match for us in flying. We have harnessed the ether, and made it serve as a means of instantaneous communication with any part of the world. We have analyzed and weighed the sun at a distance of millions of miles, and have determined, through the aid of *imagination,* the elements of which it consists. We have discovered that our own brain is both a broadcasting and a receiving station for the vibration of thought, and we are beginning now to learn how to make practical use of this discovery. We have increased the speed of locomotion until we may now travel at a speed of more than 600 miles an hour.

Our only limitation, within reason, *lies in the development and use of our imagination.* We have not yet reached the apex of development in the use of our imaginative faculty. We have merely discovered that we have an imagination, and have commenced to use it in a very elementary way.

Two Forms of Imagination

The imaginative faculty functions in two forms. One is known as "synthetic imagination," and the other as "creative imagination."

Synthetic Imagination. Through this faculty one may arrange old concepts, ideas, or plans into new combinations. This faculty creates nothing. It merely works with the material of experience, education, and observation with which it is fed. It is the faculty used most by the inventor, with the exception of the "genius," who draws upon the creative imagination when they cannot solve a problem through synthetic imagination.

Creative Imagination. Through the faculty of creative imagination, the finite mind of humankind has direct communication with Infinite Intelligence. It is the faculty through which "hunches" and "inspirations" are received. It is by this faculty that all basic or new ideas are developed. It is through this faculty that thought vibrations from the minds of others are received. And it is through this faculty that one individual may "tune in to," or communicate with, the subconscious minds of others.

The creative imagination works automatically, in the manner described in subsequent pages. This faculty functions *only* when the conscious mind is vibrating at an exceedingly rapid rate—as, for example, when the conscious mind is stimulated through the emotion of a strong desire.

The creative faculty becomes more alert, more receptive to vibrations from the sources mentioned, in proportion to its development through *use*. Indeed, both the synthetic and creative faculties of imagination become more alert with use, just as any muscle or organ of the body develops through use. Your imaginative faculty may have become weak through inaction. It can be revived and made alert through *use*. This faculty does not die, though it may become quiescent through lack of use. This statement is significant! Ponder on it before continuing.

Keep in mind as you follow these principles that the entire story of how one may convert *desire* into money cannot be told in one statement. The story will be complete only when one has *mastered, assimilated,* and *begun to make use of* all the principles.

The great leaders of business, industry, and finance and the great artists, musicians, poets, and writers became great because they developed the faculty of creative imagination.

Desire is only a thought, an impulse. It is nebulous and ephemeral. It is abstract and of no value until it has been transformed into its physical counterpart. While the synthetic imagination is the one used most frequently in the process of transforming the impulse of *desire* into money, you must keep in mind that you may face circumstances which demand use of the creative imagination as well.

Center your attention, for the time being, on the development of the synthetic imagination. Transformation of the intangible impulse of *desire* into the tangible reality of *money* calls for the use of a plan, or plans. These plans must be formed with the aid of the imagination, and mainly with the synthetic faculty.

Read the entire book through, then come back to this chapter and begin at once to put your imagination to work on building a plan, or plans, for the transformation of your *desire* into money. Detailed instructions for building plans have been given in almost every chapter. Carry out the instructions best suited to your needs. Put your plan in writing, if you have not already done so. The moment you complete this, you will have *definitely* given concrete form to the intangible *desire.* Read the preceding sentence once more. Read it aloud, very slowly. As you do so, remember that the moment you put in writing the statement of your desire and a plan for its realization, you have actually *taken the first* of a series of steps that will enable you to convert the thought into its physical counterpart.

The earth on which you live, you yourself, and every other material thing are the result of evolutionary change, through which microscopic bits of matter have been organized and arranged in an orderly fashion. Moreover—and this statement is of stupendous importance— this earth, every one of the billions of individual cells of your body, and every atom of matter *began as an intangible form of energy.*

Desire is a thought impulse! Thought impulses are forms of energy. When you begin with the thought impulse *desire* to accumulate money, you are drafting into your service the same "stuff" that Nature used in creating this earth and every material form in the universe, including the body and brain in which the thought impulses function.

As far as science has been able to determine, the entire universe consists of but two elements—matter and energy. Through the combination of energy and matter has been created everything perceptible, from the largest star that floats in the heavens down to and including humankind.

You are now engaged in the task of trying to profit by Nature's method. You are (sincerely and earnestly, we hope) trying to adapt yourself to Nature's laws by endeavoring to convert *desire* into its physical and monetary equivalent. YOU CAN DO IT! IT HAS BEEN DONE BEFORE!

You can build a fortune through the aid of immutable laws. But first you must become familiar with these laws, and learn to *use* them. Through repetition, and by approaching the description of these principles from every conceivable angle, the author hopes to reveal to you the secret through which great fortunes have been accumulated. Strange and paradoxical as it may seem, the "secret" is *not a secret.* Nature herself advertises it on the earth on which we live, the stars, the planets suspended within our view, in the elements above and around us, in every blade of grass and every form of life within our vision.

Nature advertises this "secret" in the terms of biology, in the conversion of a tiny cell, so small that it may be lost on the point of a pin, into the *human being* now reading this line. The conversion of desire into its physical equivalent is certainly no more miraculous!

Do not become discouraged if you do not fully comprehend all that has been stated. Unless you have long been a student of the mind, it is not to be expected that you will assimilate all that is in the chapter upon a first reading.

But you will, in time, make good progress.

The principles that follow will open the way for an understanding of imagination. Assimilate that which you understand, as you read this philosophy for the first time. Then, when you reread and study it, you will discover that something has happened to clarify it and give you a broader understanding of the whole. Above all, *do not stop* or hesitate in your study of these principles until you have read the book at least *three* times, for then you will not want to stop.

How to Make Practical Use of Imagination

Ideas are the beginning points of all fortunes. Ideas are products of the imagination. Let us examine a few well-known ideas that have yielded huge fortunes, with the hope that these illustrations will convey definite information concerning the method by which imagination may be used in accumulating riches.

The Enchanted Kettle

Many years ago, an old country doctor drove to town, hitched his horse, quietly slipped into a drugstore by the back door, and began "dickering" with the young drug clerk. His mission was destined to yield great wealth to many people. It was destined to bring to the South the most far-flung benefit since the Civil War.

For more than an hour, behind the prescription counter, the old doctor and the clerk talked in low tones. Then the doctor left. He went out to the buggy and brought back a large, old-fashioned kettle and a big wooden paddle (used for stirring the contents of the kettle), and deposited them in the back of the store.

The clerk inspected the kettle, reached into his inside pocket, took out a roll of bills, and handed it over to the doctor. The roll contained exactly $500—the clerk's entire savings!

The doctor handed over a small slip of paper on which was written a secret formula. The words on that small slip of paper were worth a king's ransom! *But not to the doctor!* Those magic words were needed to start the kettle boiling, but neither the doctor nor the young clerk knew what fabulous fortunes were destined to flow from that kettle.

The old doctor was glad to sell the outfit for $500. The money would pay off his debts and give him freedom of mind. The clerk was taking a big chance by staking his entire life's savings on a mere scrap of paper and an old kettle! He never dreamed his investment would start a kettle overflowing with gold that would surpass the miraculous performance of Aladdin's lamp.

What the clerk really purchased was an *idea*!

The old kettle and the wooden paddle and the secret message on a slip of paper were incidental. The strange performance of that kettle began to take place after the new owner mixed with the secret instructions an ingredient of which the doctor knew nothing.

Read this story carefully, and give your imagination a test! See if you can discover what it was that the young man added to the secret message which caused the kettle to overflow with gold. Remember, as you read, that this is not a story from *Arabian Nights*. Here you have a story of facts, stranger than fiction, facts which began in the form of an *idea*.

Let us take a look at the vast fortunes of gold this idea has produced. It has paid, and still pays, huge fortunes to men and women all over the world who distribute the contents of the kettle to millions of people.

The old kettle is now one of the world's largest consumers of sugar, thus providing jobs of a permanent nature to thousands of men and women engaged in growing sugarcane, and in refining and marketing sugar.

The old kettle consumes, annually, millions of glass bottles, providing jobs to huge numbers of glass workers. The old kettle gives employment to an army of clerks, copywriters, and advertising experts throughout the nation. It has brought fame and fortune to scores of artists who have created magnificent pictures describing the product. The old kettle has converted a small Southern city into the business capital of the South, which now benefits—directly or indirectly—every business and practically every resident of the city. The influence of this idea now benefits every civilized country in the world, pouring out a continuous stream of gold to all who touch it.

Gold from the kettle built and maintains one of the most prominent colleges of the South, where thousands of young people receive the training essential for success.

The old kettle has done other marvelous things.

All through the Depression of the 1930s, when factories, banks, and other businesses were folding up and quitting by the thousands, the owner of this enchanted kettle went marching on, *giving continuous employment* to an army of men and women all over the world, and paying out extra portions of gold to those who, long ago, *had faith in the idea*.

If the product of that old brass kettle could talk it would tell thrilling tales of romance in every language: romances of love, romances of business, romances of professional men and women who are daily stimulated by it.

The author is sure of at least one such romance, for he was a part of it, and it all began not far from the very spot on which the drug clerk purchased the old kettle. It was here that the author met his wife, and it was she who first told him of the enchanted kettle. It was the product of that kettle they were drinking when he asked her to accept him "for better or worse."

Now that you know the content of the enchanted kettle is a world-famous drink, it is fitting that the author confess that the home city of the drink supplied him with a wife, also that the drink itself provides him with stimulation of thought without intoxication, and thereby serves to give the refreshment of mind an author must have to do his best work.

Whoever you are, wherever you may live, whatever occupation you may be engaged in, just remember in the future, every time you see the words "Coca-Cola," that its vast empire of wealth and influence grew out of a single *idea,* and that the mysterious ingredient the drug clerk—Asa Candler—mixed with the secret formula was . . . *imagination*!

Stop and think about that for a moment.

Remember, also, that the 13 steps to riches described in this book were the media through which the influence of Coca-Cola has been extended to every city, town, village, and crossroads of the world. *Any idea* you may create, as sound and *meritorious* as Coca-Cola, has the possibility of duplicating the stupendous record of this worldwide thirst-killer.

Truly, thoughts are things, and their scope of operation is the world itself.

What I Would Do If I Had a Million Dollars

This story proves the truth of that old saying "Where there's a will, there's a way." It was told to me by that beloved educator and clergyman Frank W. Gunsaulus, who began his preaching career in the stockyards region of South Chicago.

While Dr. Gunsaulus was going through college, he observed many defects in our educational system, defects which he believed he could correct if he was the head of a college. His deepest desire was to become the directing head of an educational institution in which young men and women would be taught to "learn by doing."

He made up his mind to organize a new college in which he could carry out his ideas without being handicapped by orthodox methods of education. He needed a million dollars to put the project across! Where was he to lay his hands on so large a sum of money? That was the question that absorbed most of this ambitious young preacher's thought.

But he couldn't seem to make any progress.

Every night he took that thought to bed with him. He got up with it in the morning. He took it with him everywhere he went. He turned it over and over in his mind until it became a consuming obsession with him. A million dollars is a lot of money. He recognized that fact, but he also recognized the truth that the only limitation is that which one sets up in one's own mind.

Being a philosopher as well as a preacher, Dr. Gunsaulus recognized, as do all who succeed in life, that *definiteness of purpose* is the point from which one must begin. He recognized, too, that definiteness of purpose takes on animation, life, and power when backed by a *burning desire* to translate that purpose into its material equivalent.

He knew all these great truths, yet he did not know where or how to lay his hands on a million dollars. The natural procedure would have been to give up and quit, saying, "Ah well, my idea is a good one, but I cannot do anything with it because I never can procure the necessary million dollars." That is exactly what the majority of people would have said, but it is not what Dr. Gunsaulus said. What he said, and what he did, are so important that I now introduce him, and let him speak for himself.

"One Saturday afternoon I sat in my room thinking of ways and means of raising the money to carry out my plans. For nearly two years, I had been thinking, but I had done nothing but think!"

The time had come for *action*!

"I made up my mind, then and there, that I would get the necessary million dollars within a week. How? I was not concerned about that. The main thing of importance was the decision to get the money within a specified time. The moment I reached that decision, a strange feeling of assurance came over me, such as I had never before experienced. Something inside me seemed to say, 'Why didn't you reach that decision a long time ago? The money was waiting for you all the time!'

"Things began to happen in a hurry. I called the newspapers and announced I would preach a sermon the following morning, entitled 'What I Would Do if I Had a Million Dollars.'

"I went to work on the sermon immediately. I must tell you, frankly, the task was not difficult, because I had been preparing that sermon for almost two years. The spirit of it was a part of me!

"Long before midnight I had finished writing the sermon. I went to bed and slept with a feeling of confidence, for *I could see myself already in possession of the million dollars.*

"Next morning I arose early, went into the bathroom, read the sermon, then knelt and prayed that my sermon might come to the attention of someone who would supply the needed money.

"While I was praying I again had that feeling of assurance that the money would be forthcoming. In my excitement, I walked out without my sermon, and did not discover the oversight until I was in my pulpit and about ready to begin delivering it.

"It was too late to go back for my notes, and what a blessing that was, Instead, my own subconscious mind yielded the material I needed. When I arose to begin my sermon, I closed my eyes and spoke of my dreams with all my heart and soul. I not only talked to my audience, but I fancy I talked also to God. I told what I would do with a million dollars if that amount was placed in my hands. I described the plan I had in mind for organizing a great educational institution where young people would learn to do practical things, and at the same time develop their minds.

"When I had finished and sat down, a man slowly arose from his seat, about three rows from the rear, and made his way toward the pulpit. I wondered what he was going to do. He came into the pulpit, extended his hand, and said, 'Reverend, I liked your sermon. I believe you can do everything you said you would, if you had a million dollars. To prove that I believe in you and your sermon, if you will come to my office tomorrow morning, I will give you the million dollars. My name is Philip D. Armour.'"

Young Gunsaulus went to Mr. Armour's office and the million dollars was presented to him. With the money, he founded the Armour Institute of Technology. That is more money than the majority of preachers ever see in an entire lifetime, yet the thought impulse behind the money was created in the young preacher's mind in a fraction of a minute. The necessary million dollars came as a result of an idea. Behind the idea was a *desire* that young Gunsaulus had been nursing in his mind for almost two years.

Observe this important fact: HE GOT THE MONEY WITHIN 36 HOURS OF REACHING A DEFINITE DECISION IN HIS OWN MIND TO GET IT, AND DECIDING UPON A DEFINITE PLAN FOR GETTING IT!

There was nothing new or unique about young Gunsaulus's vague thinking about a million dollars, and weakly hoping for it. Others before him, and many since his time, have had similar thoughts. But there was something unique and different about the decision he reached on that memorable Saturday, when he put vagueness into the background and definitely said, "I *will* get that money within a week!"

God seems to throw Himself on the side of people who know exactly what they want, if they are determined to get *just that*!

Moreover, the principle through which Dr. Gunsaulus got his million dollars is still alive! It is available to you! This universal law is as workable today as it was when the young preacher made use of it so successfully. This book describes, step by step, the 13 elements of this great law, and suggests how they may be put to use.

Observe that Asa Candler and Dr. Frank Gunsaulus had one characteristic in common: Both knew the astounding truth that IDEAS CAN BE TRANSMUTED INTO CASH THROUGH THE POWER OF DEFINITE PURPOSE, PLUS DEFINITE PLANS.

If you are one of those who believe that hard work and honesty alone will bring riches, perish the thought! It is not true! Riches, when they come in huge quantities, are never the result of *hard* work! Riches come, if they come at all, in response to definite demands, based upon the application of definite principles, and not by chance or luck.

Generally speaking, an idea is an impulse of thought that impels action by an appeal to the imagination. All master sales reps know that ideas can be sold where merchandise cannot. Ordinary sales reps do not know this—that is why they are "ordinary."

A publisher of books made a discovery that should be worth much to publishers generally. He learned that many people buy titles, and not contents of books. By merely changing the name of one book that was not moving, his sales on that book jumped upward more than a million copies. The inside of the book was not changed in any way. He merely ripped off the cover bearing the title that did not sell, and put on a new cover with a title that had "box-office" value.

That, as simple as it may seem, was an *idea*! It was *imagination*. There is no standard price on ideas. Creators of ideas make their own price, and if they are smart, they get it.

The moving picture industry created a whole flock of millionaires. Most of them were men who couldn't create ideas—*but* they had the imagination to recognize ideas when they saw them.

Andrew Carnegie knew very little about making steel—I have Carnegie's own word for this—but he made practical use of two of the principles described in this book, and made the steel business yield him a fortune.

The story of practically every great fortune starts with the day when a creator of ideas and a seller of ideas got together and worked in harmony. Carnegie surrounded himself with experts who could do all that he could not do, people who created ideas and men who put ideas into operation and made themselves and the others fabulously rich.

Millions of people go through life hoping for favorable "breaks." Perhaps a favorable break can get one an opportunity, but the safest plan is not to depend upon luck. It was a favorable "break" that gave me the biggest opportunity of my life—but twenty-five years of determined effort had to be devoted to that opportunity before it became an asset.

The "break" consisted of my good fortune in meeting and gaining the cooperation of Andrew Carnegie. On that occasion Carnegie planted in my mind the idea of organizing the principles of achievement into a philosophy of success. Thousands of people have profited by the discoveries made in the twenty-five years of research, and several fortunes have been accumulated through the application of the philosophy. The beginning was simple. It was an *idea* that anyone might have developed.

The favorable break came through Carnegie, but what about the *determination, definiteness of purpose,* the *desire to attain the goal,* and the *persistent effort of twenty-five years*? It was no ordinary desire that survived disappointment, discouragement, temporary defeat, criticism, and the constant accusation of "waste of time." It was a *burning desire, an obsession*!

When Mr. Carnegie first planted the idea in my mind, it was coaxed, nursed, and enticed to remain alive. Gradually, the idea became a giant under its own power, and it coaxed, nursed, and drove me. Ideas are like that. First you give life, action, and guidance to ideas, and then they take on a power of their own and sweep aside all opposition.

Like Andrew Carnegie, Herb Kelleher, one of the founders of Southwest Airlines, is a good example of a "seller of ideas." He was a lawyer in San Antonio, Texas, when Rollin King, the creator of an idea, asked for his help in founding a new airline.

Rollin King was an investment adviser. As a side business, he ran an unprofitable air charter service between small Texas cities. At that time, most Americans who traveled by air were business executives or wealthy pleasure seekers. King was frustrated when he wanted to fly from one city in Texas to another. He could never get a seat on the airlines that currently flew those routes—and besides, prices were too high.

He recognized the need to create an airline that would fly just between the three biggest cities in the state. King knew his little airline wasn't up to the task, so he decided to start one. He put together a feasibility study and business plan. He raised $100,000 and then went to Herb Kelleher, his lawyer, to arrange for the necessary paperwork to create Air Southwest Co. (later Southwest Airlines Co.).

Although Kelleher was at first skeptical, he worked with King to gain additional capital and some political support. On February 20, 1968, the Texas Aeronautics Commission approved Southwest's petition to fly between the three cities. However, on February 21, competing airlines—Braniff, Trans Texas, and Continental—blocked the approval with a temporary restraining order.

Kelleher, his enthusiasm for the airline ignited by the efforts to quash it, put his litigation skills to work. The competition argued that Texas didn't need a new carrier. It took a three-and-a-half-year legal battle, including three trips to three courts, for Southwest to prove otherwise and gain the necessary permission to start operating.

Although they made a good start, it wasn't enough. The company lost $3.7 million that year, and the losses continued for another year and a half. Southwest was trying to keep costs down and attract customers without compromising its original goals.

By this time, Kelleher, had become so enthralled with the concept that he gave up his law practice to run Southwest. His aim was to make Southwest the airline of choice in the market it served.

One of his innovations was peak and off-peak airline pricing. Another was the 10-minute turnaround. After landing, each plane would pull into the gate, get checked by maintenance, unload passengers, reload, and leave the gate within 10 minutes instead of the 45 minutes other airlines took. The 10-minute turnaround allowed the three-plane airline to maintain a busy schedule and improve its on-time performance.

Because of their very limited budget, they couldn't advertise in the usual media, so they chose to promote the airline by word of mouth. To do this the company decided to cultivate a sensational, off-the-wall image.

Customer service became their top priority. Flight attendants were trained to give "tender loving care" to the passengers. The company's slogan was "Now there's somebody else up there who loves you."

In addition, Kelleher eliminated the annoying, time-consuming methods the major airlines used in issuing boarding passes by creating open seating on all flights. No seat reservations were needed, and passengers were given numbered boarding cards, which were issued and collected at the gate.

With passenger satisfaction as their main objective, Kelleher and his team built up a loyal following and a reputation for passenger consideration.

Southwest began to climb its way up.

By 1978, it was one of the country's most profitable airlines. In the early 2000s, when many airlines suffered major setbacks, some going into bankruptcy and even out of business, Southwest not only survived but led the industry in profitability.

Herb Kelleher gives this advice to success-minded people:

- *Stick to your ideas. Despite the efforts of its giant competitors to keep Southwest from entering the business, a positive attitude kept them going during three years of court fights and no operating income.*
- *Think of what the customers want and then give it to them.*
- *Overcome obstacles put in your path by taking positive steps to break them down—even while the battle is being fought, find ways to get around them.*
- *Keep open to new opportunities, and when they arise, take positive steps to meet them.*

SUCCESS REQUIRES NO
EXPLANATION.

FAILURE PERMITS NO ALIBIS.

CHAPTER 7

ORGANIZED PLANNING:
The Crystallization of Desire into Action

(The Sixth Step to Riches)

You have learned that everything that is created or acquired begins in the form of *desire,* that desire is taken on the first lap of its journey, from the abstract to the concrete, into the workshop of the *imagination,* where *plans* for its transition are created and organized.

In Chapter 2, you were instructed to take six definite, practical steps as your first move in translating desire into money. One of these steps is the formation of a *definite,* practical plan, or plans, through which this transformation may be made.

You will now be instructed on how to build practical plans:

1. Ally yourself with a group of as many people as you may need for the creation and carrying out of your plan, or plans, for the accumulation of money, making use of the Master Mind principle described in Chapter 9. (Compliance with this instruction is absolutely essential. Do not neglect it.)

2. Before forming your Master Mind alliance, decide what advantages and benefits you may offer the individual members of your group in return for their cooperation. No one will work indefinitely without some form of compensation. No intelligent person will either request or expect another to work without adequate compensation, although this may not always be in the form of money

3. Arrange to meet with the members of your Master Mind group at least twice a week, and more often if possible, until you have collectively perfected the necessary plan, or plans, for the accumulation of money.

4. Maintain *perfect harmony* between yourself and every member of your Master Mind group. If you fail to carry out this instruction to the letter, you may expect to meet with failure. The Master Mind principle cannot operate where perfect harmony does not prevail. Keep in mind these facts:

    a. You are engaged in an undertaking of major importance to you. To be sure of success, you must have plans that are faultless.

    b. You must have the advantage of the experience, education, natural ability, and imagination of other minds. This is in harmony with the methods followed by every person who has accumulated a great fortune.

No individual has sufficient experience, education, natural ability, and knowledge to ensure the accumulation of a great fortune without the cooperation of other people. Every plan you adopt in your endeavor to accumulate wealth should be the collective creation of yourself and every other member of your Master Mind group. You may originate your own plans, either in whole or in part, but *see that those plans are checked and approved by the members of your Master Mind alliance.*

If the first plan you adopt does not work successfully, replace it with a new plan. If this new plan fails to work, replace it, in turn, with still another, and so on until you find a plan which *does work*. Right here is the point at which the majority of people meet with failure, because of their lack of *persistence* in creating new plans to take the place of those which fail.

The most intelligent person living cannot succeed in accumulating money—or in any other undertaking—without plans that are practical and workable. Just keep this fact in mind, and remember when your plans fail that temporary defeat is not permanent failure. It may only mean that your plans have not been sound. Build other plans. Start all over again.

Thomas A. Edison "failed" 10,000 times before he perfected the incandescent electric lightbulb. That is, he met with temporary defeat 10,000 times before his efforts were crowned with success.

Temporary defeat should mean only one thing—the certain knowledge that there is something wrong with your plan. Millions of people go through life in misery and poverty because they lack a sound plan through which to accumulate a fortune.

Henry Ford accumulated a fortune not because of his superior mind, but because he adopted and followed a *plan* which proved to be sound. A thousand people could be pointed out with a better education than Ford's, yet they live in poverty because they do not possess the *right* plan for the accumulation of money.

James J. Hill met with temporary defeat when he first endeavored to raise the necessary capital to build a railroad from the East to the West, but he turned defeat into victory through new plans.

Henry Ford met with temporary defeat, not only at the beginning of his career but after he had gone far toward the top. He created new plans and went marching on to financial victory.

We see people who have accumulated great fortunes, but we often recognize only their triumph, overlooking the temporary defeats they had to surmount before "arriving."

NO FOLLOWER OF THIS PHILOSOPHY CAN REASONABLY EXPECT TO ACCUMULATE A FORTUNE WITHOUT EXPERIENCING "TEMPORARY DEFEAT." When defeat comes, accept it as a signal that your plans are not sound, rebuild those plans, and set sail once more toward your coveted goal. If you give up before your goal has been reached, you are a "quitter."

A QUITTER NEVER WINS—AND A WINNER NEVER QUITS.

Lift this sentence out, write it on a piece of paper in letters an inch high, and place it where you will see it every night before you go to sleep, and every morning before you go to work.

When you begin to select members for your Master Mind group, endeavor to select those who do not take defeat seriously.

Some people foolishly believe that only *money* can make money. This is not true! *Desire,* transmuted into its monetary equivalent through the principles laid down here, is the agency through which money is "made." Money, of itself, is nothing but inert matter. It cannot move, think, or talk, but it can "hear" when one who *desires* it calls it to come!

Planning the Sale of Services

The remainder of this chapter has been given over to a description of ways and means of marketing services. The information here conveyed will be of practical help to any person having any form of service to market, but it will be of priceless benefit to those who aspire to leadership in their chosen occupations.

Intelligent planning is essential for success in any undertaking designed to accumulate riches. Here will be found detailed instructions to those who must begin the accumulation of riches by selling their services.

It should be encouraging to know that practically all the great fortunes began in the form of compensation for services, or from the sale of *ideas*. What else, except ideas and services, would one not possessed of property have to give in return for riches?

Broadly speaking, there are two types of people in the world, *leaders* and *followers*. Decide at the outset whether you intend to become a leader in your chosen calling or remain a follower. The difference in compensation is vast. The follower cannot reasonably expect the compensation to which a leader is entitled, although many followers make the mistake of expecting such pay.

It is no disgrace to be a follower. On the other hand, it is no credit to remain a follower. Most great leaders began in the capacity of followers. They became great leaders because they were *intelligent followers*. With few exceptions, people who cannot follow a leader intelligently cannot become efficient leaders. People who can follow a leader most efficiently are usually those who develop into leadership most rapidly. An intelligent follower has many advantages, among them the *opportunity to acquire knowledge from the leader*.

The Major Attributes of Leadership

The following are important factors of leadership:

1. **Unwavering Courage** based upon knowledge of self and of one's occupation. No follower wishes to be dominated by a leader who lacks self-confidence and courage. No intelligent follower will be dominated by such a leader for very long.
2. **Self-Control.** People who cannot control themselves can never control others. Self-control sets a mighty example for one's followers, which the more intelligent will emulate.
3. **A Keen Sense of Justice.** Without a sense of fairness and justice, no leader can command and retain the respect of his or her followers.
4. **Definiteness of Decision.** People who waver in decisions show that they are not sure of themselves. They cannot lead others successfully.
5. **Definiteness of Plans.** The successful leader must plan the work, and work the plan. A leader who moves by guesswork without practical, definite plans is comparable to a ship without a rudder. Sooner or later it will land on the rocks.
6. **The Habit of Doing More Than Paid For.** One of the penalties of leadership is the necessity of willingness, upon the part of the leaders, to do more than they require of their followers.

7. **A Pleasing Personality.** No slovenly, careless person can become a successful leader. Leadership calls for respect. Followers will not respect leaders who do not score highly on all factors of a pleasing personality.

8. **Sympathy and Understanding.** Successful leaders must be in sympathy with their followers. Moreover, they must understand them and their problems.

9. **Mastery of Detail.** Successful leadership calls for mastery of details of the leader's position.

10. **Willingness to Assume Full Responsibility.** Successful leaders must be willing to assume responsibility for the mistakes and shortcomings of their followers. If they try to shift this responsibility, they will not remain leaders. If followers make mistakes and become incompetent, it is the leader who has failed.

11. **Cooperation.** Successful leaders must understand and apply the principle of cooperative effort and be able to induce followers to do the same. Leadership calls for *power,* and power calls for *cooperation.*

There are two forms of leadership. The first, and by far the most effective, is *leadership by consent* of, and with the sympathy of, the followers. The second is *leadership by force,* without the consent and sympathy of the followers.

History is filled with evidence that leadership by force cannot endure. The downfall and disappearance of dictators and kings is significant. It means that people will not follow forced leadership indefinitely. The world has entered a new era of relationship between leaders and followers, which very clearly calls for new leaders and a new brand of leadership in business and industry. Those who belong to the old school of leadership by force must acquire an understanding of the new brand of leadership (cooperation) or be relegated to the rank and file of the followers. There is no other way out for them.

The relationship of employer and employee, or of leader and follower, in the future will be one of mutual cooperation, based upon an equitable division of the profits of business. In the future, the relationship of employer and employee will be more like a partnership than it has been in the past. Hitler and Stalin are examples of leaders who ruled by force. Their leadership passed. People may follow the forced leadership temporarily, but they will not do so willingly. *Leadership by consent* of the followers is the only brand that can endure!

The new brand of leadership will embrace the 11 attributes described earlier in this chapter, as well as some other factors. People who make these attributes the basis of their leadership will find abundant opportunity to lead in any walk of life.

The 10 Major Causes of Failure in Leadership

We come now to the major faults of leaders who fail, because it is just as essential to know *what not to do* as it is to know what to do.

1. **Inability to Organize Details.** Efficient leadership calls for ability to organize and to master details. No genuine leader is ever "too busy" to do anything that may be required as a leader. When a leader or follower is "too busy" to change plans or give attention to any emergency, it is an indication of inefficiency. The successful leader must be the master of all details connected with the position. That means, of course, that the habit of delegating details to capable lieutenants must be acquired.

2. **Unwillingness to Render Humble Service.** Truly great leaders are willing, when occasion demands, to perform any sort of labor that they would ask another to perform. "The greatest among ye shall be the servant of all" is a truth that all able leaders observe and respect.

3. **Expectation of Pay for What They "Know" Instead of What They Do with What They Know.** The world does not pay for what people "know." It pays them for what they *do,* or induce others to do.

4. **Fear of Competition from Followers.** The leader who fears that one of his followers may take his position is practically sure to realize that fear sooner or later. Able leaders train understudies to whom they may delegate at will. Only in this way may leaders multiply themselves and prepare to be at many places, and give attention to many things, at one time. It is an eternal truth that people receive more pay for their *ability to get others to perform* than they could possibly earn by their own efforts. Efficient leaders may, through knowledge of their jobs and the magnetism of their personalities, greatly increase the efficiency of others, and induce them to render more service and better service than they could by themselves.

5. **Lack of Imagination.** Without imagination, leaders are incapable of meeting emergencies, and of creating plans by which to guide followers efficiently.

6. **Selfishness.** Leaders who claim all the honor for the work of their followers are sure to be met by resentment. Really great leaders *claim none of the honors.* They are content to see the honors go to their followers, because they know that most people will work harder for commendation and recognition than they will for money alone.

7. **Intemperance.** Followers do not respect an intemperate leader. Moreover, intemperance in any of its various forms destroys the endurance and the vitality of all who indulge in it.

8. **Disloyalty.** Perhaps this should have come at the head of the list. Leaders who are not loyal to their trust and to their associates—those above and below them—cannot long maintain their leadership. Disloyalty marks people as being less than the dust of the earth, and brings down on their head the contempt they deserve. Lack of loyalty is one of the major causes of failure in every walk of life.

9. **Emphasis of the "Authority" of Leadership.** Efficient leaders lead by encouraging, not by trying to instill fear in the hearts of their followers. Leaders who try to impress followers with their "authority" come within the category of leadership through *force*. Real leaders have no need to advertise that fact except by their conduct, sympathy, understanding, and fairness, and a demonstration of knowledge of the job.

10. **Emphasis of Title.** Competent leaders require no "title" to gain the respect of their followers. Leaders who make too much of their title generally have little else to emphasize. The doors to the office of real leaders are open to all who wish to enter, and their working quarters are free from formality or ostentation.

These are among the more common causes of failure in leadership. Any one of these faults is sufficient to induce failure. Study the list carefully if you aspire to leadership, and make sure you are free of these faults.

Some Fertile Fields in Which "New Leadership" Will Be Required

Before you leave this chapter, your attention is called to a few of the fertile fields in which there has been a decline of leadership, and in which the new type of leader may find an abundance of *opportunity*.

1. In the field of politics there is a most insistent demand for new leaders, a demand that indicates nothing less than an emergency. Too many politicians have, seemingly, become high-grade, legalized racketeers. They have increased taxes and debauched the machinery of industry and business until the people can no longer stand the burden.

2. The financial industry is undergoing a reform. The leaders in this field have almost entirely lost the confidence of the public. Already financial executives have sensed the need for reform, and have set the wheels in motion.

3. Industry calls for new leaders. The old type of leaders thought and moved in terms of dividends instead of thinking and moving in terms of human equations! The future leaders in industry, to endure, must regard themselves as quasi-public officials whose duty it is to manage their trust in such a way that it will bring hardship on no individual or group. Exploitation of workers is a thing of the past. Let those who aspire to leadership in the field of business, industry, and labor remember this.

4. Religious leaders of the future will be forced to give more attention to the temporal needs of their followers in the solution of their economic and personal problems of the present, and less attention to the dead past and the yet unborn future.

5. In the professions of law, medicine, and education, a new brand of leadership, and to some extent new leaders, will become a necessity. This is especially true in the field of education. Leaders in that field must, in the future, find ways and means of teaching people *how to apply* the knowledge they receive in school. They must deal more with *practice* and less with *theory*.

6. New leaders will be required in the field of journalism. The media of the future, to be conducted successfully, must be divorced from "special privilege" and relieved from the subsidy of advertising.

These are but a few of the fields in which opportunities for new leaders and a new brand of leadership are now available.

The world is undergoing a rapid change. This means that the media, through which the changes in human habits are promoted must be adapted to the changes. The media here described are the ones that, more than any others, determine the trend of civilization.

When and How to Apply for a Position

The information described here is the net result of many years of experience during which thousands of men and women were helped to market their services effectively. It can, therefore, be relied upon as sound and practical.

Media Through Which Services May Be Marketed

Experience has proved that the following media offer the most direct and effective methods of bringing the buyer and seller of services together:

1. **Employment Agencies.** Care must be taken to select only reputable agencies, the management of which can show adequate records of achievement of satisfactory results.

2. **Advertising** in newspapers, trade journals, and magazines and on the Internet. Classified advertising may usually be relied upon to produce satisfactory results in the case of those who apply for clerical or ordinary salaried positions. Display advertising is more desirable in the case of those who seek executive connections, the copy to appear in the section of the paper most likely to come to the attention of the class of employer being sought. When one is preparing the advertisement, it is advantageous to get advice from an expert who understands how to inject sufficient selling qualities to produce replies.

3. **Personal Letters of Application,** directed to particular firms or individuals most likely to need the services being offered. Letters should be neatly typed, ALWAYS, and signed by hand. With the letter should be sent a complete CV or outline of the applicant's qualifications. Both the letter of application and the CV should be prepared with advice from an expert (below).

4. **Application Through Personal Acquaintances.** When possible, the applicant should endeavor to approach prospective employers through some mutual acquaintance. This method of approach is particularly advantageous in the case of those who seek executive connections and do not wish to appear to be "peddling" themselves.

5. **Application in Person.** In some instances it may be more effective if applicants offer their services personally to prospective employers. In such cases a complete written statement of qualifications for the position should be presented so that prospective employers may discuss the applicant's record with associates.

Information to Be Supplied in a Written CV

This CV should be prepared as carefully as a lawyer would prepare the brief of a case to be tried in court. Unless the applicant is experienced in the preparation of CVs, an expert should be consulted. Successful merchants employ men and women who understand the art and psychology of advertising to present the merits of their merchandise. One who has services for sale should do the same. The following information should appear in the CV.

1. **Education.** State briefly, but definitely, what schooling you have had, and in what subjects you specialized, giving the reasons for that specialization.

2. **Experience.** If you have had experience in connection with positions similar to the one you seek, describe it fully, stating names and addresses of former employers. Be sure to bring out clearly any special experience you may have had which would equip you to fill the position you seek.

3. **References.** Practically every business firm desires to know all about the previous records of prospective employees who seek positions of responsibility. Be prepared to present to the employer, if asked, the names of people who can provide information about your experience and capabilities, such as:

   a. Former employers

   b. Teachers under whom you studied

   c. Prominent people whose judgment may be relied upon.

4. **Apply for a specific position.** Avoid application for a position without describing *exactly* what position you seek. Never apply for "just a position." That indicates you lack specialized qualifications.

5. **State your qualifications for the particular position for which you are applying.** Give full details as to the reason you believe you are qualified for the particular position you seek. This is THE MOST IMPORTANT DETAIL OF YOUR APPLICATION. It will determine, more than anything else, what consideration you receive.

6. **Offer to go to work on probation.** In the majority of instances, if you are determined to have the position for which you apply, it will be most effective if you offer to work for a week, or a month or for a sufficient length of time to enable your prospective employer to judge your value WITHOUT PAY. This may appear to be a radical suggestion, but experience has proven that it seldom fails to win at least a trial. If you are *sure of your qualifications,* a trial is all you need. Incidentally, such an offer indicates that you have confidence in your ability to fill the position you seek. It is most convincing. If your offer is accepted and you make good, it is more than likely that you will be paid for your "probation" period. Make clear the fact that your offer is based upon:

    a. Your confidence in your ability to fill the position

    b. Your confidence in your prospective employer's decision to employ you after trial

    c. Your *determination* to have the position you seek

7. Knowledge of your prospective employer's business. Before applying for a position, do sufficient research in connection with the business to familiarize yourself thoroughly with that business, and indicate in your brief the knowledge you have acquired in this field. This will be impressive, as it will indicate that you have imagination and a real interest in the position you seek.

   Remember that it is not the lawyer who knows the most law but the one who best prepares the case who wins. If your "case" is properly prepared and presented, your victory will have been more than half won at the outset.

8. Do not be afraid of making your CV too long. Employers are just as interested in purchasing the services of well-qualified applicants as you are in securing employment. In fact, the success of most successful employers is due, in the main, to their ability to select well-qualified lieutenants. They want all the information available.

   Remember another thing: neatness in the preparation of your CV will indicate that you are a painstaking person. I have helped to prepare CVs for clients that were so striking and out of the ordinary that they resulted in the employment of the applicant without a personal interview.

Once the CV is completed, have it printed on the finest paper you can obtain, Carefully check the spelling and grammar. Follow these instructions to the letter, improving upon them wherever your imagination suggests.

Successful salespeople groom themselves with care. They understand that first impressions are lasting. Your CV is your sales representative. Give it a good suit of clothes so it will stand out in bold contrast to anything your prospective employer ever saw in the way of an application for a position. If the position you seek is worth having, it is worth going after with care. Moreover, if you sell yourself to an employer in a manner that impresses them with your individuality, you will probably receive more money for your services from the very start than you would if you applied for employment in the usual conventional way.

If you seek employment through an advertising agency or an employment agency, get the agent to use copies of your CV in marketing your services. This will help to gain preference for you, both with the agent and the prospective employers.

How to Get the Exact Position You Desire

Everyone enjoys doing the kind of work for which they are best suited. An artist loves to work with paints, mechanics with their hands; a writer loves to write. Those with less definite talents have their preferences for certain fields of business and industry. There is a full range of occupations to choose from in manufacturing, marketing, and the professions.

1. Decide *exactly* what kind of job you want. If the job doesn't already exist, perhaps you can create it.
2. Choose the company, or individual, for whom you wish to work.
3. Study your prospective employer as to policies, personnel, and chances of advancement.
4. By analysis of yourself, your talents, and your capabilities, work out *what you can offer,* and plan ways and means of giving advantages, services, developments, and ideas that you believe you can successfully deliver.
5. Forget about "a job." Forget whether or not there is an opening. Forget the usual routine of "have you got a job for me?" Concentrate on what you can give.
6. Once you have your plan in mind, arrange with an experienced writer to help you put it on paper in neat form, and in full detail.
7. Present it to the proper person with authority to make the decision. Every company is looking for people who can give something of value, whether it is ideas, services, or "connections." Every company has room for the person who has a definite plan of action that will work to the advantage of that company.

This line of procedure may take a few days or weeks of extra time, but the difference in income, in advancement, and in gaining recognition will save years of hard work at low pay. It has many advantages, the main one being that it will often save from one to five years of time in reaching a chosen goal.

Every person who starts or "gets in" halfway up the ladder does so by deliberate and careful planning (except, of course, the boss's son).

The New Way of Marketing Services
"Jobs" Are Now "Partnerships"

Men and women who want to market their services to the best advantage in the future must recognize the stupendous change that has taken place in the relationship between employer and employee.

The time will come when the Golden Rule and not the Rule of Gold will be the dominating factor in the marketing of merchandise as well as services. The future relationship between employers and their employees will be more in the nature of a partnership consisting of

  a. the employer;
  b. the employee; and
  c. the public they serve.

This new way of marketing services is called "new" for many reasons. First, both the employer and the employee of the future will be considered as fellow employees whose business it will be to *serve the public efficiently.* In times past, employers and employees have bartered among themselves, driving the best bargains they could with each other, not considering that in the final analysis they were, in reality, *bargaining at the expense of the third party, the public they served.*

In the future both employers and employees will recognize that they are *no longer privileged to drive bargains at the expense of those whom they serve.* The real employer of the future will be the public. This should be kept uppermost in mind by every person seeking to market their services effectively.

"Courtesy" and "service" are the watchwords of merchandising today. They apply to the person who is marketing their services even more directly than to the employer they serve, because, in the final analysis, both employer and employee are *employed by the public they serve.* If they fail to serve well, they pay by the loss of their privilege of serving.

What Is Your "QQS" Rating?

The causes of success in marketing services *effectively* and permanently have been clearly described. Unless those causes are studied, analyzed, understood, and *applied,* no one can market their services effectively and permanently. It is up to *you* to sell your own services. The *quality* and the *quantity* of services rendered, and the *spirit* in which they are rendered, determine to a large extent the price and the duration of employment. To market services effectively (which means a permanent market, at a satisfactory price, under pleasant conditions), one must adopt and follow the QQS formula, which means that QUALITY, plus QUANTITY, plus the proper SPIRIT of cooperation equals perfect marketing of service. Remember the "QQS" formula, but do more—*apply it as a habit!*

Let us analyze the formula to make sure we understand exactly what it means:

1. **Quality** of service means the performance of every detail, in connection with your position, in the most efficient manner possible, with the object of greater efficiency always in mind.
2. **Quantity** of service means the Habit of giving all the service of which you are capable, at all times, with the purpose of increasing the amount of service as you develop greater skill through practice and experience. Emphasis is again placed on the word "Habit."
3. **Spirit** of service means the HABIT of agreeable, harmonious conduct that will induce cooperation from associates and fellow employees.

   Adequacy of Quality and Quantity of service is not sufficient to maintain a permanent market for your services. The conduct, or the SPIRIT, in which you deliver service is a strong determining factor in connection with both the price you receive and the duration of employment.

Andrew Carnegie stressed this point more than others in his description of the factors that lead to success in the marketing of services. He emphasized again and again the necessity for *harmonious conduct.* He stressed that he would not retain any person, no matter how great a *quantity* or how efficient the *quality* of their work, unless that person worked in a spirit of *harmony.* Mr. Carnegie insisted upon everybody being *agreeable.* To prove that he placed a high value upon this quality, he permitted many people who conformed to his standards to become very wealthy. Those who did not conform had to make room for others.

The importance of a pleasing personality has been stressed because it enables one to provide service in the proper *spirit.* If one has a personality which *pleases* and serves in a spirit of *harmony,* these assets often make up for deficiencies in both the *quality* and the *quantity* of service one gives. Nothing, however, can be *successfully substituted for pleasing conduct.*

The Capital Value of Your Services

The person whose income is derived entirely from the sale of their services is no less than a merchant who sells commodities. It might well be added that such a person is subject to *exactly the same rules* of conduct as the merchant who sells merchandise.

This has been emphasized because the majority of people who live by the sale of their services make the mistake of considering themselves free from the rules of conduct and the responsibilities attached to those engaged in marketing commodities.

The actual capital value of your brains may be determined by the amount of income you can produce (by marketing your services). A fair estimate of the capital value of your services may be made by multiplying your annual income by 16 and two-thirds, as it is reasonable to estimate that your annual income represents 6 percent of your capital value. Money rents for 6 percent per annum. Money is worth no more than brains. It is often worth much less.

Competent "brains," if effectively marketed, represent a much more desirable form of capital than that required to conduct a business dealing in commodities. This is because "brains" are a form of capital that cannot be permanently depreciated through depressions, nor can this form of capital be stolen or spent. Moreover, the money essential for the conduct of business is as worthless as a sand dune until it has been mixed with efficient "brains."

The 30 Major Causes of Failure
How Many of These Are Holding You Back?

Life's greatest tragedy consists of men and women who earnestly try, and fail! The tragedy lies in the overwhelmingly large majority of people who fail, as compared with the few who succeed.

I have had the privilege of analyzing several thousand men and women, 98 percent of whom were classed as "failures." There is something radically wrong with a civilization and a system of education which permit so many people to go through life as failures. But I did not write this book for the purpose of moralizing on the rights and wrongs of the world; that would require a book a hundred times the size of this one.

My analysis work proved that there are 30 major reasons for failure. As you go over the list, check yourself by it, point by point, to discover how many of these causes of failure stand between you and success.

1. **Unfavorable Hereditary Background.** Little, if anything, can be done for people who are born with a deficiency in brainpower. This philosophy offers but one method of bridging this weakness—through the aid of the Master Mind (see page 139). Observe with profit, however, that this is the *only* one of the 30 causes of failure that may not be easily corrected by any individual.

2. **Lack of a Well-Defined Purpose in Life.** There is no hope of success for the person who does not have a central purpose, or definite goal. Ninety-eight out of every hundred of those whom I have analyzed had no such aim. Perhaps this was the *major cause of their failure.*

3. **Lack of Ambition to Aim Above Mediocrity.** We offer no hope for the person who is so indifferent as not to want to get ahead in life, and who is not willing to pay the price.

4. **Insufficient Education.** This is a handicap that may be overcome with comparative ease. Experience has proven that the best-educated people are often those who are known as "self-made" or self-educated. It takes more than a university degree to make one a person of education. Any person who is educated has learned to get whatever they want in life without violating the rights of others. Education consists not so much of knowledge, but of knowledge effectively and persistently *applied.* People are paid not merely for what they know, but more particularly for *what they do with what they know.*

5. **Lack of Self-Discipline.** Discipline comes through self-control. This means that you must control all negative qualities. Before you can control conditions, you must first control yourself. Self-mastery is the hardest job you will ever tackle. If you do not conquer self, you will be conquered by self. You may see at one and the same time both your best friend and your greatest enemy by stepping in front of a mirror.

6. **Ill Health.** No person may enjoy outstanding success without good health. Many of the causes of ill health are subject to mastery and control. These, in the main, are:
   - Overeating of foods not conducive to health
   - Wrong habits of thought; giving expression to negatives
   - Wrong use of, and overindulgence in, sex
   - Lack of proper physical exercise
   - An inadequate supply of fresh air, due to improper breathing

7. **Unfavorable Environmental Influences During Childhood.** "As the twig is bent, so shall the tree grow." Most people who have criminal tendencies acquire them as the result of bad environment and improper associates during childhood.

8. **Procrastination.** This is one of the most common causes of failure. "Old Man Procrastination" stands within the shadow of all people, awaiting the opportunity to spoil their chances of success. Most of us go through life as failures because we are waiting for the "time to be right" to start doing something worthwhile. Do not wait. The time will never be "just right." Start where you stand, work with whatever tools you may have at your command, and better tools will be found as you go along.

9. **Lack of Persistence.** Most of us are good "starters" but poor "finishers" of everything we begin. Moreover, people are prone to give up at the first signs of defeat. There is no substitute for *persistence.* The persistent person discovers that "Old Man Failure" finally becomes tired and goes away. Failure cannot cope with persistence.

10. **Negative Personality.** There is no hope of success for the person who repels people through a negative personality. Success comes through the application of *power,* and power is attained through the cooperative efforts of other people. A negative personality will not induce cooperation.

11. **Lack of Controlled Sexual Urge.** Sex energy is the most powerful of all the stimuli that move people into *action.* Because it is the most powerful of the emotions, it must be controlled through transmutation, and converted into other channels.

12. **Uncontrolled Desire for "Something for Nothing."** The gambling instinct drives millions of people to failure. *Evidence of this may be found in a study of the dot-com fiasco of the early 2000s, during which millions of people tried to make money by investing in fly-by-night companies.*

13. **Lack of a Well-Defined Power of Decision.** People who succeed reach decisions promptly, and change them—if at all—very slowly. People who fail reach decisions—if at all—very slowly, and change them frequently and quickly. Indecision and procrastination are twins. Where one is found, the other may usually be found also. Kill off this pair before they completely tie you to the treadmill of *failure.*

14. **One or More of the Six Basic Fears.** These fears have been analyzed for you in Chapter 15. They must be mastered before you can market your services effectively.

15. **Wrong Selection of a Mate in Marriage.** This is a most common cause of failure. The relationship of marriage brings people intimately into contact. Unless this relationship is harmonious, failure is likely to follow. Moreover, it will be a form of failure marked by misery and unhappiness, destroying all signs of *ambition.*

16. **Overcaution.** The person who takes no chances generally has to take whatever is left when others have finished choosing. Overcaution is as bad as undercaution. Both are extremes to be guarded against. Life itself is filled with the element of chance.

17. **Wrong Selection of Associates in Business.** This is one of the most common causes of failure in business. In marketing your services, you should take great care to select an employer who will be an inspiration, and who is intelligent and successful. We emulate those with whom we associate most closely. Pick an employer who is worth emulating.

18. **Superstition and Prejudice.** Superstition is a form of fear. It is also a sign of ignorance. People who succeed keep open minds and are afraid of nothing.

19. **Wrong Selection of a Vocation.** No one can succeed in a line of endeavor they do not like. The most essential step in marketing your services is selecting an occupation into which you can throw yourself wholeheartedly.

20. **Lack of Concentration of Effort.** The "jack-of-all-trades" is seldom good at any. Concentrate all your efforts on one *definite chief aim*.

21. **The Habit of Indiscriminate Spending.** Spendthrifts cannot succeed, mainly because they stand eternally in *fear of poverty*. Form the habit of systematic saving by putting aside a definite percentage of your income. Money in the bank gives you a very safe foundation of *courage* when bargaining for the sale of your services. Without money, you must take what you are offered, and be glad to get it.

22. **Lack of Enthusiasm.** Without enthusiasm one cannot be convincing. Moreover, enthusiasm is contagious, and the person who has it, under control, is generally welcome in any group of people.

23. **Intolerance.** The person with a "closed" mind on any subject seldom gets ahead. Intolerance means that one has stopped acquiring knowledge. The most damaging forms of intolerance are those connected with religious, racial, and political differences of opinion.

24. **Intemperance.** The most damaging forms of intemperance are connected with eating, strong drink, and sexual activities. Overindulgence in any of these is fatal to success.

25. **Inability to Cooperate with Others.** More people lose their positions and their big opportunities in life because of this fault than for all other reasons combined. It is a fault which no well-informed business executive or leader will tolerate.

26. **Possession of Power Not Acquired Through Self-Effort.** (Sons and daughters of wealthy families, and others who inherit money that they did not earn.) Power in the hands of one who did not acquire it gradually is often fatal to success. *Quick riches* are more dangerous than poverty.

27. **Intentional Dishonesty.** There is no substitute for honesty. One may be temporarily dishonest by force of circumstances over which one has no control, without permanent damage. But there is *no hope* for people who are dishonest by choice. Sooner or later, their deeds will catch up with them, and they will pay by loss of reputation, and perhaps even loss of liberty.

28. **Egotism and Vanity.** These qualities serve as red lights that warn others to keep away. *They are fatal to success.*

29. **Guessing Instead of Thinking.** Most people are too indifferent or lazy to acquire *facts* with which to *think accurately.* They prefer to act on "opinions" created by guesswork or snap judgments.

30. **Lack of Capital.** This is a common cause of failure among those who start out in business for the first time without sufficient reserve of capital to absorb the shock of their mistakes and to carry them over until they have established a *reputation.*

31. Under this, name any particular cause of failure from which you have suffered that has not been included in the foregoing list.

In these 30 major causes of failure is found a description of the tragedy of life, which is relevant for practically every person who tries and fails. It will be helpful if you can induce someone who knows you well to go over this list with you, and help to analyze you by the 30 causes of failure. It may be more beneficial than if you try this alone. Most people cannot see themselves as others see them. You may be one who cannot.

The oldest of admonitions is "Know thyself!" If you market merchandise successfully, you must know the merchandise. The same is true in marketing your services. You should know all of your weaknesses so that you may either bridge them or eliminate them entirely. You should know your strengths so that you may call attention to them when selling your services. You can know yourself only through accurate analysis.

The folly of ignorance in connection with self was displayed by a young man who applied to the manager of a well-known business for a position. He made a very good impression until the manager asked him what salary he expected. He replied that he had no fixed sum in mind (lack of a definite aim). The manager then said, "We will pay you all you are worth, after we try you out for a week."

"I will not accept it," the applicant replied, "because *I am getting more than that where I am now employed.*"

Before you even start to negotiate for a readjustment of your salary in your present position, or to seek employment elsewhere, *be sure that you are worth more than you now receive.*

It is one thing to *want* money—everyone wants more—but it is something entirely different to be *worth more*! Many people mistake their *wants* for their *just dues.* Your financial requirements or wants have nothing whatever to do with your *worth.* Your value is established entirely by your ability to provide useful service or your capacity to induce others to provide such service.

Take an Inventory of Yourself
28 Questions You Should Answer

Annual self-analysis is as essential in the effective marketing of services as is annual inventory in merchandising. Moreover, the yearly analysis should disclose a *decrease in faults* and an *increase in virtues.* One goes ahead, stands still, or goes backward in life. One's object should be, of course, to go ahead. Annual self-analysis will disclose whether advancement has been made, and if so, how much. It will also disclose any backward steps one may have made. The effective marketing of services requires one to move forward, even if the progress is slow.

Your annual self-analysis should be made at the end of each year so you can include in your New Year's resolutions any improvements that the analysis indicates should be made. Take this inventory by asking yourself the following questions, and by checking your answers with the aid of someone who will not permit you to deceive yourself as to their accuracy.

Self-Analysis Questionnaire for Personal Inventory

1. Have I attained the goal that I established as my objective for this year? (You should work with a definite yearly objective to be attained as a part of your major life objective.)

2. Have I delivered service of the best possible *quality* of which I was capable, or could I have improved any part of this service?

3. Have I delivered service in the greatest possible *quantity* of which I was capable?

4. Has the spirit of my conduct been harmonious and cooperative at all times?

5. Have I permitted the habit of *procrastination* to decrease my efficiency, and if so, to what extent?

6. Have I improved my *personality,* and if so, in what ways?

7. Have I been *persistent* in following my plans through to completion?

8. Have I reached *decisions promptly and definitely* on all occasions?

9. Have I permitted any one or more of the six basic fears (see Chapter 15) to decrease my efficiency?

10. Have I been either "overcautious" or "undercautious"?

11. Has my relationship with my colleagues in work been pleasant or unpleasant? If it has been unpleasant, has the fault been partly or wholly mine?

12. Have I dissipated any of my energy through lack of *concentration* of effort?

13. Have I been open-minded and tolerant in connection with all subjects?

14. In what way have I improved my ability to provide service?

15. Have I been intemperate in any of my habits?

16. Have I expressed, either openly or secretly, any form of *egotism*?

17. Has my conduct toward my colleagues been such that it has induced them to *respect* me?

18. Have my opinions and *decisions* been based upon guesswork, or accuracy of analysis and *thought*?

19. Have I followed the habit of budgeting my time, my expenses, and my income, and have I been conservative in these budgets?

20. How much time have I devoted to *unprofitable* effort which I might have used to better advantage?

21. How may I *rebudget* my time and change my habits so I will be more efficient during the coming year?

22. Have I been guilty of any conduct that was not approved by my conscience?

23. In what ways have I provided *more service and better service* than I was paid for?

24. Have I been unfair to anyone, and if so, in what way?

25. If I had been the purchaser of my own services for the year, would I have been satisfied with my purchase?

26. Has the purchaser of my services been satisfied with the service I have provided, and if not, why not?

27. Am I in the right vocation, and if not, why not?

28. What is my present rating on the fundamental principles of success? (Make this rating fairly and frankly, and have it checked by someone who is courageous enough to do it accurately.)

Having read and assimilated the information conveyed in this chapter, you are now ready to create a practical plan for marketing your services. Those who have lost their fortunes, and those who are just beginning to earn money, have nothing but their services to offer in return for riches. It is therefore essential that they have available the practical information needed to market their services to best advantage.

The information contained in this chapter will be of great value to all who aspire to attain leadership in any calling. It will be particularly helpful to those aiming to market their services as business or industrial executives.

Complete assimilation and understanding of the information here conveyed will be helpful in marketing one's own services, and it will also help one to become more analytical and capable of judging people. The information will be priceless to personnel directors, employment managers, and other executives charged with the selection of employees and the maintenance of efficient organizations. If you doubt this statement, test its soundness by answering in writing the 28 self-analysis questions. Indeed, that might be both interesting and profitable even if you do not doubt the soundness of the statement.

Where and How to Find Opportunities to Accumulate Riches

Now that we have analyzed the principles by which riches may be accumulated, we naturally ask, "Where may one find favorable opportunities to apply these principles?" Very well, let us take an inventory and see what the Western economy may offer the person seeking riches, great or small.

To begin with, let us remember, all of us, that we live in a society where every law-abiding citizen enjoys freedom of thought and freedom of deed. Most of us have never taken stock of the advantages of this freedom. We have never compared our unlimited freedom with the curtailed freedom in some other societies.

Here we have freedom of thought; freedom in the choice and enjoyment of education; freedom in religion; freedom in politics; freedom in the choice of a business, profession, or occupation; freedom to accumulate and own without molestation *all the property we can accumulate;* freedom to choose our place of residence; freedom in marriage; freedom through equal opportunity to all races; freedom of travel; freedom in our choice of foods; and freedom to *aim for any station in life for which we have prepared ourselves.* We have other forms of freedom, but this list will give a bird's-eye view of the most important, which constitute *opportunity* of the highest order.

Next, let us recount some of the blessings that our widespread freedom has placed within our hands. Take the average family in Western society, for example (meaning the family of average income), and sum up the benefits available to every member of the family.

- **Food.** Because of our universal freedom, the average family has available, at its very door, a choice selection of food, and at prices within its financial range.
- **Shelter.** This family lives in a comfortable home, heated by gas, lighted with electricity, with gas for cooking, all for a reasonable rate. The toast they had for breakfast was toasted on an electric toaster; the carpets are cleaned with a vacuum cleaner run by electricity. Hot and cold water are available, at all times, in the kitchen and the bathroom. The food is kept cold in a refrigerator run by electricity. The wife styles her hair, washes her clothes, and irons them with easily operated electrical equipment, on power obtained by sticking a plug in the wall. The husband shaves with an electric shaver. They receive entertainment from all over the world, 24 hours a day if they want it, by merely switching on their television.
- **Clothing.** Men and women in Western society can meet their clothing requirements and dress very comfortably at prices within the range of an average family's salary.

Only the three basic necessities of food, clothing, and shelter have been mentioned. The average citizen has other privileges and advantages available in return for modest effort, not exceeding eight hours per day of labor. Among these is the privilege of owning a car, with which one can come and go at will, at very small cost.

The "Miracle" That Has Provided These Blessings

Having no ax to grind, no grudge to express, and no ulterior motives, I have the privilege of analyzing frankly that mysterious, abstract, greatly misunderstood SOMETHING which provides us with the aforementioned blessings, opportunities to accumulate wealth and freedom of every nature.

I have the right to analyze the source and nature of this *unseen power* because I know, and have known for more than a quarter of a century, many of the people who organized that power, and many who are now responsible for its maintenance.

The name of this mysterious benefactor of humankind is CAPITAL!

Capital consists not of money alone, but more particularly of highly organized, intelligent groups of people who plan ways and means of using money efficiently for the good of the public, and profitably for themselves.

These groups consist of scientists, educators, chemists, inventors, business analysts, public relations experts, transportation experts, accountants, lawyers, doctors, and both men and women who have highly specialized knowledge in all fields of industry and business. They pioneer, experiment, and blaze trails in new fields of endeavor. They support colleges, hospitals, and schools, build good roads, publish newspapers, pay most of the cost of government, and take care of the multitudinous detail essential to human progress. Stated briefly, the capitalists are the brains of civilization because they supply the entire fabric of which all education, enlightenment, and human progress consist.

Money without brains is always dangerous. Properly used, it is the most important essential of civilization. A simple breakfast for a city family consisting of grapefruit juice, cereal, eggs, bread and butter, and tea with sugar could not be provided at a reasonable price if organized capital had not supplied the machinery, the ships, the railways, and the huge armies of trained people to operate them.

Some slight idea of the importance of *organized capital* may be had by trying to imagine yourself burdened with the responsibility of collecting and delivering a simple breakfast to the above-mentioned city family without the aid of capital.

To supply the tea, you would have to make a trip to China or India. Unless you are an excellent swimmer, you would become rather tired before making the round trip. Then another problem would confront you. What would you use for money, even if you had the physical endurance to swim the ocean?

To supply the sugar, you would have to take another long swim to a Caribbean island, or a long walk to a sugar beet farm. But even then you might come back without the sugar, because organized effort and money are necessary to produce sugar, to say nothing of what is required to refine, transport, and deliver it to the breakfast table.

The eggs you could deliver easily enough, but you would have a very long journey before you could serve the two glasses of grapefruit juice.

You would have another long walk to a wheat-growing area when you went after the four slices of wheat bread.

The cereal would have to be omitted from the menu because it would not be available except through the labor of a trained organization of people and suitable machinery, *all of which call for capital*.

While resting, you could take off for another little swim down to South America, where you would pick up a couple of bananas, and on your return you could take a short walk to the nearest dairy farm and pick up some butter and cream. Then your city family would be ready to sit down and enjoy breakfast.

Seems absurd, doesn't it? Well, the procedure described would be the only possible way these simple items of food could be delivered to the heart of the city if we had no capitalistic system.

The sum of money required for the building and maintenance of the railways and ships used in the delivery of that simple breakfast is so huge that it staggers one's imagination. It runs into hundreds of millions of dollars, not to mention the armies of trained employees required to man the ships and trains. But transportation is only a part of the requirements of modern civilization. Before there can be anything to haul, something must be grown from the ground, or manufactured and prepared for market. This calls for more millions of dollars for equipment, machinery, boxing, and marketing, and for the wages of millions of men and women.

Ships and railways do not spring up from the earth and function automatically. They come in response to the call of civilization, through the labor and ingenuity and organizing ability of people who have *imagination, faith, enthusiasm, decision,* and *persistence*! These people are known as capitalists. They are motivated by the desire to build, construct, achieve, provide useful service, earn profits, and accumulate riches. And because they *provide service without which there would be no civilization,* they put themselves in the way of great riches.

Just to keep the record simple and understandable, I will add that these capitalists are the selfsame people of whom most of us have heard soapbox orators speak. They are the same people to whom radicals, racketeers, dishonest politicians, and union leaders refer as "the predatory interests."

I am not attempting to present a brief for or against any group of people or any system of economics. I am not attempting to condemn collective bargaining when I refer to "union leaders," nor do I aim to give a clean bill of health to all individuals known as capitalists.

The purpose of this book—a purpose to which I have faithfully devoted over a quarter of a century—is to present to all who want the knowledge the most dependable philosophy through which individuals may accumulate riches in whatever amounts they desire.

I have here analyzed the economic advantages of the capitalistic system for the twofold purpose of showing:

1. that all who seek riches must recognize and adapt themselves to the system that controls all approaches to fortunes, large or small, and
2. that they must present the side of the picture opposite to that being shown by politicians and demagogues who refer to organized capital as if it were something poisonous.

This is a capitalistic society. It was developed through the use of capital, and we who claim the right to partake of the blessings of freedom and opportunity, we who seek to accumulate riches here, may as well know that neither riches nor opportunity would be available to us if *organized capital* had not provided these benefits.

If you are one of those who believe that riches can be accumulated by the mere act of people who organize themselves into groups and demand *more pay* for *less service,* if you are one of those who *demand* government relief without early-morning disturbance when the money is delivered to you, if you are one of those who believe in trading their votes to politicians in return for the passing of laws which permit the raiding of the public treasury, you may rest securely on your belief, with certain knowledge that no one will disturb you, because *this is a free country where everyone may think as they please,* where nearly everybody can live with but little effort, where many may live well without doing any work whatsoever.

However, you should know the full truth concerning this *freedom* of which so many people boast and so few understand. As great as it is, as far as it reaches, as many privileges as it provides, *it does not and cannot bring riches without effort.*

There is but one dependable method of accumulating and legally holding riches, and that is by providing useful service. No system has ever been created by which people can legally acquire riches through mere force of numbers, or without giving in return an equivalent value of one form or another.

There is a principle known as the law of *economics*! This is more than a theory. It is a law no person can beat.

Mark well the name of the principle and remember it, because it is far more powerful than all the politicians and political machines. It is above and beyond the control of all the labor unions. It cannot be swayed, influenced, or bribed by racketeers or self-appointed leaders in any calling. Moreover, *it has an all-seeing eye and a perfect system of bookkeeping* in which it keeps an accurate account of the transactions of every human being engaged in the business of trying to get without giving. Sooner or later its auditors come around, look over the records of individuals both great and small, and demand an accounting.

"Big business," "capital predatory interests," or whatever name you choose to give the system which has given us *freedom* represents a group of people who understand, respect and adapt themselves to this powerful *law of economics.* Their financial continuation depends upon their respecting the law.

Remember, also, that this is but the beginning of the available sources for the accumulation of wealth. Only a few of the luxuries and nonessentials have been mentioned. But remember that the business of producing, transporting, and marketing these few items of merchandise gives regular employment to *many millions of men and women* who receive for their services *many millions of dollars monthly* and spend it freely on both the luxuries and the necessities.

Especially remember that behind all this exchange of merchandise and personal services may be found an abundance of *opportunity* to accumulate riches. Here our *freedom* comes to our aid. There is nothing to stop you or anyone from engaging in any portion of the effort necessary to carry on these businesses. If one has superior talent, training, or experience, one may accumulate riches in large amounts. Those not so fortunate may accumulate smaller amounts. Anyone may earn a living in return for a very nominal amount of labor.

So—there you are!

Opportunity has spread its wares before you. Step up to the front, select what you want, create your plan, put the plan into action, and follow through with *persistence.* "Capitalistic" society will do the rest. You can depend upon this much: CAPITALISTIC SOCIETY GUARANTEES EVERY PERSON THE OPPORTUNITY TO PROVIDE USEFUL SERVICE AND TO COLLECT RICHES IN PROPORTION TO THE VALUE OF THE SERVICE.

The "system" denies no one this right, but it does not and cannot promise *something for nothing.* The *law of economics* itself irrevocably controls the system that neither recognizes nor tolerates for long *getting without giving.*

The law of economics was passed by Nature! There is no court to which violators of this law may appeal. The law hands out both penalties for its violation and appropriate rewards for its observance, without interference or the possibility of interference by any human being. The law cannot be repealed. It is as fixed as the stars in the heavens, and subject to, and a part of, the same system that controls the stars.

May one refuse to adapt oneself to the law of economics?

Certainly! This is a free society, where all are born with equal rights, including the privilege of ignoring the law of economics. What happens then?

Well, nothing happens until large numbers of people join forces for the avowed purpose of ignoring the law, and taking what they want by force. *Then comes the dictator, with well-organized firing squads and machine guns!*

We have not yet reached that stage, but we have learned all we want to know about how the system works. Perhaps we shall be fortunate enough not to demand personal knowledge of so gruesome a reality. Doubtless we shall prefer to continue with our *freedom of speech, freedom of deed,* and *freedom to provide useful service in return for riches.*

These observations are not founded upon short-time experience. They are the result of twenty-five years of careful analysis of the methods of both the most successful and the most unsuccessful men America has known.

CHAPTER 8

DECISION:
The Mastery of Procrastination

(The Seventh Step to Riches)

ACCURATE analysis of over 25,000 men and women who had experienced failure disclosed the fact that *lack of decision* was near the head of the list of the 30 major causes of *failure.* This is no mere statement of theory—it is a fact.

Procrastination, the opposite of *decision,* is a common enemy that practically everybody must conquer.

You will have an opportunity to test your capacity to reach quick and definite *decisions* when you finish reading this book, and are ready to begin putting into *action* the principles it describes.

Analysis of several hundred people who accumulated fortunes well beyond the million-dollar mark disclosed the fact that every one of them had the habit of *reaching decisions promptly* and of changing these decisions *slowly,* if and when they were changed. People who fail to accumulate money, without exception, have the habit of reaching decisions, *if at all,* very slowly, and of changing these decisions quickly and often.

One of Henry Ford's most outstanding qualities was his habit of reaching decisions quickly and definitely, and changing them slowly. This quality was so pronounced in Mr. Ford that it gave him the reputation of being obstinate. It was this quality which prompted Mr. Ford to continue to manufacture his famous Model "T" (the world's ugliest car), when all of his advisers, and many of the purchasers of the car, were urging him to change it.

Perhaps Mr. Ford delayed too long in making the change, but the other side of the story is that Mr. Ford's firmness of decision yielded a huge fortune before the change in model became necessary. There is but little doubt that Mr. Ford's habit of definiteness of decision assumed the proportion of obstinacy, but this quality is preferable to slowness in reaching decisions and quickness in changing them.

The majority of people who fail to accumulate money sufficient for their needs are, generally, easily influenced by the "opinions" of others. They permit the newspapers and the "gossiping" neighbors to do their "thinking" for them. "Opinions" are the cheapest commodities on earth. Everyone has a flock of opinions ready to be wished upon anyone who will accept them. If you are influenced by "opinions" when you reach *decisions,* you will not succeed in any undertaking, much less in that of transmuting *your own desire* into money.

If you are influenced by the opinions of others, you will have no *desire* of your own.

Keep your own counsel, when you begin to put into practice the principles described here, by reaching your own decisions and following them. Take no one into your confidence *except* the members of your "Master Mind" group, and be very sure in your selection of this group that you choose *only* those who will be in *complete sympathy and harmony with your purpose.*

Close friends and relatives, while not meaning to do so, often handicap one through "opinions" and sometimes through ridicule, which is meant to be humorous. Thousands of men and women carry inferiority complexes with them all through life because some well-meaning but ignorant person destroyed their confidence through "opinions" or ridicule.

You have a brain and mind of your own. Use it and reach your own decisions. If you need facts or information from other people to enable you to reach decisions, as you probably will in many instances, acquire these facts or secure the information you need quietly, without disclosing your purpose.

It is characteristic of people who have but a smattering or a veneer of knowledge to try to give the impression that they have much knowledge. Such people generally do *too much* talking and *too little* listening. Keep your eyes and ears wide open and your mouth *closed* if you wish to acquire the habit of prompt decision. Those who talk too much do little else. If you talk more than you listen, you not only deprive yourself of many opportunities to accumulate useful knowledge, but you also disclose your *plans* and *purposes* to people who will take great delight in defeating you, because they envy you.

Remember, also, that every time you open your mouth in the presence of a person who has an abundance of knowledge, you display to that person your exact stock of knowledge or your *lack* of it! Genuine wisdom is usually conspicuous through modesty and silence.

Keep in mind the fact that every person with whom you associate is, like yourself, seeking the opportunity to accumulate money. If you talk about your plans too freely, you may be surprised when you learn that some other person has beaten you to your goal by *putting into action ahead of you* the plans of which you talked unwisely.

Let one of your first decisions be to *keep a closed mouth and open ears and eyes.*

As a reminder to yourself to follow this advice, it will be helpful if you copy the following epigram in large letters and place it where you will see it daily:

TELL THE WORLD WHAT YOU INTEND TO DO,
BUT FIRST SHOW IT

This is the equivalent of saying that "deeds, and not words, are what count most."

Freedom or Death on a Decision

The value of decisions depends upon the courage required to make them. The great decisions which served as the foundation of civilization were reached by assuming great risks, which often meant the possibility of death.

Lincoln's decision to issue his famous Proclamation of Emancipation, which gave freedom to the enslaved people of America, was taken with full understanding that his act would turn thousands of friends and political supporters against him. He knew, too, that the carrying out of that proclamation would mean death to thousands of men on the battlefield. In the end, it cost Lincoln his life. That required courage.

Socrates' decision to drink the cup of poison, rather than compromise in his personal belief, was a decision of courage. It turned time ahead a thousand years, and gave to people then unborn the right to freedom of thought and of speech.

The decision of General Robert E. Lee, when he came to the parting of the ways with the Union and took up the cause of the South, was one of courage, for he well knew it might cost him his own life, and that it would surely cost the lives of others.

But the greatest decision of all time, as far as any American citizen is concerned, was reached in Philadelphia on July 4, 1776, when 56 men signed their names to a document they well knew would bring freedom to all Americans, or leave every one of the 56 hanging from a gallows!

You have heard of this famous document, but you may not have drawn from it the great lesson in personal achievement it so plainly taught.

We all remember the date of this momentous decision, but few of us realize what courage that decision required. We remember history as it was taught; we remember dates, and the names of the men who fought; we remember Valley Forge and Yorktown; we remember George Washington and Lord Cornwallis. But we know little of the real forces behind these names, dates, and places. We know still less of that intangible *power,* which guaranteed freedom for Americans long before Washington's armies reached Yorktown.

We read the history of the Revolution and falsely imagine that George Washington was the father of America, that it was he who won Americans their freedom. The truth is that Washington was only an accessory after the fact, because victory for his armies had been ensured long before Lord Cornwallis surrendered. This is not intended to rob Washington of any of the glory he so richly merited. Its purpose, rather, is to give greater attention to the astounding *power* that was the real cause of his victory.

It is nothing short of tragedy that the writers of history have entirely missed even the slightest reference to the irresistible *power* that gave birth and freedom to the nation destined to set up new standards of independence for all the peoples of the earth. I say it is a tragedy because it is the selfsame *power* that must be used by every individual who surmounts the difficulties of Life, and forces Life to pay the price asked.

Let us briefly review the events that gave birth to this *power.* The story begins with an incident in Boston on March 5, 1770. British soldiers were patrolling the streets, openly threatening the citizens by their presence. The colonists resented armed men marching in their midst. They began to express their resentment openly, hurling stones as well as epithets at the marching soldiers, until the commanding officer gave orders, "Fix bayonets . . . Charge!"

The battle was on. It resulted in the death and injury of many. The incident aroused such resentment that the Provincial Assembly (made up of prominent colonists) called a meeting for the purpose of taking definite action. Two of the members of that Assembly were John Hancock and Samuel Adams. They spoke up courageously and declared that a move must be made to eject all British soldiers from Boston.

Remember this—a *decision,* in the minds of two men, might properly be called the beginning of the freedom that Americans now enjoy. Remember, too, that the *decision* of these two men called for *faith* and *courage,* because it was dangerous.

Before the Assembly adjourned, Samuel Adams was appointed to call on the governor of the province, Hutchinson, and demand the withdrawal of British troops. The request was granted and the troops were removed from Boston, but the incident was not closed. It had caused a situation destined to change the entire trend of civilization. Strange, is it not, how the great changes, such as the American Revolution and many wars, often have their beginnings in circumstances which seem unimportant? It is interesting, also, to observe that these important changes usually begin in the form of a *definite decision* in the minds of a relatively small number of people. Few of us know the history of America well enough to realize that John Hancock, Samuel Adams, and Richard Henry Lee (of the Province of Virginia) were the real fathers of the country.

Richard Henry Lee became an important factor in this story due to the fact that he and Samuel Adams communicated frequently (by correspondence), sharing freely their fears and their hopes concerning the welfare of the people of their provinces. From this practice, Adams conceived the idea that a mutual exchange of letters between the thirteen colonies might help to bring about the coordination of effort so badly needed in connection with the solution of their problems. In March 1772, two years after the clash with the soldiers in Boston, Adams presented this idea to the Assembly in the form of a motion that a Correspondence Committee be established among the colonies, with definitely appointed correspondents in each colony, "for the purpose of friendly cooperation for the betterment of the Colonies of British America."

Mark well this incident! It was the beginning of the organization of the far-flung *power* destined to give freedom to Americans. The Master Mind had already been organized. It consisted of Adams, Lee, and Hancock. The Committee of Correspondence was organized. Observe that this move provided the way for increasing the power of the Master Mind by adding to it men from all the colonies. Take notice that this procedure constituted the first *organized planning* of the disgruntled colonists.

In union there is strength! The citizens of the colonies had been waging disorganized warfare against the British soldiers through incidents similar to the Boston riot, but nothing of benefit had been accomplished. Their individual grievances had not been consolidated under one Master Mind. No group of individuals had put their hearts, minds, souls, and bodies together in one definite *decision* to settle their difficulty with the British once and for all, until Adams, Hancock, and Lee got together.

Meanwhile, the British were not idle. They, too, were doing some *planning* and Master-Minding on their own account, with the advantage of having money and organized soldiery behind them.

The Crown appointed Gage to supplant Hutchinson as the governor of Massachusetts. One of the new governor's first acts was to send a messenger to call on Samuel Adams, for the purpose of endeavoring to stop his opposition—by *fear*.

We can best understand the spirit of what happened by quoting the conversation between Colonel Fenton (the messenger sent by Gage) and Adams.

Colonel Fenton: "I have been authorized by Governor Gage to assure you, Mr. Adams, that the Governor has been empowered to confer upon you such benefits as would be satisfactory [endeavor to win Adams by promise of bribes] upon the condition that you engage to cease in your opposition to the measures of the government. It is the Governor's advice to you, Sir, not to incur the further displeasure of His Majesty. Your conduct has been such as makes you liable to penalties of an Act of Henry VIII, by which persons can be sent to England for trial for treason, or misprision of treason, at the discretion of a governor of a province. But, *by changing your political course,* you will not only receive great personal advantages, but you will make your peace with the King."

Samuel Adams had the choice of two *decisions.* He could cease his opposition and receive personal bribes, or he could *continue, and run the risk of being hanged*!

Clearly, the time had come when Adams was forced to reach instantly a *decision* that could have cost his life. The majority of people would have found it difficult to reach such a decision. The majority would have sent back an evasive reply, but not Adams! He insisted Colonel Fenton give his word of honor to deliver to the governor the answer exactly as Adams gave it to him.

Adams's answer was, "Then you may tell Governor Gage that I trust I have long since made my peace with the King of Kings. No personal consideration shall induce me to abandon the righteous cause of my country. And, *tell Governor Gage it is the advice of Samuel Adams to him,* no longer to insult the feelings of an exasperated people."

Comment as to the character of this man seems unnecessary. It must be obvious to all who read this astounding message that its sender possessed loyalty of the highest order. This is important. (Racketeers and dishonest politicians have prostituted the honor for which such men as Adams died.)

When Governor Gage received Adams's caustic reply, he flew into a rage and issued a proclamation which read, "I do, hereby, in His Majesty's name, offer and promise his most gracious pardon to all persons who shall forthwith lay down their arms and return to the duties of peaceable subjects, excepting only from the benefit of such pardon, *Samuel Adams and John Hancock,* whose offenses are of too flagitious a nature to admit of any other consideration but that of condign punishment."

As one might say in modern slang, Adams and Hancock were "on the spot"! The threat of the irate Governor forced the two men to reach another *decision,* equally as dangerous. They hurriedly called a secret meeting of their staunchest followers. (Here the Master Mind began to take on momentum.) After the meeting had been called to order, Adams locked the door, placed the key in his pocket, and informed all present that it was imperative that a Congress of the Colonists be organized, and that *no man should leave the room until the decision for such a Congress had been reached.*

Great excitement followed. Some weighed the possible consequences of such radicalism (fear). Some expressed grave doubt as to the wisdom of so definite a decision in defiance of the Crown. Locked in that room were *two men* immune to fear, blind to the possibility of failure. Hancock and Adams. Through the influence of their minds, the others were induced to agree that through the Correspondence Committee, arrangements should be made for a meeting of the First Continental Congress, to be held in Philadelphia on September 5, 1774.

Remember this date. It is more important than July 4, 1776. If there had been no *decision* to hold a Continental Congress, there could have been no signing of the Declaration of Independence.

Before the first meeting of the new Congress, another leader, in a different section of the country, was deep in the throes of publishing a *Summary View of the Rights of British America.* He was Thomas Jefferson of the Province of Virginia, whose relationship to Lord Dunmore (representative of the Crown in Virginia) was as strained as that of Hancock and Adams with their governor.

Shortly after his famous *Summary of Rights* was published, Jefferson was informed that he was subject to prosecution for high treason against His Majesty's Government. Inspired by the threat, one of Jefferson's colleagues, Patrick Henry, boldly spoke his mind, concluding his remarks with a sentence that shall remain forever a classic, "If this be treason, then make the most of it."

It was such men as these who, without power, without authority, without military strength, without money, sat in solemn consideration of the destiny of the colonies, beginning at the opening of the First Continental Congress, and continuing at intervals for two years, until, on June 7, 1776, Richard Henry Lee arose, addressed the Chair, and to the startled Assembly made this motion:

"Gentlemen, I make the motion that these United Colonies are, and of right ought to be free and independent states, that they be absolved from all allegiance to the British Crown, and that all political connection between them and the state of Great Britain is, and ought to be totally dissolved."

Lee's astounding motion was discussed fervently and at such length that he began to lose patience. Finally, after days of argument, he again took the floor and declared, in a clear, firm voice, "Mr. President, we have discussed this issue for days. It is the only course for us to follow. Why then, Sir, do we longer delay? Why still deliberate? Let this happy day give birth to an American Republic. Let her arise, not to devastate and to conquer, but to re-establish the reign of peace and of law. The eyes of Europe are fixed upon us. She demands of us a living example of freedom that may exhibit a contrast, in the felicity of the citizen, to the ever increasing tyranny."

Before his motion was finally voted upon, Lee was called back to Virginia because of serious family illness, but before leaving he placed his cause in the hands of his friend, Thomas Jefferson, who promised to fight until favorable action was taken. Shortly thereafter the president of the Congress (Hancock) appointed Jefferson as chairman of a committee to draw up a Declaration of Independence.

Long and hard the committee labored on a document which would mean, when accepted by the Congress, that EVERY MAN WHO SIGNED IT WOULD BE SIGNING HIS OWN DEATH WARRANT should the Colonies lose in the fight with Great Britain, which was sure to follow.

The document was drawn, and on June 28 the original draft was read before the Congress. For several days it was discussed, altered, and made ready. On July 4, 1776, Thomas Jefferson stood before the Assembly and fearlessly read the most momentous *decision* ever placed upon paper.

"When in the course of human events it is necessary for one people to dissolve the political bands which have connected them with another, and to assume, among the powers of the earth, the separate and equal station to which the laws of Nature, and of Nature's God entitle them, a decent respect to the opinions of mankind requires that they should declare the causes which impel them to the separation. . . ."

When Jefferson finished, the document was voted upon, accepted, and signed by the fifty-six men, every one staking his own life upon his *decision* to write his name. By that *decision* came into existence a nation destined to bring to humankind forever the privilege of making *decisions*.

By decisions made in a similar spirit of faith, and only by such decisions, can people solve their personal problems and win for themselves high estates of material and spiritual wealth. Let us not forget this!

Analyze the events that led to the Declaration of Independence, and be convinced that the American nation was born of a *decision* created by a Master Mind consisting of fifty-six men. Note well the fact that it was their *decision* that ensured the success of Washington's armies, because the spirit of that decision was in the heart of every soldier who fought with him, and served as a spiritual power that recognizes no such thing as *failure.*

Note, also (with great personal benefit), that the *power* that gave America its freedom is the selfsame power that must be used by every individual who becomes self-determining. This *power* is made up of the principles described in this book. In the story of the Declaration of Independence it will not be difficult to detect at least six of these principles: DESIRE, DECISION, FAITH, PERSISTENCE, THE MASTER MIND, and ORGANIZED PLANNING.

Throughout this philosophy will be found the suggestion that thought, backed by strong *desire,* has a tendency to transmute itself into its physical equivalent. Before passing on, I wish to leave with you the suggestion that one may find in this story, and in the story of the organization of the United States Steel Corporation, a perfect description of the method by which thought makes this astounding transformation.

In your search for the secret of the method, do not look for a miracle, because you will not find it. You will find only the eternal laws of Nature. These laws are available to every person who has the *faith* and the *courage* to use them. They may be used to bring freedom to a nation or to accumulate riches. There is no charge save the time necessary to understand and appropriate them.

Those who reach *decisions* promptly and definitely know what they want, and generally get it. The leaders in every walk of life *decide* quickly and firmly. That is the major reason why they are leaders. The world has the habit of making room for people whose words and actions show they know where they are going.

Indecision is a habit that usually begins in youth. The habit takes on permanency as the youth goes through school and even through university or college without *definiteness of purpose.* The major weakness of all educational systems is that they neither teach nor encourage the habit of *definite decision.*

It would be beneficial if no university or college would permit the enrollment of any student unless and until the student declared their major purpose in graduating. It would be of still greater benefit if every student starting school were compelled to accept training in the *habit of decision,* and forced to pass a satisfactory examination on this subject before being permitted to advance.

The habit of *indecision,* acquired because of the deficiencies of our school systems, goes with the students into the occupations they choose, if in fact they choose their occupations. Generally, young people just out of school seek any job that can be found. They take the first place they find because they have fallen into the habit of *indecision.* Ninety-eight out of every hundred people working for wages today are in the positions they hold because they lacked the *definiteness of decision* to *plan a definite position,* and the knowledge of how to choose an employer.

Definiteness of decision always requires courage, sometimes very great courage. The fifty-six men who signed the Declaration of Independence staked their lives on the decision to affix their signatures to that document. People who reach a definite decision to procure a particular job and make life pay the price they ask do not stake their life on that decision; they stake their *economic freedom.* Financial independence, riches, desirable business and professional positions are not within reach of the person who neglects or refuses to *expect, plan,* and *demand* these things. The person who desires riches in the same spirit that Samuel Adams desired freedom for the Colonies is sure to accumulate wealth.

A modern example of a person who displayed courage in making decisions is Fred Smith, the founder of Federal Express (FedEx).

When Smith was a student in an economics class at Yale University, his professor stated that airfreight was the wave of the future and would be the primary source of revenue for the airlines.

Smith wrote a paper disagreeing. His argument was that the passenger route patterns that were the primary airline routes were wrong for freight. He noted that because costs would not come down with volume, the only way airfreight could be profitable was through a whole new system that would reach out to smaller cities as well as big ones and be designed for packages, not people. The professor considered this entirely unfeasible and gave Smith's paper a low grade.

Smith's concept was to start an all-freight airline that would fly primarily at night when the airports weren't congested. It would carry small, high-priority packages when speed of delivery was more important than cost. It would bring all the packages to a central point (he chose his home town—Memphis) where, through a specially designed computer program, the packages would be sorted, dispersed, and loaded on planes that were flown to the ultimate destinations. By consolidating all shipments to smaller cities, it would enable the company to fly full planeloads to cities all over the country and eventually the world.

Smith believed that venture capitalists would be interested and excited about this innovative idea. But to his shock, little interest was developed in the financial community.

This did not stop Smith. Because of his enthusiasm for the project and the courage of his convictions, he raised $91 million to finance his untested idea.

At this point the competing carriers realized that Smith's concept was a potential threat to their industry. The major airlines tried to forestall this new competition by lobbying the Civil Aeronautics Board to refuse Smith the necessary permission. Smith's team found a loophole in the law. Planes with a payload under 7,500 pounds did not need CAB permission to operate.

Smith went ahead and assembled a fleet of small jets. He began construction of his main facility at Memphis and started servicing seventy-five airports. FedEx would pick up packages at airports all over the country and fly them to Memphis, where they were sorted out and processed for immediate reshipment to other cities. Once the packages were unloaded, FedEx trucks delivered them to their destinations. Smith set a goal to get all packages to their destinations within 24 hours of pickup—and this goal was almost always met.

Despite the hard work and efforts of the company, the first few years were financial disasters. Losses amounted to millions of dollars. The investors were seriously concerned. Federal was falling far short of Smith's projections.

Despite the losses—which the investors blamed on Smith—and even talk of removing him and taking over the company, Smith did not lose faith. His courage never faltered. He hired experts (his "Master Mind") and worked day and night with them to solve operational problems. This resulted in Federal's revenues reaching $75 million in the next fiscal year, with a profit of $3.6 million.

Although competition from faxes virtually eliminated the use of FedEx for letters and documents, and despite competition from other airfreight companies and the postal service, which offered overnight service at a much lower price, Smith's continued innovation and dedication to continuous improvement have kept Federal as the number one carrier in its field.

In Chapter 7, on organized planning, you will find complete instructions for marketing every type of service. You will also find detailed information on how to choose the employer you prefer, and the particular job you desire. These instructions will be of no value to you UNLESS YOU DEFINITELY DECIDE to organize them into a plan of action.

CHAPTER 9

PERSISTENCE:

The Sustained Effort Necessary to Induce Faith

(The Eighth Step to Riches)

PERSISTENCE is an essential factor in the procedure of transmuting *desire* into its monetary equivalent. The basis of persistence is the *power of will*.

Willpower and desire, when properly combined, make an irresistible pair. People who accumulate great fortunes are generally known as cold-blooded and sometimes ruthless. Often they are misunderstood. What they have is willpower, which they mix with persistence and use as the basis of their desires to ensure the attainment of their objectives.

Henry Ford has been generally misunderstood to be ruthless and cold-blooded. This misconception grew out of Ford's habit of following through all of his plans with *persistence*.

The majority of people are ready to throw their aims and purposes overboard, and give up at the first sign of opposition or misfortune. A few carry on *despite* all opposition until they attain their goal. These few are the Fords, Carnegies, Rockefellers, and Edisons.

There may be no heroic connotation to the word "persistence," but the quality is to character what carbon is to steel.

The building of a fortune generally involves the application of the entire 13 factors of this philosophy. These principles must be understood—all who accumulate money must apply them with *persistence*.

If you are reading this book with the intention of applying the knowledge it conveys, the first test of your *persistence* will come when you begin to follow the six steps described in the second chapter. Unless you are one of the two out of every hundred who already have a *definite goal* at which you are aiming and a *definite plan* for its attainment, you may read the instructions and then carry on with your daily routine, never complying with those instructions.

The author is checking you up at this point, because lack of persistence is one of the major causes of failure. Moreover, experience with thousands of people has proven that lack of persistence is a weakness common to the majority of people. It is a weakness that may be overcome by effort. The ease with which lack of persistence may be conquered will depend entirely upon the *intensity of one's desire.*

The starting point of all achievement is *desire.* Keep this constantly in mind. Weak desires bring weak results, just as a small amount of fire makes a small amount of heat. If you find yourself lacking in persistence, this weakness may be remedied by building a stronger fire under your desires.

Continue to read through to the end, then go back to Chapter 2 and start immediately to carry out the instructions given in the six steps. The eagerness with which you follow these instructions will indicate clearly how much, or how little, you really *desire* to accumulate money. If you find that you are indifferent, you may be sure that you have not yet acquired the "money consciousness" which you must possess before you can be sure of accumulating a fortune.

Fortunes gravitate to people whose minds have been prepared to "attract" them, just as surely as water gravitates to the ocean. In this book may be found all the stimuli necessary to "attune" any normal mind to the vibrations that will attract the object of one's desires.

If you find you are weak in *persistence,* center your attention upon the instructions contained in Chapter 10, on power. Surround yourself with a "Master Mind" group, and develop persistence through the cooperative efforts of the members of this group. You will find additional instructions for the development of persistence in Chapter 4, on autosuggestion, and Chapter 12, on the subconscious mind. Follow the instructions outlined in these chapters until your habit nature hands over to your subconscious mind a clear picture of the object of your *desire.* From that point on, you will not be handicapped by lack of persistence.

Your subconscious mind works continuously, while you are awake and while you are asleep. Spasmodic or occasional effort to apply the rules will be of no value to you. To get *results,* you must apply all of the rules until their application becomes a fixed habit with you. In no other way can you develop the necessary "money consciousness."

Poverty is attracted to the one whose mind is favorable to it, as money is attracted to one whose mind has been deliberately prepared to attract it, and through the same laws. POVERTY CONSCIOUSNESS WILL VOLUNTARILY SEIZE THE MIND THAT IS NOT OCCUPIED WITH MONEY CONSCIOUSNESS. A poverty consciousness develops without conscious application of habits favorable to it. The money consciousness must be created to order, unless one is born with such a consciousness.

Catch the full significance of the statements in the preceding paragraph and you will understand the importance of *persistence* in the accumulation of a fortune. Without *persistence,* you will be defeated, even before you start. With *persistence,* you will win.

If you have ever experienced a nightmare, you will realize the value of persistence. You are lying in bed, half awake, with a feeling that you are about to suffocate. You are unable to turn over or to move a muscle. You realize that you *must begin* to regain control over your muscles. Through persistent effort of willpower, you finally manage to move the fingers of one hand. By continuing to move your fingers, you extend your control to the muscles of one arm, until you can lift it. Then you gain control of the other arm in the same manner. You finally gain control over the muscles of one leg, and then extend it to the other leg. THEN—WITH ONE SUPREME EFFORT OF WILL—you regain complete control over your muscular system, and "snap" out of your nightmare. The trick has been turned, step by step.

You may find it necessary to "snap" out of your mental inertia through a similar procedure, moving slowly at first, then increasing your speed until you gain complete control over your will. Be *persistent* no matter how slowly you may, at first, have to move. WITH PERSISTENCE WILL COME SUCCESS.

If you select your "Master Mind" group with care, you will have in it at least one person who will aid you in the development of persistence. Some people who have accumulated great fortunes did so because of *necessity.* They developed the habit of persistence because they were so closely driven by circumstances they had to become persistent.

THERE IS NO SUBSTITUTE FOR PERSISTENCE! It cannot be supplanted by any other quality! Remember this in the beginning and it will hearten you when the going may seem difficult and slow.

Those who have cultivated the *habit* of persistence seem to enjoy insurance against failure. No matter how many times they are defeated, they finally arrive up near the top of the ladder. Sometimes it appears there is a hidden guide whose duty is to test people through all sorts of discouraging experiences. Those who pick themselves up after defeat and keep on

THINK AND GROW RICH

trying arrive; and the world cries, "Bravo! I knew you could do it!" The hidden guide lets no one enjoy great achievement without passing the *persistence test*. Those who can't take it simply do not make the grade.

Those who can "take it" are bountifully rewarded for their *persistence*. They receive, as their compensation, whatever goal they are pursuing. That is not all! They receive something infinitely more important than material compensation: the knowledge that EVERY FAILURE BRINGS WITH IT THE SEED OF AN EQUIVALENT ADVANTAGE.

A few people know from experience the soundness of persistence. They are the ones who have not accepted defeat as being anything more than temporary. They are the ones whose *desires* are so *persistently applied* that defeat is finally changed into victory. We who stand on the sidelines of life see the overwhelmingly large number who go down in defeat, never to rise again. We see the few who take the punishment of defeat as an urge to greater effort. These, fortunately, never learn to accept life's reverse gear. But what we *do not see,* what most of us never suspect of existing, is the silent but irresistible *power* which comes to the rescue of those who fight on in the face of discouragement. If we speak of this power at all, we call it *persistence* and let it go at that. One thing we all know: if one does not possess persistence, one does not achieve noteworthy success in any calling.

A good example of the power of persistence is show business. From all over the world people have come to Hollywood seeking fame, fortune, power, love, or whatever it is that human beings call success. Once in a great while someone steps out from the long procession of seekers, and the world hears that another person has mastered Hollywood. But Hollywood is not easily or quickly conquered. It acknowledges talent, recognizes genius, and pays off in money only after one has refused to *quit*. The secret is always inseparably attached to one word, *persistence*!

Bruce Lee, the actor who made us conscious of the Asian martial arts, might have been forgotten long ago were it not for his persistence in reaching for movie stardom.

Lee arrived in America from China with nothing but a dream and the capacity for hard work. During his youth he studied and mastered kung fu and later became a teacher of this art. However, his real goal was to be an actor. He obtained minor roles in some films and TV programs, but he felt his great break came when he learned that the producers of a new television series called Kung Fu *were looking for an actor who knew the martial arts for the starring role. His screen test was successful and he looked forward to being given the role, but to his great disappointment, another actor, David Carradine, was chosen.*

Disillusioned, he was ready to give up acting and go back to teaching. When members of the Asian community heard of this, he was deluged with letters asking him not to give up. Soon the word spread to movie fans of all races, and Lee made up his mind to keep seeking new roles.

He never gave up. He took roles in several films, and his reputation as an actor and proponent of the martial arts made him a household name throughout the world. He took the study of the martial arts from being limited to Asian countries to becoming universally respected.

Although he died of a cerebral hemorrhage at the age of thirty-two, his fame has lived after him. Bruce Lee is not only still remembered and admired by fans—many of whom were not even born when he made his movies—but TV series and early films have been made into videos and are still highly popular all over the world.

Persistence is a state of mind, so it can be cultivated. Like all states of mind, persistence is based upon definite causes, including:

1. **Definiteness of Purpose.** Knowing what you want is the first and perhaps the most important step toward the development of persistence. A strong motive forces you to surmount many difficulties.
2. **Desire.** It is comparatively easy to acquire and maintain persistence in pursuing the object of intense desire.
3. **Self-Reliance.** Belief in your ability to carry out a plan encourages you to follow the plan through with persistence. (Self-reliance can be developed through the principle described in Chapter 4, autosuggestion.)
4. **Definiteness of Plans.** Organized plans, even though they may be weak and entirely impractical, encourage persistence.
5. **Accurate Knowledge.** Knowing that your plans are sound, based upon experience or observation, encourages persistence; "guessing" instead of "knowing" destroys persistence.
6. **Cooperation.** Sympathy, understanding, and harmonious cooperation with others tend to develop persistence.
7. **Willpower.** The habit of concentrating your thoughts upon the building of plans for the attainment of a *Definite Purpose* leads to persistence.
8. **Habit.** Persistence is the direct result of habit. The mind absorbs and becomes a part of the daily experiences upon which it feeds. Fear, the worst of all enemies, can

be effectively cured by forced repetition of acts of courage. Everyone who has seen active service in war knows this.

Before leaving the subject of *persistence,* take an inventory of yourself. Determine in what particular, if any, you are lacking in this essential quality. Measure yourself courageously, point by point, and see how many of the eight factors of persistence you lack. The analysis may lead to discoveries that will give you a new grip on yourself.

Symptoms of Lack of Persistence

Here you will find the real enemies that stand between you and noteworthy achievement. Here you will find not only the "symptoms" indicating weakness of *persistence,* but also the deeply seated subconscious causes of this weakness. Study the list carefully and face yourself squarely IF YOU REALLY WISH TO KNOW WHO YOU ARE AND WHAT YOU ARE CAPABLE OF DOING. These are the weaknesses that must be mastered by all who accumulate riches.

1. Failure to recognize and clearly define exactly what you want.
2. Procrastination, with or without cause (usually backed up with a formidable array of alibis and excuses).
3. Lack of interest in acquiring specialized knowledge.
4. Indecision, the habit of "passing the buck" on all occasions, instead of facing issues squarely (also backed by alibis).
5. The habit of relying upon alibis instead of creating definite plans for the solution of problems.
6. Self-satisfaction. There is but little remedy for this affliction, and no hope for those who suffer from it.
7. Indifference, usually reflected in your readiness to compromise on all occasions rather than meet opposition and fight it.
8. The habit of blaming others for your mistakes, and accepting unfavorable circumstances as being unavoidable.
9. *Weakness of desire* due to neglect in the choice of *motives* that impel action.

10. Willingness, even eagerness, to quit at the first sign of defeat (based upon one or more of the six basic fears).

11. Lack of *organized plans,* placed in writing, where they may be analyzed.

12. The habit of neglecting to move on ideas, or to grasp opportunity when it presents itself.

13. *Wishing* instead of *willing.*

14. The habit of compromising with *poverty* instead of aiming at riches—a general absence of ambition to *be,* to *do,* and to *own.*

15. Searching for all the shortcuts to riches, trying to *get* without *giving* a fair equivalent, usually reflected in the habit of gambling or endeavoring to drive "sharp" bargains.

16. *Fear of criticism,* failure to create plans and to put them into action because of what other people will think, do or say. This enemy belongs at the head of the list, because it generally exists in the subconscious mind without being recognized (see the six basic fears in Chapter 15).

Let us examine some of the symptoms of the fear of criticism. The majority of people permit relatives, friends, and the public at large to so influence them that they cannot live their own lives, because they fear criticism.

Huge numbers of people make mistakes in marriage, stand by the bargain, and go through life miserable and unhappy because they fear criticism that may follow if they correct the mistake. (Anyone who has submitted to this form of fear knows the irreparable damage it does by destroying ambition, self-reliance, and the desire to achieve.)

Millions of people neglect to acquire belated educations, after having left school, because they fear criticism.

Countless numbers of men and women, both young and old, permit relatives to wreck their lives in the name of *duty* because they fear criticism. (Duty does not require any person to submit to the destruction of their personal ambitions and the right to live their life in their own way.)

People refuse to take chances in business because they fear the criticism that may follow if they fail. The fear of criticism in such cases is stronger than the *desire* for success.

Too many people refuse to set high goals for themselves, or even neglect selecting a career, because they fear the criticism of relatives and "friends" who may say, "Don't aim so high. People will think you are crazy."

When Andrew Carnegie suggested that I devote twenty years to the organization of a philosophy of individual achievement, my first impulse of thought was fear of what people might say. The suggestion set up a goal for me, far out of proportion to any I had ever conceived. As quick as a flash, my mind began to create alibis and excuses, all of them traceable to the inherent *fear of criticism*. Something inside me said, "You can't do it—the job is too big and requires too much time. What will your relatives think of you? How will you earn a living? No one has ever organized a philosophy of success, so what right have you to believe you can do it? Who are you, anyway, to aim so high? Remember your humble birth. What do you know about philosophy? People will think you are crazy (and they did). Why hasn't some other person done this before now?"

These, and many other questions, flashed into my mind and demanded attention. It seemed as if the whole world had suddenly turned its attention to me with the purpose of ridiculing me into giving up all desire to carry out Mr. Carnegie's suggestion.

I had a fine opportunity, then and there, to kill off ambition before it gained control of me. Later in life, after having analyzed thousands of people, I discovered that MOST IDEAS ARE STILLBORN AND NEED THE BREATH OF LIFE INJECTED INTO THEM THROUGH DEFINITE PLANS OF IMMEDIATE ACTION. The time to nurse an idea is at the time of its birth. Every minute it lives gives it a better chance of surviving. The *fear of criticism* is at the bottom of the destruction of most ideas that never reach the *planning* and *action* stage.

Another good example of a person who refused to accept the criticism of others and persisted in pursuing his dream is Fred Smith, whose success in creating and developing Federal Express was described in the previous chapter.

Many people believe that material success is the result of favorable "breaks." There is an element of ground for the belief, but those depending entirely on luck are nearly always disappointed because they overlook another important factor that must be present before one can be sure of success. It is the knowledge with which favorable "breaks" can be made to order.

Let's look at Tom Monaghan, who created and grew Domino's Pizza from a one-store pizza parlor to a chain of several thousand home-delivery outlets over a period of about thirty years. In 1989, he decided to sell his hugely successful company to concentrate instead on doing philanthropic work.

But his plan did not work out. After two and a half years, the company that purchased the chain almost drove it into bankruptcy, so Monaghan came back.

It took much hard work and persistence to first rebuild and then expand the organization. Monaghan had developed the necessary determination early in his life. He had overcome a childhood of deprivation, poverty, and abuse to become a great entrepreneur. Now once again he mobilized all his efforts not only to return Domino to its original prominence but to expand it to 6,000 stores—of which 1,100 are in countries other than the United States.

Once the chain was back on its feet, Monaghan faced a new and serious challenge. Domino built its major promotion on its guarantee of fast delivery. It guaranteed customers would get their pizza within 30 minutes.

This led to a series of lawsuits from people who claimed injury from accidents caused by Domino delivery drivers who were speeding to make the 30-minute deadline. The family of a woman allegedly killed by a Domino driver was awarded $3 million. The final blow came when another woman was awarded $78 million. After that, Domino dropped the 30-minute guarantee.

Despite this financial catastrophe, Monaghan refused to give up. He plowed more money, time, and energy into the company and brought it back once again. By his persistence and positive attitude he forged ahead and inspired his team with the winning spirit that has made Domino number one in its industry.

Examine the next hundred people you meet. Ask them what they want most in life, and 98 of them will not be able to tell you. If you press them for an answer, some will say *security*, many will say *money*, a few will say *happiness*, others will say *fame and power*, and still others will say *social recognition, ease in living, ability to sing, dance, or write*, but none of them will be able to define these terms, or give the slightest indication of a *plan* by which they hope to attain these vaguely expressed wishes. Riches do not respond to wishes. They respond only to definite plans, backed by definite desires, through constant *persistence*.

How to Develop Persistence

There are four simple steps that lead to the habit of persistence. They call for no great amount of intelligence, no particular level of education, and but little time or effort. The necessary steps are:

1. **A Definite Purpose Backed by a Burning Desire for Its Fulfillment.**
2. **A Definite Plan, Expressed in Continuous Action.**
3. **A Mind Closed Tightly Against All Negative and Discouraging Influences,** including negative suggestions of relatives, friends, and acquaintances.
4. **A Friendly Alliance with One or More Persons Who Will Encourage You to Follow Through with Both Plan and Purpose.**

These four steps are essential for success in all walks of life. The entire purpose of the 13 principles of this philosophy is to enable you to take these four steps as a matter of *habit*.

They are the steps by which you may control your economic destiny.

They are the steps that lead to freedom and independence of thought.

They are the steps that lead to riches, in small or great quantities.

They are the steps that lead the way to power, fame, and worldly recognition.

They are the steps that guarantee favorable "breaks."

They are the steps that convert dreams into physical realities.

They are the steps that lead, also, to the mastery of *fear, discouragement,* and *indifference.*

There is a magnificent reward for all who learn to take these four steps. It is the privilege of writing your own ticket and of making life yield whatever price is asked.

What mystical power gives to people of *persistence* the capacity to master difficulties? Does the quality of persistence set up in your mind some form of spiritual, mental, or chemical activity that gives you access to supernatural forces? Does Infinite Intelligence throw itself on the side of the person who still fights on after the battle has been lost, with the whole world on the opposing side?

These and many other similar questions have arisen in my mind as I have observed men like Henry Ford, who started from scratch and built an industrial empire of huge proportions, with little else in the way of a beginning but *persistence*. Or Thomas A. Edison, who, with less than three months of schooling, became the world's leading inventor and converted *persistence* into the talking machine, the moving picture machine, and the incandescent light, to say nothing of half a hundred other useful inventions.

I had the happy privilege of analyzing both Mr. Edison and Mr. Ford, year by year, over a long period, and the opportunity to study them at close range. I therefore speak from actual knowledge when I say that I found no quality save *persistence* in either of them that even remotely suggested the major source of their stupendous achievements.

As one makes an impartial study of successful people, one is drawn to the inevitable conclusion that *persistence*, concentration of effort, and *definiteness of purpose* are the major sources of their achievements.

A good example of determination and persistence is Howard Schultz, the "Starbucks man." It takes a person with vision, fortitude, and unswerving confidence to make a new concept succeed.

Schultz was hired to manage retail sales and marketing for a small coffee distributor who had a few retail outlets in Seattle. He was twenty-nine and just married. He and his wife left their home in New York City to accept this new job.

About a year later, Schultz visited Italy on a buying trip. As he wandered around Milan, he noticed how important coffee was to the Italian culture. Typically, the workday starts with a cup of rich coffee at a coffee bar. After work, friends and colleagues once again meet at the coffee bar for a leisurely stop before heading home. It is a center of Italian social life. Schultz visualized this transferred to America. It had never been done, but he felt it could work because of the high quality of Starbucks coffee.

It became Schultz's obsession. He was determined to build a national chain of cafés based on the Italian coffee bar, but the Starbucks owners were reluctant. They were in the wholesale coffee bean business; the restaurants they owned were only a small part of their operation.

To implement his goal, Schultz left Starbucks and planned a new company. In 1986, Schultz opened his first coffee bar in Seattle. It was an immediate success. Schultz soon opened another in Seattle and a third in Vancouver. The following year he bought the Starbucks company and adopted its name for his enterprise.

Schultz believes that the quality of Starbucks will one day alter how everyday Americans conduct their lives. If Schultz has his way, a cup of Starbucks will become a basic part of American culture. His concept has paid off: Starbucks' sales have increased ninefold for every year since 1988.

Schultz envisioned hundreds of Starbucks coffee shops across America where business people would stop on their way to work and come to after work to relax. Shoppers would stop for a pick-me-up. Young people would meet their dates over coffee rather than cocktails. Families would come for refreshment before or after the cinema.

Starbucks incurred losses for three straight years—more than $1 million in 1989 alone—but Schultz never gave up. He had a firm conviction that this was the way to build a company and that the losses would soon turn into profits.

Once his Seattle stores were profitable, Starbucks spread slowly into other cities—Vancouver, Portland, Los Angeles, Denver, and Chicago—and later to the Eastern cities and overseas. Starbucks has become a household name all over the world and an exemplar of American marketing ingenuity. And it has made Howard Schultz one of the world's richest people.

CHAPTER 10

POWER OF THE MASTER MIND:

The Driving Force

(The Ninth Step to Riches)

Power is essential for success in the accumulation of money.

Plans are inert and useless without sufficient *power* to translate them into *action*. This chapter will describe the method by which an individual may attain and apply power.

Power may be defined as "organized and intelligently directed *knowledge*." Power, as the term is here used, refers to *organized* effort, sufficient to enable an individual to transmute *desire* into its monetary equivalent. Organized effort is produced through the coordination of effort of two or more people, who work toward a *definite* end in a spirit of harmony.

POWER IS REQUIRED FOR THE ACCUMULATION OF MONEY! POWER IS NECESSARY FOR THE RETENTION OF MONEY AFTER IT HAS BEEN ACCUMULATED!

Let us ascertain how power may be acquired. If power is "organized knowledge," let us examine the sources of knowledge:

1. **Infinite Intelligence.** This source of knowledge may be contacted through the procedure described in Chapter 6, with the aid of Creative Imagination.

2. **Accumulated Experience.** The accumulated experience of humankind (or that portion of it which has been organized and recorded) may be found in any well-equipped public library. An important part of this accumulated experience is taught in schools and colleges, where it has been classified and organized.

3. **Experiment and Research.** In the field of science, and in practically every other walk of life, people are gathering, classifying, and organizing new facts daily. This is

the source to which one must turn when knowledge is not available through "accumulated experience." Here, too, the Creative Imagination must often be used.

Knowledge may be acquired from any of the foregoing sources. It may be converted into *power* by organizing it into definite *plans* and by expressing those plans in terms of *action*.

Examination of the three major sources of knowledge will readily disclose the difficulty people would have—if they depended upon their efforts alone—in assembling knowledge and expressing it through definite plans in terms of action. If their plans are comprehensive, and if they contemplate large proportions, they must, generally, induce others to cooperate with them, before they can inject into their plans the necessary element of power.

Gaining Power through the "Master Mind"

The "Master Mind" may be defined as "coordination of knowledge and effort, in a spirit of harmony, between two or more people, for the attainment of a definite purpose."

No individual may have great power without availing himself or herself of the Master Mind. In Chapter 7, instructions were given for the creation of *plans* for the purpose of translating *desire* into its monetary equivalent. If you carry out these instructions with *persistence* and intelligence, and use discrimination in the selection of your "Master Mind" group, your objective will have been halfway reached before you even begin to recognize it.

So you may better understand the "intangible" potentialities of power available to you through a properly chosen Master Mind group, we will here explain the two characteristics of the Master Mind principle, one of which is economic in nature, and the other psychic. The economic feature is obvious. Economic advantages may be created by people who surround themselves with the advice, counsel, and personal cooperation of a group of people who are willing to lend them wholehearted aid in a spirit of *perfect harmony*. This form of cooperative alliance has been the basis of nearly every great fortune. Your understanding of this great truth may definitely determine your financial status.

The psychic phase of the Master Mind principle is much more abstract, much more difficult to comprehend, because it refers to the spiritual forces with which the human race, as a whole, is not well acquainted. You may catch a significant suggestion from this statement: "No two minds ever come together without thereby creating a third, invisible, intangible force, which may be likened to a third mind."

Keep in mind the fact that there are only two known elements in the whole universe—

energy and matter. Matter may be broken down into units of molecules, atoms, and electrons. There are units of matter that may be isolated, separated, and analyzed.

Likewise, there are units of energy.

The human mind is a form of energy, a part of it being spiritual in nature. When the minds of two people are coordinated in a *spirit of harmony,* the spiritual units of energy of each mind form an affinity, which constitutes the "psychic" phase of the Master Mind.

The Master Mind principle, or rather the economic feature of it, was first called to my attention by Andrew Carnegie. Discovery of this principle was responsible for the choice of my life's work.

Mr. Carnegie's Master Mind group consisted of a staff of approximately fifty men, with whom he surrounded himself for the *definite purpose* of manufacturing and marketing steel. He attributed his entire fortune to the *power* he accumulated through this Master Mind.

Analyze the record of any person who has accumulated a great fortune, and many of those who have accumulated modest fortunes, and you will find that they have either consciously or unconsciously employed the Master Mind principle.

GREAT POWER CAN BE ACCUMULATED THROUGH NO OTHER PRINCIPLE!

Energy is Nature's set of building blocks, out of which she constructs every material thing in the universe, including humankind, and every form of animal and vegetable life. Through a process that only Nature completely understands, she translates energy into matter.

Nature's building blocks are available to us in the energy involved in *thinking*! The brain may be compared to an electric battery. It absorbs energy from the ether, which permeates every atom of matter and fills the entire universe.

A group of electric batteries will provide more energy than a single battery. An individual battery will provide energy in proportion to the number and capacity of the cells it contains. The brain functions in a similar fashion. This accounts for the fact that some brains are more efficient than others, and leads to this significant statement: A group of brains coordinated (or connected) in a spirit of harmony will provide more thought-energy than a single brain, just as a group of electric batteries will provide more energy than a single battery.

Through this metaphor it becomes immediately obvious that the Master Mind principle holds the secret of the *power* wielded by people who surround themselves with other people of brains.

There follows, now, another statement, which will lead still nearer to an understanding of the psychic phase of the Master Mind principle: When a group of individual brains is coordinated and functions in harmony, the increased energy created through that alliance becomes available to every individual brain in the group.

Henry Ford began his business career under the handicap of poverty, illiteracy, and ignorance. Within the inconceivably short period of ten years, Mr. Ford mastered these three handicaps, and within twenty-five years made himself one of the richest men in America. Connect with this fact the additional knowledge that Mr. Ford's most rapid strides became noticeable from the time he became a personal friend of Thomas A. Edison, and you will begin to understand what the influence of one mind upon another can accomplish. Go a step further, and consider the fact that Mr. Ford's most outstanding achievements began from the time he formed the acquaintance of Harvey Firestone, John Burroughs, and Luther Burbank (each a man of great brain capacity), and you will have further evidence that *power* may be produced through a friendly alliance of minds.

There is little if any doubt that Henry Ford was one of the best-informed men in the business and industrial world. The question of his wealth needs no discussion. Analyze Mr. Ford's intimate personal friends, some of whom have already been mentioned, and you will be prepared to understand the following statement: *People take on the nature and the habits and the POWER OF THOUGHT of those with whom they associate in a spirit of sympathy and harmony.*

Henry Ford whipped poverty, illiteracy, and ignorance by allying himself with great minds, whose vibrations of thought he absorbed into his own mind. Through his association with Edison, Burbank, Burroughs, and Firestone, Mr. Ford added to his own brain-power the sum and substance of the intelligence, experience, knowledge, and spiritual forces of these four men. Moreover, he appropriated and made use of the Master Mind principle through the methods described in this book.

This principle is available to you!

President Franklin Roosevelt brought the best minds of the country to Washington to form a Master Mind group he called his "brain trust." During and after World War II, Master Mind groups called "think tanks" were frequently called upon by leaders of government and industry to help deal with critical problems.

We have already mentioned Mahatma Gandhi. Perhaps the majority of those who have heard of Gandhi look upon him as merely an eccentric little man who went around without formal clothes, and made trouble for the British government.

In reality, Gandhi was not eccentric but *he was the most powerful man of his generation* (estimated by the number of his followers and their faith in their leader). Moreover, he was probably the most powerful man who ever lived. His power was passive, but it was real.

Let us study the method by which he attained his stupendous *power.* It may be explained in a few words: He came by power through inducing over 200 million people to coordinate, with mind and body, in a spirit of *harmony* for a *definite purpose.*

In brief, Gandhi accomplished a *miracle,* for it is a miracle when 200 million people can be induced—not forced—to cooperate in a spirit of harmony for a limitless time. If you doubt that this is a miracle, try to induce *any two people* to cooperate in a spirit of harmony for any length of time. Every person who manages a business knows what a difficult matter it is to get employees to work together in a spirit even remotely resembling harmony.

The list of the chief sources from which *power* may be attained is, as you have seen, headed by *Infinite Intelligence.* When two or more people coordinate in a spirit of *harmony,* and work toward a definite objective, they place themselves in position, through that alliance, to absorb power directly from the great universal storehouse of Infinite Intelligence. This is the greatest of all sources of power. It is the source to which the genius turns. It is the source to which every great leader turns (whether conscious of the fact or not).

The other two major sources from which the knowledge necessary for the accumulation of power may be obtained are no more reliable than our five senses. The senses are not always reliable. Infinite Intelligence *does not err.*

In subsequent chapters, the methods by which Infinite Intelligence may be most readily contacted will be adequately described.

This is not a course on religion. No fundamental principle described in this book should be interpreted as being intended to interfere either directly or indirectly with anyone's religious habits. This book has been confined, exclusively, to instructing the reader how to transmute the *definite purpose of desire for money* into its monetary equivalent.

Read, *think,* and meditate as you read. Soon, the entire subject will unfold, and you will see it in perspective. You are now seeing the detail of the individual chapters.

Money is shy and elusive. It must be wooed and won by methods not unlike those used by a determined lover in pursuit of a mate. And, coincidental as it is, the power used in the "wooing" of money is not greatly different from that used in wooing a lover. That power, when successfully used in the pursuit of money, must be mixed with *faith.* It must be mixed with *desire.* It must be mixed with *persistence.* It must be applied through a plan, and that plan must be set into *action.*

Some of the best sources for creating your own Master Mind group are your employees. Andrew Grove, the extremely successful CEO of Intel Corporation, did this. Grove works with a team of technical, mar-

keting, financial, and administrative men and women in an informal environment. There are no private offices, special parking spaces, or other privileges for executives. Employees have a generous stock option plan so they can share in the gains if the company makes money and the stock rises.

Although the team may appear casual, they follow Grove's lead of being very demanding on themselves. When Intel faced a crisis in 1976, the team willingly put in extra effort and more work hours and did everything that was necessary to solve the problems. On another occasion, it was discovered that the Intel Pentium chip had a minor defect that would affect only an insignificant number of operations. Grove's decision to replace the chips at a cost of $475 million rather than deliver a product that was not perfect was fully endorsed by his colleagues.

Grove encourages his people to work in small, autonomous work units in which everyone understands the system and their role in it. Each person contributes their knowledge, expertise, and creativity. Team members are trained and motivated to produce to the best of their capacity. When crises arise, the team willingly puts in the extra time, energy, and brainpower to meet and beat the problems faced.

When money comes in quantities known as "the big money," it flows to the one who accumulates it as easily as water flows downhill. There exists a great unseen stream of *power*, which may be compared to a river, except that it flows in two directions. One side carries all who get into that side of the stream onward and upward to *wealth*—and the other side flows in the opposite direction, carrying all who are unfortunate enough to get into it (and not able to extricate themselves from it) downward to misery and *poverty*.

Every person who has accumulated a great fortune has recognized the existence of this stream of life. It consists of one's *thinking process*. The positive emotions of thought form the side of the stream that carries one to fortune. The negative emotions form the side that carries one down to poverty.

This carries a thought of stupendous importance to the person who is following this book with the object of accumulating a fortune.

If you are in the side of the stream of power that leads to poverty, this may serve as an oar by which you may propel yourself over into the other side of the stream. It can serve you *only* through application and use. Merely reading, and passing judgment on it, either one way or another, will in no way benefit you.

Some people undergo the experience of alternating between the positive and negative sides of the stream, being at times on the positive side and at times on the negative side. The Wall Street crash of '29 swept millions of people from the positive to the negative side of the stream. Those millions struggled—some of them in desperation and fear—to get back to the positive side of the stream. This book was written especially for those millions.

Poverty and riches often change places. Poverty may, and generally does, voluntarily take the place of riches. When riches take the place of poverty, the change is usually brought about through well-conceived and carefully executed *plans*. Poverty needs no plan. It needs no one to aid it, because it is bold and ruthless. Riches are shy and timid. They have to be "attracted."

Anybody can *wish* for riches, and most people do, but only a few know that a definite plan plus a *burning desire* for wealth are the only dependable means of accumulating it.

Ross Perot's attitude exemplifies the power of tough-minded commitment—not only his own but also that of the Master Mind with which he surrounded himself. He had a burning desire for wealth and he achieved it.

Before he started Electronic Data Systems (EDS), he had been the top salesperson at IBM. He was cautioned that leaving IBM to start a company from scratch was a mistake. This did not faze Perot. He was inspired by a vision of what could be. His success clearly demonstrates that by sticking to your dream, and transmitting that dream to a team of experts—a Master Mind—who have the know-how to help make it a realization, leads to success and wealth.

Perot firmly believes that commitment can accomplish miracles. This was exemplified when EDS competed for one of the largest contracts in the computer industry. Two companies, IBM and EDS, were the contestants. IBM was far richer, and had in their staff a more experienced and knowledgeable group of specialists. EDS had a small but dedicated team.

Perot recalls, "About thirty days into the competition, I walked into the room and our fifteen guys were saying, 'Gee, we probably can't win but it will be great experience.' I didn't jump up and down and chew people out. I just walked to the blackboard and wrote down the seven criteria by which we would be judged. And in a nice low voice said, 'We are going to beat them seven to zero.' That's the day we won."

Perot commented that the raises, the bonuses, the stock options and thousands of new jobs created by winning this project were, of course, the tangible rewards of achieving this coup. However, he believes that more important was the immense satisfaction of knowing that by their hard work and creativity, they beat the best in the world. That's what makes a company great—a team working together as a Master Mind to beat the opposition.

CHAPTER 11

THE MYSTERY OF SEX TRANSMUTATION

(The Tenth Step to Riches)

The meaning of the word "transmute" is, in simple language, "the changing or transferring of one element, or form of energy, into another."

The emotion of sex brings into being a state of mind.

Because of ignorance on the subject, this state of mind is generally associated with the physical. Because of improper influences, to which most people have been subjected in acquiring knowledge of sex, things essentially physical have highly biased the mind.

The emotion of sex has behind it the possibility of three constructive potentialities:

1. The perpetuation of humankind.
2. The maintenance of health (as a therapeutic agency it has no equal).
3. The transformation of mediocrity into genius through transmutation.

Sex transmutation is simple and easily explained. It means the switching of the mind from thoughts of physical expression to thoughts of some other nature.

Sex desire is the most powerful of human desires. When driven by this desire, people develop keenness of imagination, courage, willpower, persistence, and creative ability unknown to them at other times. So strong and impelling is the desire for sexual contact that people freely run the risk of life and reputation to indulge it. When harnessed and redirected along other lines, the positive attributes of this motivating force may be used as powerful creative forces in literature, art, or any other profession or calling, including, of course, the accumulation of riches.

The transmutation of sex energy calls for the exercise of willpower, to be sure, but the reward is worth the effort. The desire for sexual expression is inborn and natural. The desire cannot and should not be submerged or eliminated. But it should be given an outlet through forms of expression that enrich the body, mind, and spirit. If not given this form of outlet, through transmutation, it will seek outlets through purely physical channels.

A river may be dammed and its water controlled for a time, but eventually it will force an outlet. The same is true of the emotion of sex. It may be submerged and controlled for a time, but its very nature causes it to be ever seeking means of expression. If it is not transmuted into some creative effort, it will find a less worthy outlet.

Fortunate, indeed, are those who have discovered how to give sex emotion an outlet through some form of creative effort, for they have, by that discovery, lifted themselves to the status of genius.

Scientific research on the backgrounds of high-achieving men (unfortunately, no similar studies have been made about highly successful women) has disclosed these significant facts:

1. The men of greatest achievement are those with highly developed sex natures—men who have learned the art of sex transmutation.
2. The men who have accumulated great fortunes and achieved outstanding recognition in literature, art, industry, architecture, and the professions were motivated by the influence of a woman.

The research from which these astounding discoveries were made went back through the pages of biography and history for more than two thousand years. Wherever there was evidence available in connection with the lives of men of great achievement, it indicated most convincingly that they possessed highly developed sex natures.

The emotion of sex is an "irresistible force," against which there can be no such opposition as an "immovable body." When driven by this emotion, men become gifted with a super power for action. Understand this truth and you will catch the significance of the statement that sex transmutation will lift one to the status of a genius.

The emotion of sex contains the secret of creative ability.

Destroy the sex glands, whether in man or beast, and you have removed the major source of action. For proof of this, observe what happens to any animal after it has been castrated. A bull becomes as docile as a cow after it has been altered sexually. Sex alteration takes out of the male, whether man or beast, all the *fight* that was in him. Sex alteration of the female has the same effect.

The 10 Mind Stimuli

The human mind responds to stimuli through which it may be "keyed up" to high rates of vibration, known as enthusiasm, creative imagination, intense desire, etc. The stimuli to which the mind responds most freely are:

1. The desire for sex expression
2. Love
3. A burning desire for fame, power, financial gain, *money*
4. Music
5. Friendship between either those of the same sex or those of the opposite sex
6. A Master Mind alliance based upon the harmony of two or more people who ally themselves for spiritual or temporal advancement
7. Mutual suffering, such as that experienced by people who are persecuted
8. Autosuggestion
9. Fear
10. Narcotics and alcohol

The desire for sex expression comes at the head of the list of stimuli that most effectively "step up" the vibrations of the mind and start the "wheels" of physical action. Eight of these stimuli are natural and constructive. Two are destructive. The list is here presented to enable you to make a comparative study of the major sources of mind stimulation. From this study, it will be readily seen that the emotion of sex is, by great odds, the most intense and powerful of all mind stimuli.

This comparison is necessary as a foundation for proof of the statement that transmutation of sex energy may lift one to the status of a genius. Let us find out what constitutes a genius.

A good definition of a genius is "a person who has discovered how to increase the vibrations of thought to the point where they can freely communicate with sources of knowledge not available through the ordinary rate of vibration of thought."

The person who thinks will want to ask some questions concerning this definition of genius. The first question will be, "How may one communicate with sources of knowledge which are not available through the *ordinary* rate of vibration of thought?"

The next question will be "Are there known sources of knowledge which are available only to geniuses, and if so, *what are these sources,* and exactly how may they be reached?"

We shall offer proof of the soundness of some of the more important statements made in this book—or at least we shall offer evidence through which you may secure your own proof through experimentation. In doing so, we shall answer both of these questions.

"Genius" is Developed Through the Sixth Sense

The reality of a "sixth sense" has been fairly well established. This sixth sense is "creative imagination." The faculty of creative imagination is one that the majority of people never use during an entire lifetime, and if used at all, it usually happens by mere accident. A relatively small number of people use, *with deliberation and purpose aforethought,* the faculty of creative imagination. Those who use this faculty voluntarily, and with understanding of its functions, are *geniuses.* The faculty of creative imagination is the direct link between the finite mind of humans and Infinite Intelligence. All so-called revelations, referred to in the realm of religion, and all discoveries of basic or new principles in the field of invention take place through the faculty of creative imagination. When ideas or concepts flash into one's mind, through what is popularly called a "hunch," they come from one or more of the following sources:

1. Infinite Intelligence
2. The subconscious mind, in which is stored every sense impression and thought impulse that ever reached the brain through any of the five senses
3. The mind of some other person who has just released the thought, or picture of the idea or concept, through conscious thought
4. The other person's subconscious storehouse

There are no other *known* sources from which "inspired" ideas or "hunches" may be received.

The creative imagination functions best when the mind is vibrating (due to some form of mind stimulation) at an exceedingly high rate—that is, when the mind is functioning at a rate of vibration higher than that of ordinary, normal thought.

When brain action has been stimulated, through one or more of the 10 mind stimulants, it has the effect of lifting the individual far above the horizon of ordinary thought, and permits them to envision distance, scope, and quality of *thoughts* not available on the lower plane, such as that occupied while engaged in solving the problems of business and professional routine.

When lifted to this higher level of thought, through any form of mind stimulation, an individual occupies, relatively, the same position as someone who has ascended in a plane. While still on the ground, they may see over and beyond the horizon line which limits their vision. Moreover, while on this higher level of thought, the individual is not hampered or bound by any of the stimuli that circumscribe and limit their vision while wrestling with the problems of gaining the three basic necessities of food, clothing, and shelter. They are in a world of thought in which the *ordinary,* work-a-day thoughts have been as effectively removed, as are the hills, valleys, and other limitations of physical vision when rising in an airplane.

While someone is on this exalted plane of thought, the creative faculty of the mind is given freedom for action. The way has been cleared for the sixth sense to function; it becomes receptive to ideas that could not reach the individual under any other circumstances. The sixth sense is the faculty that marks the difference between a genius and an ordinary individual.

The more this faculty is used, the more alert and receptive the creative faculty becomes to vibrations originating outside the individual's subconscious mind, and the more the individual relies upon it and makes demands upon it for thought impulses. This faculty can be cultivated and developed only through use.

That which is known as one's "conscience" operates entirely through the faculty of the sixth sense.

The great artists, writers, musicians, and poets become great because they acquire the habit of relying upon the "still small voice" which speaks from within, through the faculty of creative imagination. It is a fact well known to people who have "keen" imaginations that their best ideas come through so-called "hunches."

There is a great orator who does not attain greatness until he closes his eyes and begins to rely entirely upon the faculty of creative imagination. When asked why he closed his eyes just before the climaxes of his oratory, he replied, "I do it because then I speak through ideas which come to me from within."

One of America's most successful and best-known financiers followed the habit of closing his eyes for two or three minutes before making a decision. When asked why he did this, he replied, "With my eyes closed, I am able to draw upon a source of superior intelligence."

Dr. Elmer R. Gates, of Chevy Chase, Maryland, created more than two hundred useful patents, many of them basic, through the process of cultivating and using the creative faculty. His method is significant to anyone interested in attaining the status of genius, in which category Dr. Gates unquestionably belonged. Dr. Gates was one of the really great, though less publicized, scientists of the world.

In his laboratory, he had what he called his "personal communication room." It was practically soundproof, and so arranged that all light could be shut out. It was equipped with a small table on which he kept a pad of writing paper. In front of the table, on the wall, was an electric push button, which controlled the lights. When Dr. Gates desired to draw upon the forces available to him through his creative imagination, he would go into this room, seat himself at the table, shut off the lights, and *concentrate* upon the *known* factors of the invention on which he was working, remaining in that position until ideas began to "flash" into his mind in connection with the *unknown* factors of the invention.

On one occasion, ideas came through so fast that he was forced to write for almost three hours. When the thoughts stopped flowing and he examined his notes, he found they contained a minute description of principles that had no parallel among the known data of the scientific world. Moreover, the answer to his problem was intelligently presented in those notes. In this manner Dr. Gates completed over two hundred patents, which had been begun, but not completed, by "half-baked" brains. Evidence of the truth of this statement is in the United States Patent Office.

Dr. Gates earned his living by "sitting for ideas" for individuals and corporations. Some of the largest corporations in America paid him substantial fees, by the hour, for "sitting for ideas."

The reasoning faculty is often faulty because it is largely guided by our accumulated experience. Not all knowledge that we accumulate through "experience" is accurate. Ideas received through the creative faculty are much more reliable because they come from sources more reliable than any available to the reasoning faculty of the mind.

The major difference between the genius and the ordinary "crank" inventor may be found in the fact that the genius works through his faculty of creative imagination, while the "crank" knows nothing of this faculty. The scientific inventor (such as Mr. Edison and Dr. Gates) makes use of both the synthetic and the creative faculties of imagination.

For example, scientific inventors or "geniuses" begin an invention by organizing and combining the known ideas, or principles accumulated through experience, through the synthetic faculty (the reasoning faculty). If they find this accumulated knowledge to be insufficient for the completion of the invention, they then draw upon the sources of knowledge available to them through their creative faculty. The method by which this is done varies with the individual, but this is the sum and substance of the procedure:

1. **They Stimulate Their Minds So That They Vibrate on a Higher-Than-Average Plane,** using one or more of the 10 mind stimulants or some other stimulant of their choice.
2. **They Concentrate** upon the known factors (the finished part) of the invention, and create in their minds a perfect picture of unknown factors (the unfinished part) of the invention. They hold this picture in mind until it has been taken over by the subconscious mind, and then relax by clearing their minds of *all* thought, and wait for the answer to pop up.

Sometimes the results are both definite and immediate. At other times, the results are negative, depending upon the state of development of the sixth sense, or creative faculty.

Mr. Edison tried out more than 10,000 different combinations of ideas through the synthetic faculty of his imagination before he "tuned in" through the creative faculty, and got the answer that perfected the incandescent light. His experience was similar when he produced the talking machine.

There is plenty of reliable evidence that the faculty of creative imagination exists. This evidence is available through accurate analysis of people who have become leaders in their respective callings without having had extensive educations. Lincoln was a notable example of a leader who achieved greatness through the discovery and use of his faculty of creative imagination. He discovered and began to use this faculty as the result of the stimulation of love, which he experienced after he met Ann Rutledge.

The pages of history are filled with records of great leaders whose achievements may be traced directly to the influence of women who aroused the creative faculties of their minds, through the stimulation of sex desire. Napoleon Bonaparte was one of these. When inspired by his first wife, Josephine, he was irresistible and invincible. When his "better judgment" or reasoning faculty prompted him to put Josephine aside, he began to decline. His defeat and St. Helena were not far distant.

If good taste would permit, we might easily mention scores of well-known men who climbed to great heights of achievement under the stimulating influence of their wives, only to drop back to destruction *after* money and power went to their heads, and they put aside the old wife for a new one. Napoleon was not the only man to discover that sex influence, from the right source, is more powerful than any substitute of expediency which may be created by mere reason.

The human mind responds to stimulation!

Among the greatest and most powerful of these stimuli is the urge of sex. When harnessed and transmuted, this driving force is capable of lifting people into that higher sphere of thought that enables them to master the sources of worry and petty annoyance that beset their pathway on the lower plane.

Unfortunately, only the geniuses have made the discovery. Others have accepted the experience of sex urge without discovering one of its major potentialities—a fact that accounts for the great number of "others" as compared to the limited number of geniuses.

Sex energy is the creative energy of all geniuses. There never has been, and never will be, a great leader, builder, or artist lacking in this driving force of sex.

Surely no one will misunderstand these statements to mean that *all* who are highly sexed are geniuses! One attains to the status of a genius *only* when, and *if,* one's mind is stimulated so that it draws upon the forces available, through the creative faculty of the imagination. Chief among the stimuli with which this "stepping up" of the vibrations may be produced is sex energy. The mere possession of this energy is not sufficient to produce a genius. The energy must be transmuted from desire for physical contact into some other form of desire and action before it will lift one to the status of a genius.

Far from becoming geniuses because of great sex desires, all too many people lower themselves, through misunderstanding and misuse of this great force, to the status of the lower animals.

Why People Seldom Succeed Before Forty

I discovered, from the analysis of over 25,000 people, that those who succeed in an outstanding way seldom do so before the age of forty. More often, they do not strike their real pace until they are well beyond the age of fifty. This fact was so astounding that it prompted me to go into the study of its cause most carefully, carrying the investigation over a period of more than twelve years.

This study disclosed that the major reason why the majority of people who succeed do not begin to do so before the age of forty to fifty is their tendency to *dissipate* their energies through overindulgence in physical expression of the emotion of sex. Most people never learn that the urge of sex has other possibilities, which far transcend in importance that of mere physical expression. The majority of those who make this discovery do so after having wasted many years when the sex energy is at its height, prior to the age of forty-five to fifty. This is usually followed by noteworthy achievement.

The lives of many people up to, and sometimes well past, the age of forty reflect a continued dissipation of energies, which could have been more profitably channeled. Their finer and more powerful emotions are sown wildly to the four winds. Out of this habit grew the term "sowing one's wild oats."

The desire for sexual expression is by far the strongest and most impelling of all the human emotions. For this very reason this desire, when harnessed and transmuted into action other than that of physical expression, may raise one to the status of a genius.

One of America's most able businessmen frankly admitted that his attractive secretary was responsible for most of the plans he created. He confessed that her presence lifted him to heights of creative imagination, such as he could experience under no other stimulus.

History is not lacking in examples of people who attained the status of geniuses as the result of using artificial mind stimulants in the form of alcohol and narcotics. Edgar Allan Poe wrote "The Raven" while under the influence of alcohol, "dreaming dreams that mortal never dared to dream before." James Whitcomb Riley did his best writing while under the influence of alcohol. Perhaps it was thus he saw "the ordered intermingling of the real and the dream, the mill above the river, and the mist above the stream." Robert Burns wrote best when intoxicated: "For Auld Lang Syne, my dear, we'll take a cup of kindness yet, for Auld Lang Syne."

But let it be remembered that many such people have destroyed themselves in the end. Nature has prepared her own potions with which people may safely stimulate their minds so they vibrate on a plane that enables them to tune in to fine and rare thoughts from "the great unknown!" No satisfactory substitute for Nature's stimulants has ever been found.

Psychologists recognize that there is a very close relationship between sex desires and spiritual urges—a fact which accounts for the peculiar behavior of people who participate in the orgies known as religious "revivals," common among the primitive types.

The world is ruled, and the destiny of civilization is established, by the human emotions. People are influenced in their actions not by reason so much as by "feelings." The creative faculty of the mind is set into action entirely by emotions, and not by cold reason. The most powerful of all human emotions is that of sex. There are other mind stimulants, some of which have been listed, but no one of them, nor all of them combined, can equal the driving power of sex.

A mind stimulant is any influence that will either temporarily or permanently increase the vibrations of thought. The ten major stimulants described are those most commonly resorted to. Through these sources one may commune with Infinite Intelligence or enter, at will, the storehouse of the subconscious mind—either one's own or that of another person.

A teacher who has trained and directed the efforts of more than 30,000 salespeople made the astounding discovery that highly sexed people are the most efficient sales reps. The explanation is that the factor of personality known as "personal magnetism" is nothing more nor less than sex energy. Highly sexed people always have a plentiful supply of magnetism. Through cultivation and understanding, this vital force may be drawn upon and used to great advantage in the relationships between people. This energy may be communicated to others through the following media:

1. **The Handshake.** The touch of the hand indicates, instantly, the presence of magnetism, or the lack of it.
2. **The Tone of Voice.** Magnetism, or sex energy, is the factor with which the voice may be colored, or made musical and charming.
3. **Posture and Carriage of the Body.** Highly sexed people move briskly, and with grace and ease.
4. **The Vibrations of Thought.** Highly sexed people mix the emotion of sex with their thoughts, or may do so at will, and in that way may influence those around them.
5. **Body Adornment.** People who are highly sexed are usually very careful about their personal appearance. They usually select clothing of a style becoming to their personality, physique, complexion, etc.

When employing salespeople, the more capable sales manager looks for the quality of personal magnetism as the first requirement for the job. People who lack sex energy will never become enthusiastic or inspire others with enthusiasm, and enthusiasm is one of the most important requisites in salesmanship, no matter what one is selling. The public speaker, orator, preacher, lawyer, or salesperson who is lacking in sex energy is a flop as far as being able to influence others is concerned. Couple with this the fact that most people can be influenced only through an appeal to their emotions, and you will understand the importance of sex energy as a part of the salesperson's natural ability. Master sales reps attain the status of mastery in selling because they, either consciously or unconsciously, transmute the energy of sex into *sales enthusiasm*! In this statement may be found a very practical suggestion as to the actual meaning of sex transmutation.

Salespeople who know how to take their minds off the subject of sex and direct it in sales effort with as much enthusiasm and determination as they would apply to its original purpose have acquired the art of sex transmutation, whether they know it or not. The majority of salespeople who transmute their sex energy do so without being in the least aware of what they are doing, or how they are doing it.

Transmutation of sex energy calls for more willpower than the average person cares to use for this purpose. Those who find it difficult to summon willpower sufficient for transmutation may gradually acquire this ability. The reward for the practice is more than worth the effort.

The entire subject of sex is one of which the majority of people appear to be unpardonably ignorant. The urge of sex has been grossly misunderstood, slandered, and burlesqued by the ignorant and the evil-minded for so long that the very word "sex" is seldom used in polite society. Men and women who are known to be blessed—yes, *blessed*—with highly sexed natures are usually looked upon with suspicion. Instead of being called blessed, they are usually called cursed.

Millions of people, even in this age of enlightenment, have developed inferiority complexes because of this false belief that a highly sexed nature is a curse. These statements of the virtue of sex energy should not be construed as justification for the libertine. The emotion of sex is a virtue *only* when used intelligently and with discrimination. It may often be misused to such an extent that it debases, instead of enriches, both body and mind. The better use of this power is the burden of this chapter.

It seemed quite significant to the author when he made the discovery that practically every great male leader, whom he had the privilege of analyzing, was a man whose achievements were largely inspired by a woman. In many instances, the "woman in the case" was a modest, self-denying wife, of whom the public had heard little or nothing. In a few instances, the source of inspiration has been traced to the "other woman." Perhaps such cases may not be entirely unknown to you.

Intemperance in sex habits is just as detrimental as intemperance in habits of drinking and eating. In this age in which we live, an age that began with World War I, intemperance in habits of sex is common. This orgy of indulgence may account for the shortage of great leaders. No one can avail of the forces of creative imagination while dissipating them. Humans are the only creatures on earth that violate Nature's purpose in this connection. Every other animal indulges its sex nature in moderation, and with purpose that harmonizes with the laws of Nature. Every other animal responds to the call of sex only in "season." The human inclination is to declare "open season."

Every intelligent person knows that stimulation in excess, through alcoholic drink and narcotics, is a form of intemperance that destroys the vital organs of the body, including the brain. Not every person knows, however, that overindulgence in sex expression may become a habit as destructive and as detrimental to creative effort as narcotics or alcohol.

A sex-mad person is not essentially different from a dope-mad person! Both have lost control over their faculties of reason and willpower. Sexual overindulgence may not only destroy reason and willpower, it may also lead to either temporary or permanent insanity. Many cases of hypochondria (imaginary illness) grow out of habits developed in ignorance of the true function of sex.

From these brief references to the subject, it may be readily seen that ignorance on the subject of sex transmutation forces stupendous penalties on the one hand, and withholds equally stupendous benefits on the other.

Widespread ignorance about sex is due to the fact that the subject has been surrounded with mystery and beclouded by dark silence. The conspiracy of mystery and silence has increased curiosity and desire to acquire more knowledge on this verboten subject. To the shame of all lawmakers, and most physicians—by training best qualified to educate youth on that subject—such information has not been easily available.

Seldom does an individual embark upon highly creative effort in any field of endeavor before the age of forty. For the average person, the greatest capacity to create is between forty and sixty. These statements are based on careful analysis of thousands of men and women. They should be encouraging to those who fail to arrive before the age of forty, and to those who become frightened at the approach of "old age," around the forty-year mark. The years between forty and fifty are, as a rule, the most fruitful. One should approach this age not with fear and trembling, but with hope and eager anticipation.

If you want evidence that most people do not begin to do their best work before the age of forty, study the records of successful people and you will find it. Henry Ford had not "hit his pace" of achievement until he had passed the age of forty. Andrew Carnegie was well past forty before he began to reap the reward of his efforts. James J. Hill was still running a telegraph key at the age of forty. His stupendous achievements took place after that age. Biographies of industrialists and financiers are filled with evidence that the period from forty to sixty is the most productive age.

Between the ages of thirty and forty, one begins to learn (if one ever learns) the art of sex transmutation. This discovery is generally accidental, and more often than otherwise the people who make it are totally unconscious of this discovery. They may observe that their powers of achievement have increased around the age of thirty-five to forty, but in most cases they are not familiar with the cause of this change; that Nature begins to harmonize the emotions of love and sex in the individual between the ages of thirty and forty, so that they may draw upon these great forces and apply them jointly as stimuli to action.

Sex, alone, is a mighty urge to action, but its forces are like a cyclone—they are often uncontrollable. When the emotion of love begins to mix itself with the emotion of sex, the result is calmness of purpose, poise, accuracy of judgment, and balance. What person who has reached the age of forty is so unfortunate as to be unable to analyze these statements, and to corroborate them by personal experience?

Love, romance, and sex are all emotions capable of driving people to heights of super achievement. Love is the emotion that serves as a safety valve, and ensures balance, poise, and constructive effort. When combined, these three emotions may lift one to the altitude of a genius. There are geniuses, however, who know little of the emotion of love. Most of them may be found engaged in some form of action which is destructive, or at least not based upon justice and fairness toward others. If good taste would permit, a dozen geniuses could be named in the field of industry and finance who ride ruthlessly over the rights of others. They seem totally lacking in conscience.

The emotions are states of mind. Nature has provided us with a "chemistry of the mind," which operates in a manner similar to the principles of chemistry of matter. A chemist may create a deadly poison by mixing certain elements, none of which are in themselves harmful in the right proportions. The emotions may, likewise, be combined to create a deadly poison. The emotions of sex and jealousy, when mixed, may turn a person into an insane beast.

The presence of any one or more of the destructive emotions in the human mind, through the chemistry of the mind, sets up a poison that may destroy one's sense of justice and fairness. In extreme cases, the presence of any combination of these emotions in the mind may destroy one's reason.

The road to genius consists of the development, control, and use of sex, love, and romance. Briefly, the process may be stated as follows:

Encourage the presence of these emotions as the dominating thoughts in your mind, and discourage the presence of all the destructive emotions. The mind is a creature of habit. It thrives upon the dominating thoughts fed it. Through the faculty of willpower, you may discourage the presence of any emotion, and encourage the presence of any other. Control of the mind, through the power of will, is not difficult. Control comes from persistence and habit. The secret of control lies in understanding the process of transmutation. When any negative emotion presents itself in your mind, it can be transmuted into a positive, or constructive, emotion by the simple procedure of changing your thoughts.

THERE IS NO OTHER ROAD TO GENIUS THAN THROUGH VOLUNTARY SELF-EFFORT! People may attain great heights of financial or business achievement solely by the driving force of sex energy, but history is filled with evidence that they may, and usually do, carry with them certain character traits which rob them of the ability to either hold, or enjoy, their good fortune. This is worthy of analysis, thought, and meditation, for it states a truth, the knowledge of which may be helpful to all people. Ignorance of this has cost thousands of people their privilege of *happiness,* even though they possessed riches.

The emotions of love and sex leave their unmistakable marks upon the features. Moreover, these signs are so visible that all who wish may read them. People who are driven by the storm of passion, based upon sex desires alone, plainly advertise that fact to the entire world by the expression of their eyes and the lines of their faces. The emotion of love, when mixed with the emotion of sex, softens, modifies, and beautifies the facial expression. No character analyst is needed to tell you this. You may observe it for yourself.

The emotion of love brings out and develops the artistic and aesthetic nature of a person. It leaves its impress upon one's very soul, even after the fire has been subdued by time and circumstance.

Memories of love never pass. They linger, guide, and influence long after the source of stimulation has faded. There is nothing new in this. Every person who has been moved by *genuine love* knows that it leaves enduring traces upon the human heart. The effect of love endures because love is spiritual in nature. Those who cannot be stimulated to great heights of achievement by love are hopeless—they are dead, though they may seem to live.

Even the memories of love are sufficient to lift one to a higher plane of creative effort. The major force of love may spend itself and pass away, like a fire that has burned itself out, but it leaves behind indelible marks as evidence that it passed that way. Its departure often prepares the human heart for a still greater love.

Go back into your yesterdays, at times, and bathe your mind in the beautiful memories of past love. It will soften the influence of the present worries and annoyances. It will give you a source of escape from the unpleasant realities of life, and maybe—who knows?—your mind will yield to you, during this temporary retreat into the world of fantasy, ideas or plans which may change the entire financial or spiritual status of your life.

If you believe yourself unfortunate because you have "loved and lost," perish the thought. One who has loved truly can never lose entirely. Love is whimsical and temperamental. Its nature is ephemeral and transitory. It comes when it pleases and goes away without warning. Accept and enjoy it while it remains, but spend no time worrying about its departure. Worry will never bring it back.

Dismiss, also, the thought that love never comes but once. Love may come and go, times without number, but there are no two love experiences that affect you in just the same way. There may be, and there usually is, one love experience that leaves a deeper imprint on the heart than all the others, but all love experiences are beneficial, except to the person who becomes resentful and cynical when love makes its departure.

There should be no disappointment over love, and there would be none if people understood the difference between the emotions of love and sex. The major difference is that love is spiritual, while sex is biological. No experience that touches the human heart with a spiritual force can possibly be harmful, except through ignorance or jealousy.

Love is, without question, life's greatest experience. It brings us into communion with Infinite Intelligence. When mixed with the emotions of romance and sex, it may lead us far up the ladder of creative effort. The emotions of love, sex, and romance are sides of the eternal triangle of achievement-building genius. Nature creates geniuses through no other force.

Love is an emotion with many sides, shades, and colors. The love one feels for parents or children is quite different from that which one feels for one's sweetheart. One is mixed with the emotion of sex while the other is not.

The love one feels in true friendship is not the same as that felt for one's sweetheart, parents, or children, but it, too, is a form of love.

Then there is the emotion of love for things inanimate, such as the love of Nature's handiwork. But the most intense and burning of all these various kinds of love is that experienced in the blending of the emotions of love and sex. Marriages not blessed with the eternal affinity of love, properly balanced and proportioned with sex, cannot be happy ones and seldom endure. Love, alone, will not bring happiness in marriage, nor will sex alone. When these two beautiful emotions are blended, marriage may bring about a state of mind as close to the spiritual as one may ever know on this earthly plane.

When the emotion of romance is added to those of love and sex, the obstructions between the finite mind of man and Infinite Intelligence are removed. Then a genius has been born!

What a different story is this to those usually associated with the emotion of sex. Here is an interpretation of the emotion that lifts it out of the commonplace, and makes of it potter's clay in the hands of God, from which He fashions all that is beautiful and inspiring. It is an interpretation that would, when properly understood, bring harmony out of the chaos that exists in too many marriages. The disharmonies often expressed in the form of nagging may usually be traced to lack of knowledge on the subject of sex. Where love, romance, and the proper understanding of the emotion and function of sex abide, there is no disharmony between married people.

CHAPTER 12

THE SUBCONSCIOUS MIND:

The Connecting Link

(The Eleventh Step to Riches)

The subconscious mind consists of a field of consciousness in which every impulse of thought that reaches the objective mind through any of the five senses is classified and recorded. From here, thoughts may be recalled or withdrawn as letters may be taken from a filing cabinet.

It receives and files sense impressions or thoughts, regardless of their nature. You may *voluntarily* plant in your subconscious mind any plan, thought, or purpose which you desire to translate into its physical or monetary equivalent. The subconscious acts first on the dominating desires that have been mixed with emotional feeling, such as faith.

Consider this in connection with the instructions in Chapter 2 on desire, for taking the 6 steps there outlined, and the instructions in Chapter 7 on planning, and you will understand the importance of the thought conveyed.

THE SUBCONSCIOUS MIND WORKS DAY AND NIGHT. It draws upon the forces of Infinite Intelligence for the power with which it voluntarily transmutes desires into their physical equivalent. To accomplish this it always makes use of the most practical media.

You cannot entirely control your subconscious mind, but you can voluntarily hand over to it any plan, desire, or purpose you wish to be transformed into concrete form. Read, again, the instructions for using the subconscious mind in Chapter 4.

There is plenty of evidence to support the belief that the subconscious mind is the connecting link between the finite mind and Infinite Intelligence. It is the intermediary through which one may draw upon the forces of Infinite Intelligence at will. It alone contains the secret process by which mental impulses are modified and changed into their spiritual equivalent. It alone is the medium through which prayer may be transmitted to the source capable of answering prayer.

The possibilities of creative effort connected with the subconscious mind are stupendous and imponderable. They inspire one with awe.

I never approach the discussion of the subconscious mind without a feeling of littleness and inferiority due, perhaps, to the fact that the entire stock of knowledge on this subject is so pitifully limited. The very fact that the subconscious mind is the medium of communication between the thinking mind and Infinite Intelligence is, of itself, a thought that almost paralyzes one's reason.

After you have accepted, as a reality, the existence of the subconscious mind—and understand its possibilities as a medium for transmuting your *desires* into their physical or monetary equivalent—you will comprehend the full significance of the instructions given in Chapter 2. You will also understand why you have been repeatedly admonished to *make your desires clear and to put them in writing.* The necessity of *persistence* in carrying out instructions will also become clear.

The 13 principles are the stimuli with which you acquire the ability to reach and to influence your subconscious mind. Do not become discouraged if you cannot do this upon the first attempt. Remember that the subconscious mind may be voluntarily directed only through habit, under the directions given in Chapter 3 on faith. You have not yet had time to master faith. Be patient. Be persistent.

A good many statements in the chapters on faith and autosuggestion will be repeated here for the benefit of your subconscious mind. Remember, your subconscious mind functions voluntarily, whether you make any effort to influence it or not. This naturally suggests to you that thoughts of fear and poverty, and all negative thoughts, serve as stimuli to your subconscious mind, unless you master these impulses and give it more desirable food upon which it may feed.

The subconscious mind will not remain idle! If you fail to plant *desires* in your subconscious mind, it will feed upon the thoughts that reach it as the result of your neglect. We have already explained that thought impulses, both negative and positive, are reaching the subconscious mind continuously from the four sources mentioned in Chapter 11, on Sex Transmutation.

For the present, it is sufficient to remember that you are living daily in the midst of all manner of thought impulses that are reaching your subconscious mind without your knowledge. Some of these impulses are negative, some are positive. You are now engaged in trying to help shut off the flow of negative impulses, and to aid in voluntarily influencing your subconscious mind through positive impulses of *desire*.

When you achieve this, you will possess the key that unlocks the door to your subconscious mind. Moreover, you will control that door so completely that no undesirable thought may influence your subconscious mind.

Everything that is created *begins* in the form of a thought impulse. Nothing can be created that is not first conceived in *thought*. Through the aid of the imagination, thought impulses may be assembled into plans. The imagination, when under control, may be used for the creation of plans or purposes that lead to success in one's chosen occupation.

All thought impulses intended for transmutation into their physical equivalent and voluntarily planted in the subconscious mind must pass through the imagination and be mixed with faith. The "mixing" of faith with a plan, or purpose, intended for submission to the subconscious mind may be done *only* through the imagination.

From these statements, you will readily observe that voluntary use of the subconscious mind calls for coordination and application of all the principles.

Ella Wheeler Wilcox, a famous poet and journalist of the late nineteenth and early twentieth century, gave evidence of her understanding of the power of the subconscious mind when she wrote:

> You never can tell what a thought will do
> > In bringing you hate or love—
> For thoughts are things, and their airy wings
> > Are swifter than carrier doves.
> They follow the law of the universe—
> > Each thing creates its kind,
> And they speed o'er the track to bring you back
> > Whatever went out from your mind.

Ms. Wilcox understood the truth that thoughts which go out from one's mind also embed themselves deeply in one's subconscious, where they serve as a magnet, pattern, or blueprint by which the subconscious mind is influenced while translating them into their physical equivalent. Thoughts are truly things, for the reason that every material thing begins in the form of thought-energy.

The subconscious mind is more susceptible to influence by impulses of thought mixed with "feeling" or emotion than by those originating solely in the reasoning portion of the mind. In fact, there is much evidence to support the theory that *only* emotionalized thoughts have any *action* influence upon the subconscious mind. It is a well-known fact that emotion or feeling rules the majority of people. If it is true that the subconscious mind responds more quickly to, and is influenced more readily by, thought impulses well mixed with emotion, it is essential to become familiar with the more important of the emotions.

There are seven major positive emotions and seven major negative emotions. The negatives voluntarily inject themselves into the thought impulses, ensuring their passage into the subconscious mind. The positives must be injected, through the principle of autosuggestion, into the thought impulses that an individual wishes to pass on to the subconscious mind. (Instructions have been given in Chapter 4, on autosuggestion.)

These emotions, or feeling impulses, may be likened to yeast in a loaf of bread because they constitute the *action* element, which transforms thought impulses from the passive to the active state. Thus may one understand why thought impulses which have been well mixed with emotion are acted upon more readily than thought impulses originating in "cold reason."

You are preparing yourself to influence and control the "inner audience" of your subconscious mind in order to hand over to it the *desire* for money, which you wish transmuted into its monetary equivalent. It is essential, therefore, that you understand the method of approach to this "inner audience." You must speak its language or it will not heed your call. It understands best the language of emotion or feeling. Let us, therefore, describe here the seven major positive emotions and the seven major negative emotions, so that you may draw upon the positives and avoid the negatives when giving instructions to your subconscious mind.

The Seven Major Positive Emotions

The emotion of DESIRE

The emotion of FAITH

The emotion of LOVE

The emotion of SEX

The emotion of ENTHUSIASM

The emotion of ROMANCE

The emotion of HOPE

There are other positive emotions, but these are the seven most powerful, and the ones most commonly used in creative effort. Master these seven emotions (they can be mastered only by *use*), and the other positive emotions will be at your command when you need them. Remember, in this connection, that you are studying a book intended to help you develop a "money consciousness" by filling your mind with positive emotions. You do not become money conscious by filling your mind with negative emotions.

The Seven Major Negative Emotions
(to be avoided)

The emotion of FEAR
The emotion of JEALOUSY
The emotion of HATRED
The emotion of REVENGE
The emotion of GREED
The emotion of SUPERSTITION
The emotion of ANGER

Positive and negative emotions cannot occupy the mind at the same time. One or the other must dominate. It is your responsibility to make sure that positive emotions constitute the dominating influence of your mind. Here the law of *habit* will come to your aid. *Form the habit* of applying and using the positive emotions! Eventually, they will dominate your mind so completely that the negatives *cannot enter it.*

Only by following these instructions literally, and continuously, can you gain control over your subconscious mind. The presence of a single negative in your conscious mind is sufficient to destroy all chances of constructive aid from your subconscious mind.

If you are an observant person, you must have noticed that most people resort to prayer *only* after everything else has *failed*! Or else they pray by a ritual of meaningless words. And because it is a fact that most people who pray do so *only after everything else has failed,* they go to prayer with their minds filled with *fear* and *doubt,* which are the emotions the subconscious mind acts upon and passes on to Infinite Intelligence. Likewise, that is the emotion Infinite Intelligence receives and *acts upon.*

If you pray for a thing, but have fear as you pray that you may not receive it, or that your prayer will not be acted upon by Infinite Intelligence, your prayer *will have been in vain.*

Prayer does, sometimes, result in the realization of that for which one prays. If you have ever had the experience of receiving something for which you prayed, go back in your memory and recall your actual *state of mind* while you were praying, and you will know for sure that the theory here described is more than a theory.

The time will come when schools and educational institutions will teach the "science of prayer." Moreover, prayer may then be reduced to a science. When that time comes (it will come as soon as humankind is ready for it and demands it), no one will approach the Universal Mind in a state of fear, for the very good reason that there will be no such emotion as fear. Ignorance, superstition, and false teaching will have disappeared, and we will have attained our true status as children of Infinite Intelligence. A few have already attained this blessing.

If you believe this prophecy is far-fetched, take a look at the human race in retrospect. Less than two hundred years ago, it was commonly believed that lightning was evidence of the wrath of God, and people feared it. Now, thanks to the power of *faith,* we have harnessed lightning and made it turn the wheels of industry. Until relatively recent times, it was believed that the space between the planets was nothing but a great void, a stretch of dead nothingness. Now, thanks to this same power of *faith,* we know that far from being either dead or a void, the space between the planets is very much alive, that it is the highest form of vibration known, excepting, perhaps, the vibration of *thought.* Moreover, we know that this living, pulsating, vibratory energy that permeates every atom of matter and fills every niche of space connects every human brain with every other human brain.

What reason do we have to believe that this same energy does not connect every human brain with Infinite Intelligence?

There are no tollgates between the finite mind of humans and Infinite Intelligence. The communication costs nothing except patience, faith, persistence, understanding, and a *sincere desire* to communicate. Moreover, the approach can be made only by each of us ourselves. Paid prayers are worthless. Infinite Intelligence does no business by proxy. You either go direct or you do not communicate.

You may buy prayer books and repeat them until the day of your doom, without avail. Thoughts that you wish to communicate to Infinite Intelligence must undergo transformation, such as can be given only through your own subconscious mind.

The method by which you may communicate with Infinite Intelligence is very similar to that through which the vibration of sound is communicated by wireless communication. If you understand the working principle of radio, TV, and cellular phones, you know that audio and video cannot be communicated through the ether until it has been "stepped up," or changed into a rate of vibration which the human ear or eye cannot detect. The sending station picks up the audio and video, and "scrambles" or modifies it by stepping up the vibration millions of times. Only in this way can the vibrations be communicated through the ether. After this transformation has taken place, the ether "picks up" the energy and carries that energy to receiving stations, and these receiving sets "step" that energy back down to its original rate of vibration so it can be seen and heard.

The subconscious mind is the intermediary that translates one's prayers into terms that Infinite Intelligence can recognize, presents the message and brings back the answer in the form of a definite plan or idea for procuring the object of the prayer. Understand this principle and you will know why mere words read from a prayer book cannot, and will never, serve as an agency of communication between the human mind and Infinite Intelligence.

Before your prayer will reach Infinite Intelligence (a statement of the author's theory only), it is probably transformed from its original thought vibration into terms of spiritual vibration. *Faith* is the only known agency that will give your thoughts a spiritual nature. *Faith* and *fear* make poor bedfellows. Where one is found, the other cannot exist.

CHAPTER 13

THE BRAIN:
A Broadcasting and Receiving Station for Thought

(The Twelfth Step to Riches)

In a study by the author with Dr. Alexander Graham Bell and Dr. Elmer R. Gates, it was concluded that every human brain is both a broadcasting and receiving station for the vibration of thought.

Through the medium of the ether, in a fashion similar to that employed by the basic principle of radio and other wireless communication, every human brain is capable of picking up vibrations of thought released by other brains.

In connection with the above statement, compare and consider the description of the creative imagination, as outlined in Chapter 6, on imagination. The creative imagination is the "receiving set" of the brain, which receives thoughts released by the brains of others. It is the agency of communication between one's conscious, or reasoning, mind and the four sources from which one may receive thought stimuli.

When stimulated or "stepped up" to a high rate of vibration, the mind becomes more receptive to the vibration of thought that reaches it through the ether from outside sources. This "stepping up" process takes place through the positive emotions or the negative emotions. Through the emotions, the vibrations of thought may be increased.

Vibrations of an exceedingly high rate are the only vibrations picked up and carried, by the ether, from one brain to another. Thought is energy traveling at an exceedingly high rate of vibration. Thought which has been modified or "stepped up" by any of the major emotions vibrates at a much higher rate than ordinary thought. It is this type of thought that passes from one brain to another, through the broadcasting machinery of the human brain.

As far as intensity and driving force are concerned, the emotion of sex stands at the head of the list of human emotions. A brain stimulated by the emotion of sex vibrates at a much more rapid rate than it does when that emotion is quiescent or absent.

The result of sex transmutation is the increase of the rate of vibration of thoughts to such a pitch that the creative imagination becomes highly receptive to ideas it picks up from the ether. When the brain is vibrating at a rapid rate, it not only attracts thoughts and ideas released by other brains, it also gives one's own thoughts the "feeling" that is essential for those thoughts to be picked up and acted upon by the subconscious mind.

Thus, you will see that the broadcasting principle is the factor through which you mix feeling or emotion with your thoughts and pass them on to your subconscious mind.

The subconscious mind is the "sending station" of the brain, through which vibrations of thought are broadcast. The creative imagination is the "receiving set," through which the vibrations of thought are picked up from the ether.

Along with these important factors of the subconscious mind and the creative imagination, consider now the principle of autosuggestion, the medium by which you may put into operation your "broadcasting" station.

Through the instructions described in Chapter 4, you were definitely informed of the method by which *desire* may be transmuted into its monetary equivalent.

Operation of your mental "broadcasting" station is a comparatively simple procedure. You have but three principles to bear in mind, and to apply, when you wish to use your broadcasting station—the SUBCONSCIOUS MIND, CREATIVE IMAGINATION, and AUTOSUGGESTION. The stimuli through which you put these three principles into action have been described; the procedure begins with *desire*.

The Greatest Forces are "Intangible"

The Depression of the 1930s brought the world to the very borderline of understanding intangible and unseen forces. Through the ages that have passed, people have depended too much upon their physical senses, and have limited their knowledge to physical things that they could see, touch, weigh, and measure.

We are now entering the most marvelous of all ages—an age that will teach us something of the intangible forces of the world about us. Perhaps we shall learn, as we pass through this age, that the "other self" is more powerful than the physical self we see when we look into a mirror.

Sometimes we speak lightly of the intangibles—the things we cannot perceive through any of our five senses—but we should never forget that we are all controlled by unseen and intangible forces.

The whole of humankind has not the power to cope with or control the intangible force wrapped up in the rolling waves of the oceans. The human mind does not have the capacity to understand the intangible force of gravity—which keeps this little earth suspended in midair and keeps us from falling from it—much less the power to control that force. All of us are entirely subservient to the intangible force which comes with a thunderstorm, and we are just as helpless in the presence of the intangible force of electricity. Indeed, many of us do not even know what electricity is, where it comes from, or what its purpose is!

Nor is this by any means the end of our ignorance in connection with things unseen and intangible. We do not understand the intangible force (and intelligence) wrapped up in the soil of the earth—the force which provides us with every morsel of food we eat, every article of clothing we wear, and every coin we carry in our pockets.

The Dramatic Story of the Brain

Last but not least, with all our boasted culture and education, we understand little or nothing of the intangible force (the greatest of all the intangibles) of thought. We know but little concerning the physical brain and its vast network of intricate machinery through which the power of thought is translated into its material equivalent. However, we are now entering an age which shall yield enlightenment on the subject. Already scientists have begun to turn their attention to the study of this stupendous thing called a brain. While they are still in the kindergarten stage of their studies, they have uncovered enough to know that the central switchboard of the human brain, the number of lines which connect each brain cell with another, equals the figure one followed by 15 million zeros.

"The figure is so stupendous," said Dr. C. Judson Herrick of the University of Chicago, "that astronomical figures dealing with hundreds of millions of light-years become insignificant by comparison. It has been determined that there are from 10 billion to 14 billion nerve cells in the human cerebral cortex, and we know that these are arranged in definite patterns. These arrangements are not haphazard. They are orderly. Recently developed methods of electrophysiology draw off action currents from very precisely located cells, or fibbers with micro-electrodes, amplify them, and record potential differences to a millionth of a volt."

It is inconceivable that such a network of intricate machinery should be in existence for the sole purpose of carrying on the physical functions incidental to growth and maintenance of the physical body. Is it not likely that the same system, which gives billions of brain cells the media for communication one with another, provides also the means of communication with other intangible forces?

In the late 1930s, the *New York Times* published an editorial showing that at least one great university, and one intelligent investigator in the field of mental phenomena, were carrying out organized research through which conclusions had been reached that parallel many of those described in this and the following chapter. The editorial briefly analyzed the work carried out by Dr. Rhine and his associates at Duke University as follows:

"What Is 'Telepathy'?"

"A month ago we cited on this page some of the remarkable results achieved by Professor Rhine and his associates in Duke University from more than a hundred thousand tests to determine the existence of 'telepathy' and 'clairvoyance.' These results were summarized in the first of two articles in *Harper's Magazine*. In the second that has now appeared, the author, E.H. Wright, attempts to summarize what has been learned, or what it seems reasonable to infer, regarding the exact nature of these "extrasensory" modes of perception.

"The actual existence of telepathy and clairvoyance now seems to some scientists enormously probable as the result of Rhine's experiments. Various percipients were asked to name as many cards in a special pack as they could without looking at them and without other sensory access to them. About a score of men and women were discovered who could regularly name so many of the cards correctly that 'there was not one chance in many a million of their having done their feats by luck or accident.'

"But how did they do them? These powers, assuming that they exist, do not seem to be sensory. There is no known organ for them. The experiments worked just as well at distances of several hundred miles as they did in the same room. These facts also dispose, in Mr. Wright's opinion, of the attempt to explain telepathy or clairvoyance through any physical theory of radiation. All known forms of radiant energy decline inversely as the square of the distance traversed. Telepathy and clairvoyance do not. But they do vary through physical causes as our other mental powers do. Contrary to widespread opinion, they do not improve when the percipient is asleep or half asleep, but, on the contrary, when he is most wide-awake and alert. Rhine discovered that a narcotic will invariably lower a percipient's score, while a stimulant will always send it higher. The most reliable performer apparently cannot make a good score unless he tries to do his best.

"One conclusion that Wright draws with some confidence is that telepathy and clairvoyance are really one and the same gift. That is, the faculty that 'sees' a card face down on a table seems to be exactly the same one that 'reads' a thought residing only in another mind. There are several grounds for believing this. So far, for example, the two gifts have been found in every person who enjoys either of them. In every one so far the two have been of equal vigor, almost exactly. Screens, walls, distances, have no effect at all on either. Wright advances from this conclusion to express what he puts forward as no more than the mere 'hunch' that other extra-sensory experiences, prophetic dreams, premonitions of disaster and the like, may also prove to be part of the same faculty. The reader is not asked to accept any of these conclusions unless he finds it necessary, but the evidence that Rhine has piled up must remain impressive."

In view of Dr. Rhine's announcement in connection with the conditions under which the mind responds to what he terms "extra-sensory" modes of perception, I now feel privileged to add to his testimony. My associates and I have discovered what we believe to be the ideal conditions under which the mind can be stimulated so that the sixth sense described in the next chapter can be made to function in a practical way.

The conditions to which I refer consist of a close working alliance between myself and two members of my staff. Through experimentation and practice, we have discovered how to stimulate our minds (by applying the principle used in connection with the "Invisible Counselors" described in the next chapter). In doing so we can, by a process of blending our three minds into one, find the solution to a great variety of personal problems submitted by my clients.

The procedure is very simple. We sit down at a conference table, clearly state the nature of the problem under consideration, and then begin discussing it. Each contributes whatever thoughts may occur. The strange thing about this method of mind stimulation is that it places each participant in communication with unknown sources of knowledge definitely outside his own experience.

If you understand the principle described in Chapter 10 on the Master Mind, you of course recognize the roundtable procedure described here as being a practical application of the Master Mind.

This method of mind stimulation, through harmonious discussion of definite subjects between three people, illustrates the simplest and most practical use of the Master Mind.

By adopting and following a similar plan, any student of this philosophy may come into possession of the famous Carnegie formula briefly described in the Author's Preface. If it means nothing to you at this time, mark this page and read it again after you have finished the last chapter.

CHAPTER 14

THE SIXTH SENSE:
The Door to the Temple of Wisdom

(The Thirteenth Step to Riches)

The "thirteenth" principle is known as the *sixth sense.* Infinite Intelligence may, and will, communicate voluntarily through the sixth sense without any effort from, or demands by, the individual.

This principle is the apex of the philosophy. It can be assimilated, understood, and applied *only* by first mastering the other 12 principles.

The *sixth sense* is the portion of the subconscious mind that has been referred to as the "creative imagination." It has also been referred to as the "receiving set" through which ideas, plans, and thoughts flash into the mind. The "flashes" are sometimes called "hunches" or "inspirations."

The sixth sense defies description! It cannot be described to a person who has not mastered the other principles of this philosophy, because such a person has no knowledge or experience with which the sixth sense may be compared. Understanding of the sixth sense comes only by meditation through mind development from within. The sixth sense is probably the medium of contact between the finite mind of individuals and Infinite Intelligence. For this reason, it is a mixture of both the mental and the spiritual. It is believed to be the point at which the mind of an individual contacts the Universal Mind.

After you have mastered the principles described in this book, you will be prepared to accept as truth a statement that may, otherwise, be incredible to you—namely, through the aid of the sixth sense, you will be warned of impending dangers in time to avoid them, and notified of opportunities in time to embrace them.

With the development of the sixth sense there comes to your aid, and to do your bidding, a "guardian angel" who will open to you at all times the door to the Temple of Wisdom.

You will never know whether or not this is a statement of truth, except by following the instructions described in the pages of this book, or some similar procedure.

The author is not a believer in, nor an advocate of, "miracles." He has enough knowledge of Nature to understand that Nature never deviates from her established laws. Some of her laws are so incomprehensible that they produce what appear to be miracles. The sixth sense comes as near to being a miracle as anything I have ever experienced, and it appears so only because I do not understand the method by which this principle is operated.

This much the author does know—that there is a power, or a First Cause, or an Intelligence, which permeates every atom of matter and embraces every unit of perceptible energy; that this Infinite Intelligence converts acorns into oak trees, causes water to flow downhill in response to the law of gravity, follows night with day and winter with summer, each maintaining its proper place and relationship to the other. This Intelligence may, through the principles of this philosophy, be induced to aid in transmuting *desires* into concrete, or material, form. The author has this knowledge because he has experimented with it and has *experienced it.*

Step by step, through the preceding chapters, you have been led to this, the last principle. If you have mastered each of the preceding principles, you are now prepared to accept, without being skeptical, the stupendous claims made here. If you have not mastered the other principles, you must do so before you may determine, definitely, whether or not the claims made in this chapter are fact or fiction.

While I was passing through the age of "hero worship" I found myself trying to imitate those whom I most admired. Moreover, I discovered that the element of *faith,* with which I endeavored to imitate my idols, gave me great capacity to do so quite successfully.

I have never entirely divested myself of this habit of hero worship, although I have passed the age commonly given over to such. My experience has taught me that the next best thing to being truly great is to emulate the great, by feeling and action, as closely as possible.

Long before I had ever written a line for publication, or endeavored to deliver a speech in public, I followed the habit of reshaping my own character by trying to imitate the nine men whose lives and lifeworks had been most impressive to me. These nine men were Emerson, Paine, Edison, Darwin, Lincoln, Burbank, Napoleon, Ford, and Carnegie. Every night, over a long period of years, I held an imaginary council meeting with this group, whom I called my "Invisible Counselors."

The procedure was this. Just before going to sleep at night, I would shut my eyes and see, in my imagination, this group of men seated with me around my council table. Here I had not only an opportunity to sit among those whom I considered to be great, but I actually dominated the group by serving as the chairman.

I had a very *definite purpose* in indulging my imagination through these nightly meetings. My purpose was to rebuild my own character so it would represent a composite of the characters of my imaginary counselors. Realizing, as I did early in life, that I had to overcome the handicap of my birth into an environment of ignorance and superstition, I deliberately assigned myself the task of voluntary rebirth through the method here described.

Building Character Through Autosuggestion

Being an earnest student of psychology, I knew that all people have become what they are because of their *dominating thoughts and desires.* I knew that every deeply seated desire seeks outward expression through which it may be transmuted into reality. I knew that self-suggestion is a powerful factor in building character, that it is, in fact, the sole principle through which character is built.

With this knowledge of the principles of mind operation, I was fairly well armed with the equipment needed to rebuild my character. In these imaginary council meetings I called on my cabinet members for the knowledge I wished each to contribute, addressing myself to each member in audible words, as follows:

"Mr. Emerson, I desire to acquire from you the marvelous understanding of Nature which distinguished your life. I ask that you make an impress upon my subconscious mind of whatever qualities you possessed that enabled you to understand and adapt yourself to the laws of Nature. I ask that you assist me in reaching and drawing upon whatever sources of knowledge are available to this end.

"Mr. Burbank, I request that you pass on to me the knowledge which enabled you to so harmonize the laws of Nature that you caused the cactus to shed its thorns and become an edible food. Give me access to the knowledge which enabled you to make two blades of grass grow where but one grew before, and helped you to blend the coloring of the flowers with more splendor and harmony, for you, alone, have successfully gilded the lily.

"Napoleon, I desire to acquire from you, by emulation, the marvelous ability you possessed to inspire people, and to arouse them to greater and more determined spirit of action. Also to acquire the spirit of enduring *faith,* which enabled you to turn defeat into victory, and to surmount staggering obstacles. Emperor of Fate, King of Chance, Man of Destiny, I salute you!

"Mr. Paine, I desire to acquire from you the freedom of thought and the courage and clarity with which to express convictions that so distinguished you!

"Mr. Darwin, I wish to acquire from you the marvelous patience and ability to study cause and effect without bias or prejudice so exemplified by you in the field of natural science.

"Mr. Lincoln, I desire to build into my own character the keen sense of justice, the untiring spirit of patience, the sense of humor, the human understanding, and the tolerance that were your distinguishing characteristics.

"Mr. Carnegie, I am already indebted to you for my choice of a lifework, which has brought me great happiness and peace of mind. I wish to acquire a thorough understanding of the principles of organized effort, which you used so effectively in the building of a great industrial enterprise.

"Mr. Ford, you have been among the most helpful of the men who have supplied much of the material essential to my work. I wish to acquire your spirit of persistence, the determination, poise, and self-confidence that have enabled you to master poverty, organize, unify, and simplify human effort, so I may help others to follow in your footsteps.

"Mr. Edison, I have seated you nearest to me, at my right, because of the personal cooperation you have given me during my research into the causes of success and failure. I wish to acquire from you the marvelous spirit of *faith*, with which you have uncovered so many of Nature's secrets, the spirit of unremitting toil with which you have so often wrested victory from defeat."

My method of addressing the members of the imaginary cabinet would vary according to the traits of character in which I was most interested in acquiring at the time. I studied the records of their lives with painstaking care. After some months of this nightly procedure, I was astounded by the discovery that these imaginary figures became, apparently, real.

Each of these nine men developed individual characteristics, which surprised me. For example, Lincoln developed the habit of always being late, then walking around in solemn parade. When he came, he walked very slowly, with his hands clasped behind him. Once in a while, he would stop as he passed and rest his hand, momentarily, upon my shoulder. He always wore an expression of seriousness upon his face. Rarely did I see him smile. The cares of a sundered nation made him grave.

That was not true of the others. Burbank and Paine often indulged in witty repartee that seemed, at times, to shock the other members of the cabinet. One night Paine suggested that I prepare a lecture entitled "The Age of Reason," and deliver it from the pulpit of a church that I formerly attended. Many around the table laughed heartily at the suggestion. Not Napoleon! He drew his mouth down at the corners and groaned so loudly that all turned and looked at him with amazement. To him the church was but a pawn of the State, not to be reformed but to be used as a convenient inciter to mass activity by the people.

On one occasion Burbank was late. When he came, he was excited with enthusiasm, and explained that he had been late because of an experiment he was making through which he hoped to be able to grow apples on any sort of tree. Paine chided him by reminding him that it was an apple that started all the trouble between man and woman. Darwin chuckled heartily as he suggested that Burbank should watch out for little serpents when he went into the forest to gather apples, as they had the habit of growing into big snakes. Emerson observed, "No serpents, no apples," and Napoleon remarked, "No apples, no state!"

Lincoln developed the habit of always being the last one to leave the table after each meeting. On one occasion, he leaned across the end of the table, his arms folded, and remained in that position for many minutes. I made no attempt to disturb him. Finally, he lifted his head slowly, got up, and walked to the door. Then he turned around, came back, laid his hand on my shoulder and said, "My boy, you will need much courage if you remain steadfast in carrying out your purpose in life. But remember, when difficulties overtake you, the common people have common sense. Adversity will develop it."

One evening Edison arrived ahead of all the others. He walked over and seated himself at my left, where Emerson was accustomed to sit, and said, "You are destined to witness the discovery of the secret of life. When the time comes, you will observe that life consists of great swarms of energy, or entities, each as intelligent as human beings think themselves to be. These units of life group together like hives of bees, and remain together until they disintegrate, through lack of harmony. These units have differences of opinion, the same as human beings, and often fight among themselves. These meetings which you are conducting will be very helpful to you. They will bring to your rescue some of the same units of life that served the members of your cabinet, during their lives. These units are eternal. THEY NEVER DIE! Your own thoughts and *desires* serve as the magnet that attracts units of life, from the great ocean of life out there. Only the friendly units are attracted—the ones that harmonize with the nature of your *desires*."

The other members of the cabinet began to enter the room. Edison got up and slowly walked around to his own seat. Edison was still living when this happened. It impressed me so greatly that I went to see him and told him about the experience. He smiled broadly and said, "Your dream was more a reality than you may imagine it to have been." He added no further explanation to his statement.

These meetings became so realistic that I started to be fearful of their consequences, and discontinued them for several months. The experiences were so uncanny, I was afraid if I continued them I would lose sight of the fact that the meetings were purely experiences of my imagination.

Some six months after I had discontinued the practice I was awakened one night, or thought I was, and saw Lincoln standing at my bedside. He said, "The world will soon need your services. It is about to undergo a period of chaos that will cause men and women to lose faith and become panic-stricken. Go ahead with your work and complete your philosophy. That is your mission in life. If you neglect it, for any cause whatsoever, you will be reduced to a primal state, and be compelled to retrace the cycles through which you have passed during thousands of years."

The following morning I was unable to tell whether I had dreamed this or had actually been awake. I have never since found out which it was, but I do know that the dream, if it was a dream, was so vivid in my mind the next day that I resumed my meetings that night.

At our next meeting, the members of my cabinet all filed into the room together, and stood at their accustomed places at the council table. Lincoln raised a glass and said, "Gentlemen, let us drink a toast to a friend who has returned to the fold."

After that, I began to add new members to my cabinet. Now it consists of more than fifty, among them Christ, St. Paul, Galileo, Copernicus, Aristotle, Plato, Socrates, Homer, Voltaire, Bruno, Spinoza, Drummond, Kant, Schopenhauer, Newton, Confucius, Elbert Hubbard, Brann, Ingersoll, Wilson, and William James.

This is the first time I have had the courage to mention this. Previously I have remained quiet on the subject, because I knew, from my own attitude in connection with such matters, that I would be misunderstood if I described my unusual experience. I have been emboldened now to reduce my experience to the printed page because I am now less concerned about what "they say" than I was in the years that have passed. One of the blessings of maturity is that it sometimes brings one greater courage to be truthful, regardless of what those who do not understand may think or say.

Lest I be misunderstood, I wish here to state most emphatically that I still regard my cabinet meetings as purely imaginary, but I feel entitled to suggest that they have led me into glorious paths of adventure, rekindled an appreciation of true greatness, encouraged creative endeavor, and emboldened the expression of honest thought.

Somewhere in the cell structure of the brain is located an organ which receives vibrations of thought ordinarily called "hunches." So far, science has not discovered where this organ of the sixth sense is located, but this is not important. The fact remains that human beings do receive accurate knowledge through sources other than the physical senses. Such knowledge, generally, is received when the mind is under the influence of extraordinary stimulation. Any emergency that arouses the emotions and causes the heart to beat more rapidly than normal may, and generally does, bring the sixth sense into action. Anyone who has experienced a near accident while driving knows that on such occasions the sixth sense often comes to one's rescue, and aids, by split seconds, in avoiding the accident.

These facts are mentioned preliminary to a statement of fact I shall now make—namely, that during my meetings with the "Invisible Counselors" I find my mind most receptive to ideas, thoughts, and knowledge that reach me through the sixth sense. I can truthfully say that I owe my counselors full credit for such ideas, facts, or knowledge I receive through "inspiration."

On scores of occasions when I have faced emergencies—some of them so grave that my life was in jeopardy—I have been miraculously guided past these difficulties through the influence of my counselors.

My original purpose in conducting council meetings with imaginary beings was solely that of impressing my own subconscious mind—through the principle of autosuggestion— with certain characteristics I desired to acquire. In more recent years, my experimentation has taken on an entirely different trend. I now go to my imaginary counselors with every difficult problem that confronts my clients and me. The results are often astonishing, although I do not depend entirely on this form of counsel.

You, of course, have recognized that this chapter covers a subject with which the majority of people are unfamiliar. The sixth sense will be of great interest and benefit to the person whose aim is to accumulate vast wealth, but it need not claim the attention of those whose desires are more modest.

Henry Ford undoubtedly understood and made practical use of the sixth sense. His vast business and financial operations made it necessary for him to understand and use this principle. Thomas A. Edison understood and used the sixth sense in connection with the development of inventions, especially those involving basic patents where he had no human experience or accumulated knowledge to guide him. This was the case while he was working on the talking machine and the moving picture machine.

Nearly all great leaders—such as Napoleon, Joan of Arc, Christ, Buddha, Confucius, and Mohammed—understood and probably made use of the sixth sense almost continuously. The major portion of their greatness consisted of their knowledge of this principle.

The sixth sense is not something one can take off and put on at will. Ability to use this great power comes slowly, through application of the other principles outlined in this book. Seldom does any individual come into workable knowledge of the sixth sense before the age of forty. More often the knowledge is not available until one is well past fifty. This is because the spiritual forces with which the sixth sense is so closely related only mature and become usable through years of meditation, self-examination, and serious thought.

No matter who you are, or what may have been your purpose in reading this book, you can profit by it without understanding the principle described in this chapter. This is especially true if your major purpose is that of accumulation of money or other material things.

This chapter on the sixth sense was included because the book was designed to present a complete philosophy by which individuals may unerringly guide themselves in attaining whatever they ask of life. The starting point of all achievement is *desire*. The finishing point is that brand of *knowledge* that leads to understanding—understanding of self, understanding of others, understanding of the laws of Nature, recognition and understanding of *happiness*.

This sort of understanding comes in its fullness only through familiarity with, and use of, the principle of the sixth sense. Therefore that principle had to be included as a part of this philosophy, for the benefit of those who demand more than money.

You must have observed that while reading the chapter you were lifted to a high level of mental stimulation. Splendid! Come back to this again a month from now, read it once more, and observe that your mind will soar to a still higher level of stimulation. Repeat this experience from time to time, without being concerned as to how much or how little you learn at the time. Eventually you will find yourself in possession of a power that will enable you to throw off discouragement, master fear, overcome procrastination, and draw freely upon your imagination. Then you will have felt the touch of that unknown "something" which has been the moving spirit of every truly great thinker, leader, artist, musician, writer, statesman. Then you will be in a position to transmute your *desires* into their physical or financial counterpart as easily as you may lie down and quit at the first sign of opposition.

CHAPTER 15

HOW TO OUTWIT THE SIX GHOSTS OF FEAR

(Clearing the Brain for Riches)

Before you can put any portion of this philosophy into successful use, your mind must be prepared to receive it. The preparation is not difficult. It begins with study, analysis, and understanding of three enemies you shall have to clear out. These are *indecision, doubt,* and *fear*!

The sixth sense will never function while these three negatives, or any of them, remain in your mind. The members of this unholy trio are closely related; where one is found, the other two are close at hand.

Indecision is the seedling of *fear*! Remember this, as you read. Indecision crystallizes into *doubt,* and the two blend and become *fear*! The "blending" process is often slow. This is one reason why these three enemies are so dangerous: they germinate and grow without their presence being observed.

The remainder of this chapter describes an end that must be attained before the philosophy, as a whole, can be put into practical use. It also analyzes a condition that has reduced huge numbers of people to poverty, and it states a truth that must be understood by all who accumulate riches, whether measured in terms of money or a state of mind of far greater value.

The purpose of this chapter is to turn the spotlight upon the cause and the cure of the six basic fears. Before we can master an enemy, we must know its name, its habits, and its place of abode. As you read, analyze yourself carefully, and determine which, if any, of the six common fears have attached themselves to you.

Do not be deceived by the habits of these subtle enemies. Sometimes they remain hidden in the subconscious mind, where they are difficult to locate and still more difficult to eliminate.

The Six Basic Fears

There are six basic fears. Every human suffers from some combination of them at one time or another. Most people are fortunate if they do not suffer from the entire six. Named in the order of their most common appearance, they are:

The fear of POVERTY
The fear of CRITICISM
The fear of ILL HEALTH
The fear of LOSS OF LOVE OF SOMEONE
The fear of OLD AGE
The fear of DEATH

All other fears are of minor importance and can be grouped under these six headings.

The prevalence of these fears, as a curse to the world, runs in cycles. For almost six years, while the Depression was on, we floundered in the cycle of *fear of poverty*. During the periods when we were at war or faced with terror, we were in the cycle of *fear of death*. Even in periods of prosperity and peace, we are in the cycle of *fear of ill health,* as evidenced by the epidemic of various diseases, which spread themselves all over the world.

Fears are nothing more than states of mind. One's state of mind is subject to control and direction. Doctors, as everyone knows, are less subject to attack by disease than ordinary laymen for the reason that doctors *do not fear disease*. Doctors have been known to treat hundreds of people suffering from such contagious diseases as smallpox in a day, without becoming infected. Their immunity against the disease consisted largely, if not solely, in their absolute lack of *fear*.

We can create nothing that is not first conceived in the form of an impulse of thought. Following this statement comes another of still greater importance—namely, THOUGHT IMPULSES BEGIN IMMEDIATELY TO TRANSLATE THEMSELVES INTO THEIR PHYSICAL EQUIVALENT, WHETHER THOSE THOUGHTS ARE VOLUNTARY OR INVOLUNTARY. Thought impulses picked up through the ether by mere chance (thoughts released by other minds) may determine one's financial, business, professional, or social destiny just as surely as the thought impulses one creates by intent and design.

We are here laying the foundation for the presentation of a fact of great importance to the person who does not understand why some people appear to be "lucky" while others of equal or greater ability, training, experience, and brain capacity seem destined to ride with misfortune. This may be explained by the statement that human beings have the ability to control their own minds completely. With this control, they may open their minds to the thought impulses released by other brains, or close the doors tightly and admit only thought impulses of their own choice.

Nature has endowed us with absolute control over but one thing, and that is *thought*. This fact, coupled with the additional fact that everything people create begins in the form of a thought, leads one very near to the principle by which *fear* may be mastered.

If it is true that *all thought has a tendency to clothe itself in its physical equivalent* (and this is true beyond any reasonable room for doubt), it is equally true that thought impulses of fear and poverty cannot be translated into terms of courage and financial gain.

Following the Wall Street crash of 1929, the people of America were compelled to think of poverty. Slowly but surely, that mass thought was crystallized into its physical equivalent, which was known as a "depression." This had to happen. It is in conformity with the laws of Nature.

The Fear of Poverty

There can be no compromise between *poverty* and *riches*! The two roads that lead to poverty and riches travel in opposite directions. If you want riches, you must refuse to accept any circumstance that leads toward poverty. (The word "riches" is here used in its broadest sense, meaning financial, spiritual, mental, and material estates.) The starting point of the path that leads to riches is *desire*. In Chapters 1 and 2, you received full instructions for the proper use of desire. In this chapter, on *fear,* you have complete instructions for preparing your mind to make practical use of desire.

Here, then, is the place to give yourself a challenge that will definitely determine how much of this philosophy you have absorbed. Here is the point at which you can turn prophet and foretell, accurately, what the future holds in store for you. If, after reading this chapter, you are willing to accept poverty, you may as well make up your mind to receive poverty. This is one decision you cannot avoid.

If you demand riches, determine what form and how much will be required to satisfy you. You know the road that leads to riches. You have been given a road map, which, if followed, will keep you on that road. If you neglect to make the start, or stop before you arrive, no one will be to blame but *you*. This responsibility is yours. No alibi will save you from accepting the responsibility if you now fail or refuse to demand riches of life. The acceptance calls for but one thing—the only thing you can control—and that is a *state of mind*. A state of mind is something that one assumes. It cannot be purchased; it must be created.

Fear of poverty is a state of mind, nothing else! But it is sufficient to destroy one's chances of achievement in any undertaking. This fear paralyzes the faculty of reason, destroys the faculty of imagination, kills off self-reliance, undermines enthusiasm, discourages initiative, leads to uncertainty of purpose, encourages procrastination, wipes out enthusiasm, and makes self-control an impossibility. It takes the charm from one's personality, destroys the possibility of accurate thinking, diverts concentration of effort; it masters persistence, turns the willpower into nothingness, destroys ambition, beclouds the memory, and invites failure in every conceivable form; it kills love and assassinates the finer emotions of the heart, discourages friendship, and invites disaster in a hundred forms; it leads to sleeplessness, misery, and unhappiness—and all this despite the obvious truth that we live in a society of overabundance of everything the heart could desire, with nothing standing between us and our desires, except lack of a definite purpose.

The fear of poverty is, without doubt, the most destructive of the six basic fears. It has been placed at the head of the list because it is the most difficult to master. Considerable courage is required to state the truth about the origin of this fear, and still greater courage to accept the truth after it has been stated. The fear of poverty grew out of the human tendency to *prey upon others economically*. Nearly all animals lower than humans are motivated by instinct, but as their capacity to "think" is limited, they prey upon one another physically. Humans, with their superior sense of intuition, with the capacity to think and to reason, do not eat other humans bodily; they get more satisfaction out of "eating" them *financially*.

The age in which we live seems to be consumed by money madness. People are considered less than the dust of the earth unless they can display a fat bank account; but if they have money—*never mind how acquired*—they are too often idolized and treated as being above the law. They rule in politics and dominate in business, and the whole world about them bows in respect when they pass by.

Nothing brings so much suffering and humility as *poverty*! Only those who have experienced poverty understand the full meaning of this. It is no wonder that we fear poverty. Through a long line of inherited experiences we have learned, for sure, that some people cannot be trusted where matters of money and earthly possessions are concerned. This is a rather stinging indictment, the worst part of it being that it is *true*.

Many marriages are motivated by the wealth possessed by one or both of the contracting parties. It is no wonder, therefore, that the divorce courts are busy. So eager are people to possess wealth that they will acquire it in any feasible manner—through legal methods if possible, but through other methods if necessary or expedient.

Self-analysis may disclose weaknesses that one does not like to acknowledge. This form of examination is essential to all who demand of life more than mediocrity and poverty. Remember, as you check yourself point by point, that you are the court and the jury, the prosecution and the defense, the plaintiff and the defendant. Face the facts squarely. Ask yourself definite questions and demand direct replies. When the examination is over, you will know more about yourself. If you do not feel that you can be an impartial judge in this self-examination, call upon someone who knows you well to serve as judge while you cross-examine yourself. You are after the truth. Get it, no matter at what cost, even though it may temporarily embarrass you!

The majority of people, if asked what they fear most, would reply, "I fear nothing." The reply would be inaccurate, because few people realize that they are bound, handicapped, whipped spiritually and physically through some form of fear. So subtle and deeply seated is the emotion of fear that one may go through life burdened with it, never recognizing its presence. Only a courageous analysis will disclose the presence of this universal enemy. When you begin such an analysis, search deeply into your character. Here is a list of the symptoms you should look for:

Symptoms of the Fear of Poverty

INDIFFERENCE. Commonly expressed through lack of ambition; willingness to tolerate poverty; acceptance of whatever compensation life may offer without protest; mental and physical laziness; lack of initiative, imagination, enthusiasm, and self-control.

INDECISION. The habit of permitting others to do one's thinking; staying "on the fence."

DOUBT. Generally expressed through alibis and excuses designed to cover up, explain away, or apologize for one's failures; sometimes expressed in the form of envy of those who are successful, or by criticizing them.

WORRY. Usually expressed by finding fault with others; a tendency to spend beyond one's income; neglect of personal appearance; scowling and frowning; intemperance in the use of alcoholic drink; sometimes through the use of narcotics; nervousness; lack of poise; self-consciousness and lack of self-reliance.

OVERCAUTION. The habit of looking for the negative side of every circumstance, thinking and talking of possible failure instead of concentrating upon the means of succeeding; knowing all the roads to disaster but never searching for the plans to avoid failure; waiting for "the right time" to begin putting ideas and plans into action, until the waiting becomes a permanent habit; remembering those who have failed, and forgetting those who have succeeded; seeing the hole in the doughnut but overlooking the doughnut.

PROCRASTINATION. The habit of putting off until tomorrow matters that should have been done last year; spending enough time in creating alibis and excuses to have done the job. This symptom is closely related to overcaution, doubt, and worry; refusal to accept responsibility when it can be avoided; willingness to compromise rather than put up a stiff fight; compromising with difficulties instead of harnessing and using them as stepping stones to advancement; bargaining with life for a penny instead of demanding prosperity, opulence, riches, contentment, and happiness; and planning what to do *if and when overtaken by failure instead of burning all bridges and making retreat impossible.* This is manifested further by weakness of, and often total lack of, self-confidence, definiteness of purpose, self-control, initiative, enthusiasm, ambition, thrift, and sound reasoning ability; *expecting poverty instead of demanding riches,* and association with those who accept poverty instead of seeking the company of those who demand and receive riches.

The Fear of Criticism

Most people are at the least very uncomfortable when criticized. In some cases they may become depressed and despondent when others censure them. The fear of criticism robs people of their initiative, destroys their power of imagination, limits their individuality, takes away their self-reliance, and does them damage in a hundred other ways. Parents often do their children irreparable injury by criticizing them. The mother of one of my boyhood chums used to punish him with a switch almost daily, always completing the job with the statement, "You'll end up in prison before you are twenty." He was sent to a reform school at the age of seventeen.

Criticism is the one form of service of which everyone has too much. Everyone has a stock of it that is handed out, gratis, whether called for or not. One's nearest relatives are often the worst offenders. It should be recognized as a crime (in reality it is a crime of the worst nature) for any parent to build inferiority complexes in the mind of a child through unnecessary criticism. Employers who understand human nature get the best there is out of people not by criticism but by constructive suggestion. Parents may accomplish the same results with their children. Criticism will plant *fear* or resentment in the human heart but it will not build love or affection.

The Fear of Ill Health

This fear may be traced to both physical and social heredity. It is closely associated in origin with the causes of fear of old age and death because it leads one closely to the border of "terrible worlds" of which nothing is really known, but concerning which some discomforting stories have been told. Certain unethical people engaged in the business of "selling health" have had not a little to do with keeping alive the fear of ill health.

In the main, ill health is feared because of the suffering it causes and the fear and uncertainty of what may happen when death comes. In addition, there is the fear of the economic toll it may claim.

A reputable doctor estimated that 75 percent of all people who visit doctors for professional service are suffering with hypochondria (imaginary illness). It has been shown most convincingly that the fear of disease, even where there is not the slightest cause for fear, often produces the physical symptoms of the disease feared. Powerful and mighty is the human mind! It builds or it destroys.

Through a series of experiments conducted some years ago, it was proved that people might be made ill by suggestion. We conducted this experiment by causing three acquaintances to visit the "victims," each of whom asked the question, "What ails you? You look terribly ill." The first questioner usually provoked a grin, and a nonchalant "Oh, nothing, I'm all right" from the victim. The second questioner was usually answered with the statement, "I don't know exactly, but I do feel bad." The third questioner was usually met with the frank admission that the victim was actually feeling ill.

Try this on an acquaintance if you doubt that it will make them uncomfortable, but do not carry the experiment too far. In some primitive cultures, people take vengeance upon their enemies by placing a "spell" on the victim. Because they believe the spell is real, victims do become sick and often die.

There is overwhelming evidence that disease sometimes begins in the form of a negative thought impulse. Such an impulse may be passed from one mind to another by suggestion, or created by an individual in their own mind.

Doctors sometimes send patients into new climates for their health because a change of "mental attitude" is necessary. The seed of fear of ill health lives in every human mind. Worry, fear, discouragement, and disappointment in love and business affairs cause this seed to germinate and grow.

The Fear of Loss of Love

The original source of this inherent fear needs little description. It obviously grew out of ancient man's polygamous habit of stealing his fellow man's mate and taking liberties with her whenever he could.

The fear of the loss of love of someone is the most painful of all the six basic fears. It probably plays more havoc with the body and mind than any of the others.

One of the distinguishing symptoms of this fear is *jealousy*: being suspicious of friends and loved ones without any reasonable evidence. Another is the habit of accusing one's partner of infidelity without grounds. Further symptoms are a general suspicion of everyone, absolute faith in no one, and finding fault with friends, relatives, business associates, and loved ones upon the slightest provocation, or without any cause whatsoever.

The Fear of Old Age

The possibility of ill health, which is more common as people grow older, is a major cause of this common fear. Eroticism also enters into the cause of the fear of old age, as no one cherishes the thought of diminishing sexual attraction.

Another contributing cause of the fear of old age is the possibility of loss of freedom and independence, as old age may bring with it the loss of both physical and economic freedom.

Some people show a tendency to slow down and develop an inferiority complex when they get older, falsely believing themselves to be "slipping" because of age. (The truth is that some of our most useful years, mentally and spiritually, are those in later life.) Unfortunately, there are older men and women who lose their initiative, imagination, and self-reliance by falsely believing themselves too old to exercise these qualities.

The Fear of Death

To some this is the cruelest of all the basic fears. The reason is obvious. We know not what to expect after death. As Shakespeare stated so well in *Hamlet,* it is "The undiscovered country from whose bourne no traveller returns."

The fear of death is not as common now as it was during the age when there were no great colleges and universities. Scientists have turned the spotlight of truth upon the world, and this truth is rapidly freeing people from this terrible fear of death. Through the aid of biology, astronomy, geology, and other related sciences, the fears of the Dark Ages that gripped the minds of people and destroyed their reason have been dispelled.

This fear is useless. Death will come, no matter what anyone may think about it. Accept it as a necessity and pass the thought out of your mind. It must be a necessity or it would not come to all.

The entire world is made up of only two things, *energy* and *matter.* In elementary physics we learn that neither matter nor energy (the only two known realities) can be created or destroyed. Both matter and energy can be transformed.

Life is energy, if it is anything. If neither energy nor matter can be destroyed, of course life cannot be destroyed. Life, like other forms of energy, may be passed through various processes of transition or change, but it cannot be destroyed. Death is mere transition.

If death is not mere change or transition, then nothing comes after death except a long, eternal peaceful sleep, and sleep is nothing to be feared. Thus you may wipe out, forever, the fear of death.

Worry

Worry is a state of mind based upon fear. It works slowly but persistently. It is insidious and subtle. Step by step, it "digs itself in" until it paralyzes one's reasoning faculty and destroys self-confidence and initiative. Worry is a form of sustained fear caused by indecision; therefore it is a state of mind which can be controlled.

An unsettled mind is helpless. Indecision makes an unsettled mind. Most individuals lack the willpower to reach decisions promptly and to stand by them after they have been made, even during normal business conditions. During periods of economic unrest, people are handicapped not only by their inherent tendency to be slow at reaching decisions, but also by the indecision of others around them who have created a state of "mass indecision."

The six basic fears become translated into a state of worry through indecision. Relieve yourself forever of the fear of death by reaching a decision to accept death as an inescapable event. Whip the fear of poverty by reaching a decision to get along with whatever wealth you can accumulate *without worry*. Put your foot upon the neck of the fear of criticism by reaching a decision *not to worry* about what other people think, do, or say. Eliminate the fear of old age by reaching a decision to accept it, not as a handicap, but as a great blessing which carries with it wisdom, self-control, and understanding not known to youth.

Acquit yourself of the fear of ill health by the decision to forget symptoms. Master the fear of loss of love by reaching a decision to get along without love, if that is necessary.

Kill the habit of worry, in all its forms, by reaching a general, blanket decision that nothing life has to offer is worth the price of worry. With this decision will come poise, peace of mind, and calmness of thought that will bring happiness.

A person whose mind is filled with fear not only destroys their own chances of intelligent action but also transmits these destructive vibrations to the minds of other people and destroys their chances as well.

Even a dog or a horse knows when its master lacks courage; moreover, a dog or horse will pick up the vibrations of fear thrown off by its master, and behave accordingly. One finds this same capacity to pick up the vibrations of fear lower down the line of intelligence in the animal kingdom. A honeybee immediately senses fear in the mind of a person. For reasons unknown, a bee will sting the person whose mind is releasing vibrations of fear much more readily than it will molest the person whose mind registers no fear.

The vibrations of fear pass from one mind to another just as quickly and as surely as the sound of the human voice passes from the broadcasting station to the receiving station and *by the selfsame medium*.

Mental telepathy is a reality. Thoughts pass from one mind to another voluntarily, whether or not this fact is recognized by either the person releasing the thoughts or the person who picks up those thoughts.

The person who gives expression, by word of mouth, to negative or destructive thoughts is practically certain to experience the results of those words in the form of a destructive "kickback." The release of destructive thought impulses alone, without the aid of words, also produces a "kickback" in more ways than one. First of all, and perhaps most important to be remembered, the person who releases thoughts of a destructive nature must suffer damage through the breaking down of the faculty of creative imagination. Second, the presence in the mind of any destructive emotion develops a negative personality that repels people, and often converts them into antagonists. The third source of damage to the person who entertains or releases negative thoughts lies in this significant fact: these thought impulses are not only damaging to others but they *embed themselves in the subconscious mind of the person releasing them,* and there become a part of their character.

One is never through with a thought merely by releasing it. When a thought is released, it spreads in every direction through the medium of the ether, but it also plants itself permanently in the subconscious mind of the person releasing it.

Your business in life is, presumably, to achieve success. To be successful, you must find peace of mind, acquire the material needs of life, and, above all, attain *happiness.* All of these evidences of success begin in the form of thought impulses.

You may control your own mind; you have the power to feed it whatever thought impulses you choose. With this privilege goes also the responsibility of using it constructively. You are the master of your own earthly destiny just as surely as you have the power to control your own thoughts. You may influence, direct, and eventually control your own environment, making your life what you want it to be. On the other hand, you may neglect to exercise the privilege that is yours—to make your life to order, thus casting yourself upon the broad sea of "circumstance," where you will be tossed hither and yon, like a chip on the waves of the ocean.

CHAPTER 16

THE DEVIL'S WORKSHOP
(The Seventh Basic Evil)

In addition to the six basic fears, there is another evil by which people suffer. It constitutes a rich soil in which the seeds of failure grow abundantly. It is so subtle that its presence is often not detected. This affliction cannot properly be classed as a fear. IT IS MORE DEEPLY SEATED AND MORE OFTEN FATAL THAN ALL OF THE SIX FEARS. For want of a better name, let us call this evil *susceptibility to negative influences.*

People who accumulate great riches always protect themselves against this evil. The poverty-stricken never do. Those who succeed in any calling must prepare their minds to resist the evil. If you are reading this philosophy for the purpose of accumulating riches, you should examine yourself very carefully to determine whether you are susceptible to negative influences. If you neglect this self-analysis, you will forfeit your right to attain the object of your desires.

Make the analysis searching. After you read the questions prepared for this self-analysis, hold yourself to strict account in your answers. Go at the task as carefully as you would search for any other enemy you knew to be waiting to ambush you—deal with your own faults as you would a more tangible enemy.

You can easily protect yourself against highway robbers, because the law provides organized cooperation for your benefit, but the "seventh basic evil" is more difficult to master. It strikes when you are not aware of its presence, when you are asleep and while you are awake. Moreover, its weapon is intangible because it consists of merely a *state of mind.* This evil is also dangerous because it strikes in as many different forms as there are human experiences. Sometimes it enters the mind through the well-meant words of one's own relatives.

At other times it bores from within, through one's own mental attitude. Always it is as deadly as poison, even though it may not kill as quickly.

How to Protect Yourself Against
Negative Influences

To protect yourself against negative influences, whether of your own making or the result of the activities of negative people around you, recognize that you have *willpower*. Put it into constant use until it builds a wall of immunity against negative influences in your own mind. Recognize the fact that you and every other human being are, by nature, lazy, indifferent, and susceptible to all suggestions that harmonize with your weaknesses.

Recognize that you are, by nature, susceptible to all six basic fears. Set up habits for the purpose of counteracting all these fears.

Recognize that negative influences often work on you through your subconscious mind and are therefore difficult to detect. Keep your mind closed against all people who depress or discourage you in any way.

Deliberately seek the company of people who influence you to *think and act for yourself.*

Do not *expect* troubles, as they have a tendency not to disappoint.

Without doubt, the most common weakness of all human beings is the habit of leaving their minds open to the negative influence of other people. This weakness is all the more damaging because most people do not recognize that they are cursed by it, and many who acknowledge it neglect or refuse to correct the evil until it becomes an uncontrollable part of their daily habits.

To aid those who wish to see themselves as they really are, the following list of questions has been prepared. Read the questions and state your answers aloud, so you can hear your own voice. This will make it easier for you to be truthful with yourself.

Self-Analysis Test Questions

Do you often complain of "feeling bad." If so, what is the cause?

Do you find fault with other people at the slightest provocation?

Do you frequently make mistakes in your work? If so, why?

Are you sarcastic and offensive in your conversation?

Do you deliberately avoid the association of anyone? If so, why?

Do you suffer frequently with indigestion? If so, what is the cause?

Does life seem futile and the future hopeless to you? If so, why?

Do you like your occupation? If not, why?

Do you often feel self-pity? If so why?

Are you envious of those who excel you?

To which do you devote most time: thinking of success or of failure?

Are you gaining or losing self-confidence as you grow older?

Do you learn something of value from all mistakes?

Are you permitting some relative or acquaintance to worry you? If so, why?

Are you sometimes "in the clouds" and at other times in the depths of despondency?

Who has the most inspiring influence upon you? "What is the cause?

Do you tolerate negative or discouraging influences that you can avoid?

Are you careless of your personal appearance? If so, when and why?

Have you learned how to "drown your troubles" by being too busy to be annoyed by them?

Would you call yourself a "spineless weakling" if you permitted others to do your thinking for you?

Do you neglect internal bathing until autointoxication makes you ill-tempered and irritable?

How many preventable disturbances annoy you, and why do you tolerate them?

Do you resort to liquor, narcotics, or cigarettes to "quiet your nerves"? If so, why do you not try willpower instead?

Does anyone "nag" you, and if so, for what reason?

Do you have a DEFINITE MAJOR PURPOSE, and if so, what is it, and what plan have you for achieving it?

Do you suffer from any of the Six Basic Fears? If so, which ones?

Have you a method by which you can shield yourself against the negative influence of others?

Do you make deliberate use of autosuggestion to make your mind positive?

Which do you value most, your material possessions or your privilege of controlling your own thoughts?

Do others easily influence you, against your own judgment?

Has today added anything of value to your stock of knowledge or state of mind?

Do you face squarely the circumstances that make you unhappy, or sidestep the responsibility?

Do you analyze all mistakes and failures and try to profit by them, or do you take the attitude that this is not your duty?

Can you name three of your most damaging weaknesses? What are you doing to correct them?

Do you encourage other people to bring their worries to you for sympathy?

Do you choose, from your daily experiences, lessons or influences that aid in your personal advancement?

Does your presence have a negative influence on other people as a rule?

What habits of other people annoy you most?

Do you form your own opinions or permit yourself to be influenced by other people?

Have you learned how to create a mental state of mind with which you can shield yourself against all discouraging influences?

Does your occupation inspire you with faith and hope?

Are you conscious of possessing spiritual forces of sufficient power to enable you to keep your mind free from all forms of FEAR?

Does your religion help you to keep your own mind positive?

Do you feel it your duty to share other people's worries? If so, why?

If you believe that "birds of a feather flock together," what have you learned about yourself by studying the friends you attract?

What connection, if any, do you see between the people with whom you associate most closely, and any unhappiness you may experience?

Could it be possible that some person you consider to be a friend is, in reality, your worst enemy because of their negative influence on your mind?

By what rules do you judge who is helpful and who is damaging to you?

Are your intimate associates mentally superior or inferior to you?

How much time out of every 24 hours do you devote to:

   a. your occupation
   b. sleep
   c. play and relaxation
   d. acquiring useful knowledge
   e. plain waste?

Who among your acquaintances:

   a. encourages you most
   b. cautions you most
   c. discourages you most
   d. helps you most in other ways?

What is your greatest worry? Why do you tolerate it?

When others offer you free, unsolicited advice, do you accept it without question or analyze their motive?

What, above all else, do you most *desire*? Do you intend to acquire it? Are you willing to subordinate all other desires for this one? How much time daily do you devote to acquiring it?

Do you change your mind often? If so, why?

Do you usually finish everything you begin?

Are you easily impressed by other people's business or professional titles, university degrees, or wealth?

Are you easily influenced by what other people think or say of you?

Do you cater to people because of their social or financial status?

Whom do you believe to be the greatest person living? In what respect is this person superior to you?

How much time have you devoted to studying and answering these questions? (At least one day is necessary for analyzing and answering the entire list.)

If you have answered all these questions truthfully, you know more about yourself than the majority of people. Study the questions carefully. Come back to them once each week for several months. You will be astounded at the amount of valuable additional knowledge you will have gained by the simple method of answering the questions truthfully. If you are not certain of the answers to some of the questions, seek the counsel of those who know you well—especially those who have no motive in flattering you—and see yourself through their eyes. The experience will be astonishing.

You have *absolute control* over but one thing, and that is your thoughts. This is the most significant and inspiring of all known facts! It reflects our divine nature. This divine prerogative is the sole means by which you may control your own destiny. If you fail to control your own mind, you may be sure you will control nothing else.

If you must be careless with your possessions, let it be in connection with material things. Your mind is your spiritual estate! Protect and use it with the care to which divine royalty is entitled. You were given a *willpower* for this purpose.

Unfortunately, there is no legal protection against those who, either by design or ignorance, poison the minds of others by negative suggestion. This form of destruction should be punishable by heavy legal penalties because it may and often does destroy one's chances of acquiring material things that are protected by law.

People with negative minds tried to convince Thomas A. Edison that he could not build a machine that would record and reproduce the human voice, "Because," they said, "no one else has ever produced such a machine." Edison did not believe them. He knew that the mind could produce *anything the mind could conceive and believe,* and that knowledge was the thing that lifted him above the common herd.

Men with negative minds told F. W. Woolworth he would go "broke" trying to run a store on five-and-ten-cent sales. He did not believe them. He knew he could do anything, within reason, if he backed his plans with faith. Exercising his right to keep other men's negative suggestions out of his mind, he piled up a fortune of more than a hundred million dollars.

Men with negative minds told George Washington he could not hope to win against the vastly superior forces of the British, but he exercised his divine right to *believe.*

Doubting Thomases scoffed scornfully when Henry Ford tried out his first crudely built automobile on the streets of Detroit. Some said the thing would never become practical. Others said no one would pay money for such a contraption. Ford said, "I'll belt the earth with dependable motorcars," and he did! His decision to trust his own judgment piled up a fortune far greater than the next five generations of his descendants could squander. Henry Ford has been repeatedly mentioned, because he is an astounding example of what someone with a mind of their own and a will to control it can accomplish. His record knocks the foundation from under that timeworn alibi "I never had a chance." Ford never had a chance either, but he *created an opportunity and backed it with persistence until it made him richer than Croesus.*

Mind control is the result of self-discipline and habit. You either control your mind or it controls you. There is no halfway compromise. The most practical of all methods for controlling the mind is the habit of keeping it busy with a definite purpose, backed by a definite plan. Study the record of people who have achieved noteworthy success and you will observe that they have control over their own minds; moreover, that they exercise that control and direct it toward the attainment of definite objectives. Without this control, success is not possible.

55 Famous Alibis

People who do not succeed have one distinguishing trait in common: They know all the reasons for failure, and have what they believe to be airtight alibis to explain away their own lack of achievement.

Some of these alibis are clever, and a few of them are justifiable by the facts. But alibis cannot be used for money. The world wants to know only one thing: *Have you achieved success?*

A character analyst compiled a list of the most commonly used alibis. As you read the list, examine yourself carefully and determine how many of these alibis, if any, are your own property. Remember, too, the philosophy presented in this book makes every one of these alibis obsolete:

1. IF only I didn't have a wife and family . . .
2. IF only I had enough "pull" . . .
3. IF only I had money . . .
4. IF only I had a good education . . .
5. IF only I could get a job . . .
6. IF only I had good health . . .
7. IF only I had time . . .
8. IF only times were better . . .
9. IF only other people understood me . . .
10. IF only conditions around me were different . . .
11. IF only I could live my life over again . . .
12. IF only I did not fear what "they" would say . . .
13. IF only I had been given a chance . . .
14. IF only I now had a chance . . .
15. IF only other people didn't "have it in for me" . . .
16. IF only nothing happened to stop me . . .
17. IF only I were younger . . .
18. IF only I could do what I want . . .
19. IF only I had been born rich . . .
20. IF only I could meet "the right people" . . .
21. IF only I had the talent some people have . . .
22. IF only I dared assert myself . . .

23. IF only I had embraced past opportunities . . .

24. IF only people didn't get on my nerves . . .

25. IF only I didn't have to keep house and look after the children . . .

26. IF only I could save some money . . .

27. IF only the boss appreciated me . . .

28. IF only I had somebody to help me . . .

29. IF only my family understood me . . .

30. IF only I lived in a big city . . .

31. IF only I could just get started . . .

32. IF only I were free . . .

33. IF only I had the personality of some people . . .

34. IF only I were not so fat . . .

35. IF only my talents were known . . .

36. IF only I could just get a "break" . . .

37. IF only I could get out of debt . . .

38. IF only I hadn't failed . . .

39. IF only I knew how . . .

40. IF only everybody didn't oppose me . . .

41. IF only I didn't have so many worries . . .

42. IF only I could marry the right person . . .

43. IF only people weren't so dumb . . .

44. IF only my family were not so extravagant . . .

45. IF only I were sure of myself . . .

46. IF only luck were not against me . . .

47. IF only I had not been born under the wrong star . . .

48. IF only it were not true that "what is to be will be" . . .

49. IF only I did not have to work so hard . . .

50. IF only I hadn't lost my money . . .

51. IF only I lived in a different neighborhood . . .

52. IF only I didn't have a "past" . . .

53. IF only I had a business of my own . . .

54. IF only other people would listen to me . . .

55. IF only—and this is the greatest of them all—I had the courage to see myself as I really am, I would find out what is wrong with me and correct it. Then I might

have a chance to profit by my mistakes and learn something from the experience of others. I know there is something *wrong* with me or I would now be where *I would have been if* I had spent more time analyzing my weaknesses, and less time building alibis to cover them.

Building alibis with which to explain away failure is a habit as old as the human race, and is fatal to success! Why do people cling to their pet alibis? The answer is obvious. They defend their alibis because *they create* them!

An alibi is the child of one's own imagination. It is human nature to defend one's own brainchild.

Building alibis is a deeply rooted habit. Habits are difficult to break, especially when they provide justification for something we do. Plato had this truth in mind when he said, "The first and best victory is to conquer self. To be conquered by self is, of all things, the most shameful and vile."

Another philosopher had the same thought in mind when he said, "It was a great surprise to me when I discovered that most of the ugliness I saw in others was but a reflection of my own nature."

"It has always been a mystery to me," said Elbert Hubbard, "why people spend so much time deliberately fooling themselves by creating alibis to cover their weaknesses. If used differently, this same time would be sufficient to cure the weakness, then no alibis would be needed."

In parting, I would remind you that life is a checker board, and the player opposite you is *time.* If you hesitate before moving, or neglect to move promptly, your checkers will be wiped off the board by time. You are playing against a partner who will not tolerate *indecision*!

Previously you may have had a logical excuse for not having forced life to come through with whatever you asked. However, that alibi is now obsolete because you are in possession of the Master-Key that unlocks the door to life's bountiful riches.

The Master-Key is intangible but it is powerful! It is the privilege of creating, in your own mind, a *burning desire* for a definite form of riches. There is no penalty for the use of the key, but there is a price you must pay if you do not use it. The price is *failure.* There is a reward of stupendous proportions if you put the key to use. It is the satisfaction that comes to all who conquer self and force life to pay whatever is asked.

The reward is worthy of your effort. Will you make the start and be convinced?

"If we are related," said the immortal Emerson, "we shall meet." In closing, may I borrow his thought, and say, "If we are related, we have, through these pages, met"?

THE MAGIC LADDER TO SUCCESS

Revised and Updated by
Patricia G. Horan

FOREWORD

In this book are the success secrets of magnates, tycoons, moguls, and captains of industry. They are towering figures whose names live in history, not in infamy. Unlike the headline makers of today, they are geniuses, not jailbirds; winners, not whiners. They had more than clout: They had class. Though they were by no means saints, they were undoubtedly larger than life, often doing what others said couldn't be done. At a time of bottom-feeders, when books are cooked and stockholders scandalized, we need the wisdom of our American Giants more than ever. They were the stuff of legends.

How did they—Andrew Carnegie, Alexander Graham Bell, Henry Ford, P. T. Barnum— do it? What was going through their minds as they blazed trails through the wilderness and created the infrastructure of this nation?

Many of them were born into impoverished circumstances. What personal alchemy turned their less-than-promising beginnings into pure gold? What it is that makes a winner?

Out of the same unforgiving circumstances came a man who set out to find the answers to this central question. With a letter of introduction from Carnegie himself, he found out these secrets by doing what no one had thought to do before: He asked the greatest how they became great. In the process, against all odds, he became a winner himself. He invented motivational writing, ultimately finding himself listed as a peer with Marcus Aurelius, Ralph Waldo Emerson, and Ben Franklin.

He was five-foot-six and his name was Napoleon, but no Waterloo ever defeated him and he refused to languish in exile. Napoleon Hill was the guru of all success gurus, and the author of the number one motivational seller of all time, *Think and Grow Rich,* which would never have seen the light of day without the book you are holding in your hands. (*Think and Grow Rich* may not have seen the light of success, either, if the publisher's choice of titles had prevailed, since it would have been known as *Use Your Noodle to Earn More Boodle!*)

More than forty years after it was published, a USA Today survey of biz leaders named *Think and Grow Rich* one of the best-selling inspirational business books ever and one of the five most influential books in its field. The same magical material contained in that book can be found in this one, which could only have been stopped in its tracks by the financial disaster that brought the rest of America to its knees.

The Magic Ladder of Success was published at the start of the great Depression, seven years before *Think and Grow Rich,* so its chance at success was washed away along with the American economy. But the ideas in this book proved themselves to be great, and they seeded the better-known book to follow. In *Magic Ladder,* Hill's famous Seventeen Laws of Success were tried, tested, and found to work miracles. In this book Napoleon Hill brings together wisdom straight from the minds of the greatest names in American business history, the result of five hundred interviews with the business giants of Hill's time.

In 1808 steel magnate Andrew Carnegie, son of penniless Scottish immigrants, stood in the library of his 124-room New York City mansion. He took his gold watch from his pocket and gave the young Napoleon Hill a challenge. The twenty-five-year-old reporter had been commissioned by former Tennessee Governor Robert L. Taylor to write success stories about leading business leaders for his magazine. Carnegie would be his first assignment, and the steel baron had already spent three days and nights with Hill. Carnegie saw something in Hill he liked, a younger, shorter reflection of himself, perhaps, and now it was his turn to ask the questions.

Would Hill be interested in compiling the beliefs and practices of the business giants of the time into a coherent philosophy? Without any payment?

Napoleon Hill took twenty-nine seconds to answer. "Good," Carnegie said as he put away his watch. "I was planning on giving you only sixty seconds."

Perhaps it was that incident that confirmed one of Hill's beliefs: "Successful people make decisions quickly and change them slowly. Unsuccessful people make decisions slowly and change them often."

Napoleon Hill would go on to become an adviser to President Franklin Delano Roosevelt. He later took credit for writing "We have nothing to fear but fear itself" and several of FDR's famous Fireside Chats. His life would prove to be more a roller coaster than a yellow brick road. Several of his businesses went bankrupt, he lost jobs, and he was wrongly accused of fraud and put into prison. One of his two sons was born without ears. Hill's work took him away from his family so much that one of his sons was adopted by a family member.

His life was such a series of victorious failures that, when in his fifties, he marveled that an entire decade had gone by without his having to face a personal disaster. But Napoleon Hill, often down but never out, never wavered from his "definite chief aim." He was to teach millions around the world that even luck can be changed and failures put to good use. How else would he have known that firsthand?

"Success requires no explanation. Failure permits no alibis," he would later say with the authority only experience can offer.

Napoleon Hill was born in 1883 in a one-room cabin in the hills of aptly named Wise County, Virginia. A wild, gun-toting, untamed child, he began his writing career at age thirteen as a "mountain reporter" for small-town newspapers, and never lost his hunger for real facts about real people who overcame odds. It was this childhood job that taught him how to interview the 500 people whose philosophies of success are distilled into this book's coherent wisdom.

His is one of those it-seemed-to-be-bad-but-it-turned-out-good stories. His mother died when he was very young, but the educated, audacious woman his father then married was impatient with poverty, as he later put it. Hill's stepmother took responsibility for the family store and farm, sent his father to dental school at the age of forty, and gave Napoleon the backbone he needed to climb out of his Virginia mountain. She placed in his mind the thought he would become most famous for: "What the mind of man can conceive, he can achieve."

The qualities of thought that propelled the titans of yesterday are rare today, and would be very welcome in our world of instant gratification and greed. Among these concepts are the politically incorrect concept of doing more than one is paid for, the unashamed use of "innate spiritual powers," the idea of boldly grasping the "big ideas" behind the principle of "definiteness of purpose," and trusting the mind's magnetic quality. Hill encouraged "the state of mind known as faith," and said that it frees the mind from negative traits such as doubt and procrastination. "The doubting mind is not a creative mind," he says, and he adds, "Tolerance may not be your duty, but it is your privilege!" Even the highest-minded ideas are practical steps on the Magic Ladder to Success. Hill tells us, for instance, "Intolerance closes the doorway to opportunity in a thousand ways, and shuts out the light of intelligence."

Hill urges us to draw freely on the Power of Infinite Intelligence, and makes the bold observation that the greatest leaders are the most sexually driven. But he considers pure love, too, as a real source of power, sometimes referring to it in a refreshingly old-fashioned way as "the love of sweethearts."

Over the years, Napoleon Hill gave his name and energies to several magazines, seven books in many languages, a foundation, a film, franchises, tapes, and countless lectures in many countries. The likes of Dale Carnegie, Norman Vincent Peale, and Oral Roberts became devotees and sometimes shared speaking platforms with Hill. W. Clement Stone, Earl Nightingale, Denis Waitley, Zig Ziglar, Tony Robbins, and others have acknowledged their enormous debt to Hill, the greatest success specialist of them all.

Insert the name Napoleon Hill into an Amazon.com book search today and nearly 18,000 references come up. Why? Because the country's number one motivational guru never fails to be quoted in books whose subjects are as wide-ranging as diet, pentathletes, communication, simple abundance, JFK, teens, online trading, feng shui, leadership, taking a band on the road, Zen, and countless more. He succeeded in making his name as famous as the names of those he interviewed.

Napoleon Hill began with nothing, learned the secrets of those who embodied success, gained and lost a few wives and several fortunes, and died a fulfilled man in November, 1970, at the age of eighty-seven.

His tombstone could very well have quoted the other famous Napoleon:

"To hell with circumstances. I create circumstance."

—PATRICIA G. HORAN

ACKNOWLEDGMENTS

This volume is the result of an analysis of the lifework of over 100 men and women who have attained outstanding success in their respective callings and of over 20,000 men and women who were classed as failures.

In his labors of research and analysis, the author received valuable assistance, either in person or by studying their lifework, from the following men: Henry Ford, John Burroughs, Luther Burbank, Thomas A. Edison, Harvey S. Firestone, John D. Rockefeller, Charles M. Schwab, Woodrow Wilson, William Wrigley Jr., A. D. Lasker, E. A. Filene, John Wanamaker, Marshall Field, William Howard Taft, F. W. Woolworth, George Eastman, Charles P. Steinmetz, Theodore Roosevelt, and Alexander Graham Bell.

Of the men named, perhaps Henry Ford and Andrew Carnegie should be acknowledged as having contributed most to the building of this philosophy. It was Mr. Carnegie who first suggested writing it and Henry Ford whose lifework has supplied much of the material and served in other ways to prove the soundness of the entire philosophy.

—NAPOLEON HILL

NAPOLEON HILL'S FASCINATING PAST

I was born in the mountains of the South, surrounded by the poverty and illiteracy that were firmly established on both sides of my family. For three generations before me, my ancestors were content to be poor and ignorant. I would have surely followed in their footsteps if I hadn't been blessed with an educated stepmother who came from a cultured family. Poverty and illiteracy irritated her, and she was not bashful about saying so.

My stepmother voluntarily assumed the task of planting ambition in our family, starting with my father, whom she sent away to college at the age of forty! She then proceeded to manage what passed for a "farm" and the little country store we owned, also taking on the full support of five children: three of her own, my brother, and myself. Her example made a deep and lasting impression on me.

It was she who firmly planted the seed of a life-changing idea in my young mind thirty years ago. It came in the form of a simple but unforgettable remark. With it came the idea that I could whip poverty and illiteracy, in spite of everything. That seed of an idea found a permanent home in my mind.

It was my stepmother who taught me the value of having a definite, major aim in life. Later that principle became so obviously essential a factor in the achievement of success that I gave it second place in the list of seventeen principles outlined in this book, which I have been writing for a quarter of a century. This volume is the result of an analysis of the life-work of over 100 men and women who have attained outstanding success in their respective callings and of over 20,000 men and women who were classed as "failures."

There are several reasons why this work could not have been completed earlier. First is the scope of my self-appointed task: to learn, through decades of research, exactly what it was that others had discovered about failure and success.

Second, and equally important, is that I had to prove I could make the Law of Success philosophy work for *myself* before offering it to readers.

When I began organizing the material for the Law of Success, I had no intention of creating the philosophy that you will find in this volume. In the beginning my purpose was to inform myself as to how other people had acquired wealth so that I might follow their example.

But as the years passed I found myself becoming more eager for knowledge than for wealth, until my thirst for knowledge became so great that I practically lost sight of my original motive, financial gain.

In addition to the influence of my stepmother, I was fortunate enough to meet and gather such knowledge from the legendary Alexander Graham Bell and Andrew Carnegie, who not only further influenced me to continue my research but also supplied me with much of the important scientific data to be found in the Law of Success philosophy.

Later I met many others of high accomplishment who encouraged me to continue building a philosophy of success and gave me full benefit of their own rich experiences.

I have mentioned these details for what I believe to be a very important reason—namely, the fact that the difference between success and failure is often (if not always) determined by definite environmental influences that may be usually traced to one person.

In my case this person was my stepmother.

Except for her influence in planting the seed of ambition in my mind, I never would have written a philosophy of success that is now rendering useful service to millions of people in every civilized country on earth.

While the Law of Success was still in the experimental stage, and as a part of my plan for giving it a practical trial before publishing it in textbooks, I personally passed it on, through lectures, to no fewer than 100,000 people. Many whom I know to have received their first impulse of ambition from these lectures have since become wealthy, although some of them may have lost sight of the cause of their prosperity.

The Law of Success has been translated into countless foreign languages and taught around the world. Millions of people have been fired with ambition to whip poverty and to gain for themselves better stations in life. Moreover, this is most decidedly an age of scientific discovery, which has put sound legs under the Seventeen Principles of the Law of Success, thus giving it a standing that it did not enjoy years ago. Today there is a very definite demand for a solid program of success that will inspire people with higher hopes and ambitions for personal achievement.

Looking back, I have encountered great struggle and hardship, poverty and failure. But these challenges have been more than offset by the joy and prosperity I have helped others to obtain.

Not long ago I received a letter from a former president of the United States, who congratulated me for sticking to my job for a quarter of a century, and suggested that I must feel very proud to have "arrived" at the top of the mountain of success in time to enjoy the fruits of my labors. His letter brought to my mind the thought that one never "arrives" if one continues to search for knowledge, because we no sooner reach the top of one peak than we discover that there are still higher mountains yet to be scaled in the distance.

No, I have not "arrived," but I have found happiness in abundance and financial prosperity sufficient for my needs, solely through having lost myself in service to others who were earnestly struggling to find themselves. It seems worthy of mention that I did not prosper greatly until I became more concerned about something other than accumulating money: I became concerned about spreading the Law of Success philosophy where it would help others.

DON'T READ THIS BOOK WITHOUT READING THIS FIRST

Be sure you have a pencil and paper on hand when you begin this book. And don't attempt to read it at bedtime.

Be ready. As millions before you will testify, this book will cause important ideas to flash into your mind. As they've read these pages, inventors have been surprised and dazzled by their inventive ideas, speeches have sprung to life, business decisions have taken a bold new turn, ingenious new businesses have suddenly appeared possible.

The Law of Success philosophy is a mind magnet for brilliant ideas.

The real value of this book is not in its own pages but in your own reaction to what you read. The main purpose of the Law of Success philosophy is to stimulate the imaginative faculties of the brain so they will readily create new and usable ideas for any emergency in life. And anyone who can create great ideas—as readers of this book tend to do—will gather great power.

As you read, underscore or highlight all statements that prompt new ideas to flash into your mind. This method will serve to fix such ideas in your mind permanently. You cannot assimilate the entire subject matter of this philosophy at one reading of this book. Read it many times, and at each reading follow the habit of marking the lines that inspire new ideas.

Following this procedure will reveal to you one of the great mysteries of the human mind. Experience has proven that it will introduce you to a source of knowledge that can only be known by those who discover it themselves. You have just received a hint about the nature of the secret of the Law of Success philosophy throughout the world.

Many years of success with this book has proven that only the methods here described lead to the possession of this secret. No other.

THE SEVENTEEN PRINCIPLES OF
THE LAW OF SUCCESS

When you can acquire whatever you want without violating the rights of others, you possess power . . . the only genuine power.

This basic course presents the simple principles through which such power has been attained by those who have become successful—even astonishingly so. These principles are not only invaluable in business but will be financially productive in solving one's economic problems no matter what the calling or field.

The factors through which power may be acquired and used in harmony with the above definition are seventeen in number:

1. The Master Mind
2. The Importance of Having a Definite Aim
3. Self-Confidence
4. The Habit of Saving
5. Initiative and Leadership
6. Imagination
7. Enthusiasm
8. Self-Control
9. Doing More Than Paid For
10. A Pleasing Personality
11. Accurate Thinking
12. Concentration
13. Cooperation
14. Profiting by Failure
15. Tolerance
16. Using the Golden Rule to Win Cooperation
17. The Prosperous Habit of Health

Let us begin with a complete analysis of each of these seventeen proven success principles.

THE MASTER MIND

The Master Mind principle may be defined as "A composite mind, consisting of two or more individual minds working in perfect harmony, with a definite aim in view."

Keep in mind the definition of success—the result of the application of power—and you will more quickly grasp the meaning of the term "Master Mind." It will be immediately obvious that a group of two or more minds, working in harmony and perfectly coordinated, will create power in abundance.

All success is achieved through the application of power. The starting point, however, may be described as a burning desire for the achievement of some specific, definite objective.

Just as the oak tree, in the embryo, sleeps within the acorn, success begins in the form of an intense desire. Out of strong desires grow the motivating forces that cause the ambitious to cherish hopes, build plans, develop courage, and stimulate their minds to a highly intensified degree of action in pursuit of some definite plan or purpose.

Desire, Don't Wish

Desire, then, is the starting point of all human achievement. At the heart of desire lie certain stimuli through which the desire is fanned into a hot flame of action. These stimuli are known and will be listed later as a part of the Law of Success philosophy described in this book.

It has been said, and not without reason, that one may have anything one wants, within reasonable limitations, providing one wants it badly enough. Anyone who is capable of stimulating his or her mind to an intense state of desire is also capable of more than average achievement in the pursuit of that desire. It must be remembered that wishing for a thing is not the same as desiring it. A wish is merely a passive form of desire. Only out of intense desire will impelling forces of action grow, driving one to build plans and put those plans to work. Most people never advance beyond the "wishing" stage.

The Power Motivators

One or more of the following eight basic motivating forces—the stimuli mentioned above—is the starting point of all human achievement worth noting:

1. The urge toward self-preservation
2. The desire for sexual contact
3. The desire for financial gain
4. The desire for life after death
5. The desire for fame, to possess power
6. The urge to love (separate and distinct from the desire for sex)
7. The desire for revenge (a characteristic of undeveloped minds)
8. The desire to indulge in egotism

People make use of great power only when urged by one or more of these eight basic motives. The imaginative forces of the human mind become active only when spurred on by the stimulation of well-defined motive! Master salespeople have discovered this. Without this discovery no one could become a master at sales.

What is salesmanship? It is the presentation of an idea, plan, or suggestion that gives the prospective purchaser a strong motive for making a purchase. The able salesperson never asks a purchaser to buy without presenting a well-defined motive as to why the purchase should be made.

Knowledge of merchandise or service offered, of itself, is not sufficient to ensure sales success. The offering must be accompanied by a thorough description of the motive meant to prompt the purchaser to buy. The most effective sales plan is one that appeals to the prospective purchaser through the greatest number of the eight basic motivating forces listed above. The best plan is one that crystallizes these motives into a burning desire for the object offered for sale.

The eight basic motives serve not only as the basis of appeal to other minds, where co-operative action from other people is sought, but they serve also as the starting point of action in one's own mind. People of ordinary ability become superhuman when aroused by some outward or inner stimulant that provokes one or more of the eight basic motives for action.

Bring someone face-to-face with the possibility of death, in a sudden emergency, and he or she will develop physical strength and imaginative strategy that would be impossible under ordinary circumstances.

With the natural desire for sexual contact driving them, people will plan, imagine, and indulge in a thousand different amazing things, none of which they'd be able to come up with otherwise.

The desire for financial gain will also lift those of mediocre ability into positions of great power. This desire also causes them to plan, imagine, and act in extraordinary ways. The desire for fame and for personal power over others is clearly the chief motivating force in the lives of leaders in every walk of life.

The animalistic desire for revenge often drives people to develop the most intricate and ingenious plans for carrying out their objective.

Love for the opposite sex (and sometimes for the same sex) serves as a mind stimulant leading to almost unbelievable heights of achievement.

The desire for life after death is such a strong motivating force that it not only drives people to both constructive and destructive extremes, it also develops highly effective leadership ability, evidence of which may be found in the lifework of practically all the founders of religions.

If you would achieve great success, then, plant in your mind a strong motive!

Millions of people struggle all the days of their lives with no stronger motive than that of being able to acquire the necessities of life, such as food, shelter, and clothing. Now and then someone will step out of the ranks of this great army and demand more than a mere living. He or she will be motivated with the strong desire for fortune, and presto! as if by the hand of magic, his or her financial status changes and action begins to turn into cash.

"Power" and "success" are different words for the same thing. Success is not attained through honesty alone, as some would have us believe. Homeless shelters are filled with people who were, perhaps, honest enough. They failed to accumulate money because they lacked the knowledge of how to acquire and use power!

The Master Mind principle described in this lesson is the medium through which all personal power is applied. For this reason, every known mind stimulant and every basic motive inspiring action in all human endeavor has been mentioned in this chapter.

The Two Faces of Power

We will examine two forms of power in this lesson. One is mental power, and it is acquired through the process of thought. It is expressed through definite plans of action and is the result of organized knowledge. The ability to think, plan, and act in a well-organized way is the starting point of all mental power.

The other form of power is physical. It is expressed through natural laws, in the form of electricity, gravity, steam pressure, and so on. In this lesson we will analyze both mental and physical power, and explain the relationship between the two.

Knowledge, alone, is not power. Great personal power is acquired only through the harmonious cooperation of a number of people who concentrate their efforts upon some definite plan.

The Nature of Physical Power

The state of advancement known as "civilization" is the measure of the knowledge the human race has accumulated. Among the useful knowledge organized and available, humans have discovered and catalogued the eighty-plus physical elements that are the building blocks for all material forms in the universe.

By study, analysis, and accurate measurements, science has discovered the "bigness" of the material side of the universe, as represented by planets, suns, and stars, some of which are known to be over one million times as large as the little earth on which we live.

On the other hand, the "littleness" of the physical forms that constitute the universe has been discovered by reducing the roughly one hundred physical elements to molecules, to atoms, to the electron, and way beyond. An electron cannot be seen; it is but a center of force consisting of a positive or a negative.

Molecules, Atoms, Electrons, and Beyond

To understand the process through which knowledge is gathered, organized, and classified, it seems essential for the student to begin with the smallest and simplest particles of physical matter. These are the ABCs with which Nature has constructed the entire physical portion of the universe.

The molecule consists of atoms, which are said to be invisible particles of matter revolving continuously with the speed of lightning, on exactly the same principles with which the earth revolves on its axis: gravity and electromagnetism.

These little particles of matter, the atoms, which revolve in one continuous circuit in the molecule, are said to be made up of electrons, protons, and neutrons. As already stated, the electron is nothing but two forms of force. The electron is uniform, of but one class, size, and nature. Thus in a grain of sand or a drop of water is duplicated the entire principle upon which the whole universe operates.

How stupendous! You may gather some slight idea of the magnitude of it all the next time you eat a meal by remembering that every article of food you eat, the plate on which you eat it, the tableware, and the table itself, are, in final analysis, but a collection of invisible particles.

In the world of physical matter, whether one is looking at the largest star that floats through the heavens or the smallest grain of sand to be found on earth, the object under observation is but an organized collection of molecules, atoms, electrons, and smaller particles, revolving at inconceivable speed.

Every particle of physical matter is in a continuous state of highly agitated motion. Nothing is ever still, although nearly all physical matter may appear, to the physical eye, to be motionless. There is no "solid" physical matter. The hardest piece of steel is but an organized mass of revolving molecules. Moreover, the electrons in a piece of steel are of the same nature as the electrons in gold, silver, brass, or pewter but move at different rates of speed.

The one hundred forms of physical matter appear to be different from one another, and they are different, because they are made up of different combinations of atoms. Electrons in those atoms are always the same, and carry a specific negative charge, but their combination with positively charged protons and neutrally charged neutrons makes for different forms of matter.

Through the science of chemistry, matter may be broken up into atoms that are, within themselves, unchangeable. To illustrate the modus operandi of chemistry through which changes take place, in terms of modern science:

"Add four electrons (two positive and two negative) to the hydrogen atom, and you have the element lithium; knock out of the lithium atom (composed of three positive and three negative electrons) one positive and one negative electron, and you have one atom of helium (composed of two positive and two negative electrons)."

Thus it may be seen that the eighty-odd physical elements of the universe differ from one another only in the number of electrons composing their atoms, and the number and arrangement of those atoms in the molecules of each element.

As an illustration, an atom of mercury contains eighty positive charges (protons) in its nucleus, and eighty negative outlying charges (electrons). If the chemist were to expel two of its positive charges, it would instantly become the metal known as platinum. If the chemist then could go a step further and take from it a negative ("planetary") electron, the mercury atom would then have lost two positive electrons and one negative; that is, one positive charge on the whole; hence it would retain seventy-nine positive charges on the nucleus and seventy-nine outlying negative electrons, thereby becoming gold!

The formula through which this electronic change might be produced has been the object of diligent search by alchemists throughout the ages, as well as chemists of today.

It is a fact known to every chemist that countless synthetic substances may be composed out of only four kinds of atoms: hydrogen, oxygen, nitrogen, and carbon.

The electron is the universal particle with which Nature builds all material forms, from a grain of sand to the largest star that floats through space. The electron is Nature's "building block," out of which she erects an oak tree or a pine, a rock of sandstone or granite, a mouse or an elephant.

Some of the ablest thinkers have reasoned that the earth on which we live, and every material particle of the earth, began with two atoms that attached themselves to each other, and through hundreds of millions of years of flight through space, kept contracting and accumulating other atoms until, step by step, the earth was formed. This, they point out, would account for the various and differing strata of the earth's substances, such as the coal beds, the iron ore deposits, the gold and silver deposits, and the copper deposits.

They reason that, as the earth whirled through space, it contracted groups of various kinds of nebulae, which it promptly appropriated through the law of magnetic attraction. There is much to be seen, in the earth's surface composition, to support this theory, although there may be no positive evidence of its soundness.

We have referred to these facts concerning the smallest analyzable particles of matter because it is a starting point from which we shall undertake to ascertain how to develop and apply the laws of power.

It has been noticed that all matter is in a constant state of vibration or motion; that the molecule is made up of rapidly moving particles called atoms, which, in turn, are made up of rapidly moving particles called electrons.

The Vibrating Principle of Matter

In every particle of matter there is an invisible force that causes the atoms to move around one another at an inconceivable rate of speed.

Call it vibration. It is believed by some investigators that the rate of speed with which this force (call it whatever you will) moves determines the nature of the physical objects of the universe.

One rate of vibration causes what is known as sound. The human ear can detect only the sound that is produced through vibrations that range from 32,000 to 38,000 per second.

As the rate of vibrations per second increases above what we call sound, they begin to manifest themselves in the form of heat. Heat begins with about 1.5 million vibrations per second.

Still higher up the scale, vibrations begin to register in the form of light. Three million vibrations per second create violet light. Above this number vibration sheds ultraviolet rays (which are invisible to the naked eye) and other invisible radiations.

And still higher up the scale, just how high no one at present seems to know, vibrations create the power with which humans think.

It is the belief of this author that the portion of vibration out of which grows all known forms of energy is universal in nature, that the "fluid" portion of sound is the same as the "fluid" portion of light, the difference in effect between sound and light being only a difference in rate of vibration; also that the "fluid" portion of thought is exactly the same as that in sound, heat, and light, except for the number of vibrations per second.

Just as there is but one form of physical matter, of which the earth and all the other planets, suns, and stars are composed—the electron—so is there but one form of "fluid" energy that causes all matter to remain in a constant state of rapid motion.

Air and Atmosphere

Air is a localized substance that performs, in the main, the service of feeding all animal and plant life with oxygen and nitrogen, without which neither could exist. Nitrogen is one of the chief necessities of plant life, and oxygen one of the mainstays of animal life. Near the top of very high mountains the air becomes very light, because it contains but little nitrogen, which is the reason why trees grow smaller on the way up and plant life cannot exist at the highest elevations. On the other hand, the air found in the high altitude consists largely of oxygen, which is the chief reason why tubercular patients used to be sent to high altitudes.

What does all this scientific material have to do with you and your goals? You will soon see that it's the very foundation of the philosophy of success that will make reaching those goals possible.

Do not become discouraged if all these laboratory facts aren't exactly thrilling to read. If you are seriously engaged in finding out what your available powers are, and how to organize and apply these powers, you must combine determination, persistence, and a well-defined desire to gather and organize such knowledge.

Your Mind Is a Two-Way Radio

Alexander Graham Bell was, of course, one of the world's authorities on the subject of vibration, which is the basis of all mental power and of all thought. The following is as true today as the day the inventor of the telephone wrote it.

"Suppose you have the power to make an iron rod vibrate with any desired frequency in a dark room. At first, when vibrating slowly, its movement will be indicated by only one sense, that of touch. As soon as the vibrations increase, a low sound will emanate from it and it will appeal to two senses.

"At about thirty-two thousand vibrations to the second the sound will be loud and shrill; but at forty thousand vibrations it will be silent and the movements of the rod will not be perceived by touch. Its movements will be perceived by no ordinary human sense.

"From this point up to about one million and a half vibrations per second, we have no sense that can comprehend any effect of the intervening vibrations. After that stage is reached, movement is indicated first by the sense of temperature and then, when the rod becomes red hot, by the sense of sight. At three million vibrations it sheds violet light. Above that it sheds ultraviolet rays and other invisible radiations, some of which can be perceived by instruments and employed by us.

"Now it has occurred to me that there must be a great deal to be learned about the effect of those vibrations in the great gap where ordinary human senses are unable to hear, see or feel the movement. The power to send wireless messages by ether vibrations lies in that gap, but the gap is so great that it seems there must be much more. You must make machines practically to supply new senses, as the wireless instruments do.

"Can it be said, when you think of that great gap, that there are not many forms of vibrations that may give us results as wonderful as, or even more wonderful than, the wireless waves? It seems to me that in this gap lie the vibrations which we have assumed to be given off by our brain and nerve cells when we think. But then, again, they may be higher up in the scale beyond the vibrations that produce the ultraviolet rays."

(Author's note: The last sentence suggests the theory held by this author.)

When Mind Speaks Directly to Mind

"Do we need a wire to carry these vibrations? Will they not pass through the ether without a wire, just as the wireless waves do? How will they be perceived by the recipient? Will he hear a series of signals, or will he find that another man's thoughts have entered into his brain?

"We may indulge in some speculations based on what we know of the wireless waves, which, as I have said, are all we can recognize of a vast series of vibrations which theoretically must exist. If the thought waves are similar to the wireless waves, they must pass from the brain and flow endlessly around the world and the universe. The body and the skull and other solid obstacles would form no obstruction to their passage, as they pass through the ether which surrounds the molecules of every substance, no matter how solid and dense.

"You ask if there would not be constant interference and confusion if other people's thoughts were flowing through our brains and setting up thoughts in them that did not originate with ourselves?

"How do you know that other men's thoughts are not interfering with yours now? I have noticed a good many phenomena of mind disturbances that I have never been able to explain. For instance, there is the inspiration or the discouragement that a speaker feels in addressing an audience. I have experienced this many times in my life and have never been able to define exactly the physical causes of it.

"Many recent scientific discoveries, in my opinion, point to a day, not far distant perhaps, when men will read one another's thoughts, when thoughts will be conveyed directly from brain to brain without the intervention of speech, writing or any of the present known methods of communication. Putting ideas to work is a profitable business, but it makes a slight difference whether the ideas were created by you or by someone else.

"It is not unreasonable to look forward to a time when we shall see without eyes, hear without ears, and talk without tongues.

"Briefly, the hypothesis that mind can communicate directly with mind rests on the theory that thought or vital force is a form of electrical disturbance, that it can be taken up by induction and transmitted to a distance either through a wire or simply through the all pervading ether, as in the case of wireless telegraph waves.

"There are many analogies which suggest that thought is of the nature of an electrical disturbance. A nerve which is of the same substance as the brain is an excellent conductor of the electric current. When we first passed an electrical current through the nerves of a dead man, we were shocked and amazed to see him sit up and move. The electrified nerves produced contraction of the muscles very much as in life."

Thought Is Electric

"The nerves appear to act upon the muscles very much as the electric current acts upon an electromagnet. The current magnetizes a bar of iron placed at right angles to it, and the nerves produce, through the intangible current of vital force that flows through them, contraction of the muscular fibers that are arranged at right angles to them.

"It would be possible to cite many reasons why thought and vital force may be regarded as of the same nature as electricity. The electric current is held to be a wave motion of the ether—the hypothetical substance that fills all space and pervades all substances. We believe that there must be ether, because without it the electric current could not pass through a vacuum, or sunlight through space. It is reasonable to believe that only a wave motion of a similar character can produce the phenomena of thought and vital force. We may assume that the brain cells act as a battery and that the current produced flows along the nerves.

"But does it end there? Does it not pass out of the body in waves which flow around the world unperceived by our senses, just as the wireless waves passed unperceived before Hertz and others discovered their existence?"

This author has proved, to his own satisfaction at least, that every human brain is both a broadcasting and a receiving station for vibrations of thought frequency.

If this theory should turn out to be a fact, and methods of reasonable control should be established, imagine the part it would play in the gathering, classifying, and organizing of knowledge. The possibility, much less the probability, of such a reality staggers the mind of man!

Thomas Paine was one of the great minds of the American Revolutionary period. To him we give credit, more perhaps than to any other one person, for both the beginning and the happy ending of the Revolution. For it was his keen mind that helped both in drawing up the Declaration of Independence and in persuading the signers of that document to translate it into reality.

Whose Thoughts Made Paine a Genius?

In speaking of the source of his great storehouse of knowledge, Paine thus described it:

"Any person who has made observations on the state of progress of the human mind, by observing his own, cannot but have observed that there are two distinct classes of what are called thoughts: Those that we produce in ourselves by reflection and the act of thinking, and those that bolt into the mind of their own accord. I have always made it a rule to treat these voluntary visitors with civility, taking care to examine, as well as I was able, if they were worth entertaining; and it is from them I have acquired almost all the knowledge that I have. As to the learning that any person gains from school education, it serves only like a small capital, to put him in the way of beginning learning for himself afterward. Every person of learning is finally his own teacher, the reason for which is that principles, being of a distinct quality to circumstances, cannot be impressed upon the memory; their place of mental residence is the understanding, and they are never so lasting as when they begin by conception."

In the foregoing words Paine described a phenomenon that at one time or another is the experience of every person. Who is so unfortunate as not to have received positive evidence that thoughts and even complete ideas will "pop" into the mind from the outside sources?

What means of conveyance is there for such visitors except the air? It is the medium of conveyance for all known forms of vibration such as sound, light, and heat. Why would it not be, also, the medium of conveyance of the vibration of thought?

Every Mind Is Connected

Every mind, or brain, is directly connected with every other brain. Every thought released by any brain may be instantly picked up and interpreted by all other brains that are in rapport with the sending brain. This author is as sure of this fact as he is that the chemical formula H_2O will produce water.

It is the belief of this author that every thought vibration released by any brain is picked up in the atmosphere and kept in motion in circuitous wavelengths. The length of the wave depends on the intensity of the energy used in releasing the thought. These vibrations remain in motion, and are one of the two sources of the thoughts that so often "pop" into one's mind. The other source is the direct and immediate contact with the brain that is releasing the thought vibration.

If this theory is a fact, the boundless space of the whole universe is literally a library containing all the thoughts released by humankind.

This is the basis for one of the most important points made in this chapter.

According to scientists, most of the useful knowledge available to the human race has been preserved and accurately recorded in Nature's bible: the earth. By turning back the pages of this unalterable bible, we may read the story of the terrific struggle that produced this civilization. The pages of this bible are made up of the physical elements of earth and the other planets, and of the atmosphere that contains them. By turning back the pages written on stone and on the surface of this earth, we have uncovered the bones, skeletons, footprints, and other unmistakable evidence of the history of animal life through many epochs and eras. The evidence is plain and unmistakable. The great stone pages of Nature's bible constitute an authentic source of communication between the Creator and humankind. This earth bible was begun before humans had reached the thinking stage—indeed, before the amoeba stage of development was reached.

This bible is above and beyond the power of humans to alter. Moreover, it tells its story in universal language.

Vibrations, Waves, and Thoughts

Though we take them for granted, we must not fail to see the marvel in the everyday miracles at our disposal. Our ancestors could not have imagined that ordinary vibrations such as those made by a human voice hitting a thin metal plate could be converted to sounds emerging from a radio in a distant home. The electric waves that are created from these vibrations move out in all directions at the speed of light, 186,000 miles (300,000 km) per second. Similarly, our television sets pick up radio waves and turn them back into sound and pictures. Our telephones permit vibrating electric signals to flow in an electromagnet inside the receiver, making a steel diaphragm vibrate and emit sound.

These everyday realities—the instantaneous transmission of sound vibrations—make it easier for us to see the transmission of thought vibrations from mind to mind as equally real.

The Master Mind: Two Creating a Mighty Third

We're now ready to look at another way we can gather, classify, and organize the useful knowledge that is essential for success. This is the alliance of two minds, which creates a third. We call that the Master Mind.

We first heard the term "Master Mind" from one of the richest and most powerful men in history: Andrew Carnegie. It's an abstract principle that deals with the effect of one mind upon other minds.

I am among those who believe that the mind is made up of the same energy that fills the universe. But since all minds are not the same, some minds clash the moment they come in contact with each other, because there are varying degrees of affinity and antagonism.

Some minds are so naturally adapted to each other that "love at first sight" is the inevitable outcome of the contact. Who has not known such an experience? In other cases minds are so antagonistic that violent mutual dislike shows itself at first meeting. These results occur without a word being spoken, and without the slightest signs of any of the usual reasons for love and hate. Whatever the reason, there seems to be an actual chemical reaction, and the resulting vibrations have either a pleasant or an unpleasant effect.

The "meeting of two minds" is an effect that is obvious to even the casual observer. This effect must have a cause like any other, and it resides in the new field created by the meeting, where the two minds are rearranging themselves. Both states of mind are different from what they were prior to their meeting. That this reaction takes place in every instance is a known fact, which gives us a starting point from which we may show what is meant by the term "Master Mind."

A Master Mind may be created through the bringing together, or blending, in a spirit of perfect harmony, of two or more minds. Out of this harmonious blending, the chemistry of the mind creates a third mind, which may be appropriated and used by one or all of the individual minds. This Master Mind will remain available as long as the friendly, harmonious alliance between the individual minds exists. It will disintegrate and all evidence of its existence disappear the moment the friendly alliance is broken.

This principle of mind chemistry is the basis and cause of practically all the incidents of "soul mates" meeting and "eternal triangles" formed. Divorce courts, tabloids, and scandal aside, these dramatic situations are in fact evidence of one of the greatest of Nature's Laws.

The entire civilized world knows that the first two or three years of marriage are often marked by much disagreement of a more or less petty nature. These are the years of "adjustment." If the marriage survives them, it is more than apt to become a permanent alliance. These facts no experienced married person will deny. Again we see the effect without understanding the cause.

While there are other contributing causes, this period of adjustment during the early years of marriage takes place because the chemistry of the two minds is slow in blending harmoniously. When first they meet, the mental energies of the two minds are often neither extremely friendly nor antagonistic. Through constant association they adapt themselves, gradually achieving harmony, except in the rare cases where open hostility exists.

It is a well-known fact that after a man and a woman have lived together for ten to fifteen years, they become practically indispensable to each other, even though there may not be the slightest evidence of the state of mind called love. Moreover, this association and sexual relationship not only develops a natural affinity between the two minds, it actually causes the two people to take on a similar facial expression and to closely resemble each other in many other marked ways. Any competent analyst of human nature can easily go into a crowd of strange people and pick out the wife after having been introduced to her husband. The expression of the eyes, the contour of the faces, and the tone of the voices of the people who have long been associated in marriage become similar to a marked degree.

Any experienced public speaker may quickly interpret the manner in which statements from the podium are accepted by the audience, so powerful is the effect of the chemistry of the human mind. Antagonism in the mind of but one person in an audience of one thousand may be readily detected by the speaker who has learned how to "feel" and register the effects of antagonism. Moreover, the public speaker can make these interpretations without observing, or in any manner being influenced by, the expressions on the faces of those in the audience. An audience may cause such a speaker to rise to great heights of oratory, or heckle the speaker into failure, without making a sound or denoting a single facial expression.

All master salespeople recognize the moment the "psychological time for closing" has arrived; not by what the prospective buyer says, but from the effect of mind chemistry as interpreted or "felt." Words often belie the intentions of those speaking them, but a correct interpretation of the chemistry of the mind leaves no loophole for such a possibility. Everyone practiced at sales knows that the majority of buyers have a habit of affecting a negative attitude almost to the very climax of a sale.

Every able lawyer has developed a sixth sense in order to "feel" his or her way through the most artfully selected words of the clever witness who is lying. Such a lawyer will correctly interpret that which is in the mind of the witness through the chemistry of the mind.

Many lawyers have developed this ability without knowing the real source of it; they possess the technique without the scientific understanding upon which it is based. Many salespeople have done the same thing.

One who is gifted in the art of correctly interpreting the chemistry of the minds of others may, figuratively speaking, walk in at the front door of the "mansion" of a given mind and leisurely explore the entire building, denoting all its details, walking out again with a complete picture of the interior of the mental building, without the owner of the building knowing that he has entertained a visitor.

That's the principle of mind chemistry. We have proven, with the aid of the reader's own everyday experiences and observations, that the moment two minds come within close range of each other, a noticeable mental change takes place in both. Sometimes the change registers as antagonism and at other times as friendliness. Every mind has what might be termed an electric field. The nature of this field varies, depending upon the "mood" of the individual mind and upon the nature of the chemistry of the mind creating the electric field.

It is believed by this author that the normal or natural condition of the chemistry of any individual mind is the combined result of physical heredity and the nature of the thoughts that have dominated that mind.

Every mind is continuously changing, to the extent that the individual's philosophy and general habits of thought change the chemistry of his or her mind. These principles the author believes to be true. That any individual may voluntarily change the chemistry of his or her mind so that it will either attract or repel all with whom it comes in contact is a known fact! To put it another way, anyone may assume a mental attitude that will attract and please others or repel and antagonize them, and this without the aid of words, or facial expression, or other form of bodily movement or demeanor.

Go back, now, to the definition of a "Master Mind"—a mind that grows out of the blending and coordination of two or more minds, in a spirit of perfect harmony, and you will catch the full significance of the word "harmony" as it is here used. Two minds will not blend, nor can they be coordinated, unless the element of perfect harmony is present. Therein lies the secret of success or failure for practically all business and social partnerships.

Every sales manager and every military commander and every leader in another walk of life understands the necessity of "esprit de corps"—a spirit of common understanding and cooperation—in the attainment of success. This mass spirit of harmony of purpose is obtained through discipline, voluntary or forced. The nature of this discipline must be such that the individual minds become blended into a Master Mind, by which is meant that the chemistry of the individual minds is modified in such a manner that these minds blend and function as one.

The methods through which this "blending" process takes place are as numerous as are the individuals engaged in the various forms of leadership. Every leader has his or her own method of coordinating the minds of the followers. One will use force. Another uses persuasion. One will play upon the fear of penalties, while another plays upon rewards, in order to reduce the individual minds of given groups of people to where they may be blended into a unified mind. The student will not have to search deeply into history of statesmanship, politics, business, or finance in order to discover the technique employed by the leaders in these fields in the process of blending the minds of individuals into a harmonious single mind.

The really great leaders of the world, however, seem to have been provided by Nature with such a favorable mind chemistry that it acts as a nucleus of attraction for other minds. Napoleon was a notable example of a man possessing a type of mind so magnetic that it had a very decided tendency to attract all minds with which it came in contact. Soldiers followed Napoleon to certain death without flinching, because of the impelling or attracting nature of his personality, and that personality was nothing more or less than the chemistry of his mind.

No group of minds can be blended into a Master Mind if one of the individuals of that group possesses an extremely negative, repellent mind. The negative and positive minds will not blend in the sense here described as a Master Mind. Lack of knowledge of this fact has brought many an otherwise able leader to defeat.

Any leader who understands this principle of mind chemistry may temporarily blend the minds of practically any group of people, so that they will represent a mass mind, but the composition will disintegrate almost the very moment the leader's presence is removed from the group. The most successful life insurance sales organizations and other sales forces meet once a week, or more often, for the purpose of merging the individual minds into a Master Mind that will, for a limited number of days, serve as a stimulus to the individual minds!

It may be true, and generally is true, that the leaders of these groups do not understand what actually takes place in these meetings, which are usually given over to talks by the leader and other members of the group. While that is going on, the minds of the individuals are "contacting" and recharging one another.

The brain of a human being may be compared to an electric battery, in that it will become exhausted or run-down, causing the owner of it to feel despondent, discouraged, and lacking in energy. Who is so fortunate as never to have had such a feeling? When in this depleted condition, the human brain must be recharged, and the manner in which this is done is through contact with a more vital mind or minds. The great leaders understand the necessity of this "recharging" process, and they understand how to accomplish it. This knowledge is the main feature that distinguishes a leader from a follower!

Fortunate is the person who understands this principle sufficiently well to keep his or her brain vitalized or "recharged" by periodically contacting it with a more vital mind. Sexual contact is one of the most effective of the stimuli through which a mind may be recharged, provided the contact is intelligently made between two people who have genuine affection for each other. Any other sort of sexual relationship is a devitalizer of the mind.

At this point it seems appropriate to call attention to the fact that all of the great leaders, whatever their walks of life, have been and are people of highly sexed natures. (The word "sex" is a decent word. You'll find it in all the dictionaries.)

There is a growing tendency on the part of the best-informed physicians and other health practitioners to accept the theory that all diseases begin when the brain of the individual is in a depleted or devitalized state. Stated in another way, it is a known fact that a person who has a perfectly vitalized brain is practically, if not entirely, immune from all manner of disease.

Every intelligent health practitioner, of whatever school or type, knows that "Nature," or the mind, cures disease in every instance where a cure is affected. Medicines, faith, laying on of hands, chiropractic, osteopathy, and all other forms of outside stimulant are nothing more than artificial aids to Nature. To state it correctly, they are mere methods of setting the chemistry of the mind into motion so that it readjusts the cells and tissues of the body, revitalizes the brain, and otherwise causes the human machine to function normally.

The most orthodox practitioner should admit the truth of this statement.

What, then, may be the possibilities of the future in the field of mind chemistry?

Through the principle of the harmonious blending of minds, perfect health may be enjoyed. Through the aid of this same principle, sufficient power may also be developed to solve the problems of economic necessity that constantly press upon every individual.

We may judge the future possibilities of mind chemistry by taking inventory of its past achievements, keeping in mind the fact that these achievements have been largely the result of accidental discovery and of chance groupings of minds.

Is it not strange that nowhere in history do we find a record of one great man who attained his greatness through deceit, trickery, and by double-crossing his business associates?

We are approaching the time when the professoriat of the universities will teach mind chemistry the same as other subjects are now taught. Meanwhile, study and experimentation in connection with this subject open vistas of possibility for the individual student.

The Mind and Money

That mind chemistry may be appropriately applied to the workaday affairs of the economic and commercial world is a demonstrable fact.

Through the blending of two or more minds, in a spirit of perfect harmony, the principle of mind chemistry may be made to develop sufficient power to enable the individuals whose minds have been thus blended to perform seemingly superhuman feats. Power is the force with which men achieve success in any undertaking. Power, in unlimited quantities, may be enjoyed by any group of people. These people must, however, be wise enough to submerge their own personalities and their own immediate individual interests, in order to blend their minds in a spirit of perfect harmony.

Observe the frequency with which the word "harmony" appears throughout this introduction! There can be no development of a Master Mind where this element of perfect harmony does not exist. The individual units of one mind will not blend with the individual units of another mind until the two minds have been aroused and warmed, as it were, by a perfect harmony of purpose. The moment two minds begin to take divergent roads of interest, the individual units of each mind separate, and the third element, known as the "Master Mind," that grew out of the friendly or harmonious alliance, will disintegrate.

We come now to the study of some well-known people who have accumulated great power (also great fortunes) through the application of the Master Mind.

Let us begin with three of history's greatest men, known to be men of great achievement in their respective fields of business and professional endeavor.

Their names are Henry Ford, Thomas A. Edison, and Harvey Firestone.

In his time, Henry Ford was the most financially powerful of the three. I will go further and say that many who studied Ford believed him to be the most powerful man who lived at the time. As far as is known, Ford is the only man who ever lived with sufficient power to outwit the money trust of the United States. It was said at the time that Ford gathered large amounts of money as a child gathered sand on a beach, easier than most people's ability to raise a month's rent. People marveled at his ability to send out a call and raise a billion dollars within a week. Edison, as everyone knows, was a philosopher, scientist, and inventor. He was also perhaps the keenest bible student on earth . . . Nature's bible, that is. He harnessed and combined Mother Nature's wisdom for the good of mankind, more than any person now living or who ever lived. It was he who brought together the point of a needle and a piece of revolving wax in such a way that the vibration of the human voice was first recorded and reproduced.

It was Edison who first harnessed the lightning and made it serve as a light for man's use, through the aid of the incandescent electric lightbulb.

It was Edison who gave the world the motion picture.

These are but a few of his outstanding achievements. These modern "miracles," performed in the bright light of science, transcend all the "miracles" described by Jules Verne and others in books of fiction at the time.

Firestone, who was the moving spirit of the great Firestone Tire Company, whose industrial achievements in the automotive industry are legendary.

All three men began their careers, business and professional, without capital and with but little schooling of that type usually referred to as "education." And all three ended their lives and careers as well-educated people. All three were enormously wealthy and powerful.

Now let us inquire into the source of their wealth and power. Thus far we have been dealing only with effect, whereas the true philosopher wishes to understand the "cause" of a given effect.

Ford, Edison, and Firestone were close personal friends for many years. Early in their careers they were in the habit of going away to the woods once a year for a period of rest, meditation, and recuperation.

Perhaps not even the great men themselves realized that their minds had become blended during those periods of retreat into a Master Mind that was the real source of each man's individual power. This mass mind—a product of the coordinated individual minds of Ford, Edison, and Firestone—enabled these men to "tune in" to forces and sources of knowledge with which most people are totally unfamiliar.

If there is doubt about either the principle or the effects here described, let the student remember that more than half the theory here set forth is based on known facts. For example, it is known that these three men wielded great power. It is known that they were extremely wealthy. It is known that they began without capital and with little schooling. It is known that they formed periodic mind contacts. It is known that they were harmonious and friendly. It is known that their achievements were so outstanding as to make it impossible to compare them with those of their peers. All these facts are known to practically every schoolchild in the civilized world; of this there can be no dispute.

There's another major fact connected with the "cause" of the achievements of Edison, Ford, and Firestone of which we may be sure: these achievements are in no way based upon trickery, deceit, or any other form of unnatural law. Neither did these men possess secret knowledge of any particular magic. They worked with natural laws that, for the most part, are well known to all economists and leaders in the field of science, with the possible exception of the law upon which chemistry of the mind is based. Though more study of the power of the mind goes on every year, it's not officially a "science" in the traditional sense.

The Master Mind intuitively used to such advantage by Ford, Firestone, and Edison may be created by any group of people who will coordinate their minds in a spirit of perfect harmony. The group may consist of any number from two upward. Best results appear available from the blending of six or seven minds.

It has been suggested that Jesus Christ discovered how to make use of the principle of mind chemistry, and that His seemingly miraculous performances grew out of the power He developed through the blending of the minds of His twelve disciples. It has been pointed out that when one of the disciples broke faith (Judas Iscariot) the Master Mind immediately disintegrated and, seen in limited human terms, Jesus then met with the supreme catastrophe of His life.

When two or more people harmonize their minds and produce the effect known as a "Master Mind," each person in the group becomes vested with the power to contact with and gather knowledge through the "subconscious" minds of all the other members of the group. This power becomes immediately noticeable, having the effect of stimulating the mind to a higher rate of vibration, and otherwise evidencing itself in the form of a more vivid imagination and the consciousness of what appears to be a sixth sense. It is through this sixth sense that new ideas will "flash" into the mind. These ideas take on the nature and form of the subject dominating the mind of the individual. If the entire group has met for the purpose of discussing a given subject, ideas concerning that subject will come pouring into the minds of all present, as if an outside influence were dictating them. The minds of those participating in the Master Mind become as magnets, attracting ideas and thought stimuli of the most highly organized and practical nature—from no one knows where!

The process of mind blending here described as a Master Mind may be likened to the act of one who connects many electric batteries to a single transmission wire, thereby "stepping up" the power passing over that line by the amount of energy the batteries carry. So it is in the case of blending individual minds into a Master Mind. Each mind, through the principle of mind chemistry, stimulates all the other minds in the group, until the mind energy thus becomes so great that it penetrates and connects with the universal energy, which, in turn, touches every atom of matter in the universe.

Every public speaker has felt the influence of mind chemistry, for it is a well-known fact that as soon as the individual minds of an audience form a rapport (become attuned to the rate of vibration of another mind) with the speaker, there is a noticeable increase in the speaker's enthusiasm, and he or she often rises to heights of oratory that surprise all, including the speaker.

The first five to ten minutes of the average speech are devoted to what is known as "warming up." By this is meant the process through which the minds of the speaker and the audience are becoming blended in a spirit of perfect harmony.

Every speaker knows what happens when this state of "perfect harmony" fails to materialize upon the part of the audience.

The seemingly supernatural phenomena sometimes occurring in meetings of religious and spiritual groups are the result of the reaction, upon one another, of the minds in the group. These phenomena seldom begin to manifest themselves during the first ten to twenty minutes after the group is formed, for the reason that this is about the time required for the minds in the group to become harmonized or blended.

The "messages" received by members of such a group probably come from one of two sources, or from both, namely:

First: From the vast storehouse of the subconscious mind of some member of the group, or,

Second: From the universal storehouse of energy, in which, it is more than probable, all thought vibration is preserved.

It is a known fact that any individual may explore the store of knowledge in another's mind through this principle of mind chemistry, and it seems reasonable to suppose that this power may be extended to include contact with whatever vibrations are available, if there are any.

The theory that all the higher and more refined vibrations, such as thought, are intact and preserved, grows out of the known fact that neither matter nor energy (the two known elements of the universe) may be either created or destroyed. It is reasonable to suppose that all such vibrations will survive forever. The lower vibrations, however, probably survive for a natural life span and die out.

All the so-called geniuses probably gained their reputations because, by mere chance or otherwise, they formed alliances with other minds, enabling them to "step up" their own mind vibrations. They were then enabled to contact the vast Temple of Knowledge, where information is recorded and filed.

Moreover, as far as this author has been enabled to ascertain, all of the great geniuses were highly sexed people. The fact that sexual contact is the greatest known mind stimulant lends color to the theory herein described.

Inquiring further into the source of economic power, as manifested by the achievements of prominent people in the field of business, let us study the case of the Chicago group known as the Big Six. One of the members of this power group was William Wrigley Jr., whose name is synonymous with chewing gum, and who a hundred years ago earned the magical sum of more than $15 million a year. There was also the owner of a restaurant chain, an advertising tycoon, and the founder of an early forerunner of Federal Express. There was the owner of a taxicab company, whose name would take on enormous power in the as-yet-unborn field of rental cars—his name was Hertz.

At the time, a reliable financial reporting company estimated the yearly income of these six men at upward of $25 million, an astounding sum for those years. Analysis of this entire group of six men discloses the fact that, as with the group of three moguls discussed above, not one of them had any special educational advantages. All began without capital or extensive credit. Their financial achievements have been due to their own individual plans, and not to any fortunate turn of the wheel of chance.

Many years ago these six men formed a friendly alliance, meeting at stated periods for the purpose of assisting one another with the day-to-day running and furthering of their various industries and businesses. With the exception of two, none of the six men were in any manner associated in a legal partnership. These meetings were strictly for the purpose of cooperating on a give-and-take basis, assisting one another with ideas and suggestions.

There is something about the financial success of this particular group that is well worth comment, study, analysis, and even emulation, and that is the fact that they have learned how to coordinate their individual minds by blending them in a spirit of perfect harmony, thereby creating a Master Mind that unlocked to each individual of the group doors that are closed to most of the human race.

The United States Steel Corporation has always been one of the strongest and most powerful industrial organizations in the world. The idea out of which this great industrial giant grew was born in the mind of Elbert H. Gary, a more or less commonplace lawyer, who was born and reared in a small Illinois town near Chicago that was later named for him.

Gary also surrounded himself with a group whose minds successfully blended in a spirit of perfect harmony, thereby creating the Master Mind that became the moving spirit of the great United States Steel Corporation.

Search where you will, and wherever you find an outstanding success in business, finance, industry, or in any of the professions, you may be sure that in back of the success is some individual who has applied the principle of mind chemistry through which a Master Mind has been created. These outstanding successes often appear to be the handiwork of but one person, but search closely and the other individuals whose minds have been coordinated with his or hers may be found. Remember that it takes just two or more to operate the principle of mind chemistry that results in a Master Mind.

Power (human power, that is) is simply organized knowledge, expressed through intelligent action!

No effort can be said to be organized unless the individuals engaged in the effort coordinate their knowledge and energy in a spirit of perfect harmony. Lack of such harmonious coordination of effort is the main cause of practically every business failure.

An interesting experiment was conducted by this author in collaboration with the students of a well-known college. Each student was requested to write an essay entitled "How and Why Henry Ford Became Wealthy."

Each student was required to describe, as a part of his or her essay, what was believed to be the nature of Ford's real assets, of what these assets consisted in detail.

The majority of the students gathered financial statements and inventories of the Ford assets and used these as the basis of their estimates of Ford's wealth.

Included in these "sources of Ford's wealth" were such items as cash in banks, raw and finished materials in stock, real estate, and buildings.

One student, out of the entire group of several hundred, answered as follows (the italics are this author's):

Henry Ford's assets consist, in the main, of two items, viz: (1) Working capital and raw and finished materials; (2) *The knowledge gained from experience by Henry Ford himself, and the cooperation of a well-trained organization that understands how to apply this knowledge to best advantage from the Ford viewpoint. It is impossible to estimate, with* anything approximating correctness, the actual dollars and cents value of either of these two groups of assets, but it is my opinion that their relative values are:

The organized knowledge of the Ford Organization 75%

The value of cash and physical assets of every nature, including raw and finished materials 25%

This author is of the opinion that this statement was not compiled by the young man whose name was signed to it without the assistance of some very analytical and experienced mind or minds.

Unquestionably the biggest asset that Henry Ford had was his own brain. Next to this would come the brains of his immediate circle of associates, for it has been through the co-ordination of these that the physical assets that he controlled were accumulated.

If at the time you destroyed every plant the Ford Motor Company owned, every piece of machinery, every ton of raw or finished material, every finished automobile, and every dollar on deposit in any bank, Henry Ford would still have been the most powerful man, economically, on earth. The brains that have built the Ford business could duplicate it again in short order. Capital is always available, in unlimited quantities, to such brains as Ford's.

Economically, Ford was the most powerful man on earth because he had the keenest and most practical conception of the principle of organized knowledge of any man then on earth, as far as this author has the means of knowing.

Despite Ford's great power and financial success, though, it may be that he blundered often in the application of the principles through which he accumulated this power. There is little doubt that Ford's methods of mind coordination were often crude in the early years, before he gained the wisdom and skill that would naturally go with maturity of years.

Neither can there be little doubt that Ford's application of the principle of mind chemistry was, at least at the start, the result of a chance alliance with other minds, particularly the mind of Edison. It is more than probable that Ford's remarkable insight into the law of nature was first begun as the result of his friendly alliance with his own wife long before he ever met either Edison or Firestone. Many a man is made by his wife, through application of the Master Mind principle, who never knows the real source of his success. Mrs. Ford was a remarkably intelligent woman, and this author has reason to believe that it was her mind, blended with her husband's, that gave him his first real start toward power.

It may be mentioned, without in any way depriving Ford of any honor or glory, that in his earlier days he had to combat the powerful enemies of illiteracy and ignorance to a greater extent than did either Edison or Firestone. Both were gifted by natural heredity with a fortunate aptitude for acquiring and applying knowledge. Ford had to hew his talent out of the rough, raw timbers of his none-too-favorable heritage. Within an inconceivably short period of time Ford mastered three of the most stubborn enemies of mankind and transformed them into assets that became the very foundation of his success.

These enemies are ignorance, illiteracy, and poverty!

Any man who can stay the hand of these three savage forces, much less harness and use them to good account, is well worth close study by less fortunate individuals.

The man who has a *definite aim* in mind, and a definite plan for attaining it, has already gone nine-tenths of the way toward success.

We are undoubtedly living in an age of industrial power. The source of all this power is organized effort. A glance at any day's newspaper or attention to any news program will confirm the vast numbers of corporate, financial, or industrial mergers that have brought unprecedented power under one management.

One day it is a group of banks; another day it is phone companies, the next week newspaper chains, followed by the arranged marriages of communications giants. All are merging for the purpose of developing power through highly organized and coordinated effort.

Knowledge, general in nature and unorganized, is not power; it is only potential power—the material out of which real power may be developed. Any modern library contains an unorganized record of all the valuable knowledge the present civilization is heir to. But this knowledge is not power because it is not organized.

Every form of energy and every species of animal or plant life must be organized in order to survive. The oversized animals whose bones have filled Nature's boneyard through extinction have left mute but certain evidence that nonorganization means annihilation.

Everything from the electron to the largest star in the universe, and every material thing in between these extremes, offers proof positive that one of Nature's first laws is that of organization. Fortunate is the individual who recognizes the importance of this law and makes it his or her business to become familiarized with the various ways this great law works.

Those who are astute in business have not only recognized the importance of the law of organized effort but have made this law the warp and woof of their power.

Without any knowledge whatsoever of the principle of mind chemistry, many have accumulated great power by merely organizing the knowledge they possessed. The majority of all who have discovered the principle of mind chemistry and developed that principle into a "Master Mind" have stumbled upon this knowledge by the merest of accidents, often failing to recognize the real nature of their discovery or understand the source of their power.

This author is of the opinion that all living persons currently making conscious use of the principle of mind chemistry in developing power through the blending of minds may be counted on the fingers of two hands, with perhaps several fingers left to spare.

If this estimate is even approximately true, the student will readily see that there is but slight danger of the field of mind chemistry practice becoming overcrowded.

It is a well-known fact that one of the most difficult tasks that any businessperson must perform is that of inducing associates to coordinate their efforts in a spirit of harmony. To induce continuous cooperation between a group of workers in any undertaking is next to impossible. Only the most efficient leaders can accomplish this highly desired object, but once in a great while such a leader will rise above the horizon in the field of industry, business, or finance, and then the world hears of a Henry Ford, Thomas A. Edison, or John D. Rockefeller.

"Power" and "success" are synonymous terms!

One grows out of the other. Therefore, any person with the knowledge and the ability to develop power through the harmonious coordination of individuals may be successful in any reasonable undertaking.

It must not be presumed that a Master Mind will immediately spring, mushroom-fashion, out of every group of minds that make a pretense of coordination in a spirit of harmony.

Harmony, in the real sense of the meaning of the word, is as rare among groups of people as is genuine Christianity among those who proclaim themselves Christians.

Harmony is the nucleus around which the state of mind known as the "Master Mind" must be developed. Without this element of harmony there can be no Master Mind, a truth which cannot be repeated too often.

When President Woodrow Wilson proposed the League of Nations, the precursor to the United Nations, he had in mind the development of a Master Mind, a blending of international minds. Wilson's conception was the most far-reaching humanitarian idea ever created in the mind of man at the time, because it dealt with a principle that embraces sufficient power to establish a real Brotherhood of Man on earth.

The greatest future unity of minds will be measured largely by the time required for the great universities and nonsectarian institutions of learning to supplant ignorance and superstition with understanding and wisdom. This time is rapidly approaching.

The Psychology of the Revival Meeting

The old religious orgy known as the "revival" offers a favorable opportunity to study the principle of mind chemistry known as "Master Mind."

It will be observed that music plays no small part in bringing about the harmony essential to the blending of a group of minds in a revival meeting. Without music, the revival meeting would be a tame affair.

During revival services, the leader of the meeting has no difficulty in creating harmony in the minds of his devotees, but it is a well-known fact that this state of harmony lasts no longer than the presence of the leader, after which the Master Mind he has temporarily created disintegrates.

By arousing the emotional nature of his followers, the revivalist has no difficulty, under the proper stage setting and with the embellishment of the right sort of music, in creating a Master Mind that becomes noticeable to all who come in contact with it. The very air becomes charged with a positive, pleasing influence that changes the entire chemistry of all minds present.

The revivalist calls this energy the "Spirit of the Lord."

This author, through experiments conducted with a group of scientific investigators and laymen who were unaware of the nature of the experiment, has created the same state of mind and the same positive atmosphere without calling it the "Spirit of the Lord."

On many occasions this author has witnessed the creation of the same positive atmosphere in a group of men and women engaged in the business of salesmanship, without calling it the "Spirit of the Lord."

The author helped conduct a school of salesmanship for Harrison Parker, founder of the Cooperative Society of Chicago, and, by the use of the same principle of mind chemistry that the revivalist calls the "Spirit of the Lord," so transformed the nature of a group of 3,000 men and women (all of them were without former sales experience) that they sold more than $10 million worth of securities in less than nine months, and earned more than one million dollars for themselves, at a time when people were earning only a fraction of that amount.

It was found that the average person who joined this school would reach the zenith of his or her selling power within one week, after which it was necessary to revitalize the individual's brain through a group sales meeting. These sales meetings were conducted on very much the same order as the modern revival meeting, with much the same stage equipment, including music and high-powered speakers that exhorted the salespeople in very much the revival manner.

Call it psychology, mind chemistry, or anything you please (they are all based upon the same principle), there is nothing more certain than the fact that wherever a group of minds are brought into contact in a spirit of perfect harmony, each mind in the group becomes immediately supplemented and reinforced by a noticeable energy called a "Master Mind."

For all this writer professes to know, this uncharted energy may be the "Spirit of the Lord," but it operates just as favorably when called by any other name.

The human brain and nervous system constitute a piece of intricate machinery which few, if any, understand. When controlled and properly directed, this piece of machinery can be made to perform wonders of achievement and, if not controlled, it will perform in quite another fantastic manner, as may be seen by examining the inmates of any insane asylum.

The human brain has a direct connection with a continuous influx of energy, from which man derives his power to think. The brain receives this energy, mixes it with the energy created by the food taken into the body, and distributes it to every portion of the body through the aid of the blood and the nervous system. It thus becomes what we call life.

From what source this outside energy comes, no one seems to know. All we know about it is that we must have it or die. It seems reasonable to presume that this energy flows into the body along with the oxygen from the air, as we breathe.

Every normal human body possesses a first-class chemical laboratory and a stock of chemicals sufficient to carry on the business of breaking up, assimilating, and properly mixing and compounding the food we take into the body, preparatory to distributing it to wherever it is needed as a bodybuilder.

Ample tests have been made, both with man and beast, to prove that the energy known as the mind plays an important part in the chemical operation of compounding and transforming food into the required substances to build and keep the body in repair.

It is known that worry, excitement, or fear will interfere with the digestive process, and in extreme cases stop this process altogether, resulting in illness or death. It is obvious, then, that the mind enters into the chemistry of food digestion and distribution.

It is believed by many eminent authorities, although it may never have been scientifically proven, that the energy known as thought may become contaminated with negative units to such an extent that the whole nervous system is thrown out of working order, digestion is interfered with, and various and sundry forms of disease manifest themselves. Such disturbed minds produce financial difficulties and unrequited love affairs, among other things. A negative environment—for instance, where some member of the family is constantly nagging—will interfere with the chemistry of the mind to such an extent that an individual will lose ambition and gradually sink into oblivion. This is the basis of the old saying that one spouse may either "make" or "break" the other.

Any high school student knows that certain food combinations will, if taken into the stomach, result in indigestion, violent pain, and even death. Good health depends, in part at least, upon a food combination that "harmonizes." But harmony of food combination is not sufficient to ensure good health. There must also be harmony between the units of energy that make up the mind.

Harmony is one of Nature's laws, without which there can be no such thing as organized energy, or life in any form whatsoever.

The health of the body as well as the mind is built upon the principle of harmony! The energy known as life begins to disintegrate and death approaches when the organs of the body stop working in harmony.

The moment harmony ceases at the source of any form of organized energy (power), units of that energy are thrown into a chaotic state of disorder and the power is rendered neutral or passive.

Harmony is also the nucleus around which the principle of mind chemistry known as a "Master Mind" develops power. Destroy this harmony and you destroy the power growing out of the coordinated effort of a group of individual minds. This truth has been stated, re-stated, and presented in every manner that the author could conceive, with continual repetition. For unless the student grasps this principle and learns to apply it, this treatise on the Master Mind is useless.

Success in life, no matter what one may call success, is very largely a matter of adaptation to environment so that there is harmony between the individual and the environment. The palace of a king comes to resemble a hovel of a peasant if harmony does not abound within its walls. Conversely stated, the hut of a peasant may be made to yield more happiness than that of the mansion of the rich man if harmony obtains in the former and not in the latter.

Without perfect harmony the science of astronomy would be as useless as a set of old bones, because the stars and planets would clash with one another, and all would be in a state of chaos and disorder.

Without the law of harmony the blood might take the food meant to grow fingernails and deposit it on the scalp, where hair is supposed to grow. That horny growth might easily be mistaken by the superstitious to signify man's relationship to a certain imaginary gentleman with horns.

Without the law of harmony there can be no organization of knowledge, for what, may one ask, is organized knowledge except the harmony of facts and truths and natural laws?

The moment discord begins to creep in at the front door, harmony edges out at the back door, so to speak, whether the application is made to a business partnership or the orderly movement of the planets of the heavens.

If the student has the impression that the author is laying undue stress upon the importance of harmony, let it be remembered that lack of harmony is the first, and often the last and only, cause of failure!

There can be no poetry, no music, no oratory worthy of notice without the presence of harmony.

Good architecture is largely a matter of harmony. Without harmony a house is nothing but a mass of building material, more or less a monstrosity.

Sound business management plants the very sinews of its existence in harmony.

Every well-dressed man or woman is a living picture and a moving example of harmony.

With all these workaday illustrations of the importance of harmony in the affairs of the world, not to say in the operation of the entire universe, how could any intelligent person leave harmony out of his "Definite Aim" in life? You might as well have no "Definite Aim" at all if you omit harmony as the chief stone of its foundation.

The human body is a complex organization of organs, glands, blood vessels, nerves, brain cells, muscles, and so on. The mind energy that stimulates to action and coordinates the efforts of the component parts of the body is also a plurality of ever-varying and changing energies. From birth until death there is a continuous struggle, often assuming the nature of open combat, between the forces of the mind. For example, the lifelong struggle between the motivating forces and desires of the human mind that take place between the impulses of right and wrong are well known to everyone.

Every human being possesses at least two distinct mind powers or personalities, and as many as six distinct personalities have been discovered in one person. One of man's most delicate tasks is that of harmonizing these mind forces so that they may be organized and directed toward the orderly attainment of a given objective. Without this element of harmony no individual can become an accurate thinker.

It is no wonder that leaders in business and industrial enterprises, as well as those in other fields of endeavor, find it so difficult to organize groups of people so they will function without friction in the attainment of a given objective. Each individual human being possesses forces, within himself, that are hard to harmonize, even when he is placed in the environment most favorable to harmony. If the chemistry of the individual's mind is such that the units of his mind cannot be easily harmonized, think how much more difficult it must be to harmonize a group of minds so they will function as one, in an orderly manner, through what is known as a "Master Mind."

The leader who successfully develops and directs the energies of a Master Mind must possess tact, patience, persistence, self-confidence, intimate knowledge of mind chemistry, and the ability to adapt himself (in a state of perfect poise and harmony) to quickly changing circumstances without showing the least sign of annoyance.

How many are there who can measure up to this requirement?

The successful leader must possess the ability to change the color of his or her mind, chameleon-like, to fit every circumstance that arises in connection with the object of leadership. Moreover, such a leader must possess the ability to change from one mood to another without showing the slightest signs of anger or lack of self-control. The successful leader must understand the Seventeen Laws of Success and be able to put into practice any combination of these laws whenever occasion demands.

Without this ability no leader can be powerful, and without power no leader can long endure.

The Real Meaning of Education

There has long been a general misconception of the meaning of the word "educate." The dictionaries have not aided in the elimination of this misunderstanding, because they have defined the word as an act of imparting knowledge.

Actually, the word educate has its roots in the Latin word *educo,* which means "to develop from within; to educe; to draw out; to grow through the law of use."

Nature hates idleness in all its forms. She gives continuous life only to those elements which are in use. Tie up an arm, or any other portion of the body, taking it out of use, and the idle part will soon atrophy and become lifeless. Reverse the order, give an arm more than normal use, such as that engaged in by the blacksmith who wields a heavy hammer all day long, and that arm (developed from within) grows stronger.

Power grows out of organized knowledge, but mind you, it "grows out of it" through application and use! Someone may become a walking encyclopedia of knowledge without possessing any power. This knowledge becomes power only to the extent that it is organized, classified, and put into action. Some of the best-educated people the world has known possessed much less general knowledge than some who have been known as fools, the difference between the two being that the former put what knowledge they possessed into use, while the latter made no such application.

An educated person is one who knows how to acquire everything needed in the attainment of his or her main purpose in life, without violating the rights of others. It might be a surprise to many of the so-called learned to know that they come nowhere near qualification as educated. It might also be a great surprise to many who believe they suffer from lack of "learning" to know that they are well educated.

The successful lawyer is not necessarily the one who memorizes the greatest number of principles of law. On the contrary, the successful lawyer is the one who knows where to find a principle of law, as well as a variety of opinions supporting that principle.

In other words, the successful lawyer is the one who knows where to find the law when needed.

This principle applies with equal force to the affairs of industry and business.

Henry Ford had little elementary schooling, yet he was one of the best educated men in the world. He seemed to have acquired such an ability to combine natural and economic laws, to say nothing of the minds of men, that he had the power to get anything of a material nature he wants.

During World War II, Henry Ford brought suit against the *Chicago Tribune,* charging that newspaper with libelous statements concerning him, one of which was that Ford was an "ignoramus," an ignorant pacifist, and so forth. When the suit came up for trial, the attorneys for the *Tribune* undertook to prove, by interrogating Ford himself, that their statement was true, that he was ignorant. With this aim in view, they cross-examined him in the courtroom on all manner of subjects.

One question they asked was "How many soldiers did the British send over to subdue the rebellion in the Colonies in 1776?"

With a wry grin on his face Ford nonchalantly replied, "I do not know just how many, but I have heard that it was a lot more than ever went back."

The response was loud laughter from court officers, jury, courtroom spectators, and even the frustrated lawyer who had asked the question.

This line of interrogation was continued for an hour or more, with Ford remaining perfectly calm. Finally, however, he grew tired of it. Then, in reply to a question that was particularly obnoxious and insulting, Ford straightened himself up, pointed his finger at the questioning lawyer, and replied, "If I should really wish to answer the foolish questions you have just asked, or any of the others you have been asking, let me remind you that I have a row of buttons hanging over my desk. By placing my finger on the right button, I could call in any number of people who could give me the correct answer to all the questions you have asked and to many that you have not the intelligence to either ask or answer. Now, will you kindly tell me why I should bother about filling my mind with a lot of useless details in order to answer every fool question that anyone may ask, when I have able people all about me who can supply me with all the facts I want when I call for them?"

This answer is quoted from memory, but it substantially relates Ford's answer.

There was silence in the courtroom. The questioning attorney's jaw dropped down, his eyes opened wide; the judge leaned forward from the bench and gazed in Ford's direction; many of the jury awoke and looked around as if they had heard an explosion, which in a sense they had.

Ford's reply knocked the questioner cold.

Up to the time of that reply the lawyer had been enjoying considerable fun at what he believed to be Ford's expense, by adroitly displaying his (the lawyer's) sample case of general knowledge and comparing it with what he inferred to be Ford's widespread ignorance. But that answer spoiled the lawyer's fun!

It also proved once more (to all who had the intelligence to accept the proof) that true education means mind development, not merely the gathering and classifying of knowledge.

Ford could not, in all probability, have named the capitals of all the states, but he could have, and in fact had, gathered the capital with which to turn many wheels within every state in the Union.

Education—let us not forget this—consists of the power to get everything one needs without violating the rights of others. Ford falls well within that definition.

There are many men of "learning" who could easily have entangled Ford, theoretically, with a maze of questions none of which he could have answered. But Ford could also have waged a battle in industry or finance that would run circles around those same men, with all of their abstract knowledge and wisdom.

Ford probably could not have gone into his chemical laboratory and separate water into its component atoms of hydrogen and oxygen and then recombine these atoms in their former order, but he knew how to surround himself with chemists who could have done this for him. The man who can intelligently use the knowledge possessed by another is as much or more a man of education as the person who merely has the knowledge but does not know what to do with it.

Education consists of doing—not merely of *knowing*!

The Relationship Between Sex and Genius

The sex drive is, by far, the most powerful of the eight basic motivating forces that stimulate the mind to action. Because of the importance of this subject, it has been reserved as the closing chapter of the first of the seventeen factors constituting the Law of Success.

The part that sexual urge plays in the achievement of outstanding success was first discovered by the author in his studies of the biographies of great leaders, and in his analysis of men and women of the present age who have risen high in their chosen fields of endeavor.

Most people are unpardonably ignorant when it comes to the subject of sex. It's no wonder, since sexual desire has been slandered and burlesqued by the ignorant and the vulgar for so long. Men and women who are known to be blessed with highly sexed natures are often looked upon with suspicion, though it's often secretly accompanied by envy.

During the early years of research, when this philosophy was in the embryonic stage, the author made the discovery that every great leader in art and music, in literature and statesmanship, and in practically every other walk of life was a highly sexed person. Among the group whose biographies were carefully studied, let us list the following as members of that group:

Napoleon Bonaparte

Shakespeare

George Washington

Abraham Lincoln

Ralph Waldo Emerson

Robert Burns

Thomas Jefferson

Oscar Wilde

Woodrow Wilson

Stanford White

Enrico Caruso

The sexual urge is the highest and most refined form of human emotion. It "steps up" the rate of vibration of the mind as no other emotion can, and causes the imaginative faculties of the brain to function at the level of genius. Far from being something of which one should be ashamed, a highly sexed nature is a blessing of which one should feel proud, and for which no apologies should be offered.

Sex as a Source of Genius

To be highly sexed is not sufficient, of itself, to produce a genius. Only those who understand the nature of the sexual urge, and who know how to transmute this powerful emotion into other channels of action than that of sexual contact, rise to the status of a genius. The sexual energy is a driving force compared with which all other motivating forces must take second place at best. A mind that has been aroused through intense sexual desire becomes receptive to the impulse of ideas that "flash" into the mind from outside sources. This is what is ordinarily known as "inspiration."

It is the belief of this author—a belief with considerable evidence to back it—that all so-called "revelations," of whatever nature, from religion to art, are induced by an intense desire for sexual contact. All so-called "magnetic" people are highly sexed. People who are brilliant, charming, versatile, and accomplished are generally highly sexed. Prove this for yourself by analyzing those whom you know to be highly sexed.

Destroy the capacity for strong sexual desire and you have removed all that is powerful about a human being. If you wish proof of this, observe what happens to the "spirited" stallion or any other male animal, such as a bull or a hog, after it has been altered sexually. The moment sexual urge has been destroyed in any animal, from man on down to the lowest forms of animal life, the capacity for dominating action goes with it. This is a statement of biological fact too well known to be disputed. Moreover, it is a significant and important fact.

The Therapeutic Value of Sex

It is a fact well known to scientists, although not generally known to the layman, that sexual desire has a therapeutic value not attributed to any other human emotion. This fact may be easily verified, however, by even the most casual study of the subject, by observing the physical state of the body following sexual contact between two people who have an affinity and are properly mated. The physical body becomes relaxed and calm. Relaxation, superinduced in this manner, provides the nervous system with a favorable opportunity to balance and distribute the nervous energy of the body to all the organs. Properly distributed nervous energy is the force that maintains a healthy body. Also, nervous energy, properly distributed through relaxation, eliminates the cause of physical ailments.

These briefly stated facts are not merely the author's opinion. They have been gleaned from many decades of careful research collaboration of some of the most eminent scientists known to the past and present generations. One was a well-known physician who was bold enough to admit that he had often recommended a change in sexual partners for patients who were suffering from hypochondria, which had the desired effect, one that he feels would not have been possible through any other prescription. This physician went even farther by predicting that the time was not far distant when this form of therapy would be more generally understood and used. The suggestion is here offered for what it may be worth, without comment from the author of this philosophy, other than the statement that most of the human race is still woefully ignorant of the possibilities of sexual desire and activity, not only in connection with the maintenance of health but also in connection with the creation of genius.

The significance of that fact impressed me when I made the discovery that practically every great leader whom I studied at close range was largely inspired by a powerful sexual connection. In the case of some influential men, the partner is a wife of whom the public hears but little. In a few cases the source of inspiration has been traced to the "other woman." In either case, a great, enduring love is a sufficient motive to drive even a mediocre person to unbelievable heights of achievement, a statement of fact that should be kept in mind by all such spouses, partners, and lovers.

Sexual desire, then, the stuff of songs and dreams, is the most effective known way to energize a mind to the level of Master Mind!

Ten Reasons Why the Mind Moves to Greatness

A mind stimulant is any influence that will, temporarily or permanently, "step up" the rate of vibration of the brain. All great achievements are the result of one form or another of such stimuli. People are often surprised by learning what some of these stimuli are. Here these "mind movers" are listed in order of what the author considers to be their importance.

1. Sexual contact between two people who are motivated by a genuine feeling of love.

2. Love, not necessarily accompanied by sexual contact.

3. A burning desire for fame, power, and financial gain.

4. To a highly emotional person, music is a mighty stimulant.

5. Friendship, between either those of the same sex or the opposite sex, provided it is accompanied by a desire to be mutually helpful in making progress with some definite undertaking or calling.

6. A Master Mind alliance between two or more people who ally themselves, mentally, for the purpose of mutual help, in a spirit of unselfishness.

7. Mutual suffering, such as that experienced by people who are unjustly persecuted, through racial, religious, and economic differences of opinion.

8. Autosuggestion. An individual may step up his or her own mind, through constant self-suggestion backed by a definite motive. (Perhaps this source of mind stimulation should have been placed nearer the top of the list.)

9. Suggestion. The influence of outside suggestion may lift one to great heights of achievement. If negatively used, it can dash one to the bottomless pit of failure and destruction.

10. Narcotics and alcohol. Although these are known to be sources of mind stimulation, their effects are totally destructive, leading, finally, to negation of all the other nine sources of stimulation.

Here you have a brief description of all the major sources of mind stimulation. Through these sources of stimulation one may partake of the stuff of genius by communing, temporarily, with Infinite Intelligence. Take or leave that plain and simple statement, just as you please! The statement is made as a positive fact because this author has had the privilege of helping to raise scores of mediocre men and women out of mediocrity into states of mind that placed them squarely in the category of genius. Some have been able to remain in this exalted state, while others have relapsed to their former mediocre status, either temporarily or permanently.

The author personally interviewed and analyzed an average of a dozen men and women every day for the purpose of helping them discover the most suitable source of mind stimulation and the most profitable outlet for the talent they displayed through moving their minds in these ways.

On many scores of occasions the author had the experience of seeing a client create some useful invention, or some unique plan of rendering useful service, right in the midst of the analysis.

Perhaps these analyses also produced an inadvertent Master Mind side effect! One such story out of many took place when a client named Gundelach came to see me with his wife. Not thirty minutes into the analysis, he conceived an idea for a new style of interlocking brick suitable for building public highways, an idea that contained the clear possibility of rendering useful service all over America, to say nothing of making a huge fortune for himself. Perhaps it would be more correct to say that the three of us—he and his wife and I—conceived the idea simultaneously.

Intemperance and Addiction Move the Mind . . . to Failure

Of the ten stimulants described in this chapter, only nine are safe for use, and even these cannot be used excessively. The intemperate use of alcohol and narcotics as mind stimulants is condemned without exception, on the ground that such use eventually destroys the normal functioning power of the brain. While it is true that some of the greatest literary geniuses of the past used liquor as a mind stimulant, albeit with temporary success, it is equally true that such use generally became an excess that destroyed them. Two writers of the past who are considered classics, Edgar Allan Poe and Robert Burns, used alcohol as a mind stimulant, with telling effects, but both were finally destroyed through excessive use of this form of stimulant.

Sex is the most powerful of all the mind stimulants, but this, too, may be used to excess with just as damaging effects as the excessive use of alcohol or narcotics. Excessive eating may be just as damaging as any other form of excess, and in many thousands of cases this form of indulgence destroys all possibility of great achievement.

One of the seventeen factors of the Law of Success is that of self-control. Later, when we reach that subject, we will expand on the idea that self-control is a balance wheel guarding the individual against excesses of every nature whatsoever. The three major excesses that are destroying people throughout the world today are excessive and addictive drinking and drugging, eating, and sexual behavior. One is just as fatal to success as either of the other two.

Why Most Who Succeed Do So After Forty

One prominent theory explaining why the majority of strivers don't reach success in their chosen work until the age of forty points to the extraordinary amount of energy spent on sexual activity in the earlier years. The word "dissipated" is often used to describe this phe-nomenon, since such energy is scattered and spread thin. The average young male, to use him as an example, does not learn that the sexual urge can be useful in areas other than sex-ual contact itself until he has reached the age of forty to forty-five years. Up to this age the life of the average male (in which classification the majority of all males may be properly placed) is just one long, continuous orgy of sexual intercourse, through which all his finer and more powerful emotions are sown wildly to the four winds. This is not merely the opin-ion of this author; it is a statement of fact based upon careful analysis of over 20,000 people. In-telligent study and analysis of twenty thousand people gives a very accurate cross-section classification of the entire human race.

Between overeating and overindulgence in sexual contact, the average man has but little energy left for other uses until he has passed the age of forty. In altogether too many in-stances men never gain mastery of themselves at all, in these two areas of weakness. A sad statement of fact is the truth that the majority of men do not look upon overindulgence in eating and in sexual contact as being dangerous excesses that destroy their chances of success in life. There is no argument over the detrimental effects of excessive use of alcohol and nar-cotics, as everyone knows that such overindulgence is fatal to success, but not everyone knows that excesses in sexual contact and in eating can be just as ruinous.

The desire for sexual contact is the strongest, most powerful, and most impelling of all human desires. It's for this very reason that it may be harnessed and transmuted into chan-nels other than that of sexual contact in a manner that will raise one to great heights of ge-nius. On the other hand, this powerful urge, if not controlled and so transmuted, may and often does lower man to the level of an ordinary beast.

In closing this chapter, may the author not offer a word of reply to those who may feel that even the very brief reference here made to the subject of sex might be harmful to young men and women? The reply is this: Ignorance of the subject of sex, due to lack of free discussion of the subject by those who really understand it, has resulted in destructive use of the sexual drive all through the ages. Moreover, if anyone should feel that this brief reference might hurt the morals of the young people of this generation, let that person keep in mind the fact that most young people get their sex education from less commendable sources than a book of this nature, and such education is generally accompanied by inter-pretations of the power of sex which in no way relate the subjects of sex and genius. These sources of sex information in no manner even suggest that there is such a possibility as the transmutation of sex power into art and literary works of the most commendable order, as well as into business leadership and a multitude of other constructive forms of helpful service. This is an age of frank discussion of the great mysteries of life, among which the subject of sex may be properly classified. Finally, the urge of sex is biological in nature and it cannot be suppressed through silence! In truth, the emotion of sexual urge is the finest of all human emotions, and the sexual relationship the most beautiful of all relationships. Why, then, cast the slurring innuendo that the sexual relationship is something ugly and vulgar by trying to shroud the subject in a dark background of silence?

This ends the subject of the Master Mind. We pass next to the discussion of the second of the seventeen factors of the Law of Success, with both apology and regret that this lack of space forbids us to discuss the remaining sixteen subjects as extensively as we have covered the subject of the Master Mind.

THE IMPORTANCE OF A DEFINITE AIM

To be successful in any sort of endeavor, you must have a definite goal. You must have definite plans for attaining this goal. Nothing is ever accomplished that is worthwhile without a definite plan of procedure that is systematically and continuously followed out day by day.

A definite chief aim is placed at the beginning of the Seventeen Laws of Success for the reason that without it the other Sixteen Laws would be useless. For how could one hope to succeed, or how could one know when success had been reached, if the nature of the accomplishment—the goal—had never been determined?

During the past twenty-odd years during which the author has analyzed more than 20,000 people from nearly all walks of life, 95 percent of these people were failures, startling as that may be. By this is meant that they were barely making enough on which to exist, some of them not even doing this well. The other 5 percent were successful, meaning by "success" that they were making enough for all their needs and saving money for the sake of ultimate financial independence.

Now, the significant thing about this discovery was that the 5 percent who were succeeding had a definite chief aim and also a plan for attaining that aim. In other words, those who knew what they wanted, and had a plan for getting it, were succeeding, while those who did not know what they wanted were getting just that—nothing!

If sales is the game, or a steady flow of paying customers is the aim, clear and definite methods of handling customers that will cause them to return and return must be built into a plan. The plan may be one thing, or it may be something else, but in the main it should be distinctive and of such a nature that it will impress itself upon the minds of patrons in a favorable manner. Anyone can hand out merchandise to those who come voluntarily and ask for it, but not everyone has acquired the art of delivering, along with the merchandise, that unseen "something" that causes the customer to repeatedly come back for more. Here is where the necessity of a definite aim and a definite plan for attaining it enters.

In certain neighborhoods, auto repair shops are as common as convenience stores. There may be little difference between the quality received at one and that received at another. Despite this fact, however, there are car owners who will drive miles out of their way to get their car serviced at a favorite shop.

Now the question arises "What causes these people to do this?"

And the answer is "People trade at businesses where they are served by those who cultivate them." What is meant by "cultivate them"? How do you cultivate a plant? Not by doing only the essentials, such as watering. You "deadhead" it, removing dead or dying parts; you are attentive to the season, giving it extra food because the calendar suggests it. You notice if it has bugs and you remove them. Any good business owner is such a gardener. One who knows your car will notice when the tires are balding or the belts fraying, when the antifreeze needs adding to, or the right turn signal light has blown. In these and scores of other ways, a good business owner impresses the customer with the fact that this is personal service, and can be trusted. All this does not "just happen." There is a definite plan and also a definite purpose in doing it, and that purpose is to bring motorists back and back. This is a brief statement of what is meant by a definite chief aim.

Let us now go a bit deeper into the study of the psychological principle upon which the law of a definite chief aim is based. Careful study of more than one hundred leaders in practically all walks of life has disclosed the fact that every one of them worked with a definite chief aim and also a definite plan for its attainment.

The human mind is something like a magnet in that it will attract the counterparts of the dominating thoughts held in the mind, and especially those which constitute a definite chief aim. For example, if someone establishes, as a definite chief aim, and as a daily working purpose, the adding of, say, one hundred new customers who will regularly purchase a given merchandise or service, immediately that aim or purpose becomes a dominating influence that will drive the business owner to do everything necessary to secure these additional one hundred customers.

Manufacturers of automobiles and other lines of merchandise often establish what they call "quotas," covering the number of automobiles or the amount of merchandise that must be sold in each territory. These "quotas," when definitely established, constitute a definite chief aim toward which all who are engaged in the distribution of the automobiles or merchandise direct their efforts. Seldom does anyone fail to make the established quotas, but it is a well-known fact that had there been no "quotas," the actual sales would have been far less than they were with them. In other words, to achieve success in selling or in practically any other line of endeavor, one must set up a mark at which to shoot, so to speak, and without this target there will be but slim results.

There is one point upon which brain researchers, physicists, psychologists, psychiatrists, counselors, and educators agree. Simply put, it is this: There is a strong connection between the events of your life and your thoughts and beliefs. Therefore, anybody with a definite purpose, and with full faith in his or her ability to realize that purpose, cannot be permanently defeated. There may be a temporary defeat, perhaps many such defeats, but failure, never!

There is one sure way to avoid criticism: Be nothing, do nothing! Get a job washing dishes and kill off your priceless ambition. The formula always works.

Should you choose, instead, to go the success route, our first step on the road to success is to know where you are going, how you intend to travel, and when you intend to get there, which is only another way of saying that you must decide upon a definite chief aim. This aim must be written out in clear language so as to be understood by you before it can be understood by any other person. If there is anything hazy about your aim, it is not definite. A successful leader once stated that nine-tenths of success in any undertaking lay in knowing what was wanted. This is true.

The moment you write out a statement of your chief aim, you have planted an image of that aim firmly in your subconscious mind. Through some process that even the most enlightened scientists have not yet discovered, Nature causes your subconscious mind to use that chief aim as a pattern or blueprint guiding the major portion of your thoughts, ideas, and efforts toward the attainment of your objective.

This is a strange, abstract truth—something that cannot be weighed or even meditated upon—but it is a truth nevertheless!

You will be taken further into the mysteries of this strange law when you reach the law of imagination and other laws, further on.

LESSON THREE

SELF-CONFIDENCE

The third of the Seventeen Laws of Success is Self-Confidence. This term is self-explanatory—it means that to achieve success you must believe in yourself. But this does not mean that you have no limitations. It means that you are to take inventory of yourself, find out what qualities you have that are strong and useful, and then organize these qualities into a definite plan of action with which to attain the object of your definite chief aim.

In all the languages of the world there is no one word that carries the same or even approximately the same meaning as the word "faith." This does not necessarily refer to faith in a Higher Power, yet if there are any such things as "miracles," they are performed only with the aid of superfaith. The doubting type of mind is not a creative mind. Search where and how you may, and you will not discover one single record of great achievement, in any line of endeavor, that was not conceived in imagination and brought into reality through faith.

To succeed, you must have faith in your own ability to do whatever you make up your mind to do. Also, you must cultivate the habit of faith in those who are associated with you, whether they are in a position of authority over you, or you over them. The psychological reason for this will be covered thoroughly and plainly in the Law on Cooperation, further on.

Doubters are not builders! Had Columbus lacked Self-Confidence and faith in his own judgment, the richest and most glorious spot of ground on this earth might never have been discovered, and these lines might never have been written. Had George Washington and his compatriots in 1776 not possessed Self-Confidence, Cornwallis's armies would have conquered and the United States of America would be ruled today from a little island lying three thousand miles away in the east.

A definite chief aim is the starting point of all noteworthy achievement, but Self-Confidence is the unseen force that coaxes, drives, or leads one on and on until the object of the aim is a reality. Without Self-Confidence no achievements would ever get beyond the "aim" stage, and mere aims, within themselves, are worth nothing. Many people have vague sorts of aims, but they get nowhere because they lack the Self-Confidence to create definite plans for attaining these aims.

Fear is the main enemy of Self-Confidence. Every person comes into this world cursed, to some extent, with Six Basic Fears, all of which must be mastered before one may develop sufficient Self-Confidence to attain outstanding success.

These six basic fears are:

1. The Fear of Criticism
2. The Fear of Ill Health
3. The Fear of Poverty
4. The Fear of Old Age
5. The Fear of Loss of Love of Someone (ordinarily called jealousy)
6. The Fear of Death

Space will not permit a long description of how and where these Six Fears came from. In the main, however, they were acquired through early childhood environment, by teaching, the telling of ghost stories, discussion of "hellfire," and in many other ways. Fear of Criticism is placed at the head of the list because it is, perhaps, the most common and one of the most destructive of the entire Six Fears. It's said that fear of public speaking is the most common one of all, and clearly Fear of Criticism is at the heart of it. No matter how urgent one's message, or how much a job or a sale depends on it, the same damp palms and halting speech afflict board chairperson and schoolchild. (One classic remedy seems to defuse this paralyzing fear, at least temporarily. That is the suggestion that the speaker visualize the audience naked.) It remains a fact that this fear is a self-centered one, and is brought on by pure vanity.

Knowledge of this basic Fear of Criticism brings vast fortunes to the manufacturers of clothing each year, and costs timid people the same amount, because most people lack the personality or the courage to wear clothes that are one season out of style. To some extent this basic Fear of Criticism is employed by the manufacturers of automobiles who design new models every season, so as to satisfy the status-seekers and those who depend on outward shows of success.

Before you can develop Self-Confidence sufficient to master the obstacles standing between you and success, you must take inventory of yourself and find out how many of these Six Basic Fears are standing in your way. A few days of study, thought, and reflection will readily enable you to lay your finger on the particular fear or fears that stand between you and Self-Confidence. Once you discover these enemies, you may easily eliminate them, through a procedure that will be described later on.

The fears of Ill Health, Poverty, Old Age, and Death are thought by some to be the results of the holdover effects of teachings of a bygone age. Though such beliefs persist in certain quarters today, it was even more common in the past for people to be taught that death might bring with it a world consisting of fire and eternal torment. The possibility exists that the effect of this teaching so shocked the sensibilities of the human mind that fear became embedded in the subconscious mind and, in that manner, was transmitted from parent to child and thus kept alive from generation to generation. Scientists differ as to the extent that such fears can be transmitted from parent to child through physical heredity. They are all in accord on this point, however: that the discussion of such matters in the presence of a child is sufficient to plant the fear impulse in its subconscious mind, where nothing but strong resolution and great faith in a belief opposite to the thing feared can eliminate the damage done.

The Fear of Loss of Love of Someone (jealousy) is a holdover from the days of human savagery, when it was man's habit to steal his fellow man's mate by force. The practice of stealing another's mate still exists, to some extent, but the stealing is now done through allurements of one sort or another: a sympathetic ear, too much intimacy at the office, a thoughtful gift, a fine dinner. The spouse may no longer be dragged into a cave by a suitor wielding a club, but those in relationships often intuitively sense the same danger that was present in prehistory. Thus the Fear of Loss of Love (or jealousy) has a biological as well as an economic basis for its existence. Jealousy is a form of insanity, because it is often indulged in without the slightest reason for its existence, linking it often with paranoia. Despite this fact, jealousy causes untold suffering, annoyance, and failure in this world. To understand the nature of this fear and how one comes by it is a step in the direction of its mastery.

Every student of this philosophy should do a certain amount of collateral reading, selecting biographies of those who have attained outstanding success, because this is sure to disclose the fact that these leaders met with practically every conceivable sort of temporary de-feat. Yet, despite these discouraging experiences, they developed Self-Confidence sufficient to enable them to master every obstacle that stood in their way. Among the recommended classic books of this type are *Compensation,* by Ralph Waldo Emerson, and *The Age of Reason,* by Thomas Paine. These two historic books, alone, help to place the concept of self-confidence within reach. They make it easier to understand why there are but few impossibilities in life, if there are any at all.

THE HABIT OF SAVING

It is an embarrassing admission, but it is true that a poverty-stricken person hasn't got a chance to be considered a noteworthy success—unless that poverty is planned and purposeful. In that case, it's voluntary simplicity, and that's the subject of another book. It may be, and perhaps is true, that money is not success, but unless you have it or can command its use in the ordinary world, you will not get far, no matter what your definite chief aim may be. As business is conducted today—and as civilization in general stands today—money is an absolute essential for success, and there is no known formula for financial independence except that which is connected, in one way or another, with systematic saving.

The amount saved from week to week or from month to month is not of great consequence so long as the saving is regular and systematic. This is true because the habit of saving adds something to the other qualities essential for success which can be had in no other way.

It is doubtful if any person can develop Self-Confidence to the highest possible point without the protection and independence that belong to those who have saved and are saving money. There is something about the knowledge that one has some money in the bank that gives faith and self-reliance such as can be had in no other way.

The one without money can more easily be exploited and preyed upon, in fact is at the mercy of every person who wishes to exploit or prey upon him. If the one who does not save and therefore has no money offers a personal service, there is no alternative to accepting what the purchaser offers. If opportunity to profit by trade or otherwise comes along, it is of no avail to the one who has neither money nor credit, and it must be kept in mind that credit is generally based upon the money one has or its equivalent.

When the Law of Success philosophy was first created, the Law of Saving was not included as one of the Seventeen Laws, with the result that thousands of people who experimented with this philosophy found that it carried them almost within reach of their goal of success, only to dash their hopes to pieces on the rocks. For years the author of the course and the creator of the philosophy searched for the reason why the philosophy fell just barely short of its intended purpose. Through many years of experimentation and research it was finally discovered that one law was lacking, and that was the law of the habit of saving.

When this law was added, the students of the Law of Success philosophy began to prosper without exception, and now untold millions have used the philosophy for the attainment of success, and not one single case of failure has been reported.

The amount of your income is of but little importance if you do not systematically save a portion of it. An income of $10 million a year is no better than $10,000 unless a part of it is saved. As a matter of fact, the income of $10 million may be far more disabling for the one who received it than the very small income, if the entire amount is spent and dissipated, because the manner in which it is spent may very well undermine the health and in other ways destroy the chances of success.

Millions of people have read stories about Henry Ford's stupendous achievements, and great wealth, but it is safe to say that not one out of every thousand of these people has taken the trouble or done enough thinking to determine the real basis of Ford's success. Through a test made by the author of the Law of Success philosophy, five hundred people were given an outline of the twelve fundamentals that have been largely responsible for Ford's success. In this outline it was pointed out that the amount of cash received each year from the floor sweepings and trash taken from the Ford plants amounts to nearly $600,000. Not one of the entire five hundred placed any significance upon this fact. Not one of the five hundred discovered, or if they did they failed to mention it, the fact that Ford was always a systematic saver of resources.

We know a great deal about the spending habits of Americans but little of the more important habit of saving. Woolworth built one of the highest skyscrapers in the world during his era, and accumulated a fortune of over $100 million by saving the dimes millions of Americans threw away in the trash. The habit of spending money is a mania with most people, and this habit keeps their noses to the grindstone all the days of their lives.

Tests have been made that show, conclusively, that the majority of businesspeople will not place their resources or even positions involving responsibilities in other directions in the hands of those who have not formed the habit of saving money. The savings habit is the finest sort of recommendation of anyone of any position.

The late James J. Hill (who was well prepared to speak with authority on the subject) said that there is a rule by which anyone may determine whether or not he or she would succeed in life. He said the rule came in the form of a required habit: that of systematically saving money.

TAKE INITIATIVE AND LEAD

All people may be placed in one or the other of two general classes. One is known as leaders and the other as followers. The followers rarely achieve noteworthy success, and never succeed until they break away from the ranks of the followers and become leaders.

There is a mistaken notion being broadcast in the world among a certain class of people, to the effect that a people are paid for what they know. This is only partly true, and, like all other half-truths, it does more damage than an out-and-out falsehood.

The truth is that people are paid not only for what they know, but more particularly for what they do with what they know, or what they get others to do. Without initiative, no one will achieve success, no matter what he or she may consider success, because he or she will do nothing out of the ordinary, only the mediocre work required in order to have a place to sleep, something to eat, and clothes to wear. These three necessities may be had without the aid of initiative and leadership, but the moment people make up their minds to acquire more than the bare necessities of life, they must either cultivate the habits of initiative and leadership or else find themselves hedged in behind a stone wall.

The first step essential in the development of initiative and leadership is that of forming the habit of prompt and firm decision. All successful people have a certain amount of decision-making power. Those who waver between two or more half-baked and more or less vague notions of what they want to do generally end up doing nothing.

There had been "talk" about building the Panama Canal for many generations, but the actual work of building the canal never got much beyond the talk stage until the late Theodore

Roosevelt became president of the United States. With the firmness of decision that was the very warp and woof of his achievements and the real basis of his reputation as a leader, Roosevelt took the initiative. He had a bill framed for Congress to pass, providing the money. He went to work with a spirit of self-confidence, plus a definite chief aim and a definite plan for its attainment, and lo! the much-talked-of Panama Canal became a splendid reality.

It is not enough to have a definite chief aim and a definite plan for its achievement, even though the plan may be perfectly practical and you may have all the necessary ability to carry it through successfully. You must have more than these. You must actually take the initiative and put the wheels of your plan into motion and keep them turning until your goal has been reached.

Study those whom you know to be failures (you'll find them all around you) and observe that, without a single exception, they lack the firmness of decision, even in matters of the smallest importance. Such people usually talk a great deal, but they are very short on performance. "Deeds, not words" should be the motto of those who intend to succeed in life, no matter what may be their calling, or what has been selected as a definite chief aim.

Lack of decision has often resulted in insanity. Nothing is very bad or dreadful, once one has reached a decision to face the consequences. This truth was demonstrated quite effectively by a man who was condemned to die and was on death row. When asked how it felt to know that he was to die in another half hour he replied, "Well, it does not bother me in the least. I made up my mind that I had to go sometime, and it might as well be now as a few years later, because my life has been nothing but a sad failure and a constant source of trouble anyway. Just think, it will soon all be over."

The man was actually relieved to know that the responsibilities of life to which he had been subjected, and which had brought him to such an ignoble ending, were about to cease.

Prominent and successful leaders are always people who reach decisions quickly, yet it is not to be assumed that quick decisions are always advisable. There are circumstances calling for deliberation, the study of facts connected with the intended decision, and so forth. But after all available facts have been gathered and organized, there is no excuse for delaying decision, and the person who practices the habit of such delay cannot become an effective leader until that shortcoming is mastered.

Julius Caesar had long wanted to conquer the armies of another country, but he faltered because he was not sure of the loyalty of his own armies. Finally he decided upon a plan that would ensure this loyalty. Loading his soldiers onto boats, he set sail for the shores of his enemy, unloaded the soldiers and implements of war, and then gave the order for all the boats to be burned. Turning to his generals, he said, "Now it is win or perish! We have no choice! Pass the word to your men and let them know that it is the lives of our enemies or our own." They went into battle and won. Julius Caesar won because he saw to it that all his soldiers had reached a decision to win!

Grant said, "We will fight it out along these lines if it takes all summer," and despite his deficiencies he stood by that decision and won!

When asked by one of his sailors what he would do if they saw no signs of land by the following day, Columbus replied, "If we see no land tomorrow, we will sail on and on." He, too, had a definite chief aim, and a definite plan for its attainment, and he had reached a decision not to turn back.

It is a known fact that many cannot do their best until they are actually fighting with their backs to the wall, under the stress of the most urgent necessity. Impending danger will enable ordinary humans to develop superhuman courage and strength of both body and mind far out of proportion to that normally used.

Napoleon, caught by surprise when he discovered that there was a deep camouflaged ditch just ahead of the line of march of his armies, gave the order for his cavalry to charge. He waited until the dead bodies of men and horses filled the ditch, then marched his soldiers across and whipped the enemy. That required a serious decision; moreover, it required an instantaneous decision. One minute of faltering or hesitation and he would have been flanked by the enemy and captured. He did the unexpected, the "impossible," and got away with it.

In the field of selling, nearly all salespeople are met with the stereotyped alibi "I will think it over and let you know later," which really means "I do not wish to buy, but I lack the courage to reach a definite decision and frankly say so." Being a leader, and understanding the value of initiative, the real sales leader does not take such alibis for an answer. That salesperson begins, immediately, to assist the prospective purchaser in the process of "thinking it over" and in short order the job is completed and the sale has been made.

IMAGINATION

No one ever accomplished anything, never created anything, never devised any plan or developed a definite chief aim without the use of imagination! Everything ever created or built was first mentally visioned, through imagination.

Years before it became a reality, the late John Wanamaker saw in his imagination, in practically all its details, the gigantic business that for so many years bore his name. Despite the fact that he was then without the capital to create such a business, he managed to get it and lived to see the business he had dreamed of in his mind become a splendid reality.

In the workshop of the imagination one may take old, well-known ideas or concepts, or parts of ideas, and combine them with still other old ideas or parts of ideas, and out of this combination create something that seems to be new. This process is the major principle of all invention.

One may have a definite chief aim and a plan for achieving it; one may possess self-confidence in abundance; one may have a highly developed habit of saving, and both initiative and leadership in abundance. But if the element of imagination is missing, these other qualities will be held useless, because there will be no driving force to shape their use. In the workshop of the imagination all plans are created, and without such plans no achievement is possible except by mere accident.

Witness the manner in which the imagination can be used as both the beginning and the end of successful plans: Clarence Saunders, who created the well-known chain of Piggly Wiggly supermarkets, conceived the idea on which the stores were based, or rather borrowed it, from the cafeteria restaurant system. While working as a grocer's helper, Mr. Saunders went into a cafeteria for lunch. As he stood in line, waiting for his turn at the food counters, the wheels of his imagination began to turn, and he reasoned, to himself, something like this:

"People seem to like to stand in line and help themselves. Moreover, I see that more people can be served this way, with fewer salespeople. Why would it not be a good idea to introduce this plan in the grocery business, so people could come in, wander around with a basket, pick up what they want, and pay on the way out?"

Then and there, with that bit of elementary "imagining," Mr. Saunders sowed the seed of an idea which later became the Piggly Wiggly stores system and made him a multimillionaire in the bargain.

"Ideas" are the most profitable products of the human mind, and they are all created in the imagination. The old five-and-ten-cent store system that served the nation so well for so many years was the result of imagination. The system was created by F. W. Woolworth, and it happened in this way: Woolworth was working as a salesman in a retail store. The owner of the store complained that he had a considerable amount of old, unsalable merchandise on hand that was in the way, and he was about to throw some of it into the trash box to be consigned to the furnace when Woolworth's imagination began to function.

"I have an idea," he said, "how to make this merchandise sell. Let's put it all on a table and place a big sign on the table saying that all articles will be sold at ten cents each."

The idea seemed feasible, so it was tried. It worked satisfactorily, and then further development began, which resulted, finally, in the big chain of Woolworth stores that eventually appeared throughout the entire country and made the man who used his imagination a classic American success story and a household name.

Ideas are valuable in any business, and the one who strikes out to cultivate the power of imagination, out of which ideas are born, will sooner or later find himself headed toward financial success backed with tremendous power.

Thomas A. Edison invented the incandescent electric lightbulb by the use of his imagination, when he assembled two old and well-known principles in a combination in which they had never before been associated. A brief description of just how this was accomplished will help you to envision the manner in which the imagination may be made to solve problems, overcome obstacles, and lay the foundation for great achievements in any undertaking.

The basic idea behind the lightbulb was not new. Edison discovered, as other experimenters had before him, that a light could be created by applying electrical energy to a wire to heat it to a white heat. The trouble, however, came because of the fact that no one had found a way to control the heat. The wire soon burned out when heated sufficiently to give a clear light.

After many years of experimentation Edison happened to think of the well-known old method of burning charcoal. He saw, instantly, that this principle held the secret to the control of heat that was needed to create a light by applying electrical power to a wire.

Charcoal is made by placing a pile of wood on the ground, setting the wood on fire, and then covering it over with dirt, thereby cutting off most of the oxygen from the fire. This enables the wood to burn slowly. It cannot blaze and the stick cannot burn up entirely, because there can be no combustion where there is no oxygen, and but little combustion where there is but little oxygen. With this knowledge in mind, Edison went into his laboratory and placed the wire that he'd been experimenting with inside a vacuum tube, thus cutting off all the oxygen. He then applied the electrical power, and lo! he had a perfect incandescent lightbulb. The wire inside the bulb could not burn up because there was no oxygen inside to create combustion sufficient to burn it up.

Thus it happened that one of the most useful of modern inventions was created by combining two principles in a new way.

There is nothing absolutely new!

Whatever seems to be new is but a combination of ideas or elements of something old. This is literally true in the creation of business plans, invention, the manufacture of metals, and everything else created by mankind.

What is known as a "basic" patent, meaning a patent that embraces really new and heretofore undiscovered principles, is rarely offered for record at the patent office. Most of the hundreds of thousands of patents applied for and granted every year involve nothing more than a new arrangement or combination of old and well-known principles that have been used many times before in other ways and for other purposes.

When Mr. Saunders created his famous Piggly Wiggly stores system, he did not even combine two ideas; he merely took an old idea that he saw in use and gave it a new setting, or in other words, put it to a new use, but this required imagination.

To cultivate the imagination so it will eventually suggest ideas on its own initiative, you should make it your business to keep a record of all the useful, ingenious, and practical ideas you see in use in other lines of work outside of your own occupation, as well as in connection with your own work. Start with an ordinary, pocket-size notebook, and catalogue every idea, or concept, or thought that occurs to you that is capable of practical use, and then take these ideas and work them into new plans. By and by, the time will come when the powers of your own imagination will go into the storehouse of your own subconscious mind, where all the knowledge you have ever gathered is stored, assemble this knowledge into new combinations, and hand over to you the results in the shape of brand-new ideas, or what appear to be new ideas.

This procedure is practical because it has been followed successfully by some of the best-known leaders and business leaders.

"Everything you can imagine is real," said Picasso.

Let us here define the word imagination as "The workshop of the mind wherein may be assembled, in new and varying combinations, all ideas, thoughts, plans, facts, principles, and theories known to man." A single combination of ideas, which may be merely parts of old and well-known ideas, may be worth anywhere from a few cents to a few million dollars. Imagination is the one faculty on which there is no set price or value. It is the most important of the faculties of the mind, for it is here that all of man's motives are given the impulse necessary to turn them into action.

The dreamer who does nothing more than dream uses imagination, yes. But the dreamer falls short of utilizing this great faculty efficiently, because the impulse to put thoughts into action is missing. Here is where initiative enters and goes to work, provided the dreamer is familiar with the Laws of Success and understands that ideas, of themselves, are worthless until put into action.

The dreamer who creates practical ideas must place back of these ideas three of the laws that have preceded this one, namely:

1. The Law of the Importance of a Definite Chief Aim
2. The Law of Self-Confidence
3. The Law of Taking Initiative and Leadership

Without the influence of these three laws, no one may put thoughts and ideas into action, although the power to dream, imagine, and create may be highly developed.

It is your business to succeed in life! How? That is something you must answer for yourself, but, in the main, you must proceed somewhat along these lines:

1. Adopt a definite purpose and create a definite plan for its attainment.
2. Take the initiative and begin putting your plan into action.
3. Back your initiative with belief in yourself and in your ability to successfully complete your plan.

No matter who you are, what you are doing, how much your income is, or how little money you have, if you have a sound mind and if you are capable of using your imagination, you can gradually make a place for yourself that will command respect and give you all the worldly goods that you need. There is no trick connected with this. The procedure is simple, as you may start with a very simple, elementary idea, plan, or purpose and gradually develop it into something more impressive.

What if your imagination is not sufficiently developed, at this time, to enable you to create some useful invention? You can begin exercising this faculty anyway, by using it to create ways and means of improving the methods of performing your present work, whatever it may be. Your imagination will grow strong in proportion to the extent that you command it and direct it into use. Look about you and you will find plenty of opportunities to exercise your imagination. Do not wait for someone to show you what to do, but use vision and let your imagination suggest what to do. Do not wait for someone to pay you for using your imagination! Your real pay will come from the fact that every time you use it constructively in creating new combinations of ideas, it will grow stronger. If you keep up this practice, the time will soon come when your services will be sought eagerly, at any price within reason.

If a barber or hairstylist works in a unisex salon, for example, it may seem to him or her that there is little opportunity to use imagination. Nothing could be further from the truth. As a matter of fact, anyone holding such a position may give his or her imagination the finest sort of exercise by making a point of cultivating every customer who enters the salon in such a manner that the customer will repeatedly return. Moreover, the stylist may go a step further and work out ways and means of bringing in one new customer each day, or even one a week, or one a month, and in that manner very materially and quickly add to the store's income. Sooner or later, through this sort of exercise of imagination, backed up by self-confidence and initiative, plus a definite chief aim, the one who follows this practice will be sure to create some new plan that will draw new hair salon customers from far and near, and will then be on the great Highway to Success.

A complete analysis of occupations shows that the most profitable occupation on earth, taken as a whole, is that of salesmanship. The one whose fertile mind and imagination create a new and useful invention may not have sufficient ability to market that invention, and may therefore have to dispose of it for a mere pittance, as is, in fact, so often the case. But the one who has the ability to market that invention may (and generally does) make a fortune out of it.

Anyone who can create plans and ideas that will cause the number of patrons of any business to constantly increase, and who is able to send all the patrons away satisfied, is well on the way toward success, regardless of the commodity, service, or wares that are sold there.

It is not the purpose of this brief outline of the Law of Success philosophy to show the student what to do and how to do it, but to list the general rules of procedure applying in all successful undertakings so anyone may understand them. These rules are simple and easily adopted by anyone.

ENTHUSIASM

The true meaning of "enthusiasm" gives this quality an importance that far surpasses the cheerleading attitude that the word too often brings to mind. Rooted in the Greek, it means "inspired," and contains no less than the word for the Creator. Those who come by it naturally are fortunate indeed.

It seems more than a mere coincidence that the most successful people in all walks of life—and particularly in the area of sales—are the enthusiastic type.

Enthusiasm is a driving force that not only gives greater power to the one who has it, but also is contagious and affects all whom it reaches. Enthusiasm over the work in which one is engaged takes the drudgery out of that work. It has been observed that even laborers engaged in the toilsome job of ditchdigging can take the drabness out of their work by singing as they work.

When the Yanks went into action during World War I, they went in singing and full of enthusiasm. This was too much for the war-worn soldiers who had been in the field long enough to wear off their enthusiasm, and they made a poor match indeed for the Yanks.

At the turn of the century the Filene's department store in Boston was opened with music furnished by the store band every morning during the summer months. The salespeople danced to the music, and when the doors were finally opened for business the patrons of the store met a jolly crowd of enthusiastic, cheerful, smiling salespeople, many of whom still hummed the tune to which they had been dancing a few minutes before. This spirit of enthusiasm remained with the salespeople throughout the day, lightening their work and their customers. These days the Muzak piped into stores is carefully chosen to have the same effect.

During the same period it was found that by introducing music with the aid of bands, orchestras, and so on into the plants where war materials were being made, production was stimulated, in some instances as much as 50 percent above normal. Moreover, it was discovered that the workers not only turned out much more work during the day, but they came to the end of the day without fatigue as well, many of them whistling or singing on their way home. Enthusiasm gives greater power to one's efforts, no matter what sort of work one may be engaged in.

Enthusiasm is simply a high rate of mental vibration. The starting point of enthusiasm is "motive," or well-defined desire. Elsewhere in this book may be found a complete list of the mind stimulants that will superinduce the state of mind known as enthusiasm, the greatest of which is sexual desire. People who do not feel a strong desire for sexual contact are seldom, if ever, capable of becoming highly enthusiastic over anything. Transmutation of the great driving force of sex desire is the basis of practically all the works of genius. (By "transmutation" is meant the switching of thought from sexual contact to any other form of physical action.)

The importance of enthusiasm, as one of the Seventeen Essentials of the Law of Success, is explained in the chapter on the Master Mind. The strange phenomenon felt by those who coordinate their efforts in a spirit of harmony, for the purpose of availing themselves of the Master Mind principle, is felt as the high rate of mental vibration known as enthusiasm.

It is a well-known fact that people succeed most readily when engaged in the occupation they like best, and this for the reason that they readily become enthusiastic over that which they like best. Enthusiasm is also the basis of creative imagination. When the mind is vibrating at a high rate, it is receptive to similar high rates of vibration from outside sources, thus providing a favorable condition for creative imagination. It will be observed that enthusiasm plays an important part in four of the other principles constituting the Law of Success philosophy—namely, the Master Mind, Imagination, Accurate Thought, and Pleasing Personality.

Enthusiasm, to be of value, must be controlled and directed to definite ends. Uncontrolled enthusiasm may be, and generally is, destructive. The acts of so-called "bad boys" are nothing more or less than uncontrolled enthusiasm. The wasted energy of uncontrolled enthusiasm expressed by the majority of young men through promiscuous sexual contact—and sexual desire not expressed through contact—is sufficient to lift them to high achievement if only this urge were harnessed and transformed.

The next chapter, on self-control, appropriately follows the subject of enthusiasm, as much self-control is necessary in the mastery of enthusiasm.

SELF-CONTROL

Lack of Self-Control has brought grief to more people than any other shortcoming known to the human race. This evil shows itself, at one time or another, in every person's life.

Every successful person must have some sort of a balance wheel for his or her emotions. When a person "loses his temper," something takes place in the brain that should be better understood. When a person becomes extremely angry, certain glands triggered by negative emotions begin to empty their contents into the blood, and if this is kept up for any great length of time the amount will be sufficient to do serious damage to the entire system, sometimes resulting in death.

The blood coagulates at a time like this, which accounts for one turning white and red in the face, alternately, as the flow of blood throughout the body is temporarily checked. No doubt Nature created this system for the protection of the young human race during the savage stage of development, when anger usually preceded a terrific fight with some other savage, which might mean opening of the veins and loss of blood. Scientists have found, by experiment, that a dog will, when tormented until it becomes angry, throw off enough poison with each exhalation of breath to kill a guinea pig.

But there are other reasons why one should develop Self-Control. For example, the one who lacks Self-Control may be easily mastered by one who has such control, and tricked into saying or doing that which may later be embarrassing. Success in life is very largely a matter of harmonious negotiation with other people, and this requires Self-Control in abundance.

The author of the Law of Success philosophy once observed a long line of angry women in front of the "Complaint Desk" of a large Chicago department store. As he watched at a distance, he saw that the young woman who was hearing the complaints kept sweetly cool and smiled all the while, notwithstanding the fact that some of the women were very abusive. One by one this young woman directed the women to the right department, and she did it with such poise that it caused the author to walk up closer where he could see just what was happening. Standing just back of the young woman at the complaint desk was another young woman who was also listening to the conversations, and making notes and passing them over the shoulder of the young woman who was actually handling the desk.

These notes contained the gist of each complaint, minus the vitriol and abuse of the person making the complaint. It turned out the woman at the desk was stone-deaf! She was getting all the facts that she needed through her assistant, at her back. The manager of the store said that this was the only system he had found that enabled him to handle the complaint desk properly, as human nerves were not strong enough to listen all day long, day in and day out, to abusive language without causing the person doing the listening to become angry, lose Self-Control, and "strike back."

An angry person is suffering from a degree of temporary insanity, and therefore hardly capable of diplomatic negotiation with others. For this reason the one who has no Self-Control is an easy victim of the one who has such control. No one may become powerful without first gaining control of the self.

Self-Control is also a "balance wheel" for the person who is too optimistic and whose enthusiasm needs checking, for it is possible to become entirely too enthusiastic—so much so that one becomes a bore to all those nearby.

THE HABIT OF DOING MORE THAN PAID FOR PAYS OFF

This law is a stumbling block on which many a promising career has been shattered. There is a general inclination among people to perform just as little service as they can get by with. But if you will study these people carefully, you will observe that while they may be actually "getting by" temporarily, they are not, however, getting anything else. There are two major reasons why all successful people must practice this law, as follows:

1. Just as an arm or a limb of the body grows strong in exact proportion to its use, so does the mind grow strong through use. By rendering the greatest possible amount of service, the faculties through which the service is rendered are put into use and, eventually, become strong and accurate.

2. By rendering more service than that for which you are paid, you will be turning the spotlight of favorable attention upon yourself, and it will not be long before you will be sought with impressive offers for your services, and there will be a continuous market for those services.

"Do the thing and you shall have the power" was the admonition of Emerson, to this day our greatest philosopher.

That is literally true! Practice makes perfect. The better you do your work, the more adept you become at doing it, and this, in time, will lead to such perfection that you will have but few, if any, equals in your field of endeavor.

By rendering more service and better service than that for which you are paid, you thereby take advantage of the Law of Increasing Returns through the operation of which you will eventually be paid, in one way or another, for far more service than you actually perform.

This is no mere inventive theory. It actually works out in the most practical tests. You must not imagine, however, that the law always works instantaneously. You may render more service and better service than you are supposed to render for a few days, then discontinue the practice and go back to the old, usual habit of doing as little as can be safely trusted to get you by, and the results will in no way benefit you. But if you adopt the habit as a part of your life's philosophy, and let it become known by all who know you that you render such service out of choice—not as a matter of accident, but by deliberate intent—you will soon see keen competition for your service.

You'll observe that it's not easy to find very many people rendering such service, which is all the better for you, because you will stand out in bold contrast with practically all others who are engaged in work similar to yours. Contrast is a powerful law, and you may, in this manner, profit by contrast.

Some people set up the weak but popular argument that it does not pay to render more service and better service than one is paid for because it is not appreciated. They add that they work for people who are selfish and will not recognize such service.

Splendid! The more selfish an employer is, the more he or she will be inclined to continue to employ a person who makes a point of rendering such service, unusual both in quantity and quality. This very selfishness will impel such an employer to recognize such services. If, however, the employer should happen to be the proverbial exception, one who has not sufficient vision to analyze employees, then it is only a matter of time until all who render such service will attract the attention of other employers who will gladly reward them.

Careful study of the lives of successful men has shown that faithfully practicing this one law alone has brought the compensations with which success is usually measured. If the author of this philosophy had to choose one of the Seventeen Laws of Success as being the most important, and had to discard all the others except the one chosen, he would, without a moment's hesitation, choose this Law of Rendering More Service and Better Service Than Paid For.

THE PERSONALITY OF SUCCESS

A Pleasing Personality, the personality of success, is a personality that does not antagonize. Personality cannot be defined in one word, or with half a dozen words, for it represents the sum total of all one's characteristics, good and bad.

Your personality is totally unlike any other personality. It is the sum total of qualities, emotions, characteristics, appearances, and so on that distinguish you from all other people on earth.

Your clothes form an important part of your personality: the way you wear them, the harmony of colors you select, their quality, and many other details all indicate much that is intrinsically a part of your personality. Psychologists claim that they can accurately analyze any person, in many important respects, by turning that person loose in a clothing store that sells a great variety and where the subject has instructions to select the clothes freely.

Your facial expression, as shown by the lines of your face, or the lack of lines, forms an important part of your personality. Your voice—its pitch, tone, and volume—and the language you use form important parts of your personality, because they mark you instantly, once you have spoken, as a person of refinement or the opposite.

The manner in which you shake hands constitutes an important part of your personality. If, when shaking hands, the hand you offer is limp and lifeless as a dead fish, you are displaying a personality that shows no sign of enthusiasm or initiative.

A Pleasing Personality usually may be found in the person who speaks gently and kindly, selecting refined words that do not offend, in a modest tone of voice; who selects clothing of appropriate style and colors that harmonize. One who is unselfish and not only willing to but desirous of serving others; who is a friend of all humanity, the rich and the poor alike, regardless of politics, religion, or occupation. Who refrains from speaking unkindly of others, either with or without cause; who manages to converse without being drawn into vulgar conversations or useless arguments on such debatable subjects as religion and politics. Who sees both the good and the bad in people but makes due allowance for the latter; who seeks neither to reform nor to reprimand others; who smiles frequently and deeply. Who loves music and little children; who sympathizes with all who are in trouble and forgives acts of unkindness; who willingly grants others the right to do as they please as long as no one's rights are interfered with. Who earnestly strives to be constructive in every thought and deed; who encourages others and spurs them on to greater and better achievement in their chosen line of work.

A Pleasing Personality is something that can be acquired by anyone who has the determination to learn how to negotiate his or her way through life without friction, with the object of getting along peacefully and quietly with others.

One of the best-known and most successful men in America once said that he would prefer a Pleasing Personality, as it is defined in this course, to the college degree that was awarded him, more than fifty years ago, by Harvard University. It was his opinion that a man could accomplish more with a Pleasing Personality minus the college degree than he could with a college degree minus the personality.

The development of a Pleasing Personality calls for exercise of self-control, because there will be many incidents and many people to try your patience and destroy your good resolutions. The reward is worthy of the effort, however, because one who possesses a Pleasing Personality stands out so boldly compared with the majority of people that his or her pleasing qualities become all the more pronounced.

When Abraham Lincoln was a young man he heard that a great lawyer, who was known to be an impressive orator, was to defend a client charged with murder some forty miles from Lincoln's home. He walked the entire distance to hear this man, who was one of the spellbinders of the South. After he had heard the man's speech, and the orator was on his way out of the court room, Lincoln stepped into the aisle, held out his rough hand, and said, "I walked forty miles to hear you, and if I were to do it over, I would walk a hundred." The lawyer looked young Lincoln over, turned up his nose, and, in a supercilious manner, walked out without speaking to him.

Years later these two met once again, this time in the White House, where this selfsame lawyer had come to petition the president of the United States on behalf of a man who had been condemned to death.

Lincoln listened patiently to all the lawyer had to say, and when he had finished speaking, said, "I see you have lost none of your eloquence since I first heard you defend a murderer years ago, but you have changed considerably in other ways, because you now seem to be a polite gentleman of refinement, which was not the impression I got of you at our first meeting. I did you an injustice, perhaps, for which I now ask your pardon. Meanwhile, I shall sign a pardon for your client and we will call accounts square."

The lawyer's face turned white and red as he stammered a brief apology!

By his lack of a Pleasing Personality, at his first meeting with Lincoln, he was guilty of conduct that would have been costly to him had the incident happened with one less charitable than the great Lincoln.

It has been said, and perhaps correctly, that "courtesy" represents the most valuable characteristic known to the human race. Courtesy costs nothing, yet it returns dividends that are stupendous if it is practiced as a matter of habit, in a spirit of sincerity.

A young friend of the author of this philosophy was employed as a service man in one of the gas stations belonging to a large corporation. One day a big car drove up to his station, and the passenger stepped out while the chauffeur told the attendant what kind of gas he wanted. While the gas was being pumped, the wealthy passenger entered into conversation with my young friend.

"Do you like your job?" the man inquired.

"Like it, hell!" replied the young man. "I like it just as much as a dog loves a tomcat."

"Well," said the stranger, "if you do not like your job, why do you work here?"

"Because I am just waiting for something better to turn up," was the quick rejoinder.

"How long do you think you will have to wait?" the man inquired.

"I dunno how long, but I hope I soon get out of here, because there is no opportunity here for a bright fellow like myself. Why, I'm a high school graduate and I can hold a better position if I had it."

"Yes?" said the stranger. "If! Now if I offered you a better position than the one you now have, would you be any better off than you are now?"

"I can't say," replied the young fellow.

"Well," replied the stranger, "allow me to offer the suggestion that better positions usually come to those who are prepared to fill them. But I do not believe you are ready for a better position, at least not while you are in your present frame of mind. Perhaps there is a big opportunity for you right where you stand. Let me recommend . . ." And here he recommended a motivational book of that year. "It may give you an idea that will be useful to you all through life."

The stranger got into his automobile and drove away. He was the president of the corporation that owned the gas station. The young man was talking to his employer, without knowing it, and every word he uttered spoiled his chances of attracting favorable attention.

Later this same gas station was placed in charge of another young man, and it is one of the most profitable service stations operated by that company. The station is basically the same as it was before it was turned over to new management. The convenience store inside is exactly the same. The prices charged are the same. But the personality of the man who meets those who drive up to this station for service is not the same.

Practically all success in life hinges, in the final analysis, on personality.

A nasty disposition can spoil the chances of the best educated, and such dispositions do spoil not a few.

Good Showmanship a Part of Personality

Life may be properly called a great drama in which good showmanship is of the utmost importance. Successful people in all callings are generally good showmen, meaning they practice the habit of catering or playing to the crowd. Let us compare some well-known historical figures from different areas on the subject of their ability as showmen. The following once enjoyed outstanding success in their respective callings, because their genius and invention was heightened by their good showmanship:

Theodore Roosevelt
Henry Ford
Thomas A. Edison
Billy Sunday
William Randolph Hearst
George Bernard Shaw

Following is a list of some well-known men, each famous for great ability but falling short on the score of good showmanship by comparison with the foregoing list:

Woodrow Wilson

Calvin Coolidge

Herbert Hoover

Abraham Lincoln

The inclusion of Lincoln's name here proves that his other sterling qualities took over and placed him at the top of history's list, despite a lack of natural showmanship.

A good showman is one who understands how to cater to the masses. Success is not a matter of chance or luck. It is the result of careful planning and careful staging and able acting of parts by the players in the game.

What is to be done about his defect by the man who is not blessed with a personality that lends itself to able showmanship? Is such a person to be doomed to failure all his life because of Nature's oversight in not blessing him with such a personality?

Not at all! Here is where the principle of the Master Mind comes to the rescue. Those who do not have pleasing personalities may surround themselves with men and women who supply this defect. The financier J. P. Morgan had a rather pugnacious attitude toward people that prevented him from being a good showman, but he associated himself with others who supplied all that he lacked in this respect.

Henry Ford was not blessed, by Nature, with native ability as a good showman, and his personality was not 100 percent perfect by a long way, but knowing how to make use of the Master Mind principle, he bridged this defect by surrounding himself with men who did have such ability.

What are the essential characteristics of good showmanship?

First, the ability to appeal to the imagination of the public, and to keep people interested and curious concerning one's activities. Second, a keen sense of appreciation of the value of psychological appeal through advertising. Third, sufficient alertness of mind to enable one to capture and make use of the prejudices, likes, and dislikes of the public, at the right psychological moment.

Summary of Factors Constituting a Pleasing Personality

Following is a condensed description of the major factors that serve as the basis of a Pleasing Personality:

1. The manner of shaking hands
2. Clothing and posture of the body
3. Voice—its tone, volume, and quality
4. Tactfulness
5. Sincerity of purpose
6. Choice of words, and their appropriateness
7. Poise
8. Unselfishness
9. Facial expression
10. Dominating thoughts (because they register in the minds of other people)
11. Enthusiasm
12. Honesty (intellectual, moral, and economic)
13. Magnetism (high rate of vibration due to well-defined, healthy sexuality)

If you wish to try an interesting and perhaps beneficial experiment, analyze yourself and give yourself a grading on each of these thirteen factors of a Pleasing Personality. An accurate checkup on these thirteen points might easily bring to your notice facts which would enable you to eliminate faults that make success impossible.

It will also be an interesting experiment if you form the habit of analyzing those whom you know intimately, measuring them by the thirteen points here described. Such a habit will, in time, help you to find in other people the causes of both success and failure.

ACCURATE THINKING

The art of Accurate Thinking is not difficult to acquire, although certain definite rules must be followed. To think accurately, one must follow at least two basic principles, as follows:

1. Accurate Thinking calls for the separation of facts from mere information.
2. Facts, when ascertained, must be separated into two classes: important, and unimportant or irrelevant.

The question naturally arises, "What is an important fact?" and the answer is, "An important fact is any fact that is essential for the attainment of one's definite chief aim or purpose, or which may be useful or necessary in connection with one's daily occupation. All other facts, while they may be useful and interesting, are comparatively unimportant as far as the individual is concerned."

No one has the right to have an opinion on any subject unless he or she has arrived at that opinion by a process of reasoning based upon all the available facts connected with the subject. Despite this fact, however, nearly everyone has opinions on nearly every subject, whether they are familiar with those subjects or have any facts connected with them or not.

Snap judgments and opinions that are not opinions at all, but mere wild conjectures or guesses, are valueless. There's not an idea in a carload of them. Anyone may become an Accurate Thinker by making it a point to get the facts, all that are available with reasonable effort, before reaching decisions or creating opinions on any subject.

When you hear someone begin a discourse with such generalities as "I hear that so-and-so is the case," or, "I see by the papers that so-and-so did so-and-so," you may put that person down as one who is not an Accurate Thinker, and his opinions, guesses, statements, and conjectures should be accepted, if at all, with a very hefty grain of salt. Be careful, also, that you do not indulge in wild, speculative language that is not based upon known facts.

It often requires considerable effort to learn the facts on any subject, which is perhaps the main reason why so few people take the time or go to the trouble to gather facts as the basis of their opinions.

You are presumably studying this philosophy for the purpose of learning how you may become more successful, and if that is true then you must break away from the common practices of the masses who do not think and take the time to gather facts as the basis of thought. That this requires effort is freely admitted, but it must be kept in mind that success is not something that one may come along and pluck from a tree, where it has grown of its own accord. Success is something that represents perseverance, self-sacrifice, determination, and strong character.

Everything has its price, and nothing may be obtained without paying this price; or if something of value is thus obtained, it cannot be retained for long. The price of Accurate Thought is the effort required to gather and organize the facts on which to base the thought.

"How many automobiles pass this gas station each day?" the manager of a chain of such stations asked a new employee. "And on what days is traffic the heaviest?"

"I am of the opinion . . ." the young man began.

"Never mind your opinion," the manager interrupted. "What I asked you calls for an answer based upon facts. Opinions are worth nothing when the actual facts are obtainable."

With the aid of a pocket calculator this young man began to count the automobiles that passed his station each day. He went a step further and recorded the number that actually stopped and purchased gas or oil, giving the figures day by day for two weeks, including Sundays.

Nor was this all! He estimated the number of automobiles that should have stopped at his station, day by day, for two weeks. Going still further, he created a plan that cost only the price of one-page flyers and that actually increased the number of automobiles that stopped at his station the following two weeks. This was not a part of his required duties, but the question asked him by his manager had put him to thinking, and he made up his mind to profit by the incident.

The young man in question is now a half-owner in a chain of gas stations, and a moderately wealthy man, thanks to his ability to become an Accurate Thinker.

CONCENTRATION

The jack-of-all-trades seldom accomplishes much at any trade. Life is so complex, and there are so many ways of dissipating energy unprofitably, that the habit of concentrated effort must be formed and adhered to by all who would succeed.

Power is based upon organized effort or energy. Energy cannot be organized without the habit of concentration of all the faculties on one thing at a time. An ordinary magnifying glass may be used to so focus the rays of the sun that they will burn a hole in a board in a few minutes. Those same rays will not even heat the board significantly until they are concentrated on one spot.

The human mind is something like the magnifying glass, because it is the medium through which all the faculties of the brain may be brought together and made to function, in coordinated formation, just as the rays of the sun may be focused on one spot with the aid of that glass.

It is worth considering that all the outstandingly successful people in all walks of life concentrated the major portion of their thoughts and efforts upon some one definite purpose, objective, or chief aim.

Witness the impressive list of people who created and lead this country's earlier history, whose success was due to their having acquired and practiced the habit of concentration:

Woolworth concentrated upon the single idea of five-and-ten-cent stores and became one of the nation's creative geniuses in the retail field.

Henry Ford concentrated all his energies upon the single aim of creating a cheap but practical automobile, and that idea made him one of the most powerful and richest men in history.

Marshall Field concentrated his efforts upon building "The World's Greatest Store" and was rewarded by tens of millions of dollars, an unthinkable amount at that time. Van Heusen concentrated years of effort on the production of a soft collar, at a time when men thought they would never be free of the stiff collar, and the idea made him wealthy in a comparatively short time, and with a name forever synonymous with the chosen product of his concentration.

Wrigley concentrated his efforts upon the production and sale of a humble five-cent package of chewing gum and was rewarded by millions of dollars and a memorable place in history for his perseverance.

Edison concentrated his mind upon the production of "the talking machine," the electric light, the motion picture, and scores of other useful inventions, until they all became realities and assured him a place at the top of the pantheon.

Bessemer concentrated his thoughts upon a better way to produce steel, and the Bessemer process is evidence that his efforts were history-making.

George Eastman concentrated his energy upon radically improving the business of photographs, and this one idea made him a multimillionaire.

Andrew Carnegie, the child of immigrants, envisioned a great steel industry, concentrated his mind upon that purpose, and made tens of millions of dollars.

James J. Hill, while still working as a telegrapher at $40 a month, concentrated his thought upon the dream of a great transcontinental railway system and kept on thinking about it (and acting on his thought as well) until it became a splendid reality and made him one of the wealthy men of his time.

Cyrus H. K. Curtis concentrated his efforts upon one idea of producing the best and most popular magazine on earth, and the splendid *Saturday Evening Post* was but one of the results. Not only did he create a great magazine, his concentration of thought brought him millions as well.

Orville Wright concentrated upon one goal: mastering the air with a heavier-than-air machine, and accomplished it against all odds, with life-changing results.

Marconi concentrated his mind upon one thought: sending wireless messages, and countless lives were improved.

Truly, whatever one can imagine, one can create, providing the mind concentrates upon it with determination and does not stop short of victory.

Great and powerful is the human mind when functioning through the aid of concentrated thought.

Woodrow Wilson determined to become president of the United States twenty-five years before he actually occupied the president's chair in the White House. He kept his mind concentrated upon this one purpose and eventually achieved it.

Robert Green Ingersoll concentrated on the production of a good, practical watch that could be sold for one dollar. His idea, plus his concentrated efforts, made of him a multi-millionaire.

E. M. Statler concentrated on the building of hotels that rendered homelike service, and made himself one of the leading hoteliers of the world, to say nothing of many millions of dollars in wealth.

Rockefeller concentrated his efforts upon the refining and distribution of oil, and his efforts brought him tens of millions of dollars.

Russell Conwell concentrated a lifetime of effort on the delivery of his famous lecture, "Acres of Diamonds," and that one lecture brought in more than $6 million at a time when people were being paid in pennies, and rendered the people of his time a service the extent of which can never be estimated in mere money.

Lincoln concentrated his mind upon freedom for mankind, and saw his task through, though the end proved unfortunate to him.

Gillette concentrated upon producing a safety razor; the idea made him a multimillionaire and linked his name permanently with all such products.

William Randolph Hearst concentrated on newspapers, and became king of his field and lord of his manor.

Helen Keller grew up deaf, dumb, and blind, but through concentration she learned to "hear" and to speak, inspiring the world.

So the story might go on and on in one continuous chain, as evidence that concentrated effort is profitable. Find out what you wish to do—adopt a definite chief aim—then concentrate all your energies in support of purpose until it has reached a happy climax.

Observe, in analyzing the next law, on cooperation, the close connection between the principles outlined and those associated with the law of concentration.

Wherever a group of people ally themselves in an organized, cooperative spirit for the carrying out of some definite purpose, it will be observed that they are employing the Law of Concentration, and unless they do so their alliance will be without real power.

Raindrops, as they fall through the air, each one for itself, helter-skelter, represent a very great form of energy, but this energy cannot be called real power until those raindrops are collected in a river behind a dam and made to pour their energy over a wheel in organized fashion, or until they are confined in a boiler and converted into steam.

Everywhere, regardless of the form in which it is found, power is developed through concentrated energy.

Whatever you are doing as your daily occupation, do it with all your attention, with all your heart and soul focused on that one definite thing.

COOPERATION

This is distinctly an age of cooperation in which we are living. The outstanding achievements in business, industry, finance, transportation, and politics are all based upon the principle of cooperative effort.

You can hardly read a daily paper one week in succession without seeing notice of some corporate merger. Aside from hostile takeovers, these mergers are based upon cooperation, because cooperation brings together in a spirit of harmony of purpose different energies, whether human or mechanical, so that they function as one, without friction.

Marshal Foch was one of the heroes of World War I. The turning point came, as historians will remember, when all the Allied Armies were placed under the direction of Foch, thus ensuring perfectly coordinated effort and cooperation such as would not have been possible under many leaders.

To succeed in a big way in any undertaking means that one must have the friendly cooperation of others. The winning football team is the one that is best coached in the art of cooperation. The spirit of perfect teamwork must prevail in business, or the business will not get very far.

You will observe that some of the preceding laws of this course must be practiced as a matter of habit before one can get perfect cooperation from others. For example, other people will not cooperate with you unless you have mastered and apply the Law of a Pleasing Personality, the Personality of Success. You will also notice that Enthusiasm and Self-Control and the Habit of Doing More Than Paid For must be practiced before you can hope to gain full cooperation from others.

These laws overlap one another, and all of them must be merged into the Law of Cooperation, which means that to gain cooperation from others, one must form the habit of practicing the laws named.

No one is willing to cooperate with a person who has an offensive personality. No one is willing to cooperate with one who is not enthusiastic, or who lacks self-control. Power comes from organized, cooperative effort!

A dozen well-trained soldiers, working with perfectly coordinated effort, can master a mob of a thousand people who lack leadership and organization. Education, in all its forms, is nothing but organized knowledge, or, as it might be stated, cooperative facts.

Andrew Carnegie had but little schooling, yet he was a well-educated man because he formed the habit of organizing his knowledge and shaping it into a definite chief aim. He also made use of the Law of Cooperation, as a result of which he made himself a multimillionaire; moreover, he made millionaires of scores of other men who were allied with him in his application of the Law of Cooperation, which he so well understood.

It was Andrew Carnegie who gave the author of the Law of Success philosophy the idea upon which the entire philosophy was founded. The event is worth describing, as it involves a newly discovered law that is the real basis of all effective cooperation.

The author went to interview Carnegie for the purpose of writing a story about his industrial career. The first question asked was "Mr. Carnegie, to what do you attribute your great success?"

"You have asked me a big question," said Carnegie, "and before I answer I would like you to define the word 'success.' Just what do you call success?"

Before the author had time to reply, Carnegie anticipated the reply by saying, "By success I think you mean my money, do you not?"

The author said, "Yes, that seems to be the term that stands for success."

"Oh, well," replied Carnegie, "if you merely wish to know how I got my money—if that is what you call success—I can easily answer your question. To begin with, let me tell you that we have, here in this steel business a Master Mind. This Master Mind is not the mind of any one person, but it is the sum total of the ability, knowledge, and experience of nearly a score of men whose minds have been perfectly coordinated so they function as one, in a spirit of harmonious cooperation. These are the ones who manage the various departments of this business. Some of them have been associated with me for many years, while others have not been here so long.

"You may be surprised to know," Carnegie continued, "that I have had to try and then try over and over again to find those whose personalities were such that they could subordinate their own interests for the benefit of the business. One of the most important places on our staff has been filled by more than a dozen before one was finally found who could do the work required in that position and at the same time cooperate in a spirit of harmony with the other members of our staff. My one big problem has been, and always will continue to be, the difficulty in securing the services of people who will cooperate, because without cooperation, the Master Mind of which I speak could not exist."

In these words (or their equivalent, as I am quoting from memory) the greatest of all the steel magnates the industry has ever known laid bare the real secret of his stupendous achievements. His statement led this author to a line of research, covering a period of over twenty years, which resulted in the discovery that this same Master Mind principle is also the secret of the success of most of the other successful leaders of this type who are at the heads of our great industries, financial institutions, railroads, banks, department stores, and so on.

It is a fact, although the scientific world may not yet endorse it, that whenever two or more minds are allied toward any undertaking in a spirit of harmony and cooperation, there arises an unseen power that gives greater energy to the undertaking.

You may test this out, in your own way, by watching the reaction of your own mind when you are in the presence of those with whom you are friendly. Compare your reaction with what happens when you are in the presence of those whom you do not like. Friendly association inspires one with a mysterious energy not otherwise experienced, and this great truth is the very foundation stone of the Law of Cooperation.

An army that is forced to fight because the soldiers are afraid they will be shot down by their own leaders may be a very effective army, but such an army never has been a match for the army that goes into action of its own accord, with soldiers determined to win because they believe their side ought to win.

At the beginning of World War I, the Germans were sweeping everything before them. The German soldiers, at that time, went into action singing. They had been thoroughly "sold" on the idea of *"kultur."* Their leaders had made them think they were bound to win because they ought to win.

As the war went along, however, these same soldiers began to see the light. It began to dawn upon them that the killing off of millions was a serious business. Next, the thought began to creep in that, after all, perhaps their kaiser was not the ordained agent of God, and that they might be fighting an unjust war.

From this point on the tide began to turn. They no longer went into battle singing. They no longer "felt proud to die for *kultur*," and their end was then a short distance away.

So it is in every walk of life, in every human endeavor. Those who can subordinate their own personalities, subdue their own self-interests, and coordinate all their efforts, physical and mental, with those of others in support of a common cause they believe in have already gone nearly the entire distance toward success.

A few years ago the president of a well-known real estate company addressed the following letter to the author:

Dear Mr. Hill:

Our firm will give you a check for $10,000.00 if you will show us how to secure the confidence of the public in our work as effectively as you do in yours.

Very cordially,

To this letter the following reply was sent:

Dear Mr. J—:

I thank you for the compliment, and while I could use your check for $10,000, I am perfectly willing to give you, gratis, what information I have on the subject. If I have unusual ability to gain cooperation from other people, it is because of the following reasons:

1. I render more service than I ask people to pay for.
2. I engage in no transaction, intentionally, that does not benefit all whom it affects.
3. I make no statements that I do not believe to be true.
4. I have a sincere desire in my heart to be of useful service to the greatest possible number of people.
5. I like people better than I like money.
6. I am doing my best to live as well as to teach my own philosophy of success.
7. I accept no favors from anyone without giving favors in return.
8. I ask nothing of any person without having a right to that for which I ask.
9. I enter into no arguments with people over trivial matters.
10. I spread the sunshine of optimism and good cheer wherever and whenever I can.
11. I never flatter people for the purpose of gaining their confidence.

12. I sell counsel and advice to other people, at a modest price, but never offer free advice.
13. While teaching others how to achieve success, I have demonstrated that I can make my philosophy work for myself as well, thus "practicing what I preach."
14. I am so thoroughly sold on the work in which I am engaged that my enthusiasm over it becomes contagious and others are influenced by it.

If there are any other elements entering into what you believe to be my ability to get the confidence of others, I do not know what they are. Incidentally, your letter raised an interesting question, and caused me to analyze myself as I had never done before. For this reason I refuse to accept your check, on the ground that you have caused me to do something that may be worth many times ten thousand dollars.

Very cordially,
Napoleon Hill

In these fourteen points may be found the elements that form the basis of all confidence-building relationships. Cooperative effort brings power to those who can get and permanently hold the confidence of great numbers of people. This author knows of no method of inducing others to cooperate except that which is based upon the fourteen points here described.

PROFITING BY FAILURE

A wealthy philosopher by the name of Croesus was the official counselor to King Cyrus. He said some very wise things in his capacity as court philosopher, among them this:

"I am reminded, O king, and take this lesson to heart, that there is a wheel on which the affairs of humans revolve, and its mechanism is such that it prevents anyone from being always fortunate."

It is true. There is a sort of unseen fate, or wheel, turning in the lives of all of us, and sometimes it brings us good fortune and sometimes ill fortune, despite anything that we as individual human beings can do. However, this wheel obeys the law of averages, thereby insuring us against continuous ill fortune. If ill fortune comes today, there is hope in the thought that its opposite will come in the next turn of the wheel, or the one following the next, or the next.

Failure is one of the most beneficial parts of a human being's experience, for the reason that there are many needed lessons that must be learned before one commences to succeed, lessons that can be learned by no teacher other than failure. Failure is always a blessing in disguise, provided it teaches us some useful lesson that we could not or would not have learned without it!

Failure is to life what the kiln is to the potter. It tempers us.

Millions of people make the mistake of accepting failure as final, however, whereas it is, like most other events in life, transitory, and for this reason should not be accepted as final.

Successful people must learn to distinguish between failure and temporary defeat. Every person experiences, at one time or another, some form of temporary defeat, and out of such experiences come some of the greatest and most beneficial lessons.

In truth, most of us are so constituted that if we never experienced temporary defeat (or what some ignorantly call failure), we would soon become so egotistical and independent that we would imagine ourselves more important than the Deity. There are a few such people in this world, and it is said of them that they refer to the Deity, if at all, as "Me and God," with heavy emphasis on the "Me."

Headaches are beneficial, despite the fact that they are very disagreeable, for the reason that they represent Nature's language. In this case she calls loudly for intelligent use of the human body, particularly of the stomach and tributary organs through which most of us create the majority of physical human ills.

It is the same regarding temporary defeat or failure. These are Nature's symbols through which she signals us that we have been headed in the wrong direction, and if we are reasonably intelligent we heed these signals, steer a different course, and come, finally, to the objective of our definite chief aim.

The author of this philosophy has devoted more than a quarter of a century to research for the purpose of discovering what characteristics were possessed and employed by the successful men and women in the fields of business, industry, politics, statesmanship, religion, finance, transportation, literature, and science.

This research has involved the reading of more than one thousand books of a scientific, business, and biographical nature, or an average of more than one such book a week.

One of the most startling discoveries made through this enormous amount of research was the fact that all the outstanding successes, regardless of the field of endeavor in which they were engaged, were people who met with reverses, adversity, temporary defeat, and in some instances actual permanent failure (as far as they, as individuals, were concerned). Not one single successful person was discovered whose success was attained without the experience of what, in many instances, seemed like unbearable obstacles that had to be mastered.

It was discovered also that these people rose to success in exact ratio to the extent that they met squarely and did not budge from defeat. In other words, success is measured, always, by the extent to which any individual meets and squarely deals with the obstacles that arise in the pursuit of his definite chief aim.

Let us recall a few of the great successes of the world who met with temporary defeat, and some of whom were permanent failures, as far as they, as individuals, were concerned.

Columbus started out to find a shorter passage to India but discovered America instead. He died a prisoner, in chains, a victim of ignorance.

Thomas A. Edison met with defeat after defeat, more than ten thousand unsuccessful efforts in all, before he made a revolving piece of wax record and reproduce the sound of the human voice. He met with similar defeat before he created the modern incandescent electric lightbulb.

Alexander Graham Bell met with years of defeat before he perfected the long-distance telephone.

Woolworth's first five-and-ten-cent store project was not a success, and he had to master the most trying obstacles before he finally got his true bearings and rode high on the road to success.

Fulton's steamboat was a fizzle, and people laughed at him so hard that he had to sneak out at night and conduct his experiments privately.

The Wright brothers smashed many airplanes and suffered much defeat before they created a heavier-than-air flying machine that was practical.

Henry Ford almost starved to death, figuratively if not literally, before he successfully completed his first working model of an automobile. Nor was this the end of his troubles; he spent years perfecting the famous Model T car that made his fame and fortune.

Do not think, for one moment, that these rode to success on the wings of plenty, without opposition of the most heartrending nature. We are too apt to look at leaders in the hour of their triumph without taking into consideration the setbacks, defeats, and adversities through which they had to pass before success came.

Napoleon met with defeat after defeat before he made himself the great power that he was, and even then he finally met with permanent failure. At many times, it is recorded in his biographies, he contemplated committing suicide, so great were his disappointments.

The Panama Canal was not built without defeat. Time after time many of the deep cuts fell in and the engineers had to go back and do their work all over again. It looked on many occasions, to those on the outside, as if some of the heavy cuts never could be made to stand up. But perseverance, plus a definite chief aim, finally delivered to the world the most marvelous artificial body of water in the world, viewed from the standpoint of usefulness.

There comes to mind what this author believes to be the finest poem ever written on the subject of failure. It so thoroughly and clearly states the benefits of defeat that it is here reprinted, as follows:

When Nature Wants a Man!

By Angela Morgan

When Nature wants to drill a man,
And thrill a man,
And skill a man;
When Nature wants to mold a man
To play the noblest part;
When she yearns with all her heart
To create so great and bold a man
That all the world shall praise,
Watch her method, watch her ways!
How she ruthlessly perfects
Whom she royally elects;
How she hammers him and hurts him,
And with mighty blows converts him
Into trial shapes of day which only Nature understands.
While his tortured heart is crying
And he lifts beseeching hands,
How she bends but never breaks,
When his good she undertakes,
How she uses whom she chooses
And with every purpose infuses him,
By every art induces him
To try his splendor out,
Nature knows what she's about.

When Nature wants to take a man,
And shake a man,
And wake a man;
When Nature wants to make a man
To do the Future's will;
When she tries with all her skill

And she yearns with all her soul
To create him large and whole.
With what cunning she prepares him!
How she goads and never spares him,
How she whets him, and she frets him,
And in poverty begets him.
How she often disappoints
Whom she sacredly anoints,
With what wisdom she will hide him,
Never minding what betide him
Though his genius sob with slighting,
And his pride may not forget!
Bids him struggle harder yet.
Makes him lonely, so that only
God's high messages shall reach him,
So that she may surely teach him
What the Hierarchy planned.
Though he may not understand,
Gives him passions to command.
Now remorselessly she spurs him
With terrific ardor stirs him
When she poignantly prefers him!

When Nature wants to name a man,
And fame a man,
And tame a man;
When Nature wants to shame a man
To do his heavenly best;
When she tries the highest test
That the reckoning may bring
When she wants a god or king!
How she reins him and restrains him
So his body scarce contains him

While she fires him
And inspires him!
Keeps him yearning, ever burning, for a tantalizing
    goal—
Lures and lacerates his soul.
Sets a challenge for his spirit,
Draws it high when he's near it;
Makes a jungle that he clear it;
Makes a desert that he fear it
And subdue it if he can.
So doth Nature make a man.
Then, to test his spirit's wrath
Hurls a mountain in his path,
Puts a bitter choice before him
And relentless stands o'er him.
"Climb, or perish!" so she says,
Watch her purpose, watch her ways!

Nature's plan is wondrous kind,
Could we understand her mind,
Fools are they who call her blind.
When his feet are torn and bleeding,
Yet his spirit mounts unheeding
All his higher powers speeding,
Blazing newer paths and fine;
When the force that is divine
Leaps to challenge every failure
And his ardor still is sweet,
And love and hope are burning
In the presence of defeat.
Lo, the crisis! Lo, the shout
That must call the leader out.
When the people need salvation

Doth he come to lead the nation.
Then doth Nature show her plan
When the world has found—a man!

Do not be afraid of temporary defeat, but make sure that you learn some lesson from every such defeat. That which we call "experience" consists, largely, of what we learn by mistakes—our own and those made by others—but take care not to ignore the knowledge that may be gained from mistakes.

TOLERANCE

Intolerance has caused more grief than any of the many other forms of ignorance. Practically all wars grow out of intolerance. Misunderstandings between so-called "capital" and "labor" are usually the outgrowth of intolerance.

It is impossible for any man to observe the Law on Accurate Thought without having first acquired the habit of tolerance, for the reason that intolerance causes a man to fold the Book of Knowledge and write "Finis, I know it all!" on the cover.

The most damaging form of intolerance grows out of religious and racial differences of opinion. Civilization, as we know it today, bears the deep wounds of gross intolerance all through the ages, mostly those of a religious nature.

This is the most democratic country on earth. We are the most cosmopolitan people on earth. We are made up of all nationalities and people of every religious belief. We live side by side with neighbors whose religion differs from our own. Whether we are good neighbors or bad depends largely on how tolerant we are with one another.

Intolerance is the result of ignorance or, stated conversely, the lack of knowledge. Well-informed people are seldom intolerant, because they know that no one knows enough to be entitled to judge others.

Through the principle of social heredity we inherit, from our environment and through our early religious teachings, our ideas of religion. Our teachers themselves may not be always right, and if we bear this thought in mind, we would not allow such teachings to influence us to believe that we have a corner on truth, and that people whose teachings on this subject have been different from our own are all wrong.

There are many reasons why one should be tolerant, the chief of them being the fact that tolerance permits cool reason to guide one in the direction of facts, and this, in turn, leads to accurate thinking.

Those whose minds have been closed by intolerance, no matter of what brand or nature, can never become accurate thinkers, which is sufficient reason to cause us to master intolerance.

It may not be your duty to be tolerant with other people whose ideas, religious views, politics, and racial tendencies are different from yours, but it is your privilege. You do not have to ask permission of anyone to be tolerant; this is something that you control, in your own mind; therefore, the responsibility that goes with the choice is also your own.

Intolerance is closely related to the six basic fears described in the Law of Self-Confidence, and it may be stated as a positive fact that intolerance is always the result of either fear or ignorance. There are no exceptions to this rule. The moment another person (provided that person is not intolerant) discovers that you are cursed with intolerance, he or she can easily and quickly mark you as being either the victim of fear and superstition or, what is worse, ignorance!

Intolerance closes the doorway to opportunity in a thousand ways, and shuts out the light of intelligence.

The moment you open your mind to facts, and take the attitude that the last word is seldom said on any subject, and that there always remains the chance that still more truth may be learned, you begin to cultivate the Law of Tolerance. If you practice this habit for long you will soon become a thinker, with ability to solve the problems that confront you in your struggle to make a place for yourself in your chosen field of endeavor.

USING THE GOLDEN RULE TO WIN COOPERATION

This is, in some ways, the most important of the Seventeen Laws of Success. Despite the fact that for more than five thousand years the great philosophers all taught the Law of the Golden Rule, the great majority of people of today look upon it as a sort of pretty text for preachers to build sermons on.

In truth the Golden Rule philosophy is based upon a powerful law which, when understood and faithfully practiced, will enable a man to get others to cooperate with him.

It is a well-known truth that most people follow the practice of returning good or evil, act for act. If you slander anyone, you will be slandered in return. If you praise anyone, you will be praised. If you favor someone in business, you will be favored in return.

There are exceptions to this rule, to be sure, but by and large the law works out. Like attracts like. This is in accordance with a great natural law, and it works in every particle of matter and in every form of energy in the universe. The successful attract the successful. Failures attract failures. The professional ne'er-do-well will make a beeline for skid row, where he may associate with others of his kind, even though he may have landed in a strange city, after dark.

The Law of the Golden Rule is closely related to the Law of the Habit of Doing More Than Paid For. The very act of rendering more service than you are paid to render puts into operation this law, through which "like attracts like," and this is the selfsame law as that which forms the basis of the Golden Rule philosophy.

There is no escape from the fact that those who render more service than they're paid to render eventually will be eagerly sought by those who will be willing to pay for more than is actually done. Compound interest on compound interest is Nature's rate, when she goes to pay the indebtedness incurred through application of this law.

This law is so fundamental, so obvious, yet so simple. It is one of the great mysteries of human nature that it is not more generally understood and practiced. Behind its use lie possibilities that stagger the imagination of the most visionary person. Through its use may one learn the real secret—all the secret there is—about the art of getting others to do that which we wish them to do.

If you want a favor from someone, make it your business to seek out the person from whom you want the favor and, in an appropriate manner, render that person an equivalent of the favor you wish from him. If he does not respond at first, double the dose and render him another favor, and another, and another, and so on, until finally he will, out of shame if nothing more, come back and render you a favor.

You get others to cooperate with you by first cooperating with them.

The foregoing sentence is worth reading a hundred times, for it contains the gist of one of the most powerful laws available to those with the intention of attaining great success.

It may sometimes happen, and it will, that the particular individual to whom you render useful service will never render you a similar service, but keep this important truth in mind: even though one person fails to respond, someone else will observe the transaction and, out of a sportsman's desire to see justice done, or perhaps with a more selfish motive in mind, will render you the service to which you are entitled.

"Whatsoever a man soweth, that shall he also reap!"

This is more than a mere preachment; it is a great practical truth that may be made the foundation of every successful achievement. From winding pathways or straight, every thought you send out, every deed you perform, will gather a flock of other thoughts or deeds according to its own nature, and come back home to you in due time.

There is no escape from this truth. It is as eternal as the universe, as sure of operation as the law of gravitation. To ignore it is to mark yourself as ignorant, or indifferent, either of which will destroy your chances of success.

The Golden Rule philosophy is the real basis on which children should be governed. It is also the real basis on which "children grown tall" should be managed. Through force, or by taking advantage of unfair circumstances, one may build a fortune without observing the Golden Rule, and many do this, but such fortunes cannot bring happiness, because ill-gotten gain is bound to destroy the peace of mind of all.

Ideas are the most valuable products of the human mind. If you can create usable ideas and put them to work, you can take whatever you wish for your pay. Wealth created or acquired by the Golden Rule philosophy does not bring with it a flock of regrets, nor does it disturb the conscience and destroy the peace of mind.

Fortunate is the man who makes the Golden Rule his business or professional slogan and then lives up to the slogan faithfully, both literally and figuratively, observing the spirit of it as well as the letter.

THE PROSPEROUS HABIT OF HEALTH

We come now to the last of the seventeen factors of success. In previous chapters we have learned that success grows out of power; that power is organized knowledge expressed in definite action. No one can remain intensely active very long without good health. The mind will not function properly unless it has a sound body in which to function. Practically all of the other sixteen factors which enter into the building of success depend for their successful application upon a healthy body.

Good health is dependent, in the main, upon:

1. Proper food and fresh air
2. Regularity of elimination
3. Proper exercise
4. Right thinking

It is not the purpose of this chapter to present a treatise on how to remain healthy, as that is a task belonging to the specialists in physical and mental health. But no harm can be done by calling attention to the fact that poor health is usually superinduced by poor elimination. People who live in cities and eat processed foods will find it necessary to constantly aid Nature in the process of regular elimination, preferably in healthy ways. A great many incidences of headaches, sluggishness, loss of energy, and similar feelings are due to autointoxication, or intestinal poisoning through improper elimination.

Most people eat too much. Such people will find it helpful if they go on a ten-day fast about three times a year, during which time they will refrain from taking food of any nature whatsoever. The experience of fasting will bring to all who have never tried it health-building values that can be attained in no other way. No one should experiment with fasting, dieting, or any other form of self-administered therapeutics, except under the direction of a health care professional.

Sexual Energy a Health-Builder

As a closing thought for this chapter the author has chosen to inject a very brief statement concerning the therapeutic value of sexual energy. The justification for such a theory is as follows:

It is a well-known fact that thought is the most powerful energy available to humankind.

It is equally well known that negative thoughts of worry and envy and hatred and fear will destroy the digestive processes and bring about illness, this by reason of the fact that negative thoughts inhibit the flow of certain glandular contents that are essential in the digestive processes.

Negative thoughts cause "short circuits" in the nerve lines that carry nervous energy (or life force) from the central distributing station, the brain, to all parts of the body, where this energy performs its natural task of nourishment and of removal of worn-out cells and waste matter.

Sexual energy is a highly vitalizing, positive force when activated during the period of sexual contact, and because it is powerful it sweeps over the entire nervous system of the body and unties any "short circuits" that may exist in any of the nerve lines, thus ensuring a complete flow of nervous energy to all parts of the body.

Sexual emotion is the most powerful of all the human emotions, and when it is actively engaged it reaches and vitalizes every cell in every organ of the body, thereby causing the organs to function in a normal manner. Total sexual abstinence was not one of Nature's plans, and those who do not understand this truth usually pay for their ignorance out of a trust fund that Nature provided for the maintenance of health.

Thought controls all voluntary movements of the body. Are we in accord on this statement? Very well, if thought controls all voluntary movements of the body, may it not also be made to control, or at least materially influence, all involuntary movements of the body?

Thoughts of a negative nature—such as fear, worry, and anxiety—not only inhibit the flow of the digestive juices, they also "tie knots" in the nerve lines that carry nervous energy to the various organs of the body.

Thoughts of a positive nature untie these knots in the nerve lines and permit the nervous energy to pass through. Sexual feeling is the most powerful form of positive thought. It is Nature's own "medicine," proof of which is obvious if one will observe the state of mind and the perfectly relaxed condition of the body following sexual contact.

Brief as it is, the foregoing statement should be made the starting point for some intelligent analysis of this subject by the reader of this book. Let us be open-minded on this subject of sex. No one has the last word on the subject; most of us do not even know the first word. Therefore, let us not pass judgment on a subject concerning which we know so very little until we have at least done some intelligent thinking about it. For all we know, both poverty and ill health may be mastered through a complete understanding of the subject of sexual energy, and this for the reason that sex energy is the most powerful mind stimulant known.

The Thirty Most Common Causes of Failure

Through the foregoing pages you have had a brief description of the seventeen factors through which success is attained. Now let us turn our attention to some of the factors that cause failure. Check the list and you will perhaps find here the cause of any failure, or temporary defeat, that you may have experienced. The list is based on accurate analysis of over 20,000 failures, and it covers men and women in every calling.

1. Unfavorable social or family foundation (This cause of failure stands at the head of the list. Bad breeding is a handicap against which there is but little remedy, and it is one for which the individual, unfortunately, is not responsible.)
2. Lack of a well-defined purpose, or definite major aim toward which to strive
3. Lack of the ambition to aim above mediocrity
4. Insufficient education
5. Lack of self-discipline and tact, generally manifesting itself through all sorts of excesses, especially in sexual desires and eating
6. Ill health, usually due to preventable causes
7. Unfavorable environment during childhood, when character was being formed, resulting in vicious habits of body and mind
8. Procrastination
9. Lack of persistence and the courage to take responsibility for one's failures
10. Negative personality

11. Lack of well-defined sexual urge

12. An uncontrollable desire to get something for nothing, usually manifesting itself in habits of gambling

13. Lack of decision-making ability

14. One or more of the six basic fears described elsewhere in this book

15. Poor selection of a mate in marriage

16. Overcaution, destroying initiative and self-confidence

17. Poor selection of associates in business

18. Superstition and prejudice, generally traceable to lack of knowledge of natural laws

19. Wrong selection of occupation

20. Dissipation of energies, through lack of understanding of the law of concentration, resulting in what is commonly known as a "jack-of-all-trades"

21. Lack of thrift

22. Lack of enthusiasm

23. Intolerance

24. Intemperance in eating, drinking, and sexual activities

25. Inability to cooperate with others in a spirit of harmony

26. Possession of power that was not acquired through self-effort, as in the case of one who inherits wealth, or is placed in a position of power to which he is not entitled by merit

27. Dishonesty

28. Egotism and vanity

29. Guessing instead of thinking

30. Lack of capital

Some may wonder why "lack of capital" was placed at the bottom of the list, and the answer is that anyone who can qualify with a reasonably high grade on the other twenty-nine causes of failure can always get all the capital needed for any purpose whatsoever.

The foregoing list does not include all the causes of failure, but it does represent the most common causes. Some may object that "unfavorable luck" should have been added to the list, but the answer to this complaint is that luck, or the law of chance, is subject to mastery by all who understand how to apply the seventeen factors of success. In fairness to those who may never have had the opportunity to master the seventeen factors of success, however, it must be admitted that luck, or an unfavorable turn of the wheel of chance, is sometimes the cause of failure.

Those who are inclined to attribute all their failures to "circumstances" or luck should remember the blunt injunction laid down by Napoleon, who said, "To hell with circumstances. I create circumstances."

Most "circumstances" and unfavorable results of luck are self-made, also. Let us not forget this!

Here is a statement of fact, and a confession, that is well worth remembering: The Law of Success philosophy, which has to date rendered useful service to untold millions all over this earth, is very largely the result of nearly twenty years of so-called failure upon the part of the author. In the more extensive course on the Law of Success philosophy, under the lesson on "Profiting by Failure," the student will observe that the author met with failure and adversity and reverses so often that he might have been justified in crying out, "Luck is against me!" Seven major failures and more scores of minor failures than the author can, or cares to remember, laid the foundation for a philosophy that has brought success to so many generations of people, including the author. "Bad luck" has been harnessed and put to work, and the whole world is now paying substantial monetary tribute to the man who ferreted out the happy thought that even luck can be changed, and failures can be capitalized upon.

"There is a wheel on which the affairs of men revolve, and its mechanism is such that it prevents any man from being always fortunate."

True enough! There is such a wheel of life, but it is rotating continuously. If this wheel brings misfortune today, it can be made to bring good fortune tomorrow. If this were not true, the Law of Success philosophy would be a farce and a fake, offering nothing but false hope.

The author was once told that he would always be a failure because he was born under an unfavorable star! Something must have happened to act as an antidote to the bad influence of that star, and something has happened. That "something" is the power to master obstacles by first mastering self, which grew out of understanding and application of the Law of Success philosophy. If the seventeen factors of success can offset the bad influence of a star for this author, they can do the same for you, or for any other person.

Laying our misfortunes to the influence of stars is just another way of acknowledging our ignorance or our laziness. The only place that stars can bring you bad luck is in your own mind. You have possession of that mind, and it has the power to master all the bad influences standing between you and success, including that of the stars.

If you really wish to see the cause of your bad luck and misfortunes, do not look up toward the stars—look in a mirror! You are the master of your fate. You are the captain of your soul. And this by reason of the fact that you have a mind that you alone control, and this mind can be stimulated and made to form a direct contact with all the power you need to solve any problem that may confront you. The person who blames his or her troubles upon stars thereby challenges the existence of Infinite Intelligence, or God, if you prefer that name.

The Mystery of the Power of Thought

In front of the author's study, at Broadway and Forty-fourth Street, in New York City, stands the Paramount Building—a great, tall, impressive building that serves as a daily reminder of the great power of thought.

Come, stand with me by the window of my study and let us analyze this modern skyscraper. Tell me, if you can, of what materials the building is constructed. Immediately you will say, "Why, it is built of brick and steel girders and plate glass and lumber," and you will be partly right, but you have not told the entire story.

The brick and steel and other materials that went into the physical portion of the building were necessary, but before any of those materials were laid into place the building, in its entirety, was constructed of another sort of material. It was first built in the mind of Adolph Zukor, out of the intangible stuff known as thought.

Everything you have or ever will have, good or bad, was attracted to you by the nature of your thoughts. Positive thoughts attract positive, desirable objects; negative thoughts attract poverty and misery and a flock of other sorts of undesirable objects. Your brain is the magnet to which everything you possess clings, and make no mistake about this; your brain will not attract success while you are thinking of poverty and failure.

All people are exactly where they are as the result of their own dominating thoughts, just as surely as night follows day. Thought is the only thing that you absolutely control, a statement of fact that we repeat because of its great significance. You do not control, entirely, the money you possess, or the love and friendship that you enjoy. You had nothing to do with your coming into the world and you will have little to do with the time of your going. But you do have everything to do with the state of your own mind. You can make that mind positive or you can permit it to become negative, as the result of outside influences and suggestions. Divine Providence gave you supreme control of your own mind, and with this control you were given the responsibility that is now yours to make the best use of it.

In your own mind you can fashion a great building, similar to the one which stands in front of the author's study, and then transform that mental picture into a reality, just as Adolph Zukor did, because the material out of which he constructed the Paramount Building is available to every human being. Moreover, it is free. All you have to do is to appropriate it and put it to your use. This universal material, as we have said, is the power of thought.

The difference between success and failure is largely a matter of the difference between positive and negative thought. A negative mind will not attract a fortune. Like attracts like. Nothing attracts success as quickly as success. Poverty begets more poverty. Become successful and the whole world will lay its treasures at your feet and want to do something to help you become more successful. Show signs of poverty and the entire world will try to take away that which you have of value. You can borrow money at the bank when you are prosperous and do not need it, but try and arrange a loan when you are poverty-stricken, or when some great emergency faces you. You are the master of your own destiny because you control the one thing that can change and redirect the course of human destinies, the power of thought. Let this great truth sink into your consciousness and this book will have marked the most important turning point of your life.

A Message to Those Who Have Tried and Thought They Have Failed

The author would not be satisfied to send this book out on its mission of inspirational service without adding this short chapter as a personal message to those who have tried and "failed."

"Failure"! What a misunderstood word! What chaos and distress and poverty and heartaches have come out of misinterpretation of this word.

Just a few days ago the author stood on a humble spot of ground in the mountains of Kentucky, not far from his own birthplace, where a well-known "failure" was born. When a very young man, this "failure" went away to war, commissioned as a captain.

His record was so poor that he was demoted to corporal and finally returned home as a private.

He took up surveying, but he could not make a living at this work, and very soon he was humiliated by having his instruments sold for his debts.

Next he took up law, but he got very few cases, and most of these he lost on account of incompetence.

He became engaged to a young lady, but changed his mind and failed to show up for the wedding.

He drifted into politics and by chance was elected to Congress, but his record was so drab that it caused no favorable comment. Everything he undertook brought him humiliation and failure.

Then a miracle happened! A great love experience came into his life, and despite the fact that the young woman who aroused this love passed beyond the Great Divide, the lingering thoughts of that love caused this "nobody" to fight his way out of his humble role as failure, and at the age of fifty-two he became the greatest and most beloved president who ever occupied the White House.

People are made, or broken, according to the use they make of the power of thought. Failure may be transformed into success overnight, when one becomes inspired with a great impelling motive to succeed. The eight basic motives that move men to action have been described in a previous chapter. One of these eight is the motive of love.

Abraham Lincoln's love for Ann Rutledge turned mediocrity into greatness. He found himself through the sorrow that came to him through her death.

Henry Ford was at one time the richest and most powerful man alive. He had to master poverty, illiteracy, and other handicaps that the average man never encounters. He became successful because of the love inspired by a truly great woman, his wife, and this despite the fact that his early biographers never mentioned her name.

Every Ford automobile, the Ford millions, every Ford factory, and all that Henry Ford accomplished for the good of mankind may be appropriately submitted as evidence of the soundness of the Law of Success philosophy, as he was the most practical student of this philosophy. From his lifework, more than from any other source, has come the material that made this philosophy a reality.

The seed of all success lies sleeping in well-defined motive!

Without a burning desire to achieve, superinduced by one or more of the eight basic motives, no man ever becomes a genius.

Motivated by a highly developed sex life, Napoleon became the greatest leader of men of his time. His ignoble ending was the result of his lack of observance of two of the other seventeen factors of success—namely, Self-Control and the Golden Rule.

Lester Park entered the movie business, at about the same time that the author began the organization of the Law of Success philosophy. The "miracle" that transformed Mr. Park from a self-styled "failure" into an outstanding success was described in an editorial written by the author and published in a New York newspaper. This editorial is here reproduced in full as a fitting close for this chapter:

Another Miracle

For twenty-five years I have been studying, measuring, and analyzing human beings. My research has brought me in contact with over 20,000 men and women. Two people out of this vast army stand out in bold contrast with nearly all the others. These two are Henry Ford and Lester Park.

Mr. Ford's general average (measuring his commitment to the Laws of Success) was 95 percent. Lester Park's general average was 94 percent. When I first analyzed Henry Ford, his rating on the Seventeen Factors of Success was 67 percent. His gradual rise from 67 percent to 95 percent was an outstanding achievement, but nothing to compare with the transformation that took place in Lester Park's mental machinery over a period of only a few weeks.

When I first analyzed Mr. Park, his general average was 45 percent. Less than a month later I made a second analysis and lo! he had jumped from zero to 100 percent on two of the most important of the Seventeen Factors of Success, and had made astounding advances on many of the other factors.

A Sweeping Endorsement

This analysis, showing Lester Park's two ratings on the factors that create power and wealth, is a sweeping endorsement of the belief that many philosophers have held: that all success is merely a state of mind, that people are lifted to great heights of power, or dashed into oblivion, solely by the thoughts they release on the wings of the ether.

Solitary Confinement

Lester Park was formerly one of the most active movie executives in America. His name was linked to the names of others, who have since made huge fortunes out of this business. But something "snapped" in Lester Park's mental machinery. He lost his grip on himself. His self-confidence dropped to zero. He ceased to have a definite chief aim. He drew himself away from contact with others in his profession, thereby depriving himself of the greatest of all the Laws of Success, the Master Mind. (You will recall that this is a mind that is a composite of two or more minds working in perfect harmony, for the attainment of some definite objective.)

For years Park committed himself to solitary confinement in a dark dungeon. That dungeon was his own mind, and he himself carried the key to the door.

The Wheel of Fate

Some time ago I conducted a class on the Laws of Success at the Waldorf-Astoria Hotel, in New York City. By a queer turn of the wheel of chance—or was it the "wheel of fate"?—Lester Park became a student in that class. The transformation that has taken place in Lester Park occurred in a fraction of a minute, during the first half hour of my first lecture! In a single sentence I made a statement that served as a key that unlocked the door to the cell in which Park had confined himself, and he stepped out, ready to pick up the reins where he had laid them down several years ago. The transformation was no imaginary one. It has been both real and complete.

Within two weeks' time after the light again shone into the brain of Lester Park he had completed all arrangements for the production of one of the greatest pictures of his career. When I say he had "completed all arrangements," I mean just that! The money for the production was offered him from more than one source. Friends he had known in the heyday of his career as a producer suddenly appeared upon the scene as if by magic, and greeted him like long-lost brothers! The dream movie of his life became a living, pulsating reality.

A Modern Miracle Had Happened!

That miracle brings great joy to my heart, because it proves, once more, that the child of my heart and brain—the Law of Success philosophy—is destined to emancipate millions of other Lester Parks from the dark dungeons of despair to which they have confined themselves. Many years ago Andrew Carnegie gave me an idea that caused me to start a long period of labor and research. That idea was the hub around which the Law of Success philosophy has been built. I have lived to see it bring freedom to countless millions, and to how many more it will bring similar freedom I have no way of knowing, because the philosophy is now being studied in nearly every civilized country on earth, by those, of every background, with whom I have not personally come in contact.

The man who sows a single beautiful thought in the mind of another renders the world, through that act, a greater service than that rendered by all the faultfinders combined.

A Prophecy Fulfilled

Years ago, when I predicted that Henry Ford would one day become the most powerful man on earth, my statement caused me great embarrassment, because Ford had not then shown any signs of becoming the world's richest man. I stood back of that prediction and lived to see it become more than justified.

[Signed] NAPOLEON HILL.

This Is an Age of Action!

To summarize the seventeen factors of success described in this volume: The reader may better grasp the entire philosophy by keeping in mind the fact that success is based upon power, and that power is knowledge expressed in action.

All the major stimuli which arouse the mind and put it into action have been described in this volume. The main purpose of the seventeen factors of success is that of providing one with practical plans and methods of application for the use of these stimuli.

Careful analysis has disclosed the startling fact that a single incident or experience often results in such marked influence upon a mind of the most mediocre type that the owner of that mind surpasses, in achievement, others who have superior and better trained minds.

The Law of Success, as described through the seventeen factors outlined in this volume, provides all the known methods of mind stimulation that inspire the individual with high ambition and supply the courage essential for the attainment of the object of that ambition.

It is hardly sufficient to say that one may achieve more if one will undertake more. The author has aimed to offer the individual a practical mind stimulant, or source of inspiration, which may be used to build greater ambition and supply the motive for action in carrying out that ambition.

Ninety-five percent of the energy of the human mind remains passive throughout life. The major purpose of this philosophy of success is to supply the stimuli that will arouse this sleeping 95 percent of mind energy and put it to work. How? By planting in the mind some strong motive that will lead to action; by stepping up the mind, through contact with other minds, and causing it to vibrate on a higher plane.

THE
MASTER-KEY
TO RICHES

Revised and Updated by
Patricia G. Horan

THINK!

Many centuries ago a very wealthy and wise philosopher by the name of Croesus, an adviser to Cyrus, King of the Persians, said, "I am reminded, O King: and take this lesson to heart; that there is a Wheel on which the affairs of men revolve, and its mechanism is such that it prevents any man from being always fortunate."

There is a Wheel of Life that controls the destiny of us all! It operates through the power of thought.

The Master-Key to Riches was designed for the purpose of aiding you in the mastery and control of this great Wheel, to the end that it may be made to yield an abundance of all that you desire, including the Twelve Great Riches of Life described in the second chapter.

Remember, you who are beginning the study of this philosophy, that this same Wheel that "prevents any man from being always fortunate" may provide also that no one shall be always unfortunate, provided he or she will take possession of his or her own mind and direct it to the attainment of some Definite Major Purpose in life.

THE PROLOGUE

I give and bequeath to the American people the greater portion of my vast fortune, which consists in the philosophy of individual achievement, through which all of my riches were accumulated."

Thus began the last will and testament of one of the richest men that the richest nation on earth ever produced, and it now serves as the beginning of the prologue of a story that may well mark the most important turning point in the lives of all who read it.

This story first began in the late fall of 1908, when Andrew Carnegie called in a man whom he trusted, and whose integrity and judgment he respected, and entrusted to him what Mr. Carnegie said was "the greater portion" of his vast fortune, with the understanding that the legacy was to be presented to the American people.

Today, nearly a hundred years later, his story has been written to notify you of your right to share in this huge estate, and to inform you as to the conditions under which you may do so.

Lest you do the perfectly natural thing that many would do—that of reaching the false conclusion that the conditions under which you may share in this huge estate are too rigid to permit you to comply with them—let me relieve your mind by saying that the conditions are well within the reach of any adult of average intelligence, and there are no tricks or false hopes, either in connection with the conditions or in this promise.

So that you may know whether or not this promises anything you need or desire, let me tell you what it does promise:

- A clear description of the formula by which you may have the full benefit of the Master-Key to Riches—a key that should unlock the doors to the solution of all of your problems, that will help you convert all of your past failures into priceless assets, and that lead you to the attainment of the Twelve Great Riches, including economic security.

- An inventory of the vast riches which Andrew Carnegie provided for distribution to those who are qualified to receive them, together with detailed instructions through which you may appropriate and use your full share.

- A description of the means by which you may have the full benefit of the education, experience, and technical skill of those whose cooperation you may need for the attainment of your major purpose in life, thus providing a practical means by which you may bridge the disadvantages of an inadequate education and attain the highest goals of life as successfully as may those who are blessed with a formal education.

- The privilege of using the philosophy of success which was organized from the life experiences, by the trial-and-error method, of more than 500 successful men, among whom are Henry Ford, Thomas A. Edison, William Wrigley Jr., Cyrus H. K. Curtis, J. Ogden Armour, Elbert Hubbard, Charles M. Schwab, F. W. Woolworth, Frank A. Vanderlip, Edward Bok, Dr. Alexander Graham Bell, Clarence Darrow, and Luther Burbank. A definite plan by which anyone who works for wages or a salary may promote him or herself into a higher income, with the full consent and cooperation of his or her employer.

- A definite plan through which anyone who works for others may get into a business or a profession of his or her own, with more than average chances of success. A definite plan through which any businessperson may convert his or her customers into permanent clients, and through their willing cooperation add new customers who will likewise become permanent. A definite plan through which any salesperson of life insurance, or of other useful service or merchandise, may convert buyers into willing workers who will aid in finding new clients. A definite plan through which any employer may convert his or her employees into personal friends, under circumstances which will enable him or her to make the business more profitable for himself or herself and for the employees.

You have here a clear statement of my promise, and the first condition under which you may benefit by these is that you read this book twice, line by line, and think as you read!

Nothing ever happens without a definite cause. It was by no mere chance that the United States came to be known as the "richest and the freest" country of the world. This is a land of plenty because of definite, understandable causes, each of which we have clearly defined.

The desire for plenty may be selfish, but we all know that it is a natural desire. Andrew Carnegie understood this when he decided to give away his huge fortune, but guided as he was by the wisdom of a lifetime of practical experience in dealing with people, he safeguarded his gift by attaching to it certain conditions with which all who receive any part of it must comply.

Mr. Carnegie adopted a novel method for the distribution of his riches because he recognized the weakness of humankind in wanting something for nothing. He knew that people in all walks of life, all down through the past, have been looking for a "land flowing with milk and honey."

He also knew that the gift of riches in any form, without some sort of consideration in return, generally harms more than it benefits the one who receives it. Therefore he wisely attached to his gift certain conditions by which those who receive it are protected against this common weakness of desiring something for nothing.

Looking into history, Mr. Carnegie recognized that this desire for something for nothing was the object of the search of the scouts who were sent out by Moses and Joshua, because the children of Israel, after they had worked in slavery in Egypt for many years, making brick without straw, had escaped the Pharaohs and were waiting, after a long period in the wilderness, for an opportunity to cross over the sea into the land of plenty.

The glowing description of plenty in that land served as the incentive which enabled their leaders, against strong opposition, to hold the solidarity of the people until they reached their objectives.

A counterpart of this same story is found in the migration of subdued people from England to the New World. They came not only in search of a land of material plenty, but for a land which afforded plenty of opportunities for the expression of personal initiative, freedom of worship, and freedom of speech, and the very purpose of their migration served as an assurance of the success of the most outstanding step ever taken by any group in modern history.

They developed a land of plenty. The plenty came from their efforts simply because their endeavors were based upon a sound philosophy, a constructive objective, which Andrew Carnegie recognized centuries later, and he not only converted it into a huge fortune for himself, but he left to the American people of today a simple set of rules, a Master-Key, by which they too may acquire riches.

Out of their pioneering toil down through the years, the descendants of those pilgrims of progress have built a civilization never before known in the history of the world, a culture which exceeds the greatest culture of all times, standards of living which are higher than ever before known to mankind, conveniences, comforts, luxuries, and opportunities available to the humblest person, such as the world has never known. All of these advantages were the result of a sound foundation—the foundation stones of a budding new democracy, something new under the sun, a modified form of perfect state, which was destined to prove successful because it was practical.

Such a civilization had never before been known in the entire history of mankind. There have been many periods in history when the advance of civilization was heralded with glowing terms, yet the civilization of the particular age in each instance was confined to a relatively small percentage of the people.

The difference between each of these periods of the distant past and the present, which we now enjoy, lies in the fact that the masses of people of the past were under the heels of sovereigns, many of whom were tyrants, while we enjoy a standard of living which was unknown even to the kings of those days.

Thus we represent a difference between the cultural eras of the past and the culture of today. Study if you will the picture of the advantages enjoyed by the American people today, even to the lowliest and the humblest. Free education, free entertainment, radio, television, the automobile, the airplane, the network of free highways, advanced modes of communication, free worship. These and thousands of other advantages denied to the peasants of the past are now the common property of all of the people in America today.

This difference, which is due to the fundamental difference in motives and objectives, has been made possible because of practical developments under the American way of life, which have never been experienced in Europe or in any other part of the Old World.

In America men and women have been free to follow the dictates of their own consciences; they have had freedom of worship, freedom of speech, freedom of the press, freedom of political convictions, and freedom for the fullest exercise of their own personal initiative in any calling of their choice, and they have been protected by a form of government which assured them the fruits of their labors.

This has arisen out of the fact that freedom, life, liberty, and the pursuit of happiness constituted the basis of the development of our country, with its program of plenty as the goal of every citizen.

As workers began to express their personal initiative as individuals, and later as groups, and later still for security and protection as corporations, with the capital financed by workers and nonworkers, employees learned the art of salesmanship, the art of competition, the blessings of individual initiative, and the necessity of honest production to justify the art of advertising.

All these factors combined have justified greater production at lower cost, so that more people may afford to purchase American commodities, so that more people may be engaged in manufacturing.

This, briefly stated, is the heart of the American system—a well-expressed faith, thrift, cooperation, confidence in one another, personal initiative, and a sense of fairness in human relationships.

In understanding this story of the road to riches under the American way of life, it is necessary that the reader supply a part of the story by his own thoughts and by comparing our statements with his own experiences. This in turn makes it necessary for the reader to have a clear picture of the history of the American sources of riches in order that he or she may be sure of appropriating his or her share of those riches.

In this spirit do we approach the description of the Master-Key, from the use of which come all riches known to the American people.

Let it be known at the outset that when we speak of "riches" we have in mind all riches, not merely those represented by bank balances and material things.

We have in mind the riches of liberty and freedom, of which we have more than any other nation.

We have in mind the riches of human relationships, through which every American citizen may exercise to the fullest the privilege of personal initiative in whatever direction he or she chooses; the riches of the system of free enterprise, which has made American industry the envy of the whole world; and the riches of a free press, free public schools, and free places of worship.

Thus, when we speak of "riches" we have reference to the abundant life which is everywhere available to the people of the United States, and obtainable with a minimum amount of effort.

Meanwhile, let it be understood that we shall offer no suggestions to anyone as to the nature of the riches for which he should aim, nor the amount he should undertake to acquire.

Fortunately the American way of life offers an abundance of all forms of riches, sufficient in both quality and quantity to satisfy all reasonable human desires, but we sincerely hope that somehow every reader will aim for his or her share, not only of the things that money can buy but also of the things that money cannot buy.

We shall not undertake to tell anyone how to live life, but we know, from having observed both the rich and the poor of America, that material riches alone are no guarantee of happiness.

We have never yet found a truly happy person who was not engaged in some form of service by which others benefited. And we do know many who are wealthy in material things but have not found happiness.

We mention these observations not to preach but to quicken those who, because of the great abundance of material riches in America, take them for granted, and who have lost sight of the priceless things of life that are to be acquired only through the intangible riches we have mentioned.

Although the American people already enjoy the highest standard of living in the world, we are not satisfied with this standard, and we propose to describe how we believe it can be raised still higher.

In the next several pages, you'll see how you, too, can contribute to improving the American way of life, and indeed the lives of all with whom you form close ties.

CHAPTER 1

THE BEGINNING
OF ALL RICHES

You have opened this book to seek the "Master-Key to Riches"! You have opened it because of that human urge for the better things in life, which is the common desire of all people. Some of you desire economic security, which money alone can provide.

Some of you desire an outlet for your talents in order that you may have the joy of creating your own riches.

Some of you are seeking the easy way to riches, with the hope that you will find it without giving anything in return; that, too, is a common desire. But it is a desire I shall hope to modify for your benefit, as from experience I have learned that there is no such thing as something for nothing.

There is but one sure way to riches, and that may be attained only by those who have what I call the Master-Key to Riches.

This "Master-Key" is an ingenious device with which those who possess it may unlock the door where they will find the solution to all of their problems. Its powers of magic transcend those of Houdini himself.

It opens the door to sound health.

It opens the door to love and romance.

It opens the door to friendship, by revealing the traits of personality and character that make enduring friends.

It reveals the method by which every adversity, every failure, every disappointment, every mistaken error of judgment, and every past defeat may be transmuted into riches of a priceless value.

It rekindles the dead hopes of all who possess it, and it reveals the formula by which one may "tune in" and draw on the great reservoir of Infinite Intelligence, through that state of mind known as Faith. It lifts humble people to positions of power, fame, and fortune.

It turns back the hands of time and renews the spirit of youth for those who have grown old too soon.

It provides the method by which one may take full and complete possession of one's own mind, thus giving one unchallengeable control over the emotions of the heart and the power of thinking.

It bridges the deficiencies of those who have inadequate education through formal schooling, and puts them substantially on the same plane of opportunity that is enjoyed by those who have a better education.

And last, it opens the doors, one by one, to what I call the Twelve Great Riches of Life, which I shall describe for you in detail in a moment.

Listen carefully to what I have to say. Listen not only with open ears, but with open minds and eager hearts, remembering that one can't hear what one isn't prepared to hear. That preparation consists of many things, among them sincerity of purpose, humility of heart, a full recognition of the truth that no one knows everything—that the combined knowledge of humankind has not been enough to save us from destroying one another through warfare, nor to restrain us from cheating and stealing the fruits of labor from others. I shall speak to you of facts and describe to you many principles of which many of you may never have heard, for they are known only to those who have prepared themselves to accept the advice I have to offer a small but ever-increasing number of people who have attained the Degree of Fellowship.

Achieving the Degree of Fellowship

The Fellowship is made up of men and women from many walks of life, of all nationalities and creeds. Its purpose is to reveal the benefits that are available through the spirit of sharing universal wisdom. The Fellowship is nonsectarian and noncommercial. Its members work individually. It has no authorized leaders, but all who qualify for the Degree of Fellowship become leaders unto themselves. The only condition that is required for membership is that all who qualify for the degree shall share with others the benefits they receive through these teachings—as many as they may find who are willing to prepare themselves to receive the benefits.

The Fellowship prepares men and women to relate themselves to one another as brothers and sisters. It recognizes the great abundance of material riches available to all and provides a rational plan by which every person may share in these riches in proportion to his or her talents, as they are expressed through useful service.

It frowns upon the idea of too much for the few and too little for the many, but it also discourages all who endeavor to get something for nothing. And it discourages the accumulation of riches by individuals whose greed inspires them to seek more than they can use for their own economic security and encourages them to provide opportunities through which others may attain such security.

The Fellowship has a stupendous task ahead of it. Civilization must live and go forward, not backward. We must learn to live together, so that we may walk arm in arm, do the world's work, and reap our just reward without poverty, without hardship, without fear or trembling.

The members of the Fellowship have learned to do this without suffering the loss of any of the joys of living or sacrificing any of their rights as individuals. They have discovered that the Fellowship way is the only path to enduring happiness.

I have come to tell you about the Fellowship and to place in your hands what I describe as the Twelve Great Riches.

The Many Selves Who Guide You

Before I describe the Twelve Great Riches, let me reveal to you some of the riches you already possess, riches of which most of you may not be conscious.

First, recognize that each of you is a plural personality, although you may regard yourself as a single personality. You and every other person consist of at least two distinct personalities, and many of you possess more.

There is that self you recognize when you look into a mirror. That is your physical self. But it is only the house in which your other selves live. In that house there are two individuals, at least, who are eternally in conflict with each other.

One is a negative sort of person who thinks and moves and lives in an atmosphere of fear and doubt and poverty and ill health. This self expects failure and seldom is disappointed. It thinks of the circumstances of life that you do not want but seem forced to accept—poverty, greed, superstition, fear, doubt, worry, and physical sickness.

And one is your "other self," a positive sort of person who thinks in terms of opulence, sound health, love and friendship, personal achievement, creative vision, and service to others, and who guides you unerringly to the attainment of all of these blessings. It is this self which alone is capable of recognizing and appropriating the Twelve Great Riches. It is the only self capable of receiving the Master-Key to Riches.

These are not imaginary personalities of which I speak. They are real, for they have been revealed through scientific investigation of irreproachable authenticity. Many of you might have heard of Martin Seligman, a renowned psychologist and clinical researcher who has studied the effects of optimism, or positive thinking, for over twenty-five years. His research is but one scientific example of many available that have demonstrated the power that our thoughts can possess over our destiny.

Then you have many other priceless assets of which you may not be aware; hidden riches you have neither recognized nor used. Among these is a modern radio broadcasting and receiving station so powerful that it may pick up and send out the vibrations of thought from or to any part of the world, including the potential capacity to reach out into the cosmos and tune in with the power of Infinite Intelligence.

Your radio station operates automatically and continuously, when you are asleep just as when you are awake. And it is under the control at all times of one or the other of your two major personalities, the negative personality or the positive personality. When your negative personality is in control, your radio station picks up only the negative thought vibrations which are being sent out by hundreds of millions of other negative personalities throughout the world. These are accepted, acted upon, and translated into their physical equivalent in terms of the circumstances of life which you do not wish.

When your positive personality is in control, it picks up only the positive thought vibrations being released by millions of other positive personalities throughout the world, and translates them into their physical equivalent in terms of prosperity, sound health, love, hope, faith, peace of mind, and happiness—the values of life for which you and every other normal person are searching.

The Obligation to Share the Wealth

Why should you believe what I am saying to you? Why should you trust that I offer you the lessons you need to succeed? As you are aware, I am considered one of the richest, most influential men in the world. However, I was not born to riches.

I was born in poverty and illiteracy. My formal education is limited to the knowledge I gained through a country grade school. And the entire universe, as far as I was concerned, extended no farther than the boundary lines of the backwoods county into which I was born. Then love came into my heart, and with it the influence of the greatest person I shall ever hope to know. She became my wife and guide, for she came from a world outside my own—one I had not suspected existed. She was a woman of culture and education. From her I learned some of the secrets of biology, and chemistry, and astronomy, and physics. She reached deeply into my soul and uncovered that "other self" of which I had no knowledge.

Step by step, patiently and with love, she lifted me into a higher plane of understanding, until at long last I was prepared to receive the great gift which I shall share with you in the hope that you may become as rich as I.

With that blessing came also a responsibility consisting of an obligation to reveal the secrets of what I call "the great Master-Key" to as many of you as are prepared to receive it. But let me warn you that the Master-Key may be retained only by those who accept the obligation to share it with others. No one may use it selfishly, for personal aggrandizement alone.

The founders of the Rotary Club movement must have recognized the benefits of sharing, for they adopted as their motto "He profits most who serves best." And every close observer must have recognized that all individual successes which endure have had their beginning through the beneficent influence of some other individual, through some form of sharing.

My great opportunity consisted in the willingness of my wife to share with me the knowledge she had acquired, plus the knowledge I gained from the principles which placed the Master-Key within my reach.

Your opportunity may well consist in my willingness to share this knowledge with you. But remember, I have not come to give you material riches alone. I have come to share with you the knowledge by which you may acquire riches—all riches—through the expression of your own personal initiative. That is the greatest of all gifts! And it is the only kind of gift that anyone who is blessed with the advantages of a great nation like ours should expect. For here we have every potential form of riches available to mankind. We have them in great abundance.

So I assume that you, too, wish to become rich.

Let us become partners in the attainment of your desire, for I have found the way to all riches. Therefore I am prepared to serve as your guide.

I sought the path to riches the hard way before I learned that there is a short and dependable path I could have followed had I been guided as I hope to guide you.

Before we begin our journey to the land of riches we must take inventory so that we may know the true nature of riches. It is important to be prepared to recognize riches when they come within our reach.

Some believe that riches consist in money alone. But enduring riches, in the broader sense, consist in many other values than those of material things, and, may I add, that without these other intangible values the possession of money will not bring the happiness some believe it will provide.

When I speak of "riches," I have in mind the greater riches whose possessors have made life pay off on their own terms, leading to a life of full and complete happiness. I call these the "Twelve Riches of Life," and I sincerely wish to share them with all of you who are prepared to receive them, in whole or in part.

You may wonder about my willingness to share, so I shall tell you that the Master-Key to Riches enables its possessors to add to their own store of riches everything of value that they share with others. This is one of the strangest facts of life, but it is a fact each of you must recognize and respect if you hope to tap its power.

CHAPTER 2

THE TWELVE RICHES OF LIFE

1. A Positive Mental Attitude

All riches, of whatsoever nature, begin as a state of mind, and let us remember that a state of mind is the one and only thing over which any person has complete, un-challenged right of control. It is highly significant that none of us has control over anything except the power to shape our own thoughts and the privilege of fitting them to any pattern of our choice.

Mental attitude is important because it converts the brain into the equivalent of an elec-tromagnet that attracts the counterpart of one's dominating thoughts and purposes. It also attracts the counterpart of one's fears, worries, and doubts.

A positive mental attitude is the starting point of all riches, whether they be riches of a material nature or intangible riches. It attracts the riches of true friendship and the riches one finds in the hope of future achievement. It provides the riches one may find in Nature's handiwork, as it exists in the moonlit nights, in the stars that float out there in the heavens, in the beautiful landscapes and in distant horizons.

It attracts the riches to be found in the labor of one's choice, where expression may be given to the highest plane of man's soul.

It draws the riches of harmony in home relationships, where all members of the family work together in a spirit of friendly cooperation.

It creates the riches of freedom from fear, and the riches of enthusiasm, both active and passive.

It inspires the riches of song and laughter, both of which indicate states of mind.

And the riches of self-discipline, through which one may have the joy of knowing that the mind can and will serve any desired end if one will take possession of it and command it through definiteness of purpose.

It elicits the riches of play, through which one may lay aside all of the burdens of life and become as a little child again.

And the riches of discovery of one's "other self"—the self which knows no such reality as permanent failure.

It develops the riches of faith in the universe, of which every individual mind is a minute projection.

And the riches of meditation, the connecting link by which anyone may draw upon the great universal supply of Infinite Intelligence at will.

These and all other riches begin with a positive mental attitude. Therefore, it is but little cause for wonder that a positive mental attitude takes the first place in the list of the Twelve Riches.

2. Sound Physical Health

Sound health begins with a "health consciousness" produced by a mind which thinks in terms of health and not in terms of illness. It requires temperance of eating and a commitment to physical activity.

3. Harmony in Human Relationships

Harmony with others begins with oneself. As Shakespeare said, there are benefits to following this rule. "To thine own self be true, and it must follow, as the night the day, thou cans't not then be false to any man."

4. Freedom from Fear

No one who fears anything is free. Fear is a harbinger of evil, and wherever it appears one may find a cause which must be eliminated before one may become rich in the fuller sense. The seven basic fears which appear most often in our minds are (1) the fear of POVERTY,

(2) the fear of CRITICISM, (3) the fear of ILL HEALTH, (4) the fear of LOSS OF LOVE, (5) the fear of LOSS OF LIBERTY, (6) the fear of OLD AGE, and (7) the fear of DEATH.

5. The Hope of Achievement

The greatest of all forms of happiness comes as the result of hope of achievement of some yet unattained desire. The person who cannot look to the future with hope of becoming the person he or she would like to be, or with the belief of attaining the objective he or she has failed to reach in the past, is poor beyond description.

6. The Capacity for Faith

Faith is the connecting link between the conscious mind and the great universe. It is the fertile soil of the garden of the human mind wherein may be produced all of the riches of life. It is the "eternal elixir" which gives creative power and action to the impulses of thought. Faith is the basis of all so-called miracles, and of many mysteries which cannot be explained by the rules of logic or science. It is the spiritual "chemical" which, when it is mixed with prayer, gives one direct and immediate connection with one's God.

Faith is the power which transmutes the ordinary energies of thought into their spiritual equivalent.

7. Willingness to Share One's Blessings

Those who haven't learned to share have not learned the true path to happiness, for happiness comes only by sharing. All riches may be embellished and multiplied by the simple process of sharing them where they may serve others. The space one occupies in the hearts of others is determined precisely by the service rendered through some form of sharing one's blessings.

Riches which are not shared, whether they be material riches or the intangibles, wither and die like the rose on a severed stem, for it is one of Nature's first laws that inaction and disuse lead to decay and death, and this law applies to material possessions just as it applies to the living cells of every physical body.

8. A Labor of Love

No one is richer than the person who has found a labor of love and who is busily engaged in performing it. Labor is the highest form of human expression of desire. It is the liaison between the demand and the supply of all human needs, the forerunner of all human progress, and the medium by which imagination is given the wings of action. All labors of love are sanctified because they bring the joy of self-expression.

9. An Open Mind on All Subjects

Tolerance, which is among the higher attributes of culture, is expressed only by the person who holds an open mind on all subjects at all times. And it is only the person with an open mind who becomes truly educated and who is thus prepared to receive the greater riches of life.

10. Self-Discipline

The person who does not master self-discipline may never become the master of anything else. Those who master themselves may become the master of their own earthly destiny. The highest form of self-discipline consists in the expression of humility of the heart when one has attained great riches or has been overtaken by that which is commonly called "success."

11. The Capacity to Understand People

Those who are rich in their understanding of people always recognize that all people are fundamentally alike in that they have evolved from the same origin; that all human activities are inspired by one or more of the nine basic motives of life, including:

> The emotion of LOVE
> The desire for SEX
> The desire for MATERIAL GAIN
> The desire for SELF-PRESERVATION
> The desire for FREEDOM OF BODY AND MIND
> The desire for SELF-EXPRESSION
> The desire for perpetuation of LIFE AFTER DEATH

The emotion of ANGER

The emotion of FEAR

Those who understand what motivates others must first understand what motivates themselves.

The capacity to understand others eliminates many of the common causes of friction among people. It is the foundation of all friendship. It is the basis of all harmony and cooperation. It is fundamentally important in all leadership that calls for friendly cooperation.

12. Economic Security

The last, though not least important of the Twelve Riches, is economic security.

Economic security is not attained by the possession of money alone. It is attained by the service one renders—for useful service may be converted into all forms of human needs, with or without the use of money.

Henry Ford had economic security not because he controlled a vast fortune of money, but for the better reason that he provided profitable employment for millions of men and women, and also the first dependable automobiles to still greater numbers of people. The service he rendered attracted the money he controlled. That is how all enduring economic security must be attained.

I will introduce to you the principles by which money and all other forms of riches may be obtained, but first you must be prepared to apply these principles. Your mind must be conditioned for the acceptance of riches just as the soil of the earth must be prepared for the planting of seeds. Maybe you have heard the expression "When the student is ready, the teacher will appear."

This does not mean that the things one may need will appear without a cause, for there is a vast difference between one's "needs" and one's readiness to receive. To miss this distinction is to miss the major benefits I shall try to convey.

The Challenge of Embracing New Ideas

This may seem strange to you at first, but you should not become discouraged, for all new ideas seem strange. If you doubt that this approach is practical, take courage from the fact that it has brought me riches in abundance.

Human progress always has been slow, because people are reluctant to accept new ideas.

When Samuel Morse announced his discovery of the telegraph, instead of welcoming it, the world scoffed at him. They had never seen such a system before. It was unorthodox and it was new, and therefore it created suspicion and doubt.

The world also scoffed at Marconi when he improved on Morse's system. The same with the man we recognize today as an unqualified genius: Thomas A. Edison. He was not honored in his day but actually ridiculed for his electric lightbulb. Did the world welcome Ford's horseless buggy? No, he met the same experience!

So there was no surprise when ridicule met the legendary Wilbur and Orville Wright's flying machine. As a matter of fact, newspaper reporters refused to attend a demonstration of that ridiculous airplane.

Radio, instead of being recognized for the miracle it was, was thought of as a toy for the amusement of children, and nothing more.

I mention these examples in case you assumed that because history has so universally stood in awe of these titans, the people of their day felt the same.

No, what they proposed was new, unfamiliar. What I am proposing to you is equally new, and I warn you not to be discouraged. The unfamiliar does not always merit suspicion and dismissal. Follow my thought, accept my philosophy, and be assured that it will work for you, as it has worked for me.

By serving as your guide, I shall receive my compensation for my efforts in exact proportion to the benefits you receive. The eternal law of compensation ensures this. My compensation may not come directly from you, but it will come in one form or another, for it is a part of the great cosmic plan that no useful service shall be rendered by anyone without a just compensation. "Do the thing," said Emerson, "and you shall have the power."

Aside from the consideration of what I shall receive for my attempt to serve you, there is the question of an obligation which I owe the world in return for the blessings it has bestowed upon me. I did not acquire my riches without the aid of many others. I have observed that all who acquire enduring riches have ascended the ladder of opulence with two outstretched hands: one extended upward to receive the help of others who have reached the peak, and the other extended downward to aid those who are still climbing.

So let me admonish you who are on the path to riches that you, too, must proceed with outstretched hands, to give and to receive aid. It is a well-known fact that no one may attain enduring success or acquire enduring riches without aiding others who are seeking these desirable ends. To *get* one must first *give*! I am delivering this message to you today so that I may give!

The next step you must take in the process of "conditioning" your mind to receive riches is to learn the Nine Practices for receiving life's rewards.

They serve me when I am awake and they serve me while I sleep. They have protected me against fear, envy, greed, doubt, indecision, and procrastination. They have inspired me to move on my own personal initiative, have kept my imagination active, and have given me definiteness of purpose and the faith to ensure its fulfillment. They have been the real "conditioners" of my mind, the builders of my positive mental attitude!

CHAPTER 3

THE NINE PRACTICES FOR RECEIVING LIFE'S REWARDS

I want to share with you those practices I use to maintain my positive outlook on life. The first is GRATITUDE. Practice being grateful for everything that life has blessed you with. Every day I voice my appreciation for what I have received. I say:

"Today has been beautiful.

"It has provided me with health of body and mind.

"It has given me food and clothing.

"It has brought me another day of opportunity to be of service to others.

"It has given me peace of mind and freedom from all fear.

"For these blessings I am grateful."

Next is the practice of MATERIAL PROSPERITY. Every day you must attune your mind to the consciousness of opulence and plenty, free from the fear of poverty and want.

Third is the practice of SOUND PHYSICAL HEALTH. Every day be conscious of how you are treating your body, what you are eating, and how you are managing your stress. Being aware of your health helps you to value and sustain it.

Fourth, practice PEACE OF MIND. Try to keep your mind free from all inhibitions and self-imposed limitations, thereby providing your body and mind with complete rest.

Next is the practice of HOPE. Be grateful for the fulfillment of today's desires, and for the promise of fulfillment of tomorrow's aims.

Sixth, practice FAITH, whatever that might mean to you. I am grateful to God for the guidance God has given me; for inspiring me to do what has been helpful to me, and for turning me back from doing that which, had it been done, would have proven harmful to me.

Next, the practice of LOVE. This includes not only romantic love, but also love of country, love of family, love of friends, and love of all humankind. Be inspired to share your riches with all with whom you come in contact. Be conscious of all the love in your life, which makes life sweet and enhances your relationships with others.

Eighth is the practice of ROMANCE. What is there to say, but that romance is what renews our spirit of youth, in spite of the passing of years.

Finally, the practice of OVERALL WISDOM, which transforms into an enduring asset of priceless value all your past failures, defeats, errors of judgment and of deed, fears, mistakes, disappointments, and adversities of every nature. For me, these incidents have developed into my willingness and ability to inspire others to take possession of their own minds and to use the power of their mind for the attainment of the riches of life. Wisdom provides me with the privilege of sharing all my blessings with those who are ready to receive them, thereby enriching and multiplying my own blessings by the scope of their benefit to others.

I am grateful for the overall wisdom that has revealed to me the truth that no human experience need become a liability; that all experiences may be transmuted into useful service; that the power of thought is the only power over which one has complete control; that the power of thought may be translated into happiness at will; that there are no limitations to the power of thought save only those in one's own mind.

These Nine Practices condition your mind to receive the benefits of the Twelve Riches. They serve as a medium through which you can keep your mind fixed on the things you desire and away from the things you don't desire. They provide you with continuous immunity against all forms of negative mental attitude; thus they destroy both the seed of negative thought and the germination of that seed in the soil of your mind. They help you to keep your mind fixed upon your major purpose in life, and give the fullest expression to the attainment of that purpose. They keep you at peace with yourself, at peace with the world, and in harmony with your own conscience.

These practices reveal the existence of that "other self," which thinks, moves, plans, desires, and acts by the impetus of a power that recognizes no such reality as impossible. And they have proved, time and again, that every adversity carries with it the seed of an equivalent benefit. So when adversity overtakes you, as it overtakes everyone, you are not awed by it but begin immediately to search for that "seed of an equivalent benefit" and to germinate it into a full-blown flower of opportunity. That is how these practices help me to retain my positive outlook.

How to Make Use of the Twelve Riches

Now let us get on with our story by a description of the philosophy one must adopt in order to acquire the Twelve Riches.

I have described a method of preparing the mind to receive riches. But this is only the beginning of the story. I have yet to explain how one may take possession of riches and make the fullest use of them.

The story has its beginning in the life of Andrew Carnegie, a great philanthropist who was a typical product of the American system of free enterprise. Mr. Carnegie acquired the Twelve Riches, the financial portion of which was so vast that he did not live long enough to enable him to give it away, so he passed much of it on to others, who used it for the benefit of mankind. Mr. Carnegie was also blessed with the teachings of the Nine Practices. The practice of Overall Wisdom served him so well that he was inspired not only to give away all his material riches but also to provide people with a complete philosophy of life through which they, too, might acquire riches.

That philosophy consists of seventeen principles, which conform in every respect to the tenets of the great Constitution of the United States and the American system of free enterprise.

The organization of this philosophy required twenty years of labor, in which Mr. Carnegie and more than 500 other great American leaders of industry had a part, each of them contributing the sum total of what was learned from a lifetime of practical experience under the American system of free enterprise.

Mr. Carnegie explained his reason for having inspired the organization of a philosophy of individual achievement when he said:

"I acquired my money through the efforts of other people, and I shall give it back to the people as fast as I can find ways to do so without inspiring the desire for something for nothing. But the major portion of my riches consists in the knowledge with which I acquired both the tangible and the intangible portions of it. Therefore, it is my wish that this knowledge be organized into a philosophy and made available to every person who seeks an opportunity for self-determination under the American form of economics."

It was this philosophy by which Mr. Carnegie was inspired to give to the people who provided me with the Twelve Riches and an opportunity to achieve all that I have in life. And it is the philosophy you must adopt and apply if you hope to accept the riches I desire to share with you.

Before I describe the principles of this philosophy, I wish to give a brief history of what it has already accomplished for others throughout more than half the world:

It has been translated into four of the leading Indian dialects and has been made available to more than 2 million people of India.

It has been translated into the Portuguese language for the benefit of the people of Brazil, where it has served more than 1.5 million people.

It has been published in a special edition for distribution throughout the British Empire, where it has served more than 2 million people.

It has benefited one or more people in practically every city, town, and village in the United States, numbering in all an estimated 20 million people.

And it may well become the means of bringing about a better spirit of friendly cooperation between all the peoples of the world, since it is founded on no creed or brand but consists of the fundamentals of all enduring success, and all constructive human achievements in every field of human endeavor.

It supports all religions yet it is a part of none!

It is so universal in its nature that it leads men inevitably to success in all occupations.

But more important to you than all of this evidence, the philosophy is so simple that you may start, right where you stand, to put it to work for you.

The seventeen principles will serve as a dependable road map leading directly to the source of all riches, whether they be intangible or material riches. Follow the map and you cannot miss the way, but be prepared to comply with all the instructions and to assume all the responsibilities that go with the possession of great riches. And above all, remember that enduring riches must be shared with others; that there is a price one must pay for everything acquired.

The Master-Key will not be revealed through any one of these seventeen principles, for its secret consists in the combination of all of them. These principles represent seventeen doors through which one must pass to reach the inner chamber wherein is locked the source of all riches. The Master-Key will unlock the door to that chamber, and it will be in your hands when you have prepared yourself to accept it. Your preparation shall consist of the assimilation and the application of the first five of these seventeen principles, which I shall now describe at length.

CHAPTER 4

DEFINITENESS OF PURPOSE

It is impressive to recognize that all the great leaders, in all walks of life and during all periods of history, have attained their leadership by the application of their abilities behind a definite major purpose.

It is no less impressive to observe that those who are classified as failures have no such purpose, but they go around and around, like a ship without a rudder, coming back always empty-handed, to their starting point. Some of these "failures" begin with a definite major purpose, but they desert that purpose the moment they are overtaken by temporary defeat or strenuous opposition. They give up and quit, not knowing that there is a philosophy of success which is as dependable and as definite as the rules of mathematics, and never suspecting that temporary defeat is but a testing ground which may prove a blessing in disguise if it is not accepted as final.

It is one of the great tragedies of civilization that 98 out of every 100 people go all the way through life without coming within sight of anything that even approximates definiteness of a major purpose! And it was Andrew Carnegie's recognition of this tragedy that inspired him to influence some 500 great American leaders of industry to collaborate in the organization of this philosophy of individual achievement.

Mr. Carnegie's first test, which he applied to all of his associate workers who were under consideration for promotion to supervisory positions, was that of determining to what extent they were willing to *Go the Extra Mile.* His second test was to determine whether or not they had their minds fixed upon *a Definite Goal,* including the necessary preparation for the attainment of that goal.

"When I asked Mr. Carnegie for my first promotion," said Charles M. Schwab, one of his employees, "he grinned broadly and replied, 'If you have your heart fixed on what you want, there is nothing I can do to stop you from getting it.'"

Mr. Schwab knew what he wanted. It was the biggest job within Carnegie's control. And Mr. Carnegie helped him to get it.

One of the strange facts concerning those who move with definiteness of purpose is the readiness with which the world steps aside that they may pass, even coming to their aid in carrying out their aims.

How Andrew Carnegie Found the Perfect Employee

The story behind this philosophy is dramatic, and demonstrates the importance that Andrew Carnegie placed upon definiteness of purpose.

He had developed his great steel industry and accumulated a huge fortune in money when he turned his interest to the use and the disposition of his fortune. After he had recognized that the better portion of his riches consisted in the knowledge with which he had accumulated them and in his understanding of human relationships, his major aim in life became that of inspiring someone to develop a philosophy that would convey this knowledge to all who might desire it.

He was then well along in years and recognized that the job called for the services of a young person who had the time and the inclination to spend twenty years or more researching the causes of individual achievement.

After interviewing more than 250 possible associates who he suspected might have such ability, by chance he met a young man who had been sent by a magazine to interview him for the story of his achievements. Carnegie's keen insight into human character helped him to recognize that this young man might have the qualities for which he had long been searching, so he set up an ingenious plan to test him.

He began by giving the young man the story of his achievements. Then he began to suggest to him that the world needed a practical philosophy of individual achievement that would permit the humblest worker to accumulate riches in whatever amount and form the worker might desire.

For three days and nights he elaborated upon his idea, describing how one might go about the organization of such a philosophy. When the story was finished, Mr. Carnegie was ready to apply his test, to determine whether or not he had found the person who could be depended upon to carry his idea through to completion.

"You now have my idea of a new philosophy," he said, "and I wish to ask you a question in connection with it that I wish you to answer by a simple yes or no. The question is this:

"If I give you the opportunity to develop the world's first philosophy of individual achievement, and introduce you to those who can and will collaborate with you to develop it, do you wish the opportunity, and will you follow through with it to completion?"

The young man cleared his throat, stammered for a few seconds, then replied in a brief sentence that was destined to provide him with an opportunity to project his influence for good throughout the world.

"Yes," he exclaimed. "I will not only undertake the job, but I will finish it!"

That was definite. It was the one thing Mr. Carnegie was searching for—*Definiteness of Purpose.*

Many years later this young man learned that Mr. Carnegie had held a stopwatch in his hand when he asked that question, and had allowed exactly 60 seconds for an answer. If the answer had required more time, the opportunity would have been withheld. His answer had actually required 29 seconds.

Mr. Carnegie explained the reason for timing him.

"It has been my experience," he said, "that a person who cannot reach a decision promptly, once all of the necessary facts for a decision at hand are explained, cannot be depended upon to carry through any decision that person may make. I have also discovered that those who reach decisions promptly usually have the capacity to move with definiteness of purpose in other circumstances."

The first hurdle of Mr. Carnegie's test had been covered with flying colors, but there was still another that followed.

"Very well," said Carnegie, "you have one of the two important qualities that will be needed by the person who develops the philosophy I have described. Now I shall learn whether or not you have the second.

"If I give you the opportunity to develop the philosophy, are you willing to devote twenty years of your time to research the causes of success and failure, without pay, earning your own living as you go along?"

The question shocked him. He assumed that since he had been chosen by Mr. Carnegie for so important a job, he would be subsidized from Mr. Carnegie's huge fortune.

He recovered quickly from the shock, however, by asking Mr. Carnegie why he was unwilling to provide the money for so important an assignment.

"It is not unwillingness to supply the money," Mr. Carnegie replied, "but it is my desire to know if you have a natural capacity to *go the extra mile* by rendering service before trying to collect pay for it."

Then he went on to explain that the more successful people in all walks of life were, and had always been, those who followed the habit of rendering more service than that for which they were paid. He also called attention to the fact that subsidies of money, whether made to individuals or to groups of individuals, often do more injury than good.

And he reminded the young man that he had been given an opportunity which had been withheld from more than 250 other people, some of whom were much older and more experienced than he.

He finished by saying, "If you make the most of the opportunity I have offered you, it is conceivable that you may develop it into riches so fabulous in nature as to dwarf my material wealth by comparison, for that opportunity provides the way for you to penetrate the keenest minds of this nation, to profit by the experiences of our greatest American leaders of industry, and it might well enable you to project your influence for good throughout the civilized world, thereby enriching those who are not yet born."

Mr. Carnegie had found the person for whom he had been so long searching, and this person had received his first lesson on *Definiteness of Purpose* and willingness to *go the extra mile*.

Twenty years later, almost to the day, the philosophy that Mr. Carnegie had designated as being the reason for his riches was completed and presented to the world in an eight-volume edition.

"And what of the man who spent twenty years of time without pay?" some ask. "What compensation did he receive for his labor?"

A complete answer to this question would be impossible, for the man himself does not know the total value of the benefits received. Moreover, some of these benefits are so flexible in nature that they will continue to aid him the rest of his life.

But for the satisfaction of those who measure riches in material values alone, it can be stated that one book written by this man, and the result of the knowledge gained from the application of the principle of going the extra mile has already yielded an estimated profit of upward of $3 million. The actual time spent in writing the book was four weeks.

Why These Principles Are So Effective

Definiteness of Purpose and the habit of *Going the Extra Mile* constitute a force which staggers the imagination of even the most imaginative of people, although these are but two of the seventeen principles of individual achievement.

I mention these two principles together for one purpose: to indicate how the principles of this philosophy are interconnected like the links of a chain, and how this combination of principles leads to the development of stupendous power which cannot be attained by the application of any single one of them.

We will now analyze the power of definiteness of purpose and the psychological principles from which this power is derived.

First premise

The starting point of all individual achievement is the adoption of a definite purpose and a definite plan for its attainment.

Second premise

All achievement is the result of a motive or combination of motives, and there are nine basic motives which govern all voluntary actions. (These motives have been previously described in Chapter 2.)

Third premise

Any dominating idea, plan, or purpose held in the mind, through repetition of thought, and emotionalized with a burning desire for its realization, is taken over by the subconscious section of the mind and acted upon, and it is thus carried through to its logical climax by whatever natural means may be available.

Fourth premise

Any dominating desire, plan, or purpose held in the conscious mind and backed by *absolute faith* in its realization is taken over and acted upon immediately by the subconscious section of the mind. There is no known record of this kind of a desire having ever been held without fulfillment.

Fifth premise

The power of thought is the only thing over which any person has complete, unquestionable control—a fact that, for some, might suggest the need for a close relationship between the mind of man and Infinite Intelligence, linked together by faith.

Sixth premise

The subconscious mind may be reached through faith and given instructions as though it were a person or a complete entity unto itself.

Seventh premise

A definite purpose, backed by absolute faith, is a form of wisdom, and wisdom in action produces positive results.

The Major Advantages of Definiteness of Purpose

Definiteness of Purpose develops self-reliance, personal initiative, imagination, enthusiasm, self-discipline, and concentration of effort; all of these are prerequisites for the attainment of material success.

It induces one to budget one's time and to plan all day-to-day endeavors so they lead toward the attainment of one's *Major Purpose* in life.

It makes one more alert in the recognition of opportunities related to the object of one's *Major Purpose,* and it inspires the necessary courage to act on those opportunities when they appear.

It inspires the cooperation of other people.

It prepares the way for the full exercise of that state of mind known as faith, by making the mind positive and freeing it from the limitations of fear and doubt and indecision.

It provides one with a success consciousness, without which no one may attain enduring success in any calling.

It destroys the destructive habit of procrastination.

Last, it leads directly to the development and the continuous maintenance of the first of the Twelve Riches, a positive mental attitude.

These are the major characteristics of *Definiteness of Purpose,* although it has many other qualities and usages—and it is directly related to each of the Twelve Riches, because they are attainable only by singleness of purpose.

Compare the principle of *Definiteness of Purpose* with the Twelve Riches, one at a time, and observe how essential it is for the attainment of each. Then take inventory of the people of outstanding achievement whom this country has produced, and observe how each of them has emphasized some major purpose as the object of his endeavors.

Henry Ford concentrated on building the first low-priced, dependable automobiles. Thomas Edison devoted his efforts to scientific inventions, and Andrew Carnegie to the manufacture and sale of steel. F.W. Woolworth concentrated on the first large-scale general stores, and Philip Armour on meatpacking and distribution. William Randolph Hearst focused on newspapers and Alexander Graham Bell on developing the first telephone.

In our present day, every Olympian athlete trains with one major purpose before him or her.

In our historic past, our nation depended on the major purposes of Jefferson, Lincoln, Washington, Patrick Henry, and Thomas Paine, who devoted their lives and in some instances their fortunes to the freedom of the rest of us.

This list might be multiplied until it contained the name of every great American leader who has contributed to the establishment of the American way of life as we of today know it and benefit by it.

How to Acquire a Definite Major Purpose

The procedure in the development of a *Definite Major Purpose* is simple but important. If you follow these steps, you will begin to reap the rewards of your efforts.

(a) Write out a complete, clear and definite statement of your *major purpose in life,* sign it, and commit it to memory; then repeat it orally at least once every day, more often if practicable. Repeat it over and over, thus placing all your faith in Infinite Intelligence.

(b) Write out a clear, definite plan by which you intend to begin the attainment of the object of your *Definite Major Purpose.* In this plan, state the maximum time allowed for the attainment of your purpose, and describe precisely what you intend to give in return for the realization of your purpose, remembering that there is no such thing as something for nothing, and that everything has a price which must be paid in advance, in one form or another.

(c) Make your plan flexible enough to permit changes at any time you are inspired to do so. Remember that Infinite Intelligence, which operates in every atom of matter and in every living or inanimate thing, may present you with a plan far superior to any you can create. Therefore, be ready at all times to recognize and adopt any superior plan that may be presented to your mind.

(d) Keep your *major purpose* and your plans for attaining it strictly to yourself except insofar as you will receive additional instructions for carrying out your plan, in the description of the *Master Mind Principle*, which follows.

Do not make the mistake of assuming that because you may not understand these instructions, the principles here described are not sound. Follow the instructions to the letter; follow them in good faith, and remember that by so doing you are duplicating the procedure of many of the greatest leaders this nation has ever produced.

These instructions call for no effort that you may not easily put forth. They make no demands upon time or ability with which the average person would find it difficult to comply.

Decide now what you desire from life and what you have to give in return. Decide where you are going and how you are to get there. Then make a start from where you now stand. Make the start with whatever means of attaining your goal you have at hand. And you will discover that to the extent you make use of these, other and better means will reveal themselves to you.

That has been the experience of all those whom the world has recognized as successes. Most of them started with humble beginnings with little more to aid them than a passionate desire to attain a definite goal.

There is enduring magic in such a desire!

Soon you will learn about a principle that is the key to all great achievements, the principle that has been responsible for our great American way of life, our system of free enterprise, our riches, and our freedom. But first you must make sure that you know what it is that you desire of life.

Ideas That Lead to Success Begin as Definiteness of Purpose

It is a well-known fact that ideas are the only assets that have no fixed values. It is equally well-known that ideas are the beginning of all achievements.

Ideas form the foundation of all fortunes, the starting point of all inventions. They have mastered the air above us and the waters of the oceans around us; they have enabled us to harness and use the atmosphere itself, through which one brain may communicate with another brain through telepathy.

The phonograph was nothing but an abstract idea until Edison organized it through definiteness of purpose and submitted it to the subconscious portion of his brain, where it was projected into the great reservoir of Infinite Intelligence, from which a workable plan was flashed back to him. And this workable plan he translated into a machine that worked.

The philosophy of individual achievement began as an idea in the mind of Andrew Carnegie. He backed his idea with definiteness of purpose, and now the philosophy is available for the benefit of millions of people throughout the industrialized world. Any idea that is held in the mind, emphasized, feared, or reverenced begins at once to clothe itself in the most convenient and appropriate physical form that is available.

That which people believe, talk about, and fear, whether it be good or bad, has a very definite way of making its appearance in one form or another. Those who are struggling to free themselves from the limitations of poverty and misery must not forget this great truth, for it applies to an individual just as it does to a nation of people.

Self-Suggestion: The Link Between the Conscious and the Subconscious Mind

There is a working principle through which thoughts, ideas, plans, hopes, and purposes which are placed in the conscious mind find their way into the subconscious section of the mind, where they are picked up and carried out to their logical conclusion, through a law of nature I shall describe later. To recognize this principle and understand it is to recognize, also, the reason why *Definiteness of Purpose* is the beginning of all achievements.

You can transfer thought from the conscious to the subconscious section of the mind more quickly by the simple process of "stepping up" or stimulating the vibrations of thought through faith, fear, or any other highly intensified emotion, such as enthusiasm, a burning desire based on definiteness of purpose. Thoughts backed by faith have precedence over all others in the matter of definiteness and speed with which they are handed over to the subconscious section of the mind and are acted upon. The speed with which the power of faith works has given rise to the belief held by many that certain phenomena are the result of miracles.

Psychologists and scientists recognize no such phenomenon as a miracle, claiming that everything that happens is the result of a definite cause, albeit a cause which cannot be explained. Be that as it may, it is a known fact that those capable of freeing their minds from all self-imposed limitations, through the mental attitude known as faith, generally find the solution to all life's problems, regardless of their nature.

Psychologists recognize also that Infinite Intelligence, while it is not claimed to automatically solve riddles, nevertheless carries out any clearly defined idea to a logical conclusion, aim, or desire that is submitted to the subconscious section of the mind in a mental attitude of perfect faith.

But Infinite Intelligence never attempts to modify any thought that is submitted to it, and it has never been known to act upon a mere wish or indefinite idea, thought, or purpose. This truth, well grounded in your mind, will give you sufficient power to solve your daily problems with much less effort than most people devote to worrying over their problems.

So-called hunches often are signals indicating that Infinite Intelligence is endeavoring to reach and influence the conscious section of the mind, but you will observe that they usually come in response to some idea, plan, purpose, or desire, or some fear that has been handed over to the subconscious section of the mind.

All "hunches" should be treated civilly and examined carefully, as they often convey, either in whole or in part, information of the utmost value to the individual who receives them. These "hunches" often make their appearance many hours, days, or weeks after the original thought which inspires them has reached the reservoir of Infinite Intelligence. Meanwhile, the individual often has forgotten the original thought.

This is a profound subject about which even the wisest know very little. It becomes a self-revealing subject only upon meditation and thought.

If you understand the principle of mind operation I've described, you will have a clue as to why meditation sometimes brings that which one desires, while at other times it brings that which one does not wish. This type of mental attitude is attained only by preparation and self-discipline. We will learn how to develop this mental attitude later in the seminar.

It is one of the most profound truths of the world that the affairs of all people shape themselves to fit the exact pattern of thoughts, whether the thoughts are mass thought or of individual thought. Those who are successful become successful only because they acquire the habit of thinking in terms of success. Definiteness of purpose can, and it should, so completely occupy the mind that one has no time or space in the mind for thoughts of failure.

Another profound truth consists in the fact that those who have been defeated and who recognize themselves as failures may, by reversing the position of the "sails" of their minds, convert the winds of adversity into a power of equal volume which will carry them onward to success. As one poet said,

> One ship sails east, the other west,
> Impelled by the self same blow,
> It's the set of the sails and not the gales,
> That bids them where to go.

To some who pride themselves on being what the world calls "cool-headed and practical," this analysis of the principle of *Definiteness of Purpose* may appear to be abstract or impractical. There is a power greater than the power of conscious thought, and often it is not perceptible to the finite mind. Acceptance of this truth is essential for the successful culmination of any definite purpose based on the desire for great achievements.

Every circumstance of everyone's life is the result of a definite cause, whether it is a circumstance that brings failure or one that brings success. And many of the circumstances of everyone's life are the result of causes over which that person has or may have control. This obvious truth gives importance of the first magnitude to the principle of definiteness of purpose. If the circumstances of people's lives are not what they desire, those circumstances may be changed by changing their mental attitude and forming new and more desirable thought habits.

How Definiteness of Purpose Leads to Success

Of all the great American industrialists who have contributed to the development of our industrial system, none was more spectacular than the late Walter Chrysler. His story should give hope to every young American who aspires to the attainment of fame or fortune, and it serves as evidence of the power one may gain by moving with *Definiteness of Purpose*.

Chrysler began as a mechanic in a railroad shop in Salt Lake City. From his savings he had accumulated a little more than $4,000, which he intended to use as a fund to set himself up in business. Looking around diligently, he decided that the automobile business was a coming industry, so he decided to go into that field. His entry into the business was both dramatic and novel.

His first move was one that shocked his friends and astounded his relatives, for it consisted in his investing all his savings in an automobile. When the car arrived in Salt Lake City he gave his friends still another shock by proceeding to take it apart, piece by piece, until the parts were scattered all over the shop.

Then he began to put the parts together again.

He repeated this operation so often that some of his friends thought he had lost his mind. That was because they did not understand his purpose. They saw what he was doing with the automobile, but they did not see the plan which was taking form in Walter Chrysler's mind. He was making his mind automobile conscious! Saturating it with *Definiteness of Purpose*! He was observing carefully every detail of the car. When he was through with his job of tearing down his automobile and rebuilding it, he knew all its good points and all its weak ones.

From that experience he began to design automobiles, embodying all the good points of the car he had bought and omitting all its weaknesses. He did his job so thoroughly that when the Chrysler automobiles began to reach the market they became the sensation of the entire automobile industry. His rise to fame and fortune was both rapid and definite, because he knew where he was going before he started, and he prepared himself with painstaking accuracy for the journey.

Observe these men who move with *Definiteness of Purpose* wherever you find them and you will be impressed by the ease with which they attract the friendly cooperation of others, break down resistance, and get that which they seek.

Analyze Walter Chrysler accurately and observe how definitely he acquired the Twelve Riches of Life and made the most of them. He began by developing the greatest of all the riches, a positive mental attitude. That provided him with a fertile field in which to plant and germinate the seed of his Definite Major Purpose, the building of fine motorcars. Then, one by one, he acquired other riches: sound physical health, harmony in human relationships, freedom from fear, hope of achievement, the capacity for faith, willingness to share his blessings, a labor of love, an open mind on all subjects, self-discipline, the capacity to understand people, and last, financial security.

One of the strangest facts concerning the success of Walter Chrysler consists in the simplicity with which he attained it. He had no appreciable amount of working capital with which to begin. His education was a limited one. He had no wealthy backers to set him up in business. But he did have a practical idea and enough personal initiative to begin, right where he stood, to develop it. Everything he needed to translate his *Definite Major Purpose* into reality seemed almost miraculously placed in his hands as fast as he was ready for it—a circumstance that is not uncommon to those who move with *Definiteness of Purpose.*

Edward Bok, a famous leader of his time, was an immigrant at the beginning of the twentieth century who made history by following these principles. He came to this country at the age of six, not able to speak the language. Starting as a humble office boy for Western Union, he was to edit *The Ladies' Home Journal* and make it the first magazine in the world to have one million subscribers. He was also a champion of social causes—he helped conserve Niagara Falls, and established the Woodrow Wilson Professorship of Literature at Princeton.

Bok did all this with his practical ideas and enough personal initiative to develop them. Everything he needed in order to translate his *Definite Major Purpose* into reality seemed almost miraculously placed in his hands as fast as he was ready for it, a circumstance not uncommon to those who move with definiteness of purpose.

Each of Bok's greatest desires became his aims. He truly desired to be recognized as a great American citizen, an ambition fueled by the vastness of opportunities his adopted country offered him. He attained that aim.

Let me point out that each of Bok's aims was created by himself, in his own mind, and each was attained by his own efforts through sheer merit. He did not depend on lucky "breaks," did not expect something for nothing, but shaped his own destiny by careful planning based upon Definiteness of Purpose.

Like Walter Chrysler, Bok conditioned his mind for success by acquiring all of the Twelve Riches.

$2 Million in Less Than an Hour

Shortly after the book *Think and Grow Rich* (a one-volume interpretation of a portion of the Andrew Carnegie philosophy of individual achievement) was published, the publisher began to receive orders for the book from book stores in and near Des Moines, Iowa.

The orders called for express shipment of the book. The cause of the sudden demand for the book was a mystery until several weeks later, when the publisher received a letter from Edward P. Chase, a life insurance salesman representing the Sun Life Assurance Company, in which he said, "I am writing to express my grateful appreciation of your book, *Think and Grow Rich.* I followed its advice to the letter. As a result I received an idea which resulted in the sale of a $2 million life insurance policy—the largest single sale of its kind ever made in Des Moines."

The key sentence in Mr. Chase's letter is in the second sentence: "I followed its advice to the letter." He moved on that idea with *Definiteness of Purpose,* and it helped him to earn more money in one hour than most life insurance men earn in five years of continuous effort. In one brief sentence Mr. Chase told the entire story of a business transaction which lifted him out of the category of ordinary life insurance salespeople and made him a member of the coveted Million Dollar Roundtable.

Somewhere in reading the book Mr. Chase's mind established contact with the mind of the author of the book, and that contact quickened his own mind so definitely and intensely that an idea was born. The idea was to sell a life insurance policy larger than any he had ever thought of selling. The sale of that policy became his immediate Definite Major Purpose in life. He moved on that purpose without hesitation or delay, and his objective was attained in less than an hour.

How I Discovered My Own Personal Power

As Andrew Carnegie once said, the person who is motivated by definiteness of purpose and moves on that purpose with the spiritual forces of his being may challenge those who are indecisive at the post and pass them at the grandstand. It makes no difference whether someone is selling life insurance or digging ditches.

A definite, potent idea, when it is fresh in one's mind, may so change the biochemistry of that mind that it takes on the spiritual qualities which recognize no such reality as failure or defeat. The major weakness of most people, as Mr. Carnegie so often declared, is that they recognize the obstacles they must surmount without recognizing the spiritual power available to them that will allow them to remove those obstacles at will.

I recall, as though it were only yesterday, the circumstances of my own recognition of the spiritual powers available to me. And strangely enough, that recognition came from the same book that inspired Edward P. Chase to lift himself into the upper brackets of achievement in his chosen profession, *Think and Grow Rich.*

My wife brought the book home from the public library and asked me to read it. The moment my hands touched the covers, before the book had been opened, I felt a strange thrill of inspiration which caused me to begin, then and there, to open the book and read it. Before I had finished the first chapter I recognized that some strange quirk of fate had caused the book to be placed in my hands. I took it to bed with me and read it from cover to cover before I went to sleep. The next morning I awoke a new man. I had been reborn! Indecision and doubt were forever gone.

In six brief years that idea enabled me to project my influence for the benefit of millions of people throughout a large portion of the world. At long last I had acquired the blessed art of sharing my riches with others. And I had acquired the Twelve Riches in their fullest and most bountiful form. Moreover, I had discovered my "other self"—that self I had never known before. I also had discovered the existence of the Nine Practices, which guide me in all that I do.

I was so elated over my changed life that it seemed imperative that I meet the author of the book and thank him in person for my good fortune. Finding him was like searching for a needle in a haystack, for he had retired and was living in seclusion. His publisher could not give me his address, so I traced him from one address to another, until I finally located him, after having crossed the continent three times in my search.

My urge to meet the author was due mainly to a feeling I had that he had not exhausted his entire knowledge on the subject of individual achievement through the pages of *Think and Grow Rich*. In this assumption I was correct, for I discovered that he had mentioned only three of the seventeen principles of individual achievement in this book—that he had written an entirely new course in which the entire seventeen principles had been presented.

Applying the principle of *going the extra mile*—a principle in which I believe devoutly—I induced the author to permit me to carry out a very important portion of my Definite Major Purpose in life: that of assisting in taking this philosophy to an ailing world at a time when it was most needed. I said to the author, as I now say to you, that I would rather have had the privilege of being the author of that philosophy than to have been president of the United States. And next to that, I would rather have the privilege of helping to take it to the world than to own all of the world's wealth. This privilege has been granted me.

I exercised my privilege in a variety of ways. First, I made the philosophy available, although in a brief form, through a series of radio programs which were broadcast several times a week.

Next, I helped to make the philosophy available in printed lessons, which would be distributed to the people through newsstands and bookstores throughout the country.

Then I aided in having it filmed for presentation at company meetings, and distributed to them through the cooperation of management.

In addition to these outlets for the philosophy, I helped organize a nationwide series of private study groups at which the philosophy is presented. It is my purpose to cooperate with the religious institutions of the nation by helping to provide the means by which the philosophy may be made available to their members.

I have also arranged with the author of the philosophy to write a book for children, in which the philosophy will be interpreted in terms that will grip their imagination. This book will be distributed through bookstores and it will be available for use in the public schools.

Beyond this, I hope to make other contributions as opportunities present themselves, leading to the distribution of this philosophy on a scale so vast that it will become available to every person who is searching for his or her place in the world.

Thus I have had the privilege of revealing the inner workings of a mind that has been inspired with a Definite Major Purpose in life, and though the task may seem extensive, let me assure you that my contribution will be truly a labor of love.

My compensation consists of an ever-increasing reward which is known only to the man who has discovered the blessed privilege of gaining riches by sharing his blessings with others. Riches—the real riches of life—increase in exact proportion to the scope and extent of the benefit they bring to those with whom they are shared. I know this to be true, for I have grown rich by sharing. I have never benefited anyone in any manner whatsoever without having received in return, from one source or another, ten times as much benefit as I have contributed to others.

In sharing my riches with others, I seek no glorification, for my donations are made anonymously, except in rare instances when my identity must be revealed. Instead of seeking glorification of my name, I prefer to glorify my soul through useful service to others. The riches I give away add to my own wealth and state of being.

How to Find Your Definite Major Purpose

One of the strangest of all truths which have been revealed to me is the fact that the surest way to solve one's personal problems is to find someone with a greater problem and help that person to solve it, through some method of application of the habit of *Going the Extra Mile.*

This is a simple formula, but it has charm and magic, and it never fails to work. But you cannot appropriate the formula by the mere acceptance of my testimony as to its soundness. You must adopt it and apply it in your own way. You will then need no testimony as to its soundness. You will find that many opportunities surround you.

You might begin by organizing a Fellowship Club among your own neighbors or fellow workers, casting yourself for the role of leader and teacher of the group. Here you will learn another great truth—namely, that the best way to appropriate the principles of the philosophy of individual achievement is by teaching it to others. When one begins to teach anything, one begins also to learn more about that which one is teaching. You are now a student of this philosophy, but you can become a master of it by teaching it to others. Thus, your compensation will be assured you in advance.

No matter what line of work you are in, this is your big opportunity to find yourself by helping others to adjust their relationships in peace and harmony. The manager who guides followers by this philosophy will have the confidence of those followers and their fullest co-operation.

If you have not already adopted a *Definite Major Purpose* in life, here is an opportunity for you to do so. You can start right where you are, by helping to teach this philosophy to those who are in need of it. The time has come when it is not only beneficial to the individual to help his neighbor to solve his personal problems, it is imperative that each of us do so as a means of self-preservation.

If your neighbor's house were on fire you would volunteer to help put out the fire, even if you were not on friendly terms, for common sense would convince you that this would be the means of saving your own house.

On the other hand, those with a sound philosophy of life will find themselves surrounded with an abundance of opportunities that did not exist a decade ago. Those who try to get ahead without a *Definite Major Purpose* will meet with difficulties far greater than the average person could handle. The more lucrative opportunities of the world of today and tomorrow will go to those who prepare themselves for leadership in their chosen calling. And leadership in any field of endeavor requires a foundation of sound philosophy. The days of "hit and miss" leadership are gone forever. Skill, technique, and human understanding will be required in our constantly changing world.

Take inventory, you who are without a *Definite Major Purpose,* to find out where you fit in this changed world, prepare yourselves for your new opportunities, and make the most of them.

If I had the privilege of so doing I could no doubt choose for you a *Definite Major Purpose* suited in every way to your qualifications and needs, and I might create for you a simple plan by which you could attain the object of that purpose, but I can serve you more profitably by teaching you how to do this for yourself. Somewhere along the way the idea for which you are searching will reveal itself to you. That has been the experience of most of the students of this philosophy. When the idea comes you will recognize it, for it should come with such force that you cannot escape it. You may be sure of that, provided you are sincerely searching for it.

One of the imponderable features of this philosophy is that it inspires the creation of new ideas, reveals the presence of opportunities for self-advancement which had been previously overlooked, and inspires one to move on one's own personal initiative to embrace and make the most of such opportunities. This feature of the philosophy is not the result of chance. It was designed to produce a specific effect, since it is obvious that an opportunity which one creates for oneself, or an idea with which one may be inspired through one's own thought, is more beneficial than any one may borrow from others, for the very procedure by which an individual creates useful ideas leads unerringly to the discovery of the source from which one may acquire additional ideas when needed.

While it is of great benefit to have access to a source from which to receive the inspiration necessary to create your own ideas, and self-reliance is an asset of priceless value, there may come a time when you will need to draw upon the resources of other minds. And that time is sure to come to those who aspire to leadership in the higher brackets of personal achievement.

How to Harness Your Own Personal Power

Next, I shall reveal to you the means by which personal power may be attained, through the consolidation of many minds directed to the achievement of definite ends.

It was by this same means that Andrew Carnegie ushered in the great steel age and gave America its greatest industry, although he had no capital with which to begin, and very little education.

And it was by this means that Thomas A. Edison became the greatest inventor of all time, though he had no personal knowledge of physics, mathematics, chemistry, electronics, or many other scientific subjects, all of which were essential in his work as an inventor.

It should give you hope to know that lack of education, lack of working capital, and lack of technical skill need not discourage you from establishing, as your major goal in life, any purpose you may choose, for this philosophy provides a way by which any goal within reason may be attained by anyone of average ability.

The one thing it cannot do for you is to choose your goal for you. But once you have established your own goal, this philosophy can guide you unerringly to its attainment. That is a promise without qualifications. I cannot tell you what to desire, or how much success to hope for, but I can and shall reveal to you the formula by which successes may be attained.

Your major responsibility right now is to find out what you desire in life, where you are going, and what you will do when you get there. This is one responsibility that no one but you can assume, and because of procrastination, it is a responsibility 98 out of every 100 people never assume. That is the major reason why only 2 out of every 100 people can be rated as successful. Success begins through *Definiteness of Purpose*!

Singleness of purpose is a priceless asset. Few possess it, yet it is an asset which one may appropriate at a moment's notice.

Make up your mind what you desire of life, decide to get just that, without substitutes, and lo! you will have taken possession of one of the most priceless of all assets available to human beings.

But your desire must be no mere wish or hope!

It must be *a burning desire,* and it must become so definitely an obsessional desire that you are willing to pay whatever price its attainment may cost. The price may be much or it may be little, but you must condition your mind to pay it.

The moment you choose your *Definite Major Purpose* in life, you will observe a strange circumstance, consisting of the fact that ways and means of attaining that purpose will begin immediately to reveal themselves to you.

Opportunities you had not expected will be placed in your way.

The cooperation of others will become available to you, and friends will appear as if by a stroke of magic. Your fears and doubts will begin to disappear and self-reliance will take their place.

This may seem, to the uninitiated, a fantastic promise, but not so to the person who has done away with indecision and has chosen a definite goal in life. I speak not from the observation of others alone but from my own personal experience as well. I have transformed myself from a dismal failure to an outstanding success, and I have therefore earned the right to give you this assurance of what you may expect if you follow the road map provided by this philosophy.

When you come to that inspiring moment when you choose your definite major purpose, do not become discouraged if relatives or friends who are nearest you call you a dreamer.

Just remember that the dreamers have been the forerunners of all human progress.

They have given us the great American system of free enterprise.

They have given us our greatest asset, the privilege of enjoying personal liberty and the right to dream when we choose.

They have given us the greatest air force and the greatest navy in the world.

They have pushed back the frontiers of civilization and have made of the American way of life a glorious pattern which is the envy of the rest of the world.

Christopher Columbus dreamed of an unknown world, set sail on an uncharted ocean, and discovered a new world. Copernicus dreamed of an unseen world, and with the aid of an improvised telescope, revealed it, eliminating much fear and superstition. Edison dreamed of a lamp that could be lighted by electricity, went to work on his dream, and despite the fact that he met with ten thousand failures, he gave the world that lamp.

So let no one discourage you from dreaming, but make sure you back your dreams with action based on *Definiteness of Purpose*. Your chances for success are as great as have been those of anyone who has preceded you. In many ways your chances are greater, for you now have access to the knowledge of the principles of individual achievement that millions of successful people of the past had to acquire the long and hard way.

Those who are wise share most of their riches generously. They share their confidences sparingly, and take great care not to misplace them. And when they talk of their aims and plans, they generally do it by action rather than by words. Those who are wise listen much and speak with caution, for they know that only by way of listening can one learn something of value, while one may learn nothing when speaking, unless it be the folly of talking too much! The wise, when in doubt about whether or not to speak, take their doubts into account and keep quiet.

Exchange of thought, through intercourse of speech, is one of the more important means by which all people gather useful knowledge, create plans for the attainment of their *Definite Major Purpose* and find ways and means of carrying out these plans. And roundtable discussions are an outstanding feature among those in the higher brackets of achievement. But these are far different from the idle discussions in which some open their minds to anyone who wishes to enter.

CHAPTER 5

THE HABIT OF GOING THE EXTRA MILE

An important principle of success in all walks of life and in all occupations is a willingness to *Go the Extra Mile,* which means the rendering of more and better service than that for which one is paid, and giving it with a positive mental attitude.

Search wherever you will for a single sound argument against this principle and you will not find it, nor will you find a single instance of enduring success which was not attained in part by its application.

This principle is not the creation of human kind. It is a part of Nature's handiwork, for it is obvious that every living creature below the intelligence of humans is forced to apply the principle in order to survive.

Many may disregard the principle if they choose, but they cannot do so and at the same time enjoy the fruits of enduring success. Observe how Nature applies this principle in the production of food that grows from the soil, where the farmer is forced to *Go the Extra Mile* by clearing the land, plowing it, and planting the seed at the right time of the year—and there is no advance pay for any of this.

But observe that if he does his work in harmony with Nature's laws, and performs the necessary amount of labor, Nature takes over the job where the farmer's labor ends, germinates the planted seed, and develops it into crops.

And observe thoughtfully this significant fact: For every grain of wheat or corn the farmer plants in the soil, Nature yields perhaps a hundred grains, thus enabling the farmer to benefit by the law of increasing returns.

Nature *Goes the Extra Mile* by producing enough of everything for her needs, together with a surplus for emergencies and waste; for example, the fruit on the trees, the bloom from which the fruit is grown, the frogs in the pond, and the fish in the seas. If this were not true, the species of all living things would soon vanish.

Some believe that the beasts and birds of the jungle live without labor, but thoughtful people know that this is not true. It is true that Nature provides the sources of food for every living thing, but every creature must labor before it may eat that food.

Thus we see that Nature discourages the habit which some have acquired of trying to get something for nothing.

The advantages of the habit of *Going the Extra Mile* are definite and understandable. Let us examine some of them and be convinced:

- The habit brings the individual to the favorable attention of those who can and will provide opportunities for self-advancement.
- It tends to make one indispensable in many different human relationships, and it therefore enables one to command more than average compensation for personal services. It leads to mental growth and to physical skill and perfection in many forms of endeavor, thereby adding to one's earning capacity.
- It protects one against the loss of employment when employment is scarce, and places one in a position to command the best jobs. It enables one to profit by being noticed, since the majority of people do not practice the habit.
- It leads to the development of a positive mental attitude, which is essential for enduring success.
- It tends to develop a keen, alert imagination, because it is a habit which inspires one continuously to seek new and better ways of rendering service.
- It develops the important quality of personal initiative.
- It develops self-reliance and courage.
- It serves to build the confidence of others in one's integrity.
- It aids in the elimination of the destructive habit of procrastination. It develops definiteness of purpose, insuring one against the common habit of aimlessness.

There is still another, and a greater reason for following the habit of *Going the Extra Mile*: *It gives one the only logical reason for asking for increased compensation*.

If an employee performs no more service than that for which the employee is being paid, then obviously he or she is receiving just that much pay. That employee must render the amount of service called for by the amount of salary in order to hold the job.

But one has the privilege always of rendering a surplus of service as a means of accumulating goodwill, and to provide a just reason for demanding more pay, a better position, or both.

How Going the Extra Mile Is Related to the Twelve Riches

The habit of *Going the Extra Mile* is only one of the seventeen principles of the philosophy that Mr. Carnegie has recommended to those who are seeking riches, but let us consider how it is directly related to the Twelve Riches.

First, this habit is inseparably related to the development of the most important of the Twelve Riches: a *positive mental attitude*. When someone becomes the master of his own emotions, and learns the blessed art of self-expression through useful service to others, that person has gone far toward the development of a positive mental attitude.

With a positive mental attitude as a builder of the proper thought pattern, the remainder of the Twelve Riches falls into that pattern as naturally as night follows day, and as inevitably. Recognize this truth and you will understand why the habit of *Going the Extra Mile* provides benefits far beyond the mere accumulation of material riches. You will understand also why this principle has been given first place in Mr. Carnegie's philosophy of individual achievement.

Let us now observe that the admonition to render more service and better service than that for which one is paid is paradoxical, because it is impossible for anyone to render such service without receiving appropriate compensation. The compensation may come in many forms and from many different sources, some of them strange and unexpected sources, but come it will.

The worker who renders this type of service may not always receive appropriate compensation from the person to whom he renders the service, but this habit will attract to him many opportunities for self-advancement, among them new and more favorable sources of employment. Thus his pay will come to him indirectly.

Ralph Waldo Emerson had this truth in mind when he said (in his essay "Compensation" from 1841):

> If you serve an ungrateful master, serve him the more. Put God in your debt. Every stroke shall be repaid. The longer the payment is withholden, the better for you; for compound interest on compound interest is the rate and usage of this exchequer.

Speaking once more in terms that seem paradoxical, be reminded that the most profitable time one can devote to labor is that for which one receives no direct or immediate financial compensation. Remember, there are two forms of compensation available to those who work for wages. One is the wages received in money. The other is the skill attained from experiences—a form of compensation which often exceeds monetary remuneration, for skill and experience are the worker's most important stock-in-trade through which to be promoted to higher pay and greater responsibilities.

This is an asset of which no worker can be cheated, no matter how selfish or greedy his immediate employer may be. It is the "compound interest on compound interest" which Emerson mentioned.

It was this very asset which enabled Charles M. Schwab to climb, step by step, from his lowly beginning as a day laborer to the highest position his employer had to offer; and it was this asset, as well, which brought Mr. Schwab a bonus of more than ten times the amount of his salary. The million-dollar bonus which Mr. Schwab received was his payoff for having put his best efforts into every job he performed—a circumstance, let us remember, which he controlled entirely. And it was a circumstance that could not have happened if he had not followed the habit of *Going the Extra Mile*.

And here let us note that those who follow the habit of *Going the Extra Mile* thereby place the purchaser of their services under a double obligation to pay a just compensation—one being an obligation based upon a sense of fairness, the other based on the fear of losing a valuable employee.

And we understand, too, what a great industrial leader had in mind when he said, "Personally I am not so much interested in a 40-hour-week minimum work law as I am in finding how I can crowd 40 hours into a single day."

It was this same man who said, "If I were compelled to risk my chances of success upon but one of the seventeen principles of achievement, I would, without hesitancy, stake everything on the principle of *Going the Extra Mile*."

Fortunately, however, he was not obligated to make this choice, for the Seventeen Principles of Success are related to one another like the links of a chain. Therefore they blend into a medium of great power through coordination of their use. The omission of any one of these principles would weaken that power, just as the removal of a single link would weaken the chain.

Each of these principles represents, through its use, a definite, positive quality of the mind, and every circumstance that draws upon the power of thought calls for the use of some combination of the principles.

The Seventeen Principles may be likened to the twenty-six letters of the alphabet, through the combinations of which all human thought may be expressed. The individual letters of the alphabet convey little or no meaning, but when they are combined into words, they may express any thought one can conceive.

The Seventeen Principles are the "alphabet" of individual achievement, through which all talents may be expressed in their highest and most beneficial form, and they provide the means by which one may attain the great Master-Key to Riches.

Some Who Have Benefited by the Habit of Going the Extra Mile

No one ever performs any action without consequences. Let us see if we can reveal the consequences that will justify the habit of *Going the Extra Mile* by observing a few who have been inspired by it.

Many years ago an elderly lady was strolling through a Pittsburgh Department Store, obviously killing time. She passed counter after counter without anyone paying any attention to her. All the clerks had spotted her as an idle "looker" who had no intention of buying. They made it a point of looking in another direction when she stopped at their counters.

Finally the lady came to a counter that was attended by a young clerk who politely asked if he might serve her. "No," she replied. "I am just killing time, waiting for the rain to stop so I can go home."

"Very well, madam," the young man said with a smile. "May I bring out a chair for you?" And he brought it without waiting for her answer. After the rain slacked, the young man took the old lady by the arm, escorted her to the street, and bade her goodbye. As she left, she asked him for his card.

Several months later the owner of the store received a letter, asking that this young man be sent to Scotland to take an order for the furnishings of a home. The owner of the store wrote back that he was sorry, the young man did not work in the house furnishings department. But he explained that he would be glad to send an "experienced man" to do the job.

Back came a reply that no one would do except this particular young man. The letters were signed by Andrew Carnegie, and the "house" he wanted furnished was Skibo Castle in Scotland. The elderly lady was Mr. Carnegie's mother. The young man was sent to Scotland. He received an order for several hundred thousand dollars worth of household furnishings, and with it a partnership in the store. He later became the owner of a half interest in the store.

Some years ago the editor of a magazine was invited to deliver a speech at a college in Davenport, Iowa. He accepted the invitation for his regular modest fee, plus traveling expenses. While at the college, he picked up enough ideas for several stories he was planning to write for his magazine. When he was asked to turn in his expense account, he refused, saying he had already been adequately paid by the stories he was now able to write. He took the train back to Chicago feeling well repaid for his trip.

News of his refusal to accept his fee reached the journalism students to whom he had spoken, since this was an example of a real-life journalistic experience. The following week he began to receive from Davenport many subscriptions to his magazine. By the end of the week he had received many thousands of dollars in cash subscriptions. Then followed a letter from the college president, explaining that the subscriptions had come from his students. During the following two years the students and the graduates of the college sent in more than $50,000 in subscriptions to the young man's magazine. This story was so impressive that it was written up in a magazine that had a circulation throughout the English-speaking world, prompting more subscriptions to come from many different countries.

Thus, by rendering service without collecting, the editor had started the law of increasing returns to work in his behalf, and it yielded him a return of over 500 times his investment. The habit of *Going the Extra Mile* is no pipe dream. It pays, and pays handsomely!

Moreover, it never forgets! Like other types of investments, the habit of *Going the Extra Mile* often yields dividends throughout one's lifetime.

Let's look at what happened when someone else neglected an opportunity to *Go the Extra Mile*.

Late one rainy afternoon an automobile salesman sat at his desk in the show room of the New York branch of a well-known luxury car company. The door opened and in walked a man, jauntily swinging a cane.

The salesman looked up from his afternoon paper, took a swift glance at the newcomer, and immediately spotted him as another of those window shoppers who do nothing but waste one's valuable time. He went back to his newspaper and took another sip from his coffee, not taking the trouble to rise from his chair.

The man with the cane walked through the show room, looking casually, first at one car and then another. Finally he walked over to where the salesman was sitting and reading, leaned on his cane, and nonchalantly asked the price of three different automobiles on the floor. Without looking up from his newspaper, the "salesman" muttered the prices.

The man with the cane walked back over to the three models he had been looking at, kicked the tires of each one, then returned to the uninterested salesman and said, "Well, I hardly know whether I will take this one, that one, the other one over there, or whether I'll buy all three."

The salesman turned to the next page of his newspaper and smirked. "Sure," he said.

Then the man with the cane said, "Well, I think I've decided. Write me up a sales slip for the convertible." He took out his checkbook, wrote out a check, and handed it to the salesman, who, now very much alert, had finally put down his newspaper and walked out. When the salesman saw the name on the check, he went white and saw stars. The name on the check was the same as the name on the museum down the fancy street. He realized, far too late, that if he had gone the extra mile, he indeed could easily have sold three of the cars in his showroom to Harry Payne Whitney. Freely offering anything except one's very best service is costly business—a fact many have learned too late.

Over forty years ago another young salesman held a similar position in a hardware store. One slow day he observed that the store had a lot of odds and ends that were out-of-date and not selling. Having time on his hands, he rigged up a special table in the middle of the store. He loaded it with some of this unsalable merchandise, marking it at the bargain price of a dime an article. To his surprise and that of the owner of the store, the gadgets sold like hotcakes.

The legendary, all-American concept of the five-and-ten-cent store had been invented on the spot by young Frank W. Woolworth. All he was doing was *Going the Extra Mile,* and his idea won him a fortune and a major place in American business history. Moreover, the same idea made several others rich, and variations of the idea are at the heart of many of the more profitable merchandising systems in America.

No one told young Woolworth to exercise his right to personal initiative. No one paid him for doing so. Yet his action led to ever-increasing returns for his efforts.

There is something about this habit of doing more than one is paid for which works in one's behalf even while one sleeps. Once it begins to work, it piles up riches so fast that it seems like magic, which, like Aladdin's lamp, draws to one's aid an army of genii who come laden with bags of gold.

One day a young newspaper reporter was sent to interview Andrew Carnegie in order to write a story about his stupendous achievements in the industrial world.

During the interview Carnegie dropped a hint that if the reporter had the vision to *Go the Extra Mile,* to the extent of twenty years of unprofitable labor, he might acquire a fortune comparable to that of the great steel master. The reporter accepted that challenge and went to work. After twenty years of this "unprofitable" labor, almost to the day, the reporter gave the world the net results of what he had learned about Andrew Carnegie's methods of accumulating riches, as well as what he had learned of the methods of some 500 others who had accumulated great riches by the simple expedient of *Going the Extra Mile.*

Today that information is being circulated in book form in practically every English-speaking country of the world, where it is serving many millions of people who wish to learn the secret of achievement through the exercise of personal initiative. It has been translated into many foreign languages. It is designed to help those who are not afraid of doing more than they are paid for and who wish to convert their share of American opportunity into some form of riches.

The compensation this former newspaper reporter is now receiving for his twenty years of "unprofitable" labor affords him riches sufficient for all his needs. Among the greatest of these are peace of mind, priceless friendships throughout the world, and the form of enduring happiness which is the lot of everyone who has found desired work, likes it, and is busily engaged in performing it.

You will remember that Charles M. Schwab began as a laborer not afraid to go the extra mile. A few years later, his private railroad car was being switched onto the siding at his steel plant in Pennsylvania. It was a cold, frosty morning. As he alighted from the car he was met by a young man with a notebook in his hands who hurriedly explained that he was an assistant in the general office of the steel company, and that he had come down to meet the car to see if Mr. Schwab needed any memos written, messages sent, or the like.

"Who asked you to meet me?" Mr. Schwab asked.

"No one," the young man replied. "I saw the notice announcing your arrival, so I came down to meet you, hoping I might be of some service."

Think of that! He came down hoping he might be able to find something to do for which he was not paid extra. And he came on his own initiative, without being told.

Mr. Schwab thanked him politely for his thoughtfulness but said he had no need for any such help at the moment. After carefully noting the young man's name, he sent the lad back to his work.

That night, when Schwab's private railroad car was hitched to the night train for its return to New York City, it carried the willing young man. He had been assigned, at Mr. Schwab's request, for service in New York as one of the steel magnate's personal assistants. The lad's name was Williams. He remained in Mr. Schwab's services for several years, and during this time opportunity after opportunity for promotion came to him unsolicited.

It is peculiar how such opportunities have a way of trailing the people who make it their business to *Go the Extra Mile,* but they always do, very definitely. Finally an opportunity came to young Williams which he could not ignore. He was made president and a large stockholder in one of the largest pharmaceutical companies in the United States—a job which yielded him a fortune far greater than his needs.

This incident is clear evidence of what can happen, and of what has been happening all down through the years under the American way of life.

Here is the appropriate place to remind you of an important thing about the habit of *Going the Extra Mile* by doing more than one is paid for. It is the strange influence it has on those who do it. The greatest benefit from this habit does not come to those to whom the service is rendered. It comes to those who render the service, in the form of a changed "mental attitude," which gives them more influence with other people, more self-reliance, greater initiative, more enthusiasm, more vision, and more definiteness of purpose. All these qualities are qualities of successful achievement.

"Do the thing and you shall have the power," said Emerson. Ah yes, the power! What can we do in our world without power? But it must be the type of power which attracts other people instead of repelling them. It must be a form of power which gains momentum from the law of increasing returns, through the operation of which one's acts and deeds come back greatly multiplied.

You who work for wages should learn more about this sowing-and-reaping business. Then you would understand why no one can go on forever sowing the seed of inadequate service while reaping a harvest of full-grown pay. You would know that there must come a halt to the habit of demanding a full day's pay for a poor day's work.

And you who do not work for wages, but who wish to get more of the better things of life! Let us have a word with you. Why do you not become wise and start getting what you wish the easy and sure way? Yes, there is an easy and a sure way to promote oneself into whatever one wants from life, and its secret becomes known to all who make it their business to *Go the Extra Mile.* The secret can be uncovered in no other manner, for it is wrapped up in that extra mile.

The pot of gold at the "end of the rainbow" is not a mere fairy tale. The end of that extra mile is the spot where the rainbow ends, and that is where the pot of gold is hidden.

Few people ever catch up with the "end of the rainbow." When we get to where we thought the rainbow ended, we find it is still far in the distance. The trouble with most of us is that we do not know how to follow rainbows. Those who know the secret know that the end of the rainbow can be reached only by *Going the Extra Mile.*

Late one afternoon, William C. Durant, the founder of General Motors, walked into his bank after banking hours and asked for some favor that normally would have been taken care of during banking hours.

The man who granted the favor was Carol Downes, a lesser officer of the bank. He not only served Mr. Durant with efficiency, but he went the extra mile and added courtesy to the service. He made Mr. Durant feel that it was a real pleasure to serve him. The incident seemed trivial, and of itself it was of little importance. Unknown to Mr. Downes, though, this courtesy was destined to have repercussions of a far-reaching nature.

The next day Mr. Durant asked Downes to come to his office. That visit led to the offer of a position, which Downes accepted. He was given a desk in a general office where nearly a hundred other people worked. His salary to begin with was modest.

At the end of the first day, when the gong rang announcing the close of the day's work, Downes noticed that all the employees grabbed their hats and coats and made a rush for the door. He sat still, waiting for the others to leave the office. After they left he remained at his desk, wondering why everyone showed such great haste to get away at the very second of quitting time.

Fifteen minutes later Mr. Durant opened the door of his private office, saw Downes still at his desk, and asked Downes whether he understood that he was privileged to stop work at 5:30.

"Oh yes," Downes replied, "but I did not want to be run over in the rush." Then he asked if he could be of any service to Mr. Durant. He was told he might find a pencil for the motor magnate. He got the pencil, ran it through the pencil sharpener, and took it to Mr. Durant. Mr. Durant thanked him and said "good night."

The next day at quitting time Downes remained at his desk again after the "rush" was over. This time, though, he waited with purpose. In a little while Mr. Durant came out of his private office and asked again if Downes did not understand that 5:30 was the time for closing.

"Yes," Downes said with a smile, "I understand it is quitting time for the others, but I have heard no one say that I have to leave the office when the day is officially closed, so I chose to remain here with the hope that I might be of some slight service to you."

"What an unusual hope," Durant exclaimed. "Where did you get the idea?"

"I got it from the scene I witness here at closing time every day," Downes replied. Mr. Durant grunted some reply which Downes did not hear distinctly and returned to his office.

From then on, Downes always remained at his desk after closing time until he saw Mr. Durant leave for the day. He was not paid to work overtime. No one told him to do it. No one promised him anything for remaining, and as far as the casual observer might know, he was wasting his time.

Several months later, Downes was called into Mr. Durant's office and informed that he had been chosen to go out to a new plant that had been purchased recently to supervise the installation of the plant machinery. Imagine that! A former bank official becoming a machinery expert in a few months.

Without quibbling, Downes accepted the assignment and went on his way. He did not say, "Why, Mr. Durant, I know nothing about the installation of machinery." He did not say, "That's not my job," or "I'm not paid to install machinery." No, he went to work and did what was requested of him. Moreover, he went at the job with a pleasant mental attitude.

Three months later the job was completed. It was done so well that Mr. Durant called Downes into his office and asked him where he learned about machinery. "Oh," Downes explained, "I never learned, Mr. Durant. I merely looked around, found men who knew how to get the job done, put them to work, and they did it."

"Splendid," Mr. Durant exclaimed. "There are two types of people who are valuable. One can do something and do it well, without complaining about being overworked. The other is the one who can get other people to do things well, without complaining. You are both types wrapped into one package."

Downes thanked him for the compliment and turned to go.

"Wait a moment," Durant requested. "I forgot to tell you that you are the new manager of the plant you have installed, and your salary to start with has just been doubled."

The following ten years of association with Mr. Durant were worth between $10 million and $12 million to Carol Downes, a huge sum at that time. He became an intimate adviser to the motor king and made himself rich as a result.

The main trouble with so many of us is that we see men who have arrived and we evaluate them in the hour of their triumph, without taking the trouble to find out how or why they arrived.

There is nothing very dramatic about the story of Carol Downes. The incidents mentioned occurred during the day's business, without even a passing notice by the average person who worked along with Downes. And we doubt not that many of these fellow workers envied him because they believed he had been favored by Mr. Durant, through some sort of pull or luck, or whatever it is that those who do not succeed use as an excuse to explain their own lack of progress.

Well, to be candid, Downes did have an inside "pull" with Mr. Durant!

He created that "pull" with his own initiative.

He created it by *Going the Extra Mile* in a matter as trivial as that of placing a neat point on a pencil when nothing was requested except a plain pencil.

He created it by remaining at his desk with the hope that he might be of service to his employer after the rush was over at 5:30 each evening.

He created it by using his right of personal initiative by finding men who understood how to install machinery instead of asking Durant where or how to find such men.

Trace down these incidents, step by step, and you will find that Downes's success was due solely to his own initiative. Moreover, the story consists of a series of little tasks well performed, in the right mental attitude.

Perhaps there were a hundred other men working for Mr. Durant who could have done as well as Downes, but the trouble with them was that they were searching for the "end of the rainbow" by running away from it in the 5:30 rush each afternoon.

Long years afterward, a friend asked Carol Downes how he got his opportunity with Mr. Durant. "Oh," he modestly replied, "I just made it my business to get in his way, so he could see me. When he looked around, wanting some little service, he called on me because I was the only one in sight. In time he got into the habit of calling on me."

There you have it! Mr. Durant got into the habit of calling on Downes. Moreover, he found that Downes could and would assume responsibilities by *Going the Extra Mile.*

What a pity that all the American people do not catch something of this spirit of assuming greater responsibilities. What a pity that more of us do not begin speaking more of our "privileges" under the American way of life, and less of the lack of opportunities in America.

Is there anyone living in America today who would seriously claim that Carol Downes would have been better off if he had been forced, by law, to join the mad rush and quit his work at 5:30 in the afternoon? If he had done so, he would have received the standard wages for the sort of work he performed, but nothing more. Why should he have received more?

His destiny was in his own hands. It was wrapped up in this one lone privilege, which should be the privilege of every American citizen: the right of personal initiative through the exercise of which he made it a habit always to *Go the Extra Mile.* That tells the whole story. There is no other secret to Downes's success. He admits it, and everyone familiar with the circumstances of his promotion from poverty to riches knows it.

There is one thing no one seems to know: Why are there so few men and women who, like Carol Downes, discover the power implicit in doing more than one is paid for? It has in it the seed of all great achievement. It is the secret of all noteworthy success, and yet it is so little understood that most people look upon it as some clever trick with which employers try to get more work out of their employees.

This spirit of indifference toward the habit of *Going the Extra Mile* was dramatically expressed by a "wiseacre" who once applied to Henry Ford for a job. Mr. Ford questioned the man about his experience, his habits, and other routine matters, and was satisfied with the replies.

Then he asked, "How much money do you want for your services?" The man was evasive on this point, so Mr. Ford finally said, "Well, suppose you start in and show us what you can do, and we will pay you all you are worth after we have tried you out." Mr. Wiseacre exclaimed, "I'm getting more than that where I am now employed." And we doubt not that he told the truth.

That explains precisely why so many people do not get ahead in life. They are "getting more than they are worth" where they are, and they never learn how to get ahead by becoming worth more!

A famous story called "A Message to Garcia" tells how President William McKinley commissioned a young soldier by the name of Rowan to carry a message from the United States Government to Garcia, the rebel chieftain during the Spanish-American war, whose exact whereabouts were not known.

The young soldier took the message, made his way through the Cuban jungle, finally found Garcia, and delivered the note to him. That was all there was to the story, just a private soldier carrying out his orders under difficulties, and getting the job done without coming back with an excuse.

The story fired imaginations and spread all over the world. The simple act of a man doing what he was told, and doing it well, became news of the first magnitude. *A Message to*

Garcia was printed in booklet form and the sales reached an all-time high for such publications, amounting to more than 10 million copies. This one story made the author famous, to say nothing of helping to make him rich.

The story was popular because it had in it something of the magic power that belongs to the rare one who does something and does it well.

The whole world is clamoring for such rare ones. They are needed and wanted in every walk of life. American Industry has always had princely berths for those who can and will assume responsibilities and who get the job done with the right mental attitude, by *Going the Extra Mile.*

Andrew Carnegie lifted no fewer than forty such men, including Charles Schwab, from the lowly station of day laborers to millionaires. He understood the value of those who were willing to *Go the Extra Mile.* Wherever he found one, he brought "his find" into the inner circle of his business and gave him an opportunity to earn "all he was worth."

Charles M. Schwab began work with Carnegie in the humble capacity of a stake driver at day wages. But, step by step, he climbed to the top and became Carnegie's right-hand man. People do things or refrain from doing them because of a motive. The soundest of motives for the habit of *Going the Extra Mile* is the fact that it yields enduring dividends, in ways too numerous to mention, to all who follow the habit.

No one has ever been known to achieve permanent success without doing more than he was paid for. The practice has its counterpart in the laws of nature. It has in back of it an impressive array of evidence as to its soundness, supplied by those who have made it a practice of *Going the Extra Mile.* It is based on common sense and justice.

The best of all methods of testing the soundness of this principle is that of putting it to work as a part of one's daily habits. Some truths we can learn only through our own experience.

Some will say, "I am already doing more than I am paid for, but my employer is so selfish and greedy that he will not recognize the sort of service I am rendering." We all know there are the greedy who desire more service than that for which they are willing to pay.

Selfish employers are like pieces of clay in the hands of a potter. Through their greed they can be induced to reward the one who renders them more service than he or she is paid to render.

Greedy employers do not wish to lose the services of one who makes a habit of *Going the Extra Mile.* They know the value of such employees. Here, then, is the crowbar and the fulcrum with which employers can be pried loose from their greed.

The clever will make it their business to become indispensable to a greedy employer by doing more work and better work than any other employee. Greedy employers will "give their eyeteeth" before parting with such an employee. Thus the alleged greed of employers becomes a great asset to the one who follows the habit of *Going the Extra Mile*.

We have seen this technique applied at least a hundred times as a means of manipulating greedy employers through the use of their own weakness. Not once have we seen it fail to work!

On some occasions the greedy employer failed to move as quickly as expected, but that proved to be unlucky, because that employee attracted the attention of a competitive employer who made a bid for the services of the employee and secured them.

There is no way to cheat those who follow the habit of *Going the Extra Mile*. If they do not get proper recognition from one source, it comes voluntarily from some other source—usually when it is least expected.

Those who *Go the Extra Mile* and do it with the right kind of mental attitude never spend time looking for a job. They don't have to, for the job is always looking for them. Depressions may come and go, business may be good or poor, the country may be at war or at peace, but those who render more service and better service than they are paid for become indispensable and thereby insure themselves against unemployment.

High wages and indispensability are twin sisters. They always have been and always will be.

Not only is *Going the Extra Mile* personally worthwhile, it profits one's business, as well. In fact, *Going the Extra Mile* makes perfect business sense, as we will see in the next section.

Going the Extra Mile Makes Good Business Sense

Many companies incorporate the concept of *Going the Extra Mile* into their company mission. One of our popular airlines is one such company. The founder has done everything right, and so the company's known for its waiting list of applicants eager to join the company. One of the main ingredients for this company's success is its spectacular customer service.

The founder himself says, "I know it sounds simple, but I keep saying follow the golden rule of service. Serve others as you yourself would like to be served. I'll ask our people, 'Do you like to go into a restaurant or department store and encounter salespeople who are indifferent to you, who don't care about your needs and wants, who treat you as if you're an object?' Well, everybody has to answer that one way: 'No, we don't like that.' Then I say, 'Well then, don't be a hypocrite. Provide better service. Provide the service you yourself would like to receive.' "

The Revealing Story of Edward Choate

Some men who are smart, and others who are wise, have discovered the way to riches by the deliberate application of the principle of *Going the Extra Mile* for financial gain.

Those who are truly wise, however, recognize that the greatest payoff through this principle comes in terms of friendships which endure throughout life, in harmonious human relationships, in performing a labor of love, in the capacity to understand people, in a willingness to share one's blessings with others—all of which are among the Twelve Riches of Life.

Edward Choate is one who recognized this truth and has found the Master-Key to Riches. He lived in Los Angeles, where he sold life insurance.

At the outset of his career as a life insurance salesman, he made a modest living from his efforts, but he broke no records in that field. He lost all his money through an unfortunate business venture and found himself at the bottom of the ladder, forced to make a new start.

I said "an unfortunate business venture," but perhaps I should have said "a fortunate business venture," for his loss influenced him to stop, look, listen, *think,* and to meditate on why fate seemed to lift some to high places of achievement but condemn others to temporary defeat or permanent failure.

Through his meditations he became a student of the philosophy of individual achievement that Andrew Carnegie helped to provide through his colorful career. When Mr. Choate reached the lesson on *Going the Extra Mile,* he was awakened by a keen sense of understanding he had never before experienced, and he recognized that the loss of material riches may lead one to the source of greater riches, consisting of one's spiritual forces.

With this discovery Mr. Choate began to appropriate, one by one, the Twelve Riches of Life, beginning at the head of the list with the development of positive mental attitude.

For the time being he ceased to think about the amount of life insurance he might sell, and began to look around for opportunities to be of service to others who were burdened with problems they could not solve.

His first opportunity came when he discovered a young man out in the deserts of California who had failed in a mining venture and was facing starvation. He took the young man in, fed him, encouraged him, and kept him in his home until he found a good position for him.

In thus casting himself in the role of the Good Samaritan, Mr. Choate had no thought of financial gain, for it was obvious that a poverty-stricken, broken-spirited boy might never become a prospective purchaser of life insurance.

Then other opportunities to help the less fortunate began to reveal themselves so rapidly that it seemed as if Mr. Choate had made himself a magnet which attracted only those with difficult problems to be solved.

But the appearance was deceiving, for he was only passing through a testing period by which he might demonstrate his sincerity of purpose in helping others. A period, let us not forget, which everyone who applies the principle of *Going the Extra Mile* must experience in one way or another.

Then the scene shifted, and the affairs of Edward Choate began to take a turn he probably had not expected. His life insurance sales began to mount higher and higher, until at last they had reached an all-time high level. And miracle of miracles, one of the largest policies he had ever written up to that time was sold to the employer of the young man of the desert whom he had befriended. The sale was made without Mr. Choate's solicitation.

Other sales began to come his way in the same manner, until he was actually selling more insurance, without any strenuous effort, than he had ever sold previously by the hardest kind of labor.

Moreover, he had tapped a field of life insurance salesmanship in which the policies he sold were of large amounts. Leaders of great responsibilities and extensive financial affairs began to send for him to counsel them in connection with their life insurance problems.

His business grew until it brought him that goal so greatly coveted by all life insurance salespeople: life membership in the Million Dollar Roundtable. Such a distinction is attained only by those who sell a minimum of a million dollars a year in insurance for three consecutive years.

There had been only fifty-seven others before him to reach this outstanding achievement at the time. So, in seeking spiritual riches Choate also found material riches, and found them in greater abundance than he had ever anticipated. Six brief years after he had begun to cast himself for the role of the Good Samaritan, Mr. Choate sold more than $2 million of life insurance during the first four months of the year.

The story of his achievements began to spread throughout the nation. It brought him invitations to speak before life insurance conventions, for other life insurance salespeople desired to know how he had managed to lift himself to so enviable a position in that profession.

He told them! And quite contrary to the usual practice of those who are successful, he revealed the humility of heart by which he was inspired, frankly admitting that his achievements were the result of the application of the philosophy of others.

Average successful people have a tendency to try to convey the impression that their success is due to their own smartness or wisdom, but they do not always give credit to their teachers and mentors. For it is obvious to all that no one ever attains a high degree of enduring success without the friendly cooperation of others, nor does anyone ever attain enduring success without helping others.

Edward Choate is as rich in material values as he needs to be. He is far richer in spiritual values, however, for he has discovered, appropriated, and made intelligent use of all of the Twelve Riches of Life, of which money is the last and the least in importance.

CHAPTER 6

LOVE, THE TRUE EMANCIPATOR OF MANKIND

As human beings love is our greatest experience. It can bring one to communicate with Infinite Intelligence.

When it is blended with the emotions of sex and romance, it may lead one to the higher mountain peaks of individual achievement through creative vision.

The emotions of love, sex, and romance are the three sides of the eternal triangle of achievement known as genius. Nature creates geniuses through no other media. Love is an outward expression of the spiritual nature of mankind.

Sex is purely biological, but it supplies the springs of action in all creative effort, from the humblest creature that crawls to the most profound of all creations, human beings.

When love and sex are combined with the spirit of romance, the world may well rejoice, for these are the potentials of the great leaders who are the profound thinkers of the world.

Love makes all humankind related. It clears out selfishness, greed, jealousy, and envy. True greatness will never be found where love does not abide.

The love of which I speak must not be confused with the emotions of sex, for love in its highest and purest expression is a combination of the eternal triangle, yet it is greater than any one of its three component parts.

The love to which I refer is the "élan vital," the life-giving factor, the spring of action of all the creative endeavors that have lifted humankind to its present state of refinement and culture.

It is the one factor which draws a clear line of demarcation between humans and all the creatures of the earth below us. It is the one factor which determines for every person the amount of space he or she shall occupy in the hearts of others.

Love is the solid foundation upon which the first of the Twelve Riches may be built, a positive mental attitude, and let us take heed that no one may ever become truly rich without it.

Love is the warp and the woof of all the remaining eleven riches. It embellishes all riches and gives them the quality of endurance, evidence of which may be revealed by cursory observation of all who have acquired material riches but have not acquired love.

The habit of *Going the Extra Mile* leads to the attainment of that spirit of love, for there can be no greater expression of love than love which is demonstrated through service that is rendered unselfishly for the benefit of others. Emerson had the vision of the kind of love to which I refer when he said:

> Those who are capable of humility, of justice, of love, of aspiration, are already on the platform that commands the sciences and arts, speech and poetry, action and grace. For who so dwells in this mortal beatitude does already anticipate those special powers which men prize so highly.
>
> The magnanimous know very well that they who give time, or money, or shelter, to the stranger—so it be done for love, and not for ostentation—do, as it were, put God under obligation to them, so perfect are the compensations of the universe. In some way the time they seem to lose, is redeemed, and the pains they take, remunerate themselves. These men fan the flame of human love and raise the standard of civic virtue among mankind.

The great minds of every age have recognized love as the eternal elixir that binds the hearts of humankind and makes us all responsible to one another. One of the greatest minds this nation ever produced, Robert Green Ingersoll, expressed his views on love in a classic that shall live as long as time endures. He said:

> Love is the only bow on life's dark cloud.
> It is the morning and the evening star.
> It shines upon the babe, and sheds its radiance on the quiet tomb.
> It is the mother of art, inspirer of poet, patriot and philosopher.

It is the air and light of every heart-builder of every home, kindler of every fire on every hearth.

It was the first to dream of immortality.

It fills the world with melody—for music is the voice of love.

Love is the magician, the enchanter, that changes worthless things to joy, and makes right royal kings and queens of common clay.

It is the perfume of that wondrous flower, the heart, and without that sacred passion, that divine swoon, we are less than beasts; but with it, earth is heaven and we are gods.

Love is transfiguration. It ennobles, purifies and glorifies.

Love is a revelation, a creation. From love the world borrows its beauty and the heavens their glory. Justice, self denial, charity and pity are the children of love. "Without love all glory fades, the noble falls from life, art dies, music loses meaning and becomes mere motions of the air, and virtue ceases to exist."

If one is truly great, one will love all humankind. One will love the good and the bad among all humanity. The good will be loved with pride and admiration and joy. The bad will be loved with pity and sorrow, for one will know, if truly great, that both good and bad qualities in people often are but the results of circumstances over which they have, because of their ignorance, little control.

To be truly great, one will be compassionate, sympathetic, and tolerant. When compelled to pass judgment upon others, one will temper justice with tender mercy, throwing oneself always on the side of the weak, the uninformed, and the poverty-stricken.

Thus one will not only *Go the Extra Mile* in a true spirit of fellowship, but will go willingly and graciously. And if the second mile be not enough, one must go the third and the fourth, and as many additional miles as may be necessary.

The speaker's message was profound. After he stopped talking and had left the stage, many remained in their seats, allowing his powerful words to sink in. By the time they left the conference hall, it was nearly midnight.

THE MASTER MIND

The Master Mind principle is the basis of all great achievements, the foundation stone of major importance in all human progress, whether it be individual progress or collective progress. It provides the key to the attainment of great personal power. The Master Mind principle is defined as an alliance of two or more minds, blended in a spirit of perfect harmony and cooperating for the attainment of a definite purpose. The key to its power may be found in the word "harmony." Without that element, collective effort may constitute cooperation, but it will lack the power which harmony provides through coordination of effort.

The tenets of major importance in connection with the Master Mind principle are these:

Premise 1

The Master Mind principle is the medium through which one may procure the full benefit of the experience, training, education, specialized knowledge, and native ability of others, just as completely as if their minds were one's own.

Premise 2

An alliance of two or more minds, in a spirit of perfect harmony for the attainment of a definite purpose, stimulates each individual mind with a high degree of inspiration, and may become that state of mind known as Faith. (A slight idea of this stimulation and its power is experienced in the relationship of close friendship and in the relationship of love.)

Premise 3

Every human brain is both a broadcasting station and a receiving station for the expression of the vibrations of thought, and the stimulating effect of the Master Mind principle stimulates action of thought, through what is commonly known as telepathy, operating through the sixth sense.

In this manner many business and professional alliances are translated into reality, and seldom has anyone ever attained a high station or enduring power without the application of the Master Mind principle through which he secured the benefit of other minds.

This fact alone is sufficient evidence of the soundness and the importance of the Master Mind principle, and it is a fact which all may observe without straining their powers of observation or overtaxing their credulity.

Premise 4

The Master Mind principle, when actively applied, has the effect of connecting one with the subconscious section of the mind, and the subconscious sections of the minds of allies—a fact that may explain many of the seemingly miraculous results obtained through the Master Mind.

Premise 5

The more important human relationships that benefit from the application of the Master Mind principle are these:

> In marriage
> In religion
> In connection with one's occupation, profession, or calling

The Master Mind principle made it possible for Thomas Edison to become a great inventor despite his lack of education and his lack of knowledge of the sciences—a circumstance which offers hope to all who erroneously believe themselves to be seriously handicapped by the lack of a formal education.

With the aid of the Master Mind principle, one may understand the history and the structure of this earth on which we live through the knowledge of skilled geologists.

Through the knowledge and experience of the chemist, one may make practical use of chemistry without being a trained chemist.

With the aid of scientists, technicians, physicists, and practical mechanics, one may become a successful inventor without personal training in any of these fields, as did Edison.

The Importance of Alliances

There are two general types of Master Mind alliances:

1. Alliance, for purely social or personal reasons, with one's relatives, religious advisers, and friends, where no material gain or objective is sought. The most important of this type of alliance is that of husband and wife.
2. Alliances for business, professional, and economic advancement, consisting of individuals who have a personal motive in connection with the object of the alliance.

Now let us consider some of the more important examples of power that have been attained by the application of the Master Mind.

The American form of government, as it was originally written into the Constitution of the United States, should have first analysis, because it is one form of power which vitally affects every citizen of our country, and to a large degree affects the entire world.

Our country is noted for three obvious facts:

1. It is the richest country of the world.
2. It is the most powerful nation of the world.
3. It provides its citizens with more personal freedom than does any other nation.

Riches, freedom, and power! What an awe-inspiring combination of realities!

The source of these benefits is not difficult to determine, for it centers in the Constitution of our country and in the American system of free enterprise, these having been so harmoniously coordinated that they have provided people with both spiritual and economic power such as the world has never before witnessed.

Our form of government is a stupendous Master Mind alliance made up of the harmonious relationship of all the people of the nation, functioning through fifty separate groups known as states. The central core of our American Master Mind is easily discernible by breaking down our form of government and examining its component parts, all of which are under the direct control of a majority of the people.

These parts are:

1. The executive branch of our government (maintained by a president)
2. The judiciary branch (maintained by the Supreme Court)
3. The legislative branch (maintained by the Congress)

Our Constitution has been so wisely constructed that the power behind all three of these branches of government is held by the people. It is a power of which the people cannot be deprived except by their own neglect to use it.

Our political power is expressed through our government. Our economic power is maintained and expressed through our system of free enterprise. And the sum total of the power of these two is always in exact ratio to the degree of harmony with which the two are coordinated. The power thus attained is the property of all the people. It is this power which has provided the people with the highest standard of living that civilization has yet evolved, and which has made our nation truly the richest and the freest and the most powerful nation of the world.

We speak of this power as "The American Way of Life."

Another illustration of the Master Mind applied to industry may be found in the great American systems of transportation and communications. Those who manage our railroads and our airlines, our telephone and telecommunications systems have established a service that has never been equaled in any other country. Their efficiency and the resultant power consist entirely in their application of the Master Mind principle or harmonious coordination of effort.

Still another example of power attained through the Master Mind principle may be found by observing the relationship of our military forces—our army, navy, air force, marines, and coast guard. Here, as elsewhere, the key to our power has been harmonious coordination of effort.

Sports teams are an excellent example of power attained through harmony of effort.

The great American system of merchandising is still another example of economic power attained through the Master Mind principle.

Every successful industry is the result of application of the Master Mind. The American system of free enterprise in its entirety is a marvelous illustration of economic power produced by friendly, harmonious coordination of effort.

Andrew Carnegie frankly admitted that his entire fortune was accumulated by the application of this principle, through which he brought together one of the greatest industrial organizations this nation has ever witnessed. And let it be remembered that his Master Mind consisted of his entire organization of associate workers, from the humblest to the greatest.

The key workers of his Master Mind, his managerial and supervisory staff, were recruited from his rank and file, and he understood the Master Mind principle so thoroughly that he inspired every worker to make the most of this opportunity by aiming for a higher position.

The man to whom he entrusted the organization of the philosophy of individual achievement had the benefit, through Mr. Carnegie's assistance, of the greatest Master Mind alliance that ever collaborated in such an undertaking.

It consisted of more than 500 leaders of industry of Mr. Carnegie's caliber, and the alliance continued over a period of twenty years, during which everyone in the alliance provided the author of the philosophy with the full benefits of his entire industrial experience.

This alliance provided the world with an astounding demonstration of the power which may be attained through the first three principles of the philosophy: (1) *The Habit of Going the Extra Mile,* (2) *Definiteness of Purpose,* and (3) *the Master Mind.*

The definite purpose which inspired this work was that of providing all with a workable philosophy based on the experiences of those who had demonstrated material success. It was an unselfish purpose, because it was directed entirely for the benefit of others.

Those behind the purpose were already successful, but they recognized the advantages of sharing their knowledge, and they recognized also the disadvantages of an economic system which benefits a few at the expense of many.

And each person in that alliance demonstrated an understanding of the principle of *Going the Extra Mile.* They demonstrated it by contributing time and experience, without money and without price, in order that the people of this nation might enjoy the benefits of a philosophy known to be the very foundation of the great American way of life.

In order that we may get a comprehensive understanding of the power and the benefits of this particular Master Mind alliance, imagine what it might mean to you if you had the privilege of choosing 500 American leaders of industry who would consent to serve as your guides and your instructors for a period of twenty years, without cost or obligation.

You would have, through the collaboration of so large a group of successful leaders, the full benefit of all the knowledge and experience which have grown out of the development of the American system of free enterprise. If you made the best use of this knowledge, your success would be inevitable!

The humblest person may benefit from this principle by forming a harmonious alliance with anyone of his or her choice. The most profound, and perhaps the most beneficial, application of this principle that anyone may make is the Master Mind alliance in marriage, provided the motive behind that alliance is love. This sort of alliance not only coordinates the minds of husband and wife, it also blends the spiritual qualities of their souls. The benefits of such an alliance bring joy and happiness to both partners, and they profoundly bless their children with sound character and endow them with the fundamentals of a successful life.

The Ultimate Example of the Master Mind Principle

Let us turn back the pages of time for nearly half a century and have a look at a family whose Master Mind relationship resulted in the building of a great industrial empire, which now gives profitable employment to millions of men and women.

The scene opens in the kitchen of their humble home.

The husband has set up a roughly constructed model of a gasoline engine. His wife is feeding gasoline into the engine, a drop at a time, with the aid of an eyedropper. The husband is manipulating the spark plug with which he hopes to ignite the gas. After weeks of tireless effort—tireless because it has been supported with love—the gas ignites and the flywheel of the crude engine begins to turn.

There was no money behind this experiment; nothing behind it except the definiteness of purpose of two people who had formed a Master Mind alliance for the fulfillment of that purpose.

And there was no promise of immediate or direct monetary compensation behind the experiment. It had to be conducted by applying the principle of *Going the Extra Mile*.

But as a result of this effort, the model was perfected and the first practical self-propelled vehicle ever built in America became a reality.

Then the Master Mind alliance was extended to include skilled mechanics and a few friends and acquaintances who contributed small amounts of working capital for the production of automobiles.

Today, the production of automobiles has reached fantastic proportions in comparison with its humble beginnings, the product of that two-unit Master Mind partnership.

The man behind that production is one of the 500 from whose life experiences the philosophy of individual achievement was organized, and one hardly needs to be told that his name is Henry Ford.

As the Ford production grew, the Ford Master Mind was increased until it included a veritable army of mechanics, engineers, chemists, researchers, and financial experts, a sales force, and many other types of skilled labor, all of which are essential for so extensive an operation.

Through his Master Mind alliance, Henry Ford multiplied his own brain by many thousands. Without this alliance, he could not have carried on his vast industrial activities. It will continue to endure, because the power it provides benefits all whom it affects.

And here let us take notice that no Master Mind alliance can endure unless it benefits all whom it affects.

Look well to the purpose of your Master Mind alliance before you begin it, you who see power through the cooperation of human endeavor. If you would have enduring power, be sure that it is applied to ends that benefit all who are affected by it.

Power may be very dangerous or it may serve to glorify certain people, according to the way it is used. The Master Mind is the way to great power, and like all other forms of power, it is subject to either a positive or a negative application by those who wield it.

This is no mere statement of an obvious truism, for the records of the deeds of mankind all bear witness to its truth. Every great philosopher—from the days of Plato, Aristotle, and Socrates on down to the days of William James and Ralph Waldo Emerson—also recognized it and called attention to it.

Electricity will do our work, provided we adapt ourselves to its nature, but also it may snuff out life if it is applied for that purpose. The imagination cannot conceive any good that may not be converted to destructive ends. Food is necessary for the maintenance of life, and it is good when properly used. But the wrong use of food, or too much food, will do as much harm as will the most potent poison.

The Importance of Using the Master Mind Responsibly

You now have an understandable interpretation of the greatest source of personal power known to men—the Master Mind. The responsibility for its right use is yours.

Use it as Henry Ford has done and you will be blessed, as he was, with the privilege of occupying great space in the world; space that can be estimated in both geography and in human relationships which are friendly and cooperative, for it is an accepted fact that Henry Ford occupied more friendly space in the hearts of his fellow professionals than virtually any other industrialist.

Not only did Ford's Master Mind consist in his harmonious alliance with his associate workers and his technical staff, it also extended far beyond these and included the masses of the American people who stood on the sidelines and watched him go by—people like you and me who recognize sound business and personal philosophy and respect its use wherever it is observed.

We emphasize Henry Ford's application of the Master Mind because there is not to be found in the entire history of industrial America a finer example than his of individual achievement based on the American way of life. He benefited almost everyone whose life had been touched by his influence, and it is very doubtful if he himself recognized the full scope and measure of his influence on American life.

Master Mind power under the control of Henry Ford is a blessing, and not a curse or a danger, as it might be if it were wielded by someone with less vision than he possessed. All of which is an observation of Ford—not to eulogize him but to inspire all who seek any form of personal aggrandizement under the American way of life.

In an analysis of Henry Ford and fifty other outstanding Americans, representing a wide variety of occupations, based on the seventeen principles of this philosophy, Henry Ford led all the others by a wide margin. On the first three principles—*Going the Extra Mile, Definiteness of Purpose,* and *the Master Mind,* he rated 100 percent-plus. The "plus" indicated that he had made extraordinary use of these three principles—a fact that was established by close observation and analysis of his achievements and their influence for good throughout the world.

And let us be reminded that the first member of his Master Mind alliance—his wife— occupied first place in this alliance throughout his lifetime. Her influence upon him was continuous and profound, so profound in fact that it might not be an exaggeration to say that had there been no Mrs. Ford, there would have been no great Ford industrial empire as the world of today knows it.

Henry Ford made mistakes. Some of them were the result of errors of judgment; others were the result of causes beyond his control. But those who know all the facts concerning his active life will tell you that he made only two mistakes of major importance, and these were promptly mended by his own design and personal initiative, as soon as they were discovered.

What a record!

Duplicate it and you will have made indispensable contributions to the American way of life. Moreover, the compensation to you will be measured by compound interest on compound interest for every act and deed.

Remember: Do not be afraid to aim high when you establish your goal. You live in a land of opportunities, where no one is limited in the quality, the quantity, or the nature of the riches he is able to acquire provided he is willing to give adequate value in return.

Before you fix your goal in life, memorize the following lines by Jessie B. Rittenhouse, titled "My Wage," from his book *The Door of Dreams,* and take to heart the lesson they teach:

> I bargained with Life for a penny,
>   And Life would pay no more,
> However I begged at evening
>   When I counted my scanty store.
> For Life is a just employer,
>   He gives you what you ask,
> But once you have set the wages,
>   Why, you must bear the task.
> I worked for a menial's hire,
>   Only to learn, dismayed,
> That any wage I had asked of Life,
>   Life would have willingly paid.

Successful people do not bargain with life for poverty! They know that there is a power through which life may be made to pay off on their own terms. They know that this power is available to everyone who comes into possession of the Master-Key to Riches. They know the nature of this power and its unlimited scope. They know it by a name of one word, the greatest word in the English language!

This word is known to all, but as we shall soon see, the secrets of its power are understood by few.

CHAPTER 8

ANDREW CARNEGIE'S ANALYSIS OF THE MASTER MIND PRINCIPLE

When I decided to share these lessons, I knew that the most invaluable words I could find would come directly from the man who played such a large role in this quest for defining success—Andrew Carnegie.

One day I had the privilege of sharing a few undivided hours of Carnegie's time so I could ask him precisely what he meant by the Master Mind principle, so that it might be appropriated and used by others to attain their *Definite Major Purpose*.

"Describe, if you will," I asked him "the various forms of application that may be made of this principle by those of average ability, in their daily efforts to make the most of opportunities in this country."

And this was Mr. Carnegie's reply:

"The privileges which are available to the American people are a source of great power. But privileges do not spring, mushroom-like, from nothing. They must be created and maintained by the application of power.

"The founders of our American form of government, through their foresight and wisdom, laid the foundation for all our American form of liberty, freedom, and riches. But they only laid the foundation. The responsibility of embracing and using this foundation must be assumed by every person who claims any portion of this freedom and wealth.

"I will now describe some of the individual uses of the Master Mind principle, as it may be applied in the development of various human relationships which may contribute to the attainment of one's *Definite Major Purpose*.

"But first I wish to emphasize the fact that the attainment of one's *Definite Major Purpose* can be carried out only by a series of steps; that every thought one thinks, every transaction in which one engages, in relationship with others, every plan one creates, every mistake one makes, has a vital bearing on the ability to attain a chosen goal.

"The mere choice of a *Definite Major Purpose,* even though it be written out in clear language and fully fixed in one's mind, will not ensure the successful realization of that purpose.

"One's major purpose must be backed up and followed through by continuous effort, the most important part of which consists in the sort of relationship one maintains with others.

"With this truth well established in one's mind, it will not be difficult to understand how necessary it is to be careful in choosing associates, especially those with whom one maintains close personal contact in connection with one's occupation.

"Here, then, are some of the sources of human relationship, which someone with a *Definite Major Purpose* must cultivate, organize, and use in his progress toward the attainment of his chosen goal:

"Occupation: Outside of the relationship of marriage or a significant partnership, (which is the most important of all Master Mind relationships), there is no form of relationship as important as the one that exists between a worker and those with whom he or she works in a chosen occupation.

"Everyone has a tendency to take on the mannerisms, beliefs, mental attitude, political and economic viewpoint, and other traits of the more outspoken of those with whom he or she associates during the workday.

"The major tragedy of this tendency lies in the fact that the soundest thinker is not always the most outspoken among one's daily associates; and very often he or she has a grievance and takes pleasure in airing the grievance among fellow workers.

"Also, the most outspoken person is often an individual who has no *Definite Major Purpose* of his or her own. Therefore this person devotes much time belittling the person who has such a purpose.

"Those of sound character, who know exactly what they wish, usually have the wisdom to keep their own counsel, and seldom waste any of their time trying to discourage others. They are so busily engaged in promoting their own purpose that they have no time to waste with anyone or anything which does not contribute in one way or another to their benefit.

"Realizing that one may find in almost every group of associates some person whose influence and cooperation may be helpful, those of keen discrimination, who have a *Definite Major Purpose* to attain, will prove their wisdom by forming friendships with those who can be, and who are willing to become, mutually beneficial. The others will be tactfully avoided.

"Naturally this person will seek closest alliances with those who possess the most potentially helpful traits of character, knowledge, and personality. And of course people of discrimination will not overlook those holding positions of higher rank, keeping an eye on the day when they themselves may not only equal such people in positions of power but excel them, remembering meanwhile the words of Abraham Lincoln, who said, 'I will study and prepare myself, and some day my chance will come.'

"The person with a constructive *Definite Major Purpose* will never envy his or her superiors, but instead will study their methods and learn to acquire their knowledge. You may accept it as a sound prophecy that those who spend time finding fault with their superiors will never become a successful leader in their own account.

"The greatest soldiers are those who can take, and carry out, orders of their superiors in rank. Those who cannot or will not do this never will become successful leaders in military operations. The same rule is true of any person in other walks of life. If that person fails to emulate the person above, in a spirit of harmony, he or she will never benefit greatly from associating with that person.

"No fewer than a hundred people have risen from the ranks in my own organization, and have found themselves richer than they need be. They were not promoted because of bad dispositions or the habit of finding fault with those above or those below them, but they promoted themselves by appropriating and making practical use of the experience of everyone with whom they came in contact.

"The individual with a *Definite Major Purpose* will take careful inventory of every person with whom he or she comes in contact, and will look upon every such person as a possible source of useful knowledge or influence, which that individual may borrow and use in self-promotion.

"If a person looks around the workplace, he or she will discover that this place of daily labor is a schoolroom in which to acquire the greatest of all educations—the education that comes from observation and experience.

Always Remain a Student

"'How may one make the most of this sort of schooling?' some will ask.

"The answer may be found by studying the nine basic motives which move people to voluntary action. We often lend our experience, knowledge, and cooperation to others, because we have been given a sufficient motive to do so. Those who relate to others in the workplace with the right sort of mental attitude toward them stand a better chance of learning from them than those who are belligerent, irritable, discourteous, or neglectful of the little amenities of courtesy which exist between all cultured people.

"The old saying that 'you can catch more flies with honey than with vinegar' might well be remembered by those who wish to learn from those who know more about matters than oneself, and whose cooperation is needed and sought.

"Educational: No one's education is ever finished.

"The individual whose *Definite Major Purpose* is of noteworthy proportions must remain always a student, and learn from every possible source—especially those sources from which one may acquire specialized knowledge and experience related to one's major purpose.

"The public libraries are free. They offer a great array of organized knowledge on every subject. They carry, in every language, the total of human knowledge on every subject. The successful person with a *Definite Major Purpose* makes it his or her business and responsibility to read books relating to that purpose, and thus acquire important knowledge which comes from the experiences of others who have gone before.

"A reading program should be as carefully planned as a daily diet, for knowledge, too, is food, without which we cannot grow mentally.

"The person who spends all of his or her spare time reading the tabloids is not headed toward any great achievement.

"The same may be said of those who do not include in their daily program some form of reading that provides them with the knowledge which may be used in the attainment of a major purpose. Random reading may be pleasant, but it seldom is helpful in connection with one's occupation.

"Reading, however, is not the only source of education. By choosing well among our colleagues, we may make alliances that enrich our lives just through ordinary conversations with extraordinary people.

"Business and professional clubs offer an opportunity for one to form alliances of great educational benefit, provided one chooses those clubs and close associates in those clubs with a definite objective in mind. Through this sort of association many have formed both business and social acquaintances of great value to them in carrying out the object of their major purpose.

"No one can go through life successfully without the habit of cultivating friends. The word 'contact,' as it is commonly used in relationship to personal acquaintanceship, is an important word. If an individual makes it a part of his or her daily practice to enlarge his or her personal contact list, that habit will be of great benefit in ways that cannot be predicted. The time will come when they will be ready and willing to render aid if that person has done a good job of selling himself or herself.

"The church is among the more desirable sources through which one may meet and cultivate people, because it brings people together under circumstances which inspire the spirit of fellowship among people.

"Everyone needs some source through which one can associate with neighbors under circumstances that will enable an exchange of thoughts for the sake of mutual understanding and friendship, quite aside from all considerations of monetary gain. Those who shut themselves up in a shell become confirmed introverts, and soon become selfish and narrow in attitudes about life.

Perform Your Civic Duty

"Political Alliances: It is both the duty and the privilege of an American citizen to take an interest in politics and thereby exercise the right to help vote worthy men and women into public office.

"The political party to which one belongs is of much less importance than the question of exercising the privilege of voting. If politics becomes smeared with dishonest practices, there is no one to blame but the people who have it within their power to keep dishonest, unworthy, and inefficient people out of office.

"In addition to the privilege of voting and the duty it carries with it, one should not overlook the benefits which may be gained from an active interest in politics, through 'contacts' and alliances with people who may become helpful in the attainment of one's *Definite Major Purpose.*

"In many occupations, professions, and businesses, political influence becomes a definite and important factor in the promotion of one's interests. Business and professional men and women certainly should not neglect the possibility of promoting their interests through active political alliances.

"The alert individual, who understands the necessity of reaching out in every possible direction for friendly allies whom he or she can use in attaining a major purpose in life will make the fullest use of the voting privilege.

"But the major reason every American citizen should take an active interest in politics, and the one I would emphasize above all others, is the fact that if the better type of citizen fails to exercise the right to vote, politics will disintegrate and become an evil that will destroy this nation.

"The founders of this nation pledged their lives and their fortunes to provide all the people with the privileges of liberty and freedom in the pursuit of their chosen purpose in life. And chief among these privileges is that of helping, by the ballot, to maintain the institution of government which the founders of this nation established to protect those privileges.

"Everything that is worth having has a definite price.

"You desire personal freedom and individual liberty! Very well, you may protect this right by forming a Master Mind alliance with other honest and patriotic Americans, and making it your business to elect honest civil servants to public office. And it is no exaggeration to state that this may well be the most important Master Mind alliance that any American citizen can make.

"Your forefathers ensured your personal liberty and freedom by their votes. You should do no less for your offspring and the generations that will follow them.

"Every honest American citizen has sufficient influence with neighbors and coworkers to enable that citizen to influence at least five other people to exercise their right to vote. If this citizen fails to exercise this influence, he or she may still remain an honest citizen, but cannot truthfully be called a patriotic citizen, for patriotism has a price consisting of the obligation to exercise it.

Network with Your Peers

"Social Alliances: Here is a fertile, almost unlimited, field for the cultivation of friendly 'contacts.' It is particularly available to the married couple who understand the art of making friends through social activities.

"Such a couple can convert a home and social activities into a priceless asset to them both, if one or both of their occupations requires them to extend the number of their friends.

"Many whose professional ethics forbid direct advertising or self-promotion may make effective use of their social privileges, provided they have partners with a bent for social activities.

"A lawyer's husband has been credited with helping her to build one of the most lucrative law practices in a Middle Western city, by the simple process of entertaining, through social activities, the spouses of other wealthy business people. The possibilities in this equation are endless.

"One of the major advantages of friendly alliances with people in a variety of walks of life consists of the opportunity such contacts provide for roundtable discussions which lead to the accumulation of knowledge one may use in the attainment of a *Definite Major Purpose.*

"If one's acquaintances are sufficiently numerous and varied, they may become a valuable source of information on a wide range of subjects, thus leading to a form of intellectual intercourse which is essential for the development of flexibility and versatility required in many callings.

"When a group of professionals gets together and enters into a roundtable discussion on any subject, this sort of spontaneous expression and interchange of thought enriches the minds of all who participate. We all need to reinforce our own ideas and plans with new food for thought, which can be acquired only through frank and sincere discussions with people whose experience and education differ from our own.

"The leading writer who remains in that exalted position must add continuously to his or her own stock of knowledge by appropriating the thoughts and ideas of others, through personal contacts and by reading.

"Any mind that remains brilliant, alert, receptive, and flexible must be fed continuously from the storehouse of other minds. If this renewal is neglected, the mind will atrophy, the same as will an arm that is taken out of use. This is in accordance with Nature's laws. Study Nature's plan and you will discover that every living thing, from the smallest insect to the complicated machinery of a human being, grows and remains healthy only by constant use.

"Roundtable discussions not only add to one's store of useful knowledge, they also develop and expand the power of the mind. The person who stops studying the day he or she finishes formal schooling will never become an educated person, no matter how much classroom knowledge may have been acquired.

"Life itself is a great school, and everything that inspires thought is a teacher. The wise person knows this; moreover, he or she makes it a part of a daily routine to contact other minds, with the object of developing his or her own mind through the exchange of thoughts.

The Profitable Exchange of Useful Thoughts

"We see, therefore, that the Master Mind principle has an unlimited scope of practical use. It is the medium by which the individual may supplement the power of his or her own mind with the knowledge, experience, and mental attitude of other minds.

"As one so aptly expressed this idea: 'If I give you one of my dollars in return for one of yours, each of us will have no more than we started with, but if I give you a thought in return for one of your thoughts, each of us will have gained a hundred percent dividend on his investment of time.'

"No form of human relationship is as profitable as the exchange of useful thoughts, and it may be surprising but true that one may acquire from the mind of the humblest person ideas of the first magnitude of importance.

"Let me illustrate what I mean, through the story of a preacher who picked from the mind of an illiterate gardener at his church an idea that led to the attainment of his *Definite Major Purpose.*

"The preacher's name was Russell Conwell, and his major purpose was the founding of a college he had long desired to establish. All he needed was the necessary money, a tidy sum of something more than a million dollars, which in those days, was a lot of money.

"One day the Reverend Russell Conwell stopped to chat with the gardener who was busily at work cutting the church lawn. As they stood there talking in light conversation, the Reverend Conwell casually remarked that the grass adjoining the churchyard was much greener and better kept than their own lawn, intending his remark as a mild reprimand to the old caretaker.

"With a broad grin on his face the old gardener replied, 'Yes, sir, that grass does look greener, but that's because we are all so used to the grass on this side of the fence.'

"Now there was nothing brilliant about that remark, for it was not intended to be anything more than the gardener's alibi for laziness, but it planted in the fertile mind of Russell Conwell the seed of an idea—just a bare, tiny seed of thought, mind you—which led to the solution of his major problem.

"From that humble remark an idea was born for a lecture which the preacher composed and delivered more than 4,000 times. He called it 'Acres of Diamonds.' The central idea of the lecture was this: One need not seek one's opportunity in the distance, but can find it right where one stands, by recognizing the fact that the grass on the other side of the fence is no greener than that where one stands.

"The lecture yielded an income during the life of Russell Conwell of more than $6 million. It was published in book form and became a bestseller throughout the nation for many years thereafter. The money was used to found and maintain Temple University of Philadelphia, Pennsylvania, one of the great educational institutions of the country.

"The idea around which that lecture was organized did more than found a university. It enriched the minds of millions of people by influencing them to look for opportunity right where they were. The philosophy of the lecture is as sound today as it was when it first came from the mind of an illiterate gardener.

"Remember this: Every active brain is a potential source of inspiration from which one may procure an idea, or the mere seed of an idea, of priceless value in the solution of personal problems, or the attainment of a major purpose in life.

"Sometimes great ideas spring from humble minds, but generally they come from the minds of those closest to the individual, where the Master Mind relationship has been deliberately established and maintained.

Carnegie's Master Mind Experience

"The most profitable idea of my own career came one afternoon when Charlie Schwab and I were walking across a golf course. As we finished our shots on the thirteenth hole, Charlie looked up with a sheepish grin on his face, and said, 'I'm three strokes up on you at this hole, chief, but I have just thought of an idea that should give you a lot of free time to play golf.'

"Curiosity prompted me to inquire as to the nature of the idea. He gave it to me in one brief sentence, each word of which was worth, roughly speaking, a million dollars. 'Consolidate all your steel plants,' said he, 'into one big corporation and sell it out to Wall Street bankers.'

"Nothing more was said about the matter during the game, but that evening I began to turn the suggestion over in my mind and think about it. Before I went to sleep that night I had converted the seed of his idea into a *Definite Major Purpose*. The following week I sent Charlie Schwab to New York City to deliver a speech before a group of Wall Street bankers, among them J. Pierpont Morgan.

"The sum and substance of the speech was a plan for the organization of the United States Steel Corporation, through which I consolidated all my steel plants and retired from active business, with more money than anyone needs.

"Now let me emphasize one point: Charlie Schwab's idea might never have been born, and I never would have received the benefit of it, if I had not made it my business to encourage in my associates the creation of new ideas. This encouragement was provided through a close and continuous Master Mind alliance with the members of my business organization, among whom was Charlie Schwab.

"Contact, let me repeat, is an important word!

"It is much more important if we add to it the word 'harmonious.' Through harmonious relationships with the minds of others, we may have the full use of their capacity to create ideas. Those who overlook this great fact thereby condemn themselves eternally to penury and want.

"No one is smart enough to project their influence very far into the world without the friendly cooperation of others. Drive this thought home in every way you can, for it is sufficient unto itself to open the door to success in the higher brackets of individual achievement.

"Too many people look for success in the distance, far from where they are, and altogether too often they search for it through complicated plans based upon a belief in luck, or 'miracles' which they hope may favor them.

"As Russell Conwell so effectively stated, some people seem to think the grass is greener on the other side of the fence from where they stand, and they pass up the 'Acres of Diamonds' in the form of ideas and opportunities which are available to them through the minds of their daily associates.

"I found my 'Acres of Diamonds' right where I stood, while looking into the glow of a hot steel blast furnace. I remember well the first day I began to sell myself on the idea of becoming a leader in the great steel industry instead of remaining a helper in another man's 'Acres of Diamonds.'

"At first the thought was not very definite. It was a wish more than it was a definite purpose. But I began to bring it back into my mind and to encourage it to take possession of me, until there came the day when the idea began to drive me instead of my having to drive it.

"That day I began with earnestness to work my own 'Acres of Diamonds,' and I was surprised to learn how quickly a *Definite Major Purpose* may find a way to translate itself into its physical equivalent.

"The main thing of importance is to know what one wants.

"The next thing of importance is to begin digging for diamonds right where one is, using whatever tools may be at hand, even if they be only the tools of thought. In proportion to the faithful use a person makes of the tools at hand, other and better tools will be placed in that person's hands when he or she is ready for them.

"Those who understand the Master Mind principle and make use of it will find the necessary tools much more quickly than will those who know nothing of this principle.

"Every mind needs friendly contact with other minds, for the food of expansion and growth. The discriminating person who has a *Definite Major Purpose* in life chooses, with the greatest of care, the types of minds with whom to associate most intimately, recognizing that we take on a definite portion of the personality of every person with whom we associate.

"I wouldn't give much for those who do not make it their business to seek the company of people who know more. People rise to the level of their superiors or fall to the level of their inferiors, according to their choice of associates.

"Last, there is one other thought which every professional who works for wages or a salary should recognize and respect. It lies in the fact that a job is, and should be, a schooling for a higher station in life, for which the professional is being paid in two important ways: first, by the wages received directly, and second, by the experience gained from the work. And it frequently becomes true that one's greatest pay consists not in a pay envelope but in the experience from work!

"This overplus pay gained from work experience depends largely for its value upon the mental attitude with which workers relate themselves to associate workers, both those above and those beneath them. If their attitude is positive and cooperative, and they follow the habit of Going the Extra Mile, their advancement will be both sure and rapid.

"Thus we see that those who get ahead not only make practical use of the principle of the Master Mind, but also apply the principle of Going the Extra Mile, and the principle of Definiteness of Purpose—the three principles which are inseparably associated with success in all walks of life.

The Rewards of a Committed Relationship

"A committed relationship: this is by far the most important alliance anyone ever experiences during his or her entire life.

"It is important financially, physically, mentally, and spiritually, for it is a relationship bound together by all of these elements.

"The home is the place where most Master Mind alliances should begin, and the person who has chosen a mate wisely will, if wise in an economic sense, make a significant other the first member of a personal Master Mind group.

"The home alliance not only should include a committed couple, it should include other members of the family as well if they live in the same household, particularly children.

"The Master Mind principle brings into action the spiritual forces of those who are thus allied for a definite purpose; and spiritual power, while it may seem intangible, is nevertheless the greatest of all powers.

"The person in a committed relationship who is on the right terms with a partner—terms of complete harmony, understanding, sympathy, and the singleness of purpose in which each is interested—has a priceless asset in this relationship which may lift him or her to great heights of personal achievement.

"Discord between a couple is unpardonable, no matter what may be the cause. It is unpardonable because it may destroy the couple's chances of success, even though they may have every other attribute necessary for success.

"And may I here interpolate a suggestion for the benefit of both partners?

"The suggestion may, if it is heeded and followed, make just the difference between a lifetime of poverty and misery and a lifetime of opulence and plenty.

"The partner has more influence over a significant other than has any other person. When two people choose to commit to each other, in preference to all others, these two people have each other's love and confidence.

"Love heads the list of the nine basic motives of life, which inspire all voluntary actions of people. Through the emotion of love, two people may send each other to work in a spirit which knows no such reality as failure. But remember that 'nagging,' jealousy, faultfinding, and indifference do not feed the emotion of love. They kill it.

"If a couple is wise, they will arrange for a regular Master Mind hour each day, a period during which they will pool all their mutual interests and discuss them in detail, in a spirit of love and understanding. The periods most suited for this Master Mind talk are those following the morning meal and just before retiring at night.

"And every meal hour should be a period of friendly intercourse between a couple. They should not be converted into periods of inquisition and faultfinding, but rather should be converted into periods of family worship, during which there will be good cheer, and the discussion of pleasant subjects of mutual interest to both people. More family relationships are wrecked at the family meal hour than at any other time, for this is the hour which many families devote to settling their family differences of opinion, or to disciplining the children.

"Each person should take a keen interest in the other person's occupation, becoming familiar with every feature of it. When two people marry, each becomes invested in the firm of their union. If each relates to the other by a true application of the Master Mind principle, that stock in which each is invested will continue to rise in value.

"The partner who is wise will manage the firm's business by a carefully prepared budget, taking care not to spend more than the income will allow. Many marriages go on the rocks because the firm runs out of money. And it is no mere axiom to say that when poverty knocks on the front door, love takes to its heels and runs out through the back door. Love, like a beautiful picture, requires the embellishment of an appropriate frame and proper lighting. It requires cultivation and food, just as does the physical body. Love does not thrive on indifference, nagging, faultfinding, or domineering by either party.

"Love thrives best where a couple feeds it through singleness of purpose. The partner who remembers this may remain forever the most influential person in the life of a significant other. The partner who forgets it may see the time when the other person begins to look around for an opportunity 'to trade in for a newer model,' so to speak.

"While one or both partners may have the responsibility of earning a living, each should bear the responsibility of softening the shocks and the resistances the couple will meet in connection with work—a responsibility which can be discharged by planning a pleasant home life, through whatever social activities may be fitting to the couple's careers.

"The love of a significant other, if it be the right kind of love, is sufficient in abundance to serve the whole family; and it is a happy partner who is able to spread his or her love around equally, without unfair preference in favor of either the partner or the children.

"Where love abounds as the basis of the family Master Mind relationship, the family finances will not be likely to give cause for disturbance, for love has a way of surmounting all obstacles, meeting all problems, and overcoming all difficulties.

"Family problems may arise, and they do in every family, but love should be the master of them. Keep the light of love shining brightly and everything else will shape itself to the pattern of your most lofty desires.

"I know this counsel is sound, as I have followed it in my own family relationship, and I can truthfully say that it has been responsible for whatever material success I have achieved."

Mr. Carnegie's frank admission becomes impressive when one considers the fact that he accumulated a fortune of more than $500 million. Mr. Carnegie made a huge fortune, but those who knew of his relationship with his wife know that Mrs. Carnegie made him!

Other Examples of Master Mind Relationship Successes

To take up the subject of family Master Mind relationships where Andrew Carnegie left it, this seems an appropriate place to call attention to the fact that his experience is by no means an isolated one.

It was no secret among the personal friends of Henry Ford and his wife that the Master Mind relationship between them was an important factor in the building of the great Ford industrial empire. The public heard very little of Mrs. Ford, but the fact remains that she was a powerful influence in Mr. Ford's life, from the earliest days of their marriage.

Thomas A. Edison freely admitted that Mrs. Edison was the major source of his inspiration. They held their Master Mind meetings daily, usually at the close of Mr. Edison's day's work. And nothing was permitted to interfere with these meetings. Mrs. Edison saw to that, for she recognized the value of her keen interest in all of Mr. Edison's experimental work.

Mr. Edison often worked late into the night, but his homecoming found his wife awaiting him in keen anticipation of hearing him tell of his successes and failures during the day. She was familiar with every experiment he conducted and took an interest in them.

She served as a sort of sounding board for Mr. Edison, through whom he had the privilege of looking at his work from the sidelines, and it has been said that she often supplied the missing link to many of his unsolved problems.

It is believed by many that Mrs. Edison was responsible for the Master Mind alliance that was maintained between Mr. Edison, Henry Ford, Harvey Firestone, and John Burroughs, the naturalist. These meetings were noteworthy enough to have been reported on by major newspapers at the time. If the Master Mind relationship was considered to be of value to people of this caliber, surely it should be regarded as such by those who are struggling to find their places in the world.

The Princes of Love and Romance have played an important role in the lives of all truly great leaders. The story of Robert and Elizabeth Barrett Browning is replete with evidence that these unseen entities, which they recognized and respected, were largely responsible for the inspirational literary works of these great poets.

History attributes the rise to military power of Napoleon Bonaparte to the inspirational influence of his first wife, Josephine. Napoleon's military successes began to wane when he allowed his ambition for power to cause him to put Josephine aside, and his defeat and banishment to the lonely island of St. Helena was not far ahead of this act.

It may not be amiss to mention the fact that many of those in the business world considered a "Napoleon" of these times have met with the same kind of defeat for the same reason. With the high divorce rate these days, often partners will maintain their Master Mind relationships until they attain power, fame, and fortune, then "trade them in for newer models," as Andrew Carnegie expressed it.

Charles M. Schwab's story was different. He, too, gained fame and fortune through his Master Mind alliance with Andrew Carnegie, aided by a similar relationship with his wife, who was an invalid during the major portion of their married life. He did not abandon her because of her condition, but stood loyally by her until her death, because he believed that loyalty is the first requirement of sound character.

While we are on the subject of loyalty, it may not be out of place to suggest that the lack of loyalty among those in business Master Mind relationships is among the more frequent causes of business failure. As long as associates in business maintain the spirit of loyalty between one another, they generally find a way to bridge their defeats and overcome their handicaps.

It has been said that the first trait of character which Andrew Carnegie looked for in the young professionals whom he raised from the ranks of his workers to highly paid executive positions was the trait of loyalty. He often said that if a worker did not inherently have the quality of loyalty, he did not have the proper foundation for a sound character in other directions.

His methods of testing employees for loyalty were both ingenious and multiple in scope. The testings took place before promotions were made and afterward, until such time as there no longer remained any doubt as to an employee's loyalty. And it is a tribute to Carnegie's deep insight that he made but few mistakes in judging employees on their loyalty.

A Few Final Dos and Don'ts

Do not reveal the purpose of your Master Mind alliance to those outside of the alliance, and make sure that the members of your alliance refrain from so doing, because the idle, the scoffers, and the envious stand on the sidelines of life, looking for an opportunity to sow the seeds of discouragement in the minds of those who are excelling them. Avoid this pitfall by keeping your plans to yourself, except insofar as they may be revealed by your actions and achievements.

Don't go into your Master Mind meetings with your mind filled with a negative mental attitude. Remember, if you are the leader of your Master Mind group, it is your responsibility to keep every member of the alliance aroused to a high degree of interest and enthusiasm. You cannot do this when you are negative. Moreover, others will not follow with enthusiasm the leader who shows a tendency toward doubt, indecision, or lack of faith in the object of a *Definite Major Purpose*. Keep your Master Mind allies keyed up to a high degree of enthusiasm by keeping yourself keyed up in the same manner.

Don't neglect to see that each member of your Master Mind alliance receives adequate compensation, in one form or another, in proportion to the contributions each makes to your success. Remember that no one ever does anything with enthusiasm unless he or she benefits thereby. Familiarize yourself with the nine basic motives, which inspire all voluntary action, and see that each of your Master Mind allies is properly motivated to give you loyalty, enthusiasm, and complete confidence.

If you are related to your Master Mind allies by the motive of desire for financial gain, be sure that you give more than you receive, by adopting and following the principle of *Going the Extra Mile.* Do this voluntarily, before you are requested to do so, if you wish to make the most of the habit.

Do not place competitors in your Master Mind alliance, but follow the Rotary Club policy of surrounding yourself with those who have no reason to feel antagonistic toward one another—those who are not in competition with one another.

Do not try to dominate your Master Mind group by force, fear, or coercion, but hold your leadership by diplomacy, based upon a definite motive for loyalty and cooperation. The day of leadership by force is gone. Do not try to revive it, for it has no place in civilized life.

Do not fail to take every step necessary to create the spirit of fellowship among your Master Mind allies, for friendly teamwork will give you power attainable in no other way.

The most powerful Master Mind alliance in the history of mankind was formed by the United Nations after World War II. Its leaders announced to the whole world that their *Definite Major Purpose* was based on the determination to establish human liberty and freedom for all the people of the world, both the victors and the vanquished alike!

That pronouncement was worth a thousand victories on the fields of battle, for it had the effect of establishing confidence in the minds of people who were affected by the outcome of that war. Without confidence there can be no Master Mind relationship, either in the field of military operations or elsewhere.

Confidence is the basis of all harmonious relationships. Remember this when you organize your Master Mind alliance if you wish that alliance to endure and to serve your interests effectively.

I have now revealed to you the working principle of the greatest of all the sources of personal power among all people—-the Master Mind.

By the combination of the first four principles of this philosophy—the habit of *Going the Extra Mile, Definiteness of Purpose,* the *Master Mind,* and the one which follows—one may acquire a clue as to the secret of the power which is available through the Master-Key to Riches.

Therefore, it is not out of place for me to warn you to approach the analysis of our next seminar in a state of expectancy, for it may well mark the most important turning point of your life.

I shall now reveal to you the true approach to a full understanding of a power which has defied analysis by the entire world of science. Moreover, I shall hope to provide you with the formula by which you may appropriate this power and use it for the attainment of your *Definite Major Purpose* in life.

CHAPTER 9

APPLIED FAITH

Faith is a royal visitor that enters only the mind that has been properly prepared for it, the mind that has been set in order through self-discipline.

In the fashion of all royalty, Faith commands the best room—no, the finest suite—in the mental dwelling place. It will not be shunted into servants' quarters, and it will not associate with envy, greed, superstition, hatred, revenge, vanity, doubt, worry, or fear.

Get the full significance of this truth and you will be on the way to an understanding of that mysterious power which has baffled scientists down through the ages. Then you will recognize the necessity for conditioning your mind, through self-discipline, before expecting Faith to become your permanent guest.

Recalling the words of the sage of Concord, Ralph Waldo Emerson, who said, "In every man there is something wherein I may learn of him, and in that I am his pupil," I shall now introduce a man who has been a great benefactor of mankind, so that you may observe how one goes about the conditioning of his mind for the expression of Faith.

Let him tell his own story:

"During the Great Depression, which began in 1929, I took a postgraduate course in the University of Hard Knocks, the greatest of all schools. It was then I discovered a hidden fortune which I possessed but had not been using. I made the discovery one morning when a notice came that my bank had closed its doors, possibly never to be reopened again, for it was then that I began to take inventory of my intangible, unused assets. Come with me while I describe what the inventory revealed.

"Let us begin with the most important item on the list, unused Faith!

"When I searched deeply into my own heart I discovered, despite my financial losses, I had an abundance of Faith left in Infinite Intelligence and Faith in others.

"With this discovery came another of still greater importance: the discovery that Faith can accomplish that which not all the money of the world can achieve.

"When I possessed all the money I needed, I made the grievous error of believing money to be a permanent source of power. Now came the astonishing revelation that money, without Faith, is nothing but so much inert matter, of itself possessed of no power whatsoever.

"Recognizing, perhaps for the first time in my life, the stupendous power of enduring Faith, I analyzed myself carefully to determine just how much of this form of riches I possessed. The analysis was both surprising and gratifying.

"I began the analysis by taking a walk into the woods. I wished to get away from the crowd, away from the noise of the city, away from the disturbances of civilization and the fears of others, so that I might meditate in silence.

"Ah! what gratification there is in that word 'silence.'

"On my journey I picked up an acorn and held it in the palm of my hand. I found it near the roots of the giant oak tree from which it had fallen. I judged the age of the tree to have been so great that it must have been a fair-sized tree when George Washington was a small boy.

"As I stood there looking at the great tree, and its small embryonic offspring, which I held in my hand, I realized that the tree had grown from a small acorn. I also realized that all those on this planet could not have managed to build such a tree.

"I was conscious of the fact that some form of intangible Intelligence created the acorn from which the tree grew, and caused the acorn to germinate and begin its climb up from the soil of the earth.

"Then I realized that the greatest powers are the intangible powers, and not those which consist in bank balances or material things.

"I picked up a handful of black soil and covered the acorn with it. I held in my hand the visible portion of the substance out of which that magnificent tree had grown.

"At the root of the giant oak I plucked a fern. Its leaves were beautifully designed—yes, designed—and I realized as I examined the fern that it, too, was created by the same Intelligence which had produced the oak tree.

"I continued my walk in the woods until I came to a running brook of clear, sparkling water. By this time I was tired, so I sat near the brook to rest and listen to its rhythmic music, as it danced on its way back to the sea.

"The experience brought back memories of my youth. I remembered playing by a similar brook. As I sat there listening to the music of the water, I became conscious of an unseen being—an Intelligence—which spoke to me from within and told me the enchanting story of the water, and this is the story it told:

"'Water! Pure sparkling water. The same has been rendering service ever since this planet cooled off and became the home of mankind, beast, and vegetation.

"'Water! Ah, what a story you could tell if you spoke my language. You have quenched the thirst of endless millions of earthly wayfarers, fed the flowers; expanded into steam and turned the wheels of machinery, condensing and going back again to your original form. You have cleaned the sewers, washed the pavements, rendered countless services to man and beast, returning always to your source in the seas, there to become purified and start your journey of service once again.

"'When you move you travel in one direction only: toward the seas whence you came. You are forever going and coming, but you always seem to be happy at your labor.

"'Water! Clean, pure, sparkling substance. No matter how much dirty work you perform, you cleanse yourself at the end of your labor.

"'You cannot be created, nor can you be destroyed. You are akin to all life. Without your beneficence, no form of life on this earth would exist!'

"And the water of the brook went rippling, laughing, on its way back to the sea.

"The story of water ended, but I had heard a great sermon; I had been close to the greatest of all forms of Intelligence. I felt evidence of that same Intelligence which had created the great oak tree from a tiny acorn, the Intelligence which had fashioned the leaves of the fern with mechanical and aesthetic skill such as no human could duplicate.

"The shadows of the trees were becoming longer; the day was coming to a close.

"As the sun slowly descended beyond the western horizon, I realized that it, too, had played a part in that marvelous sermon which I had heard.

"Without the beneficent aid of the sun there could have been no conversion of the acorn into an oak tree. Without the sun's help, the sparkling water of the flowing brook would have remained eternally imprisoned in the oceans, and life on this earth could never have existed.

"These thoughts gave a beautiful climax to the sermon I had heard, thoughts of the romantic affinity existing between the sun and the water and all life on this earth, beside which all other forms of romance seemed incomparable and unimportant.

"I picked up a small white pebble which had been neatly polished by the waters of the running brook. As I held it in my hand I received, from within, a still more impressive sermon. The Intelligence which conveyed that sermon to my mind seemed to say:

"'Behold, mortal, a miracle, which you hold in your hand.

"'I am only a tiny pebble of stone, yet I am, in reality, a small universe in which there is everything that may be found in the more expanded portion of the universe which you see out there among the stars.

"'I appear to be dead and motionless, but the appearance is deceiving. I am made of molecules. Inside my molecules are myriad atoms, each a small universe unto itself. Inside the atoms are electrons, which move at an inconceivable rate of speed.

"'I am not a dead mass of stone, but an organized group of units of ceaseless energy.

"'I appear to be a solid mass, but the appearance is an illusion, for my electrons are separated one from another by a distance greater than their mass.

"'Study me carefully, humble earthly wayfarer, and remember that the great powers of the universe are the intangibles, that the values of life are those which cannot be added by bank balances.'

"The thought conveyed by that climax was so illuminating that it held me spellbound, for I recognized that I held in my hand an infinitesimal portion of the energy which keeps the sun, the stars, and the earth, on which we live for a brief period, in their respective places in relation to one another.

"Meditation revealed to me the beautiful reality that there is law and order, even in the small confines of a tiny pebble of stone. I recognized that within the mass of that tiny pebble, the romance and the reality of Nature were combined. I recognized that within that small pebble, fact transcended fancy.

"Never before had I felt so keenly the significance of the evidence of natural law and order and purpose, which reveal themselves in everything the human mind can perceive. Never before had I felt myself so near the source of my Faith in Infinite Intelligence.

"It was a beautiful experience, out there in the midst of Mother Nature's family of trees and running brooks, where the very calmness of the surroundings bade my weary soul be quiet and rest awhile, so that I might look, feel, and listen while Infinite Intelligence unfolded to me the story of its reality.

"Never, in all my life, had I previously been so overwhelmingly conscious of the real evidence of Infinite Intelligence, or of the source of my Faith.

"I lingered in this newly found paradise until the Evening Star began to twinkle; then, reluctantly, I retraced my footsteps back to the city, there to mingle once again with those who are driven, like galley slaves, by the inexorable rules of civilization, in a mad scramble to gather up material things they do not need.

"I am now back in my study, with my books and my typewriter, on which I am recording the story of my experience. But I am swept by a feeling of loneliness and a longing to be out there by the side of that friendly brook where, only a few hours ago, I had bathed my soul in the satisfying realities of Infinite Intelligence.

"I know that my Faith in Infinite Intelligence is real and enduring. It is not a blind Faith; it is one based on close examination of the handiwork of Infinite Intelligence, and as such has been expressed in the orderliness of the universe.

"I had been looking in the wrong direction for the source of my Faith. I had been seeking it in human deeds, in human relationships, in bank balances and material things.

"I found it in a tiny acorn, a giant oak tree, a small pebble or stone, the leaves of a simple fern, and the soil of the earth; in the friendly sun, which warms the earth and gives motion to the waters; in the Evening Star; in the silence and calm of the great outdoors.

"And I am moved to suggest that Infinite Intelligence reveals itself through silence more readily than through the boisterousness of people's struggles, in their mad rush to accumulate material things.

"My bank account vanished, my bank collapsed, but I was richer than most millionaires, because I had discovered a direct approach to Faith. With this power behind me, I can accumulate other bank balances sufficient for my needs.

"I am richer than are most millionaires, because I depend upon a source of inspired power which reveals itself to me from within, while many of the more wealthy find it necessary to turn to bank balances and the stock ticker for stimulation and power.

"My source of power is as free as the air I breathe, and as limitless. To avail myself of it, I have only to turn on my Faith, and this I have in abundance.

"Thus, once again I learned the truth that every adversity carries with it the seed of an equivalent benefit. My adversity cost me my bank balance. It paid off through the revelation of the means to all riches!"

Stated in his own words, you have the story of a man who has discovered how to condition his mind for the expression of Faith.

And what a dramatic story it is! Dramatic because of its simplicity.

Here is a man who found a sound basis for an enduring Faith not in bank balances or material riches, but in the seed of an oak tree, the leaves of a fern, a small pebble, and a running brook, things everyone may observe and appreciate.

But his observation of these simple things led him to recognize that the greatest powers are intangible powers, which are revealed through the simple things around us.

I have related this man's story as I wished to emphasize the manner in which one may clear his mind, even in the midst of chaos and insurmountable difficulties, and prepare it for the expression of Faith.

The most important fact the story reveals is this: When the mind has been cleared of a negative mental attitude, the power of Faith moves in and begins to take possession.

Surely no student of this philosophy will be unfortunate enough to miss this important observation.

An Analysis of Faith

Let us turn now to an analysis of Faith, although we must approach the subject with full recognition that Faith is a power that has defied the analytic powers of the entire scientific world.

Faith has been given fourth place in this philosophy because it comes near to representing the "fourth dimension," although it is presented here for its relationship to personal achievement.

Faith is a state of mind that might properly be called the "mainspring of the soul," through which one's aims, desires, and purposes may be translated into their physical or financial equivalent.

Previously we observed that great power may be attained by the application of (1) the habit of *Going the Extra Mile,* (2) *Definiteness of Purpose,* and (3) *The Master Mind.* But that power is feeble in comparison with that which is available through the combined application of these principles with the state of mind known as Faith.

We have already observed that capacity for Faith is one of the Twelve Riches. Let us now recognize the means by which this "capacity" may be plied with that strange power which has been the main bulwark of civilization, the chief cause of all human progress, the guiding spirit of all constructive human endeavors.

Let us remember, at the outset of this analysis, that Faith is a state of mind which may be enjoyed only by those who have learned the art of taking full and complete control of their minds. This is the one and only prerogative right over which an individual has been given complete control.

Faith expresses its powers only through the mind that has been prepared for it. But the way of preparation is known and may be attained by all who desire to find it.

The fundamentals of Faith are these:

a. *Definiteness of Purpose,* supported by personal initiative or action.

b. The habit of *Going the Extra Mile* in all human relationships.

c. A *Master Mind* alliance with one or more people who radiate courage based on Faith, and who are suited spiritually and mentally to one's needs in carrying out a given purpose.

d. A positive mind, free from all negatives, such as fear, envy, greed, hatred, jealousy, and superstition. (A positive mental attitude is the first and the most important of the Twelve Riches.)

e. Recognition of the truth that every adversity carries with it the seed of an equivalent benefit, that temporary defeat is not failure until it has been accepted as such.

f. The habit of affirming one's *Definite Major Purpose* in life, in a ceremony of meditation, at least once daily.

g. Recognition of the existence of Infinite Intelligence, which gives orderliness to the universe; that all individuals are minute expressions of this Intelligence, and the individual mind has no limitations except those which are accepted and set up by the individual in his or her own mind.

h. A careful inventory (in retrospect) of one's past defeats and adversities, which will reveal the truth that all such experiences carry the seed of an equivalent benefit.

i. Self-respect expressed through harmony with one's own conscience.

j. Recognition of the oneness of all humankind.

These are the fundamentals of major importance which prepare the mind for the expression of Faith. Their application calls for no degree of superiority, but application does call for intelligence and a keen thirst for truth and justice.

Faith fraternizes only with the mind that is positive!

It is the "élan vital" that gives power, inspiration, and action to a positive mind. It is the power that causes a positive mind to act as an "electromagnet," attracting to it the exact physical counterpart of the thought it expresses.

Faith gives resourcefulness to the mind, enabling the mind to make "grist of all that comes to its mill." It recognizes favorable opportunities, in every circumstance of one's life, whereby one may attain the object of Faith, going so far as to provide the means by which failure and defeat may be converted into success of equivalent dimensions.

Faith enables all humans to penetrate deeply into the secrets of Nature and to understand Nature's language as it is expressed in all natural laws.

From this sort of revelation have come all the great inventions that serve mankind, and a better understanding of the way to human freedom through harmony in human relationships, such as was provided by the Constitution of the United States.

Faith makes it possible to achieve that which anyone can conceive and believe!

If you would have Faith, keep your mind on that which you desire. And remember that there is no such reality as a "blanket" Faith, for *Faith is the outward demonstration of Definiteness of Purpose*!

Faith is guidance from within. The guiding force is Infinite Intelligence directed to definite ends. It will not bring that which one desires, but it will guide one to the attainment of the object of desire.

How to Demonstrate the Power of Faith

(a) Know what you want and determine what you have to give in return for it.

(b) When you affirm the objects of your desires, through prayer, inspire your imagination to see yourself already in possession of them, and act precisely as if you were in the physical possession thereof. (Remember, the possession of anything first takes place mentally.)

(c) Keep the mind open at all times for guidance from within, and when you are inspired by "hunches" to modify your plans or to move on a new plan, move without hesitancy or doubt.

(d) When overtaken by temporary defeat, as you may be overtaken many times, remember that one's Faith is tested in many ways, and your defeat may be only one of your "testing periods." Therefore, accept defeat as an inspiration to greater effort and carry on with belief that you will succeed.

(e) Any negative state of mind will destroy the capacity for Faith and result in a negative climax of any affirmation you may express. Your state of mind is everything; therefore take possession of your mind and clear it completely of all unwanted interlopers that are unfriendly to Faith, and keep it cleared, no matter what may be the cost in effort.

(f) Learn to give expression to your power of Faith by writing out a clear description of your *Definite Major Purpose* in life and using it as the basis of your daily meditation.

(g) Associate with your *Definite Major Purpose* as many as possible of the nine basic motives, described previously.

(h) Write out a list of all the benefits and advantages you expect to derive from the attainment of the object of your *Definite Major Purpose* and call these into your mind many times daily, thereby making your mind "success conscious." (This is commonly called autosuggestion.)

(i) Associate yourself, as far as possible, with people who are in sympathy with your *Definite Major Purpose,* people who are in harmony with you, and inspire them to encourage you in every way possible.

(j) Let not a single day pass without making at least one definite move toward the attainment of your *Definite Major Purpose.* Remember, "Faith without works is dead."

(k) Choose some prosperous person of self-reliance and courage as your "pacemaker," and make up your mind not only to keep up with that person, but to exceed that person. Do this silently, without mentioning your plan to anyone. (Boastfulness will be fatal to your success, as Faith has nothing in common with vanity or self-love.)

(l) Surround yourself with books, pictures, wall mottoes, and other suggestive reminders of self-reliance founded upon Faith as it has been demonstrated by other people, thus building around yourself an atmosphere of prosperity and achievement. This habit will bring stupendous results.

(m) Adopt a policy of never evading or running away from unpleasant circumstances, but recognize such circumstances and build a counterattack against them right where they overtake you. You will discover that recognition of such circumstances, without fear of their consequences, is nine-tenths of the battle in mastering them.

continued

(n) Recognize the truth that everything worth having has a definite price. The price of Faith, among other things, is eternal vigilance in carrying out these simple instructions. Your watchword must be *persistence*!

These are the steps that lead to the development and the maintenance of a positive mental attitude, the only one in which Faith will abide. They are steps that lead to riches of both mind and spirit as well as riches of the purse. Fill your mind with this kind of mental food.

These are the steps by which the mind may be prepared for the highest expressions of the soul.

"The key to every man," said Emerson, "is his thought."

That is true. Every person today is the result of his thoughts of yesterday.

The morning after the great Chicago fire had laid waste to the business portion of the city, Marshall Field went down to the site where, the day before, his retail store had stood.

All around him were groups of other merchants whose stores had also been destroyed. He listened in on their conversations and learned that they had given up hope, and many of them had already decided to move farther west and start over again.

Calling the nearest groups to him, Field said, "Gentlemen, you may do as you please, but as for me I intend to stay right here. Over there where you see the smoking remains of what was once my store shall be built the world's greatest retail store."

The store that Mr. Field built on Faith still stands on that spot, in Chicago. It was long recognized the world over as the greatest retail store on earth.

These leaders and others like them have been the pioneers who produced our great American way of life.

Human progress is no matter of accident or luck!

It is the result of applied faith, expressed by those who have conditioned their minds, through the seventeen principles of this philosophy, for the expression of Faith.

The United States is a nation founded on Faith and maintained by Faith. Moreover, it provides all the essentials that inspire Faith, so that the humblest citizen may attain the highest ambitions of heart and soul.

Therefore, our nation is justly known as a "land of opportunity," the richest and the freest nation of the world.

All freedom and riches have their roots in an abiding Faith.

And though Faith is the one power which defies scientific analysis, the procedure by which it may be applied is simple and within the understanding of the humblest, thus it is the common property of all. All that is known of this procedure has been simply stated, and not a single step of it is beyond the reach of the humblest person.

The Importance of a Positive Mental Attitude

Faith begins with definiteness of purpose functioning in a mind that has been prepared for it by the development of a positive mental attitude. It attains its greatest scope of power by physical action directed toward the attainment of a definite purpose.

All voluntary physical action is inspired by one or more of the nine basic motives. It is not difficult for one to develop Faith in connection with the pursuit of one's desires.

Let someone be motivated by love and see how quickly this emotion is given wings for action through Faith. And action in pursuit of the objective of that love quickly follows. The action becomes a labor of love, which is one of the Twelve Riches.

Let someone set his or her heart upon the accumulation of material riches and see how quickly every effort becomes a labor of love. The hours of the day are not long enough for the needs of such a one, and even though one labors long, fatigue is softened by the joy of self-expression, which is another of the Twelve Riches.

Thus, one by one the resistances of life fade into nothingness for the person who has prepared his or her mind for self-expression through Faith. Success becomes inevitable. Joy crowns every effort. There is no time or inclination for hatred. Harmony in human relationships comes naturally. Hope of achievement is high and continuous, for that person is already in possession of the object of a definite purpose. Intolerance has been supplanted by an open mind.

And self-discipline becomes as natural as the eating of food. That person understands people because he or she loves them, and because of this love is willing to share blessings. That person knows nothing of fear, for all those fears have been driven away by Faith. That's how the Twelve Riches become one's own.

Faith is an expression of gratitude for the human being's relationship to the Creator. Fear is an acknowledgment of the influences of evil, and it connotes a lack of belief in the Creator.

The greatest of life's riches consists in the understanding of the four principles I have mentioned. These principles are known as the "Big Four" of this philosophy, because they are the warp and the woof and the major foundation stones of the Master-Key to the power of thought and the inner secrets of the soul. Use this Master-Key wisely and you shall be free!

Some to Whom the Master-Key Has Been Revealed

"How may one tap that secret power that comes from within?" some will wish to ask. Let us see how others have drawn upon it.

A young clergyman by the name of Frank W. Gunsaulus had long desired to build a new type of college. He knew exactly what he wanted, but the hitch came in the fact that it required a million dollars in cash.

He made up his mind to get the million dollars. Definiteness of decision, based upon definiteness of purpose, constituted the first step of his plan.

Then he wrote a sermon titled "What I Would Do with a Million Dollars!" and announced in the newspapers that he would preach on that subject the following Sunday morning.

At the end of the sermon a strange man whom the young preacher had never seen before, arose, walked down to the pulpit, extended his hand, and said, "I like your sermon, and you may come down to my office tomorrow morning and I will give you the million dollars you desire."

The man was Philip D. Armour, the packinghouse founder of Armour & Company. His gift was the beginning of the Armour School of Technology, one of the great schools of the country.

What went on in the mind of the young preacher that enabled him to contact the secret power available through the mind of human beings is something we can only make conjectures about, but the modus operandi by which that power was stimulated was applied Faith.

Shortly after her birth, Helen Keller was stricken by a physical affliction which deprived her of sight, hearing, and speech. With two of the more important of the five physical senses stilled forever, she faced life under difficulties such as most people never know throughout their lives.

With the aid of a kindly woman who recognized the existence of that secret power which comes from within, Helen Keller began to contact that power and use it. In her own words, she gives a definite clue as to one of the conditions under which the power may be revealed.

"Faith," said Miss Keller, "rightly understood, is active, not passive. Passive faith is no more a force than sight is in an eye that does not look or search out. Active faith knows no fear. It denies that God has betrayed His creatures and given the world over to darkness. It denies despair. Reinforced with faith, the weakest mortal is mightier than disaster."

Faith, backed by action, was the instrument with which Miss Keller bridged her affliction so that she was restored to a useful life.

Through applied faith she learned to speak. Through her faith she substituted the sense of touch to do the work of the sense of hearing and the sense of sight, thus proving that no matter how great may be one's physical handicaps, there always is a means by which they may be eliminated or bridged.

The way may be found through that secret power from within one's mind, the approach to which must be discovered by each of us, alone. Go back through the pages of history and you will observe that the story of civilization's unfoldment leads inevitably to the works of men and women who opened the door to that secret power from within, with applied faith as the master-key! Observe, too, that great achievements always are born of hardship and struggle and barriers which seem insurmountable, obstacles which yield to nothing but an indomitable will backed by an abiding faith.

And here, in one short phrase—indomitable will backed by an abiding faith—you have the approach of major importance that leads to the discovery of the door of the mind, behind which the secret power from within is hidden.

Those who penetrate that secret power and apply it to the solution of personal problems sometimes are called "dreamers." But observe that they back their dreams with action, thus proving the soundness of Helen Keller's statement that "Faith, rightly understood, is active, not passive."

An International Symbol of Faith

One of the strange features of "faith, rightly understood" is that it generally appears because of some emergency which forces people to look beyond the power of ordinary thought for the solution to their problems. It is during these emergencies that we draw upon that secret power from within which knows no resistance strong enough to defeat it.

Witness the extraordinary example of the imprisoned leader of the Myanmar (formerly known as Burma) pro-democracy movement, Aung San Suu Kyi, who became involved in the politics of her country. Her father, Aung San, was believed to be the founder of modern Burma and was assassinated in a political coup when Suu Kyi was two. She later left her country to study abroad.

It wasn't until she had finished college at Oxford, married an Englishman, and had children of her own that Suu Kyi returned home to find Burma in disarray, rife with political corruption. She began to speak out on behalf of democracy and nonviolence and attracted a large following. Soon, the government, threatened by her popularity and angry over the victory of Suu Kyi's political party in a nationally held democratic election, had her placed under house arrest. She was forbidden from seeing any family or friends.

It was her faith that kept Suu Kyi from giving up her beliefs or giving in to the demands of her dictatorial government, till she was awarded the Nobel Peace Prize for her courage. At that moment, the world learned of Suu Kyi's fight for civil rights, and it was this worldwide recognition that protected her from further harm by the military junta that ruled the region. For many years she has been under house arrest, off and on. There is constant rumor that she will soon be released and democracy will be reinstated.

Faith without risk is a passive faith, which, as Helen Keller stated, "is no more a force than sight is in an eye that does not look or search out."

And let us examine the records of some of the great leaders. They, too, discovered that secret power that comes from within, drew upon it, applied it, and converted a vast wilderness into the "cradle of democracy."

Choosing the Road of Faith, Not Fear

We all know of the achievements of these great leaders; we know the rules of their leadership; we recognize the nature and the scope of the blessings their labors have conferred upon the people of this nation, and thanks to the vision of Andrew Carnegie, we have preserved for the people the philosophy of individual achievement through which these leaders helped to make this the world's richest and freest country.

But, unfortunately, not all of us recognize the handicaps under which they worked, the obstacles they had to overcome, and the spirit of active faith in which they carried on their work. Of this we may be sure, however: Their achievements were in exact proportion to the emergencies they had to overcome. They met with opposition from those who were destined to benefit most by their struggles—people who, because of the lack of active faith, always view with skepticism and doubt that which is new and unfamiliar.

The emergencies of life often bring people to a crossroads, where they are forced to choose their direction, one road being marked Faith and another Fear!

What is it that causes the vast majority to take the Fear road? The choice hinges upon one's mental attitude.

The person who takes the Faith road has conditioned the mind to believe; conditioned it little at a time, by making prompt and courageous decisions in the details of daily experiences. The person who takes the Fear road has neglected to condition the mind to be positive.

In Washington, a man sits in a wheelchair with a tin cup and a bunch of pencils in his hands, gaining a meager living by begging. The excuse for his begging is that he lost the use of his legs. His brain has not been affected. He is otherwise strong and healthy. But his choice led him to accept the Fear road when a dreaded disease overtook him, while his mind atrophies through disuse.

In another part of the same city was another man who was afflicted with the same handicap. He, too, had lost the use of his legs, but his reaction to his loss was far different. When he came to the crossroads at which he was forced to make a choice, he took the Faith road, and it led straight to the White House and the highest position within the gift of the American people.

I am speaking, of course, of Franklin Delano Roosevelt. That which he lost through incapacity of his limbs he gained in the use of his brain and his will, and it is a matter of record that his physical affliction in no way hindered him from being one of the most active men who ever occupied the position of president.

The difference in the stations of these two men was very great. But don't be deceived as to the cause of this difference, for it is entirely a difference of mental attitudes. One man chose Fear as his guide. The other chose Faith.

And when you come right down to the circumstances which lift some to high stations in life and condemn others to poverty, the likelihood is that their widely separated positions reflect their respective mental attitudes. Those who are lifted choose the high road of Faith, while others choose the low road of Fear, leaving education, experience, and personal skill as matters of secondary importance.

When Thomas A. Edison's teacher sent him home from school, at the end of the first three months, with a note to his parents saying he had an "addled" mind and could not be taught, he had the best of excuses for becoming an outcast, a do-nothing, a nobody, and that is precisely what he proceeded to become for a time. He did odd jobs, sold newspapers, and then tinkered with gadgets and chemicals until he became what is commonly known as a "jack-of-all-trades" and not very good at any.

Then something took place in the mind of Thomas A. Edison that was destined to make his name immortal. Through some strange process which he never fully disclosed to the world, he discovered that secret power from within, took possession of it, and organized it. Suddenly, instead of being a man with an "addled" brain, he became the outstanding genius of invention of all time.

And now, wherever we see an electric light or hear recorded music or see a movie, we should be reminded that we are observing the product of that secret power from within, which is as available to us as it was to the great Edison. Moreover, we should feel sorely ashamed if, by neglect or indifference, we are making no appropriate use of this great power.

One of the strange features of this secret power from within is that it aids people in procuring whatever they set their hearts upon, which is but another way of saying it translates one's dominating thoughts into reality.

The illustration might be extended to cover every profession and all human endeavor. In every calling there are a few who rise to the top while all around them are others who never get beyond mediocrity.

Those who succeed usually are called "lucky." To be sure, they are lucky. But, learn the facts and you will discover that their "luck" consists of the secret power from within which they have applied through a positive mental attitude, a determination to follow the road of Faith instead of the road of Fear and self-limitation.

The power that comes from within recognizes no such reality as permanent barriers.

It converts defeat into a challenge to greater effort.

It removes self-imposed limitations such as fear and doubt.

And above all else let us remember that it makes no black marks against anyone's record which cannot be erased.

If approached through the power from within, every day brings forth a newly born opportunity for individual achievement, which need not in any way whatsoever be burdened by the failures of yesterday.

It favors no race or creed, and it is bound by no sort of arbitrary consistency compelling one to remain in poverty because he or she was born in poverty. The power from within is the one medium through which the effects of Cosmic Habitforce may be changed from a negative to a positive application, instantaneously. It recognizes no precedent, follows no hard and fast rules, and offers the one and only grand highway to personal freedom and liberty.

It was the inspiration of the poet R. L. Sharpe, who wrote in his poem "A Bag of Tools":

Isn't it strange that princes and kings
And clowns that caper in sawdust rings;
And common folks, like you and me,
All are builders for eternity.

To each is given a book of rules,
A block of stone and a bag of tools;
And each must shape ere time has flown,
A stumbling block or a stepping-stone.

Search until you find the point of approach to that secret power from within, and when you find it you will have discovered your true self—the "other self" which makes use of every experience of life.

Then, whether you build a better mousetrap, or write a better book, or preach a better sermon, the world will beat a path to your door, recognize you, and adequately reward you, no matter who you are or what may have been the nature and scope of your failures of the past.

What if you have failed in the past?

So did Edison, Henry Ford, the Wright Brothers, Andrew Carnegie, and all the other great American leaders who have helped to establish the American way of life. They all met with failure in one way or another, but they didn't call it by that name; they called it "temporary defeat."

Anyone can quit when the going is hard!

Anyone can feel sorry for himself when temporary defeat overtakes him, but self-coddling was no part of the character of those whom the world has recognized as great.

The approach to that power from within cannot be made by self-pity. It cannot be made through fear and timidity. It cannot be made through envy and hatred. It cannot be made through avarice and greed.

No, your "other self" pays no heed to any of these negatives. It manifests itself only through the mind that has been swept clean of all negative mental attitudes. It thrives in the mind that is guided by Faith!

It is not a new philosophy of achievement that the world needs. It is a rededication of the old and tried principles which led unerringly to the discovery of that power from within which "moves mountains."

The power that has brought forth great leaders in every walk of life and in every generation is still available. Those of vision and faith, who have pushed back the frontiers of ignorance and superstition and fear, have given the world all that we know as civilization.

The power is clothed in no mystery and it performs no miracles, but it works through the daily deeds of us all, and reflects itself in every form of service rendered for the benefit of humankind.

It is called by myriad names, but its nature never changes, no matter by what name it is known. It works through but one medium, and that is the mind. It expresses itself in thoughts, ideas, plans, and purposes, and the grandest thing to be said about it is that it is as free as the air we breathe and as abundant as the scope and space of the universe.

CHAPTER 10

THE LAW OF COSMIC HABITFORCE

Habit is a cable;
we weave a thread
of it every day,
and at last
we cannot break it.

—*Horace Mann*

So, now I come to the analysis of the greatest of all of Nature's laws, the law of Cosmic Habitforce!

Briefly described, the law of Cosmic Habitforce is Nature's method of giving fixation to all habits so that they may carry on automatically once they have been set into motion—the habits of human beings the same as the habits of the universe.

All people are where they are and what they are because of established habits of thoughts and deeds. The purpose of this entire philosophy is to aid individuals in the formation of the kind of habits that will transfer them from where they are to where they wish to be in life.

Every scientist, and many laymen, know that Nature maintains a perfect balance among all the elements of matter and energy throughout the universe; that the entire universe is operated through an inexorable system of orderliness and habits which never vary, and cannot be altered by any form of human endeavor; that the five known realities of the universe are (1) time, (2) space, (3) energy, (4) matter, and (5) intelligence, which shape the other known realities into orderliness and a system based upon fixed habits.

These are Nature's building blocks, with which she creates a grain of sand or the largest stars that float through space, and every other thing known to humans, or that the human mind can conceive.

These are the known realities, but not everyone has taken the time or the interest to learn that Cosmic Habitforce is the particular application of energy with which Nature maintains the relationship between the atoms of matter, the stars in their ceaseless motion outward to some unknown destiny, the seasons of the year, night and day, sickness and health, life and death. Cosmic Habitforce is the medium through which all habits and all human relationships are maintained in varying degrees of permanence, and the medium through which thought is translated into its physical equivalent in response to the desires and purposes of individuals.

But these are truths capable of proof, and one may count that hour sacred during which one discovers the inescapable truth that human beings are only an instrument through which higher powers are projecting themselves. This entire philosophy is designed to lead one to this important discovery, and to enable one to make use of the knowledge it reveals, by placing oneself in harmony with the unseen forces of the universe, which may carry one inevitably on to success.

The hour of this discovery should bring one within easy reach of the Master-Key to all Riches!

Cosmic Habitforce is Nature's comptroller, through which all other natural laws are coordinated, organized, and operated through orderliness and systems. Therefore it is the greatest of all natural laws.

We see the stars and the planets move with such precision that the astronomers can predetermine their exact location and their relationship to one another several years from now. We see the seasons of the year come and go with a clocklike regularity. We know that an oak tree grows from an acorn, and a pine tree grows from the seed of its ancestor; that an acorn never makes a mistake and produces a pine tree; nor does a pine seed produce an oak tree. We know that nothing is ever produced that does not have its antecedents in something similar which preceded it; that the nature and the purpose of one's thoughts produce fruits after their kind, just as surely as fire produces smoke.

Cosmic Habitforce is the medium by which every living thing is forced to take on and become a part of the environmental influences in which it lives and moves. Thus, it is clearly evident that success attracts more success, and failure attracts more failure—a truth that has long been known, although few have understood the reason for this strange phenomenon.

It is known that the person who has been a failure may become an outstanding success by close association with those who think and act in terms of success, but not everyone knows that this is true because the law of Cosmic Habitforce transmits the "success consciousness" from the mind of the successful person to the mind of the unsuccessful one who is closely related to that person in the daily affairs of life.

Whenever any two minds contact each other, there is born of that contact a third mind patterned after the stronger of the two. Most successful people recognize this truth and frankly admit that their success began with their close association with some person whose positive mental attitude they either consciously or unconsciously appropriated.

Cosmic Habitforce is unperceived through any of the five physical senses. That is why it has not been more widely recognized, for most do not attempt to understand the intangible forces of Nature, nor do they interest themselves in abstract principles. These intangibles and abstractions represent the real powers of the universe, however, and they are the real basis of everything that is tangible and concrete, the source from which tangibility and concreteness are derived.

Understand the working principle of Cosmic Habitforce and you will have no difficulty in interpreting Ralph Waldo Emerson's essay "Compensation," for he was rubbing elbows with the law of Cosmic Habitforce when he wrote it.

And Sir Isaac Newton, likewise, came near to the complete recognition of this law when he made his discovery of the law of gravity. Had he gone but a brief distance beyond where his discovery ended, he might have helped to reveal the same law as it holds our little earth in space and relates it systematically to all other planets in both time and space; the same law that relates human beings to one another and relates all to themselves through thought habits.

A Description of "Habitforce"

The term "Habitforce" is self-explanatory. It is a force which works through established habits. And every living thing below the intelligence of humans reproduces itself and fulfills its earthly mission in direct response to the power of Cosmic Habitforce through what we call "instinct."

Human beings alone have been given the privilege of choice in connection with living habits, and these they may fix by the patterns of their thoughts—the one and only privilege over which any individual has been given complete right of control.

Humans may think in terms of self-imposed limitations of fear, doubt, envy, greed, and poverty; Cosmic Habitforce will translate these thoughts into their material equivalent. Or they may think in terms of opulence and plenty, and this same law will translate their thoughts into their physical counterpart. In this manner one may control one's earthly destiny to an astounding degree, simply by exercising the privilege of shaping one's own thoughts. But once these thoughts have been shaped into definite patterns, they are taken over by the law of Cosmic Habitforce and are made into permanent habits, and they remain as such unless and until they have been supplanted by different and stronger thought patterns.

Now we come to the consideration of one of the most profound of all truths: the fact that most people who attain the higher brackets of success seldom do so until they have undergone some tragedy or emergency which reached deeply into their souls and reduced them to that circumstance of life called "failure."

The reason for this strange phenomenon is readily recognized by those who understand the law of Cosmic Habitforce, for it consists in the fact that these disasters and tragedies of life serve to break up established habits—habits which have led eventually to the inevitable results of failure—and thus break the grip of Cosmic Habitforce and allow these "failures" to formulate new and better habits.

We see the same phenomenon in the results of warfare. When nations or large groups of people so relate themselves that their efforts do not harmonize with the Divine plan of Nature, they are forced to break up their habits, by warfare or some other equally disturbing circumstances, such as business depressions or epidemics of disease, so that a new start may be made which conforms more nearly to Nature's ultimate and overall scheme.

This conclusion is not intended to provide a justification for warfare but rather to serve as an indictment of humankind on the charge of ignorance of a law which, if it were universally understood and respected, would make warfare unnecessary and impossible.

Wars grow out of maladjustments in human relationships. These maladjustments are the results of negative thoughts which have grown until they assume mass proportions. The spirit of any nation is the sum total of the dominating thought habits of its people.

And the same is true of individuals, for here too the spirit of the individual is determined by dominating thought habits. Most individuals are at war, in one way or another, throughout their lives. They are at war with their own conflicting thoughts and emotions. They are at war in their family relationships and in their occupational and social relationships.

Recognize this truth and you will understand the real power and the benefits which are available to those who live by the Golden Rule, for this great rule will save you from the conflicts of personal warfare.

Recognize it and you will understand also the real purpose and benefits of a *Definite Ma-*

jor Purpose, for once that purpose has been fixed in the consciousness by one's thought habits, it will be taken over by Cosmic Habitforce and carried out to its logical conclusion, by whatever practical means that may be available.

Cosmic Habitforce does not suggest what an individual shall desire, or whether one's thought habits shall be positive or negative, but it does act on all one's thought habits by crystallizing them into varying degrees of permanency and translating them into their physical equivalent, through inspired motivation to action.

The Power of "Mass Thought"

Habitforce not only fixes the thought habits of individuals, it also fixes the thought habits of groups and masses of people, according to the pattern established by the preponderance of their individual dominating thoughts. For example, the whole world began, soon after the end of World War I, to speak of "the next war," until that war was crystallized into action.

In a similar manner, epidemics of disease are thought and talked into existence. In the past, when the Department of Health of a city began its habit of posting large red-lettered signs warning people to be on the lookout for the outbreak of various diseases, an epidemic of that particular disease was the very next manifestation of this expression of thought. It is almost sure to follow.

Here, too, the same rule applies to the individual who thinks and talks of disease. At first this person is regarded as a hypochondriac, but when the habit is maintained, the disease or one very close to it generally makes its appearance. Cosmic Habitforce causes this! For it is true that any thought held in the mind through repetition begins immediately to translate itself into its physical equivalent, by every practical means that may be available.

It is a sad commentary on the intelligence of people to observe that more than three-fourths of the people who have the full benefits of a great country such as ours should go all the way through life in poverty and want, but the reason for this is not difficult to understand if one recognizes the working principle of Cosmic Habitforce.

Poverty is the direct result of a "poverty consciousness," which results from thinking in terms of poverty, fearing poverty, and talking of poverty.

It would be difficult to imagine successful people thinking in terms of that which they do not want, or in terms of poverty. Education and general ability have nothing to do with their success, for some successful people have had less of each than have millions of others who remain poverty-stricken all their lives, some of them with a string of college degrees after their names.

The world has thought and spoken of cancer as an incurable disease for so long that Cosmic Habitforce has transmuted this thought pattern into a major fixation which is difficult to break. But the time is at hand when groups of the better-informed people are beginning to set up thought patterns which may serve as an antidote for this disease.

When this kind of "mass thinking" becomes sufficiently extensive, cancer will go the way of all human ills which have been starved to death because people stopped talking and thinking of them.

Sound health is the result of a carefully cultivated "health consciousness" that has been created by constant thoughts of sound health and is made permanent by the law of Cosmic Habitforce. If you desire sound health, give orders to your subconscious mind to create it and Cosmic Habitforce will carry out the order.

If you desire opulence, give orders to your subconscious mind to produce opulence, thus developing a "prosperity consciousness," and see how quickly your economic condition will improve.

First comes the "consciousness" of that which you desire, then follows the physical or mental manifestation of your desires. The "consciousness" is your responsibility. It is something you must create by your daily thoughts, or by meditation if you prefer to make known your desires in that manner. In this way one may ally oneself with no less a power than that of the Creator of all things.

"I have come to the conclusion," said a great philosopher, "that the acceptance of poverty, or the acceptance of ill health, is an open confession of the lack of Faith."

We do a lot of proclaiming of Faith, but our actions belie our words. Faith is a state of mind that may become permanent only by actions. Belief alone is not sufficient, for as the great Philosopher has said, "Faith without works is dead."

The law of Cosmic Habitforce is Nature's own creation. It is the one universal principle through which order and harmony are carried out in the entire operation of the universe, from the largest star that hangs in the heavens to the smallest atoms of matter.

It is a power that is equally available to the weak and the strong, the rich and the poor, the sick and the well. It provides the solution to all human problems.

The major purpose of the Seventeen Principles of this philosophy is to help people adapt themselves to the power of Cosmic Habitforce through self-discipline—specifically when it comes to forming habits of thought.

How the Seventeen Principles Lend Themselves
to Cosmic Habitforce

Let us turn now to a brief review of these principles, so that we may understand their relationship to Cosmic Habitforce. Let us observe how these principles are so related that they blend together and form the Master-Key that unlocks the doors to the solution of all problems.

The analysis begins with the first principle of the philosophy:

(a) The Habit of Going the Extra Mile

This principle is given first because it aids in conditioning the mind for the rendering of useful service. And this conditioning prepares the way for the second principle:

(b) Definiteness of Purpose

With the aid of this principle one may give organized direction to the principle of *Going the Extra Mile,* and make sure that it leads in the direction of one's major purpose and becomes cumulative in its effects. These two principles alone will take anyone very far up the ladder of achievement, but those who are aiming for the higher goals of life will need much help on the way, and this help is available through the application of the third principle:

(c) The Master Mind

Through the application of this principle one begins to experience a new and a greater sense of power which is not available to the individual mind, as it bridges one's personal deficiencies and provides one, when necessary, with any portion of the combined knowledge of humankind which has been accumulated down through the ages. But this sense of power will not be complete until one acquires the art of receiving guidance through the fourth principle:

(d) Applied Faith

Here the individual begins to tune in to the powers of Infinite Intelligence, which is a benefit that is available only to those who have conditioned their minds to receive it. Here individuals begin to take full possession of their own mind by mastering all fears, worries, and doubts, by recognizing their oneness with the source of all power.

These four principles have been rightly called the "Big Four" because they are capable of providing more power than the average person needs in order to be carried to great heights of personal achievement. But they are adequate only for the very few who have other needed qualities of success, such as those provided by the fifth principle:

(e) Pleasing Personality

A pleasing personality enables one to sell oneself and one's ideas to others. Hence it is essential for all who desire to become the guiding influence in a Master Mind alliance. But observe carefully how definitely the four preceding principles tend to give one a pleasing personality. These five principles are capable of providing one with stupendous personal power, but not enough power to be insured against defeat, for defeat is a circumstance that everyone meets many times throughout life—hence the necessity of understanding and applying the sixth principle:

(f) Habit of Learning from Defeat

Notice that this principle begins with the word "habit," which means that it must be accepted and applied as a matter of habit, under all the circumstances of defeat. In this principle may be found hope sufficient to inspire one to make a fresh start when one's plans go astray, as go astray they must at one time or another.

Observe how greatly the source of personal power has increased through the application of these six principles. Those who apply them have found out where they are going in life and have acquired the friendly cooperation of all whose services are needed to help reach their goal; they have become pleasing, thereby ensuring the continued cooperation of others; they have acquired the art of drawing upon the source of Infinite Intelligence and of expressing that power through applied Faith; and have learned to make stepping stones of the stumbling blocks of personal defeat. Despite all of these advantages, however, the person whose Definite Major Purpose leads in the direction of the higher brackets of personal achievement will come many times to the point in the career when he or she will need the benefits of the seventh principle:

(g) Creative Vision

This principle enables one to look into the future and to judge it by a comparison with the past, and to build new and better plans for attaining hopes and aims through the workshop of imagination. And here, for the first time perhaps, a person may discover his or her sixth sense and begin to draw upon it for the knowledge which is not available through the organized sources of human experience and accumulated knowledge. But in order to make sure that this benefit is put to practical use, he or she must embrace and apply the eighth principle:

(h) Personal Initiative

This is the principle that starts action and keeps it moving toward definite ends. It insures one against the destructive habits of procrastination, indifference, and laziness. An approximation of the importance of this principle may be had by recognizing that it is the "habit-producer" in connection with the seven preceding principles, for it is obvious that the application of no principle can become a habit except by the application of personal initiative. The importance of this principle may be further evaluated by recognition of the fact that it is the sole means by which one may exercise full and complete control over the only thing that the Creator has given us to control, the power of one's own thoughts.

Thoughts do not organize and direct themselves. They need guidance, inspiration, and aid, which can be given only by one's personal initiative.

But personal initiative is sometimes misdirected. Therefore it needs the supplemental guidance that is available through the ninth principle:

(i) Accurate Thinking

Accurate thinking not only insures one against the misdirection of personal initiative, but it also insures one against errors of judgment, guesswork, and premature decisions. It also protects one against the influence of one's own undependable emotions by modifying them through the power of reason.

Here the individual who has mastered these nine principles will possess tremendous power, but personal power may be, and often it is, a dangerous power if it is not controlled and directed through the application of the tenth principle:

(j) Self-Discipline

Self-discipline cannot be had for the mere asking, nor can it be acquired quickly. It is the product of carefully established and carefully maintained habits, which in many instances can be acquired only by many years of painstaking effort. So we have come to the point at which the power of the will must be brought into action, for self-discipline is solely a product of the will.

Countless people have risen to great power by the application of the preceding nine principles, only to meet with disaster, or to carry others to defeat by their lack of self-discipline in the use of their power.

This principle, when mastered and applied, gives one complete control over one's greatest enemy, oneself!

Self-discipline must begin with the application of the eleventh principle:

(k) Concentration of Endeavor

The power of concentration is also a product of the will. It is so closely related to self-discipline that the two have been called the "twin-brothers" of this philosophy. Concentration saves one from the dissipation of one's energies, and aids in keeping the mind focused on one's *Definite Major Purpose* until it has been taken over by the subconscious section of the mind and there made ready for translation into its physical equivalent, through the law of Cosmic Habitforce. It is the camera's eye of the imagination, through which the detailed outline of one's aims and purposes are recorded in the subconscious section of the mind; hence it is indispensable.

Now look again, and see how greatly one's personal power has grown by the application of these eleven principles. But even these are not sufficient for every circumstance of life, for there are times when one must have the friendly cooperation of many people, such as customers in business or clients in a profession, or votes in an election to public office, all of which may be had through the application of the twelfth principle:

(1) Cooperation

Cooperation differs from the Master Mind principle in that it is a human relationship that is needed, and may be had, without a definite alliance with others, based upon a complete fusion of the minds for the attainment of a definite purpose.

Without the cooperation of others, one cannot attain success in the higher brackets of personal achievement, for cooperation is the means of major value by which one may extend the space one occupies in the minds of others, which is sometimes known as "goodwill." Friendly cooperation brings a store's customers back as repeat customers. Hence it is a principle that belongs definitely in the philosophy of successful people, regardless of the occupation they may follow.

Cooperation is attained more freely and willingly by the application of the thirteenth principle:

(m) Enthusiasm

Enthusiasm is a contagious state of mind which not only aids one in gaining the cooperation of others, but more important than this, inspires the individual to draw upon and use the power of his own imagination. It inspires action also in the expression of personal initiative, and leads to the habit of concentration of endeavor. Moreover, it is one of the important qualities making up a pleasing personality, and it makes easy the application of the principle of *Going the Extra Mile.* In addition to all these benefits, enthusiasm gives force and conviction to the spoken word.

Enthusiasm is the product of motive, but it is difficult to maintain without the aid of the fourteenth principle:

(n) The Habit of Health

Sound physical health provides a suitable housing place for the operation of the mind, hence it is an essential for enduring success—assuming that the word "success" embraces all of the requirements for happiness.

Here again the word "habit" comes into prominence, for sound health begins with a "health consciousness" that can be developed only by the right habits of living, sustained through self-discipline.

Sound health provides the basis for enthusiasm, and enthusiasm encourages sound health, so the two are like the chicken and the egg: no one can determine which came into existence first, but everyone knows that both are essential for the production of either. Health and enthusiasm are like that. Both are essential for human progress and happiness.

Now take inventory again and count up the gains in power the individual has attained by the application of these fourteen principles. It has reached proportions so stupendous that it staggers the imagination. Yet it is not sufficient to insure one against failure; therefore we shall have to add the fifteenth principle:

(o) Budgeting Time and Money

One gets a headache at the mention of saving time and money. Nearly everyone wishes to spend both time and money freely; budget and save them, never! But independence and freedom of body and mind, the two great desires of all mankind, cannot become enduring realities without the self-discipline of a strict budgeting system. Hence this principle is of necessity an important essential of the philosophy of individual achievement.

Now we are reaching the ultimate in the attainment of personal power. We have learned the sources of power and how we may tap them and apply them at will to any desired end, and that power is so great that nothing can resist it except the fact that individuals may unwisely apply it to their own destruction and the destruction of others. To guide one in the right use of power, therefore, it is necessary to add the sixteenth principle:

(p) The Golden Rule Applied

Observe the emphasis on the word "applied." Belief in the soundness of the Golden Rule is not enough. To be of enduring benefit, and in order that it may serve as a safe guide in the use of personal power, it must be applied as a matter of habit, in all human relationships.

While this may appear to be quite an undertaking, the benefits of applying this profound rule of human relationships are worthy of the efforts necessary to develop it into a habit. The penalties for failure to live by this rule are too numerous for description in detail.

Now we have attained the ultimate in personal power, and we have provided ourselves with the necessary insurance against its misuse. What we need from here on out is the means by which this power may be made permanent during our entire lifetime. We shall complete this philosophy, therefore, with the only known principle by which we may attain this desired end—the seventeenth and last principle of this philosophy:

(q) Cosmic Habitforce

Cosmic Habitforce is the principle by which all habits are fixed and made permanent in varying degrees. As stated, it is the controlling principle of this entire philosophy, into which the preceding sixteen principles blend and become a part. And it is the controlling principle of all natural laws of the universe. It is the principle that ensures the fixation of habit in the application of the preceding principles of this philosophy. Thus, it is the controlling factor in conditioning the individual mind for the development and the expression of the "prosperity consciousness" which is so essential in the attainment of personal success.

Mere understanding of the sixteen preceding principles will not lead anyone to the attainment of personal power. The principles must be understood and applied as a matter of strict habit, and habit is the sole work of the law of Cosmic Habitforce.

Cosmic Habitforce is synonymous with the great River of Life to which frequent references have been made previously, for it consists of a negative and a positive potentiality, as do all forms of energy.

The negative application is called "hypnotic rhythm" because it has a hypnotic effect on everything that it contacts. We may see its effects, in one way or another, on every human being. It is the sole means by which the "poverty consciousness" becomes fixed as a habit.

It is the builder of all established habits of fear, envy, greed, revenge, and desire for something for nothing. It fixes the habits of hopelessness and indifference. And it is the builder of the habit of hypochondria, through which millions of people suffer all through their lives with imaginary illness.

It is also the builder of the "failure consciousness," which undermines the self-confidence of millions of people. In brief, it fixes all negative habits, regardless of their nature or effects. Thus it is the "failure" side of the great River of Life.

The "success" side of the River—the positive side—fixes all constructive habits, such as the habit of *Definiteness of Purpose,* the habit of *Going the Extra Mile,* the habit of *Applying the Golden Rule in Human Relationships,* and all the other habits one must develop and apply in order to get the benefits of the sixteen preceding principles of this philosophy.

An Examination of "Habit"

Now let us examine this word "habit." Webster's dictionary gives the word many definitions, among them "a behavior pattern acquired by frequent repetition or physiologic exposure that shows itself in regularity or increased facility of performance."

Webster's definition runs on into considerable additional detail, but no part of it comes within sight of describing the law that fixes all habits; this omission being due no doubt to the fact that the law of Cosmic Habitforce had not been revealed to the editors of this dictionary.

But we observe one significant and important word in the Webster definition, the word "repetition." It is important because it describes the means by which any habit is begun.

The habit of *Definiteness of Purpose,* for example, becomes a habit only by repetition of the thought of that purpose, by bringing the thought into the mind repeatedly; by repeatedly submitting the thought to the imagination with a burning desire for its fulfillment, until the imagination creates a practical plan for attaining this desire; by applying the habit of Faith in connection with the desire, and doing it so intensely and repeatedly that one may see oneself already in possession of the desired object, even before attaining it.

The building of voluntary positive habits calls for the application of self-discipline, persistence, willpower, and Faith, all of which are available to the person who has assimilated the sixteen preceding principles of this philosophy. Voluntary habit-building is self-discipline in its highest and noblest form of application! All voluntary positive habits are the products of willpower directed toward the attainment of definite ends. They originate with the individual, not with Cosmic Habitforce. And they must be grounded in the mind through repetition of thoughts and deeds until they are taken over by Cosmic Habitforce and are given fixation, after which they operate automatically.

The word "habit" is an important word in connection with this philosophy of individual achievement, for it represents the real cause of every person's economic, social, professional, occupational, and spiritual condition in life. We are where we are and what we are because of our fixed habits. And we may be where we wish to be and what we wish to be only by the development and the maintenance of our voluntary habits.

Thus we see that this entire philosophy leads inevitably to an understanding and application of the law of Cosmic Habitforce. The major purpose of each of the sixteen preceding principles of this philosophy is that of aiding the individual in the development of a particular, specialized form of habit that is necessary to take full possession of his or her own mind. This, too, must become a habit.

Mind power is always actively engaged on one side of the River of Life or the other. The purpose of this philosophy is to enable one to develop and maintain habits of thought and of deed which keep one's mind concentrated upon the "success" side of the River. This is the sole burden of the philosophy.

Mastery and assimilation of the philosophy, like every other desirable thing, have a definite price which must be paid before their benefits may be enjoyed. That price, among other things, is eternal vigilance, determination, persistence, and the will to make life pay off on one's own terms instead of accepting substitutes of poverty and misery and disillusionment.

There are two ways of relating oneself to life. One is that of playing horse while life rides. The other is that of becoming the rider while life plays horse. The choice as to whether one becomes the horse or the rider is the privilege of every person, but this much is certain: if one does not choose to become the rider of life, one is sure to be forced to become the horse. Life either rides or is ridden. It never stands still.

The Relationship of the "Ego" and Cosmic Habitforce

As a student of this philosophy, you are probably interested in the method by which one may transmute the power of thought into its physical equivalent. And you are also probably interested in learning how to relate yourself to others in a spirit of harmony.

Unfortunately, our public schools have been silent on both of these important needs. "Our educational system," said psychologist Dr. Henry C. Link, "has concentrated on mental development and has failed to give any understanding of the way emotional and personality habits are acquired or corrected."

His indictment is not without a sound foundation. The public school system has failed in its obligations, according to Dr. Link, because the law of Cosmic Habitforce was but recently revealed, and even now it has not been recognized by the great mass of educators.

Everyone knows that practically everything we do, from the time we begin to walk, is the result of habit. Walking and talking are habits. Our manner of eating and drinking is a habit. Our sex activities are the results of habit. Our relationships with others, whether they are positive or negative, are the results of habits, but few people understand why or how we form habits.

Habits are inseparably related to the human ego. Therefore, let us turn to the analysis of this greatly misunderstood subject of the ego. But first let us recognize that the ego is the medium through which Faith and all other states of mind operate.

Throughout this philosophy great emphasis has been placed upon the distinction between passive Faith and active Faith. The ego is the medium of expression of all action. Therefore we must know something of its nature and possibilities in order that we may make the best use of it. We must learn how to stimulate the ego to action and how to control and guide it to the attainment of definite ends.

Above all, we must disabuse our minds of the popular error of believing the ego to be only a medium for expression of vanity. The word "ego" is of Latin origin, and it means "I." But it also connotes a driving force which may be organized and made to serve as the medium for translating desire into Faith, through action.

The Misunderstood Power of the Ego

The word "ego" refers to all the factors of one's personality. Therefore, the ego is subject to development, guidance, and control through voluntary habits—habits we develop deliberately and with purpose.

A great philosopher, who devoted his entire life to the study of the human body and the mind, provided us with a practical foundation for the study of the ego when he stated,

Your body, whether living or dead, is a collection of millions of little energies that can never die.

These energies are separate and individual; at times they act in some degree of harmony.

The human body is a drifting mechanism of life, capable but not accustomed to control the forces within, except as habit, will, cultivation or special excitement (through the emotion) may marshal these forces to the accomplishment of some important end.

We are satisfied from many experiments that this power of marshalling and using these energies can be, in every person, cultivated to a high degree.

The air, sunlight, food, and water you take are agents of a force which comes from the sky and earth. You idly float upon the tide of circumstances to make up your day's life, and the opportunities of being something better than you are drift beyond your reach and pass away.

Humanity is hemmed in by so many influences that, from time immemorial, no real effort has been made to gain control of the impulses that run loose in the world. It has been, and still is, easier to let things go as they will rather than exert the will to direct them.

But the dividing line between success and failure is found at the stage where aimless drifting ceases. Where *Definiteness of Purpose* begins.

We are all creatures of emotions, passions, circumstances, and accident. What the mind will be, what the heart will be, what the body will be, are problems which are shaped to the drift of life, even when special attention is given to any of them.

If you will sit down and think for a while, you will be surprised to know how much of your life has been mere drift.

Look at any created life, and see its efforts to express itself. The tree sends its branches toward the sunlight, struggles through its leaves to inhale air; and even underground sends forth its roots in search of water and the minerals it needs for food. This you call inanimate life; but it represents a force that comes from some source and operates for some purpose.

There is no place on the globe where energy is not found.

The air is so loaded with it that in the cold north the sky shines in boreal rays; and wherever the frigid temperature yields to the warmth, the electric conditions may alarm man. Water is but a liquid union of gases, and is charged with electrical, mechanical, and chemical energies, any one of which is capable of doing great service and great damage.

Even ice, in its coldest phase, has energy, for it is not subdued, nor even still; its force has broken mountain rocks into fragments. Not a chemical molecule is free from energy; not an atom can exist without it. We are a combination of individual energies.

Humans consist of two forces, one tangible, in the form of the physical body, with its individual cells numbering billions, each of which is endowed with intelligence and energy; and the other intangible, in the form of an ego—the organized dictator of the body, which may control thoughts and deeds.

Science teaches us the tangible portion of a human weighing 160 pounds is composed of about seventeen chemical elements, all of which are known. They are:

9 pounds of oxygen
38 pounds of carbon
15 pounds of hydrogen
4 pounds of nitrogen
4½ pounds of calcium
6 ounces of chlorine
4 ounces of sulfur
3½ ounces of potassium
3 ounces of sodium
¼ ounce of iron
2½ ounces of fluorin
2 ounces of magnesium
1½ ounces of silicon
Small traces of arsenic, iodine, and aluminum

These tangible parts of humans are commercially worth a few dollars, and may be purchased in any modern chemical plant. Add to these chemical elements a well-developed and properly organized and controlled ego, and they may be worth any price the owner sets upon them. The ego is a power which cannot be purchased at any price, but it can be developed and shaped to fit any desired pattern. The development takes place through organized habits which are made permanent by the law of Cosmic Habitforce, which carries out the thought patterns one develops through controlled thought.

Our greatest creators, inventors, artists, and business leaders all purposefully develop, guide, and magnetize their egos within their fields. As a result, all men and women who have contributed to the march of progress have given the world a demonstration of the power of a well-developed and carefully controlled ego.

One of the major differences between those who make valuable contributions to humankind and those who merely take up space in the world is a difference in egos, because the ego is the driving force behind all forms of human action.

Liberty and freedom of body and mind—the two major desires of all people—are available in exact proportion to the development and use one makes of the ego. Every person who has properly related to his or her own ego has both liberty and freedom in whatever proportions desired.

An ego determines the manner in which one relates oneself to all other people. More important than this, it determines the policy under which one relates one's own body and mind, wherein is patterned every hope and purpose by which one's destiny in life is fixed.

An ego is the greatest asset or greatest liability, according to the way one relates oneself to it. The ego is the sum total of one's thought habits which have been anchored through the automatic operation of the law of Cosmic Habitforce.

How to Develop a Success Consciousness

Every highly successful person possesses a well-developed and highly disciplined ego, but there is a third factor associated with the ego which determines its potency for good or evil—the self-control necessary to enable one to transmute its power into any desired purpose.

The starting point of all individual achievements is some plan by which one's ego can be inspired with a "success consciousness." The person who succeeds must do so by properly developing his or her own ego, impressing it with the object of desire, and removing from it all forms of limitation, fear, and doubt, which lead to the dissipation of the power of the ego.

Autosuggestion (or self-hypnosis) is the medium by which one may attune one's ego to any desired rate of vibration and charge it with the attainment of any desired purpose.

Unless you catch the full significance of the principle of autosuggestion, you will miss the most important part of this analysis, because the power of the ego is fixed entirely by the application of self-suggestion.

When this self-suggestion attains the status of Faith, the ego becomes limitless in its power.

The ego is kept alive and active, and it is given power by constant feeding. Like the physical body, the ego cannot and will not subsist without food.

It must be fed with *Definiteness of Purpose.*

It must be fed with Personal Initiative.

It must be fed with continuous action, through well-organized plans.

It must be supported with Enthusiasm.

It must be fed by Controlled Attention, directed to a definite end.

It must be controlled and directed through Self-Discipline.

And it must be supported with Accurate Thought.

No one can become the master of anything or anyone until becoming the master of the ego.

No one can express oneself in terms of opulence while most of one's thought power is given over to the maintenance of a "poverty consciousness." Nevertheless, one should not lose sight of the fact that many of great wealth began in poverty—a fact which suggests that this and all other fears can be conquered and removed from interference with the ego.

In one word, "ego," may be found the composite effects of all the principles of individual achievement described in this philosophy, coordinated into one single unit of power, which may be directed to any desired end by any individual who is the complete master of his or her ego.

I am preparing you to accept the fact that the most important power available to you—the one power which will determine whether you succeed or fail in your life's ambition—is that represented by your own ego.

I am also preparing you to brush aside that timeworn belief which associates the ego with excess self-love, vanity, and vulgarity, and to recognize the truth that the ego is all there is of a person outside of the few dollars' worth of chemicals of which the physical body is composed.

Sex is the great creative force of humans. It is definitely associated with and is an important part of one's ego. Both sex and the ego got their bad reputations from the fact that both are subject to destructive as well as constructive application, and both have been abused by the ignorant, from the beginning of history. Egoists who make themselves offensive through the expression of ego are those who have not discovered how to relate themselves to their ego in a manner which gives it constructive use.

Constructive application of the ego is made through the expressions of one's hopes, desires, aims, ambitions, and plans, and not by boastfulness or an excess of self-love. The motto of the person who has his or her ego under control is "Deeds, not words."

The desire to be great, to be recognized and to have personal power, is a healthy desire; but an open expression of one's belief in one's own greatness is an indication that one has not taken possession of the ego, that one has allowed it to take possession of one; and you may be sure that any proclamations of greatness are but a cloak with which to shield some fear or inferiority complex.

The Relationship Between the Ego and Mental Attitude

Understand the real nature of your ego and you will understand the real significance of the Master Mind principle. Moreover, you will recognize that to be of the greatest service to you, the members of your Master Mind alliance must be in complete sympathy with your hopes and purposes; they must not be in competition with you in any manner whatsoever. They must be willing to subordinate their own desires and personalities entirely for the attainment of your major purpose in life.

They must have confidence in you and your integrity, and they must respect you. They must be willing to pander to your virtues and make allowances for your faults. They must be willing to permit you to be yourself and live your own life in your own way at all times. Last, they must receive from you some form of benefit which will make you as beneficial to them as they are to you.

Failure to observe the last-mentioned requirement will bring an end to the power of your Master Mind alliance.

People relate themselves to one another in whatever capacities they may be associated because of a motive or motives. There can be no permanent human relationship based upon an indefinite or vague motive, or upon no motive at all. Failure to recognize this truth has cost many the difference between poverty and wealth.

The power which takes over the ego and clothes it with the material counterparts of the thoughts which give it shape, is the law of Cosmic Habitforce. This law does not give quality or quantity to the ego; it merely takes what it finds and translates it into its physical equivalent.

Those of great achievement are, and have always been, those who deliberately feed, shape, and control their own egos, leaving no part of the task to luck or chance, or to the varying vicissitudes of life.

Every person may control the shaping of his or her own ego, but from that point on that person has no more to do with what happens than the farmer has anything to do with what happens to the seed sown in the soil of the earth. The inexorable law of Cosmic Habitforce causes every living thing to perpetuate itself after its kind, and it translates the picture a person paints of his or her ego into its physical equivalent, as definitely as it develops an acorn into an oak tree, and no outside aid whatsoever is required, except time.

From these statements it is obvious that we are not only advocating the deliberate development and control of the ego, but also we are definitely warning that no one can hope to succeed in any calling without such control over one's ego.

The Definition of a Properly Developed Ego

So that there may be no misunderstanding as to what is meant by the term "a properly developed ego," I shall describe briefly the factors which enter into its development.

First, one must ally oneself with people who will coordinate their minds with one in a spirit of perfect harmony for the attainment of a definite purpose, and that alliance must be continuous and active.

Moreover, the alliance must consist of people whose spiritual and mental qualities, education, sex, and age are suited for aiding in the attainment of the purpose of the alliance. For example, Andrew Carnegie's Master Mind alliance was made up of more than twenty people, each of whom brought to the alliance some quality of mind, experience, education, or knowledge which was directly related to the object of the alliance and not available through any of the other members of the alliance.

Second, having placed oneself under the influence of the proper associates, one must adopt some definite plan by which to attain the object of the alliance and proceed to put that plan into action. The plan may be a composite plan created by the joint efforts of all the members of the Master Mind group.

If one plan proves to be unsound or inadequate, it must be supplemented or supplanted by others, until a plan is found which will work. But there must be no change in the purpose of the alliance.

Third, one must remove oneself from the range of influence of every person and every circumstance which has even a slight tendency to cause one to feel inferior or incapable of attaining the object of one's purpose. Positive egos do not grow in negative environments. On this point there can be no excuse for a compromise, and failure to observe it will prove fatal to the chances of success.

The line must be so clearly drawn between a person and those who exercise any form of negative influence on him or her that the door is tightly closed against every such negative influence, no matter what previous ties of friendship or obligation or blood relationship may have existed between them.

Fourth, one must close the door tightly against every thought of any past experience or circumstance which tends to make one feel inferior or unhappy. Strong, vital egos cannot be developed by dwelling on thoughts of past unpleasant experiences. Vital egos thrive on the hopes and desires of the yet unattained objectives.

Thoughts are the building blocks from which the human ego is constructed. Cosmic Habitforce is the cement which binds these blocks together in permanency, through fixed habits. When the job is finished it represents, right down to the smallest detail, the nature of the thoughts which went into the building.

Fifth, one must surround oneself with every possible physical means of impressing the mind with the nature and the purpose of the ego one is developing. For example, the author should set up a workshop in a room decorated with pictures and the works of authors in the field whom he or she most admires. The bookshelves should be filled with books related to his or her own work. He or she should be surrounded with every possible means of conveying to the ego the exact picture of oneself which one expects to express, because that picture is the pattern the law of Cosmic Habitforce will pick up, the picture it will translate into its physical equivalent.

Sixth, the properly developed ego is at all times under the control of the individual. There must be no overinflation of the ego in the direction of "egomania," by which some destroy themselves.

In the development of the ego, one's motto might well be "Not too much, not too little of anything." When people begin to thirst for control over others, or begin to accumulate large sums of money which they cannot or do not use constructively, they are treading upon dangerous ground. Power of this nature grows of its own accord and soon gets out of control.

Nature has provided people with a safety valve through which she deflates the ego and relieves the pressure of its influence when an individual goes beyond certain limits in the development of the ego. Emerson called it the Law of Compensation, but whatever it is, it operates with inexorable definiteness.

Napoleon Bonaparte began to die, because of his crushed ego, on the day he landed on St. Helena Island. People who quit work and retire from all forms of activity, after having led active lives, generally atrophy and die soon thereafter. If they live they are usually miserable and unhappy. A healthy ego is one which is always in use and under complete control.

Seventh, the ego is constantly undergoing changes, for better or for worse, because of the nature of one's thought habits. The two factors which force these changes upon one are time and the law of Cosmic Habitforce. I bring to your attention the importance of time as a significant factor in the operation of Cosmic Habitforce. Just as seeds planted in the soil of the earth require definite periods of time for their germination, development, and growth, so do ideas, impulses of thought, and desires planted in the mind require definite periods of time during which the law of Cosmic Habitforce gives them life and action.

There is no adequate means of describing or predetermining the exact period of time required for the transformation of a desire into its physical equivalent. The nature of the desire, the circumstances which are related to it, and the intensity of the desire, are all determining factors in connection with the time required for transformation from the thought stage to the physical stage.

The state of mind known as Faith is so favorable for the quick change of desire into its physical equivalent that it has been known to make the change almost instantaneously.

Humans mature physically within about twenty years, but mentally—which means the ego—we require from thirty-five to sixty years for maturity. This fact explains why many seldom begin to accumulate material riches in great abundance, or to attain outstanding records of achievement in other directions, until they are about fifty years old.

The ego which can inspire people to acquire and retain great material wealth is of necessity one which has undergone self-discipline, through which one acquires self-confidence, definiteness of purpose, personal initiative, imagination, accuracy of judgment, and other qualities, without which no ego has the power to procure and hold wealth in abundance.

These qualities come through the proper use of time. Observe that we did not say they come through the passage of time. Through the operation of Cosmic Habitforce, every individual's thought habits, whether they are negative or positive, whether of opulence or of poverty, are woven into the pattern of one's ego, and there they are given permanent form, which determines the nature and the extent of one's spiritual and physical status.

The Story of How a Wife Managed Her Husband's Ego

About the beginning of the Depression, the owner of a small beauty salon turned over a back room in her place of business to an old man who needed a place to sleep. The man had no money, but he did have considerable knowledge of the methods of compounding cosmetics.

The owner of the salon gave him a place to sleep and provided him with an opportunity to pay for his room by compounding the cosmetics she used in her business.

Soon, the two entered into a Master Mind alliance which was destined to bring each of them economic independence. First, they entered into a business partnership, with the object of compounding cosmetics to be sold from house to house—the woman providing the money for the raw materials, the man doing the work.

After a few years, the Master Mind arrangement between the two had proved so profitable that they decided to make it permanent by marriage, although there was a difference of more than twenty-five years in their ages.

The man had been in the cosmetics business for the better portion of his adult life, but he had never achieved success. The young woman had barely made a living from her beauty salon. The happy combination of the two brought them into possession of a power which neither had known prior to their alliance, and they began to succeed financially.

At the beginning of the Depression they were compounding cosmetics in one small room and selling their products personally from door to door. By the end of the Depression, some eight years later, they were compounding their cosmetics in a large factory, which they had bought and paid for, and had more than 100 employees working steadily and more than 4,000 agents selling their products throughout the nation. During this period, they accumulated a fortune of over $2 million, despite the fact that they were operating during Depression years when luxuries such as cosmetics were naturally hard to sell.

They eventually placed themselves beyond the need for money for the remainder of their lives. Moreover, they gained financial freedom on precisely the same knowledge and the same opportunities they possessed prior to their Master Mind alliance, when both were poverty-stricken.

I wish the names of these two interesting people could be revealed, but the circumstances of their alliance and the nature of the analysis I shall now present makes this impractical. Nevertheless, I am free to describe what I conceive to be the source of their astounding achievement, viewing every circumstance of their relationship entirely from the viewpoint of an unbiased analyst who is seeking only to present a true picture of the facts.

The motive which brought these two people together in a Master Mind alliance was definitely economic in nature. The woman had previously been married to a man who failed to earn a living and who deserted her when her child was an infant. The man also had been previously married.

There was not the slightest indication of the emotion of love as a motive for both parties' second marriage. The motive was entirely a mutual desire for economic freedom. The business and the elaborate home in which the couple lived were entirely dominated by the old man, who sincerely believed that he was responsible for both. The man's name was on every package of merchandise which left the factory. It was printed in large letters on every delivery truck they operated, and it appeared in large type on every piece of sales literature and in every advertisement they published. The wife's name was conspicuous by its total absence.

The man believed that he had built the business, that he operated it, that it could not operate without him. The truth of the matter is precisely the opposite. His ego built the business and ran it, and the business might have continued to run as well or better without his presence as with it, for the very good reason that his wife developed that ego, and she could have done the same for any other man under similar circumstances.

Patiently, wisely, and with purpose aforethought, this man's wife fed his ego the type of food which removed from it every trace of his former inferiority complex, which was born of a lifetime of deprivation and failure. She hypnotized her husband into believing himself to be a great business tycoon.

Whatever degree of ego this man may have possessed before it came under the influence of a clever woman had died of starvation. She revived his ego, nurtured it, fed it, and developed it into a power of stupendous proportions despite his eccentric nature and his lack of business ability.

In truth, every business policy, every business move, and every forward step the business took was the result of the wife's ideas, which she so cleverly planted in her husband's mind that he failed to recognize their source. In reality she was the brains of the business, he the mere window dressing, but the combination was unbeatable, as evidenced by their astounding financial achievements.

The manner in which this woman completely effaced herself was not only convincing evidence of her complete self-control, it was evidence of her wisdom, for she probably knew she could not have accomplished the same results alone, or by any other methods than those she adopted.

This woman had very little formal education, and I have no idea how or where she learned enough about the operation of the human mind to inspire her to merge her entire personality with that of her husband for the purpose of developing in him the ego he had. Perhaps the natural intuition which many women possess was responsible for her successful procedure. Whatever it was, she did a thorough job, and it served the ends she sought by bringing her economic security.

Here, then, is evidence that the major difference between poverty and riches is merely the difference between an ego that is dominated by an inferiority complex and one that is dominated by a feeling of superiority. This old man might have died a homeless pauper if a clever woman had not blended her mind with his in such a way as to feed his ego with thoughts of, and belief in, his ability to attain opulence.

This is a conclusion from which there is no escape. Moreover, this case is only one of many that could be cited to prove that the human ego must be fed, organized, and directed to definite ends if one is to succeed in any walk of life.

The Amazing Ego of Henry Ford

The Henry Ford ego—famous because of what the public at large does not know about it—was a combination of his own ego and that of his wife. The definiteness and singleness of purpose, persistence, self-reliance, and self-control—so obviously important parts of the Ford ego—could be traced largely to the influence of Mrs. Ford.

The Ford ego, quite unlike that of the cosmetician I previously described, functioned without glamour or ostentation of any kind. It functioned in an obvious spirit of humility of the heart.

During his lifetime, there were no large pictures of Henry Ford hanging on the walls of his office, but make no mistake about this: Mr. Ford's influence was felt by every person associated directly or indirectly with his vast industrial empire, and even today, something of Henry Ford himself goes into every automobile which leaves the Ford factories.

These are the means whereby he expressed his ego: through mechanical perfection;

through transportation service which is dependable, at a popular price; through the satisfaction he got from giving employment, directly and indirectly, to millions of men and women.

Mr. Ford was not above appreciating a word of praise, but he never went out of his way to attract it. His ego did not require constant pampering, such as that given the cosmetician by his wife.

Mr. Ford's method of appropriating the knowledge and experience of other men was entirely different from that of Andrew Carnegie and most other business magnates. His ego was so modest and unassuming, in that he neither encouraged favorable comment upon his work nor went out of his way to express any form of appreciation of the compliments which were paid him.

Henry Ford had one of the truly great minds of the world.

He had a great mind because he learned to recognize the laws of Nature and to adapt himself to them in a manner beneficial to himself, but many believe that his greatness was derived in a large measure from the influence of his wife and his association with other great minds, including those of Thomas A. Edison, Luther Burbank, John Burroughs, and Harvey Firestone, with whom he had a Master Mind alliance for a great number of years.

For many years, these five men would leave their respective businesses and go away together to some quiet spot where they would exchange thoughts and feed their egos on the food each needed and craved.

Henry Ford's personality, his business policies, and even his physical appearance began to show a decided improvement from year to year because of his association with these four men. Their influence upon him was definite, deep, profound, and enduring.

Henry Ford had his ego completely under his control. By studying those of great achievement, one may observe that the space they occupy in the world is in exact proportion to the extent to which they dominate their egos.

The cosmetician occupied and controlled only the space bounded by his own business and his household. It did not extend beyond these bounds, and it never could. His own mental attitude fixed these limits, and Cosmic Habitforce made the fixation permanent.

Henry Ford occupied, in one way or another, practically all the space of the world, and he influenced in many ways the entire trend of civilization. Because he was master of his ego, Henry Ford was capable of acquiring any material thing he set his heart upon.

The cosmetician expressed his ego in many forms of childish, petty selfishness. Consequently he limited his influence to the mere accumulation of a few million dollars, and the domination (without their consent) of a few hundred people, including his own household and his employees.

Henry Ford expressed his ego in ever-expanding and increasing terms of benefit to mankind and, without making a bid for it, found himself an influencing factor throughout the world. This is an astounding thought! It provides vitally important suggestions as to the type of ego one should endeavor to develop.

Henry Ford had developed an ego which extended itself into plans belting the entire earth. He thought in terms of the manufacture and distribution of millions of automobiles. He thought in terms of tens of thousands of men and women working for him. He thought in terms of millions of dollars of working capital. He thought in terms of a business he dominated by establishing his own policies for procuring working capital, by which he kept his business out of the control of others. He thought in terms of economy through efficient coordination of the efforts of the thousands of men and women who worked for him, and by setting up pay schedules and working conditions far more favorable to his employees than they could reasonably demand. He thought in terms of harmonious cooperation between himself and his business associates, and put his thoughts into action by removing from his organization anyone who did not see eye-to-eye with him.

These are the qualities and traits of character which nourished, fed, and maintained the Ford ego. There is nothing about any of these qualities which is difficult to understand. They are qualities anyone may have by simply adopting them and using them.

Turn the spotlight on the many who began to build automobiles after Henry Ford began; study each of them carefully and you will learn quickly why one remembers but few of them, or the brands of automobiles they temporarily produced.

You will discover that every one of the Ford competitors who fell by the wayside did so because of self-imposed limitations or dissipation of the ego. You will also find that practically every one of these forgotten inventors apparently possessed as much intelligence as Henry Ford. Not only did the majority of them have better educations than he, many of them had more dynamic personalities as well.

The major difference between Henry Ford and his competitors of the past was this: He developed an ego which extended itself far beyond his personal achievements; the others so limited their egos that they soon caught up with them, and their plans went on the rocks for want of that something an extended, flexible ego does to lead one forward.

The well-balanced ego is not subject to serious influence by either commendation or condemnation. The person with a well-balanced ego sets his sails in the direction of a Definite Major Purpose, moves on personal initiative in the direction of that purpose, and never looks to the right or to the left. He or she accepts both defeat and victory as the natural essentials of life but does not allow either to modify future plans.

And you who are learning to assimilate this philosophy may reach that estate in the same manner. You have, in the Seventeen Principles of Success, all that is required to place you in possession of the Master-Key!

You are now in possession of all the practical knowledge which has been used by successful people from the dawn of civilization to the present.

This is a complete philosophy of life, sufficient for every human need. It holds the secret to the solution of all human problems. And it has been presented in terms the humblest person can understand.

You may not aspire to become a corporate or governmental star, but you can and you should aspire to make yourself useful in order that you may occupy as much space in the world as your ego desires. Everyone comes finally to resemble those who make the strongest impression upon the ego. We are all creatures of imitation, and naturally we endeavor to imitate the heroes of our choice. This is a natural and healthful trait.

Those whose heroes are persons of great Faith are fortunate, because hero worship carries with it something of the nature of the hero one worships.

The Fertile Garden Spot of the Mind

In conclusion, let me summarize what has been said on the subject of the ego by calling attention to the fact that it represents the fertile garden spot of the mind wherein one may develop all the stimuli which inspire active Faith, or by neglecting to do so one may allow this fertile soil to produce a negative crop of fear and doubt and indecision which will lead to failure.

The amount of space you occupy in the world is now a matter of choice with you. The Master-Key to Riches is in your hands. You stand before the last gate separating you from happiness. The gate will not open to you without your demand that it do so. You must use the Master-Key by making the Seventeen Principles of Success your own!

You now have at your command a complete philosophy of life that is sufficient for the solution of every individual problem.

It is a philosophy of principles, some combination of which has been responsible for every individual success in every occupation or calling, although many may have used the philosophy successfully without recognizing the Seventeen Principles by the names we have given them.

No essential factor of successful achievement has been omitted. The philosophy embraces them all and describes them in words and similes that are well within the understanding of a majority of the people.

It is a philosophy of concreteness that touches only rarely the abstractions, and then only when necessary. It is free from academic terms and phrases, which all too often serve only to confuse the average person.

The overall purpose of the philosophy is to enable one to get from where one stands to where one wishes to be, both economically and spiritually; thus it prepares one to enjoy the abundant life which the Creator intended all people to enjoy. And it leads to the attainment of "riches" in the broadest and fullest meaning of the word, including the twelve most important of all riches.

The world has been greatly enriched by abstract philosophies, from the days of Plato, Socrates, Copernicus, Aristotle, and many others of the same profound caliber of thinkers, on down to the days of Ralph Waldo Emerson, William James, and those who follow their example.

Now the world has the first complete, concrete philosophy of individual achievement that provides individuals with the practical means by which they may take possession of their own mind and direct it to the attainment of peace of mind, harmony in human relationships, economic security, and the fuller life known as happiness.

Not as an apology, but to serve as an explanation, I call your attention to the fact that throughout this analysis of the Seventeen Principles, we have emphasized the more important of these principles by continuous reference to them. The repetition was not accidental!

It was deliberate and necessary because of the tendency of all humankind to be unimpressed by new ideas or new interpretations of old truths. Repetition has been necessary also because of the interrelationship of the Seventeen Principles, being connected, as they are, like the links of a chain, each one extending into and becoming a part of the principle preceding it and the principle following it. And last, let us recognize that repetition of ideas is one of the basic principles of effective teaching and the central core of all effective advertising. Therefore it is not only justified, but it is definitely necessary as a means of human progress.

When you have assimilated this philosophy you will have a better education than the majority of people who leave graduate school with the master of arts degree. You will be in possession of all the more useful knowledge which has been organized from the experiences of the most successful people this nation has produced, and you will have it in a form you can understand and apply.

But remember that the responsibility for the proper use of this knowledge will be yours. The mere possession of the knowledge will avail you nothing. Its use is what will count.

CHAPTER 11

SELF-DISCIPLINE

The man who acquires
the ability to take
full possession
of his own mind
may take possession
of everything else
to which he is
justly entitled.

—Andrew Carnegie

I would now like to reveal the methods by which one may take possession of one's own mind. I begin with a quotation from a man who proved the truth of his statement by his astounding achievements. Mr. Carnegie not only acquired more material riches than he needed, but he acquired also the other eleven riches, and the more important of the Twelve Riches of Life.

And those who knew him best, who worked with him most closely, say that his most outstanding trait of character consisted of the fact that he took full possession of his own mind at an early age, and never gave up any portion of his right to think his own thoughts.

What an achievement and what a blessing it would be if every person could truthfully say, "I am the master of my fate; I am the captain of my soul." The Creator probably intended it to be so! If it had been intended otherwise, humans would not have been limited solely to the right of control over only one power—the power of their own thoughts. We go through life searching for freedom of body and mind, yet most never find it. Why? The Creator provided the means by which people may be free, and gave everyone access to these means, and also inspired everyone with impelling motives for the attainment of freedom.

Why, then, do we go through life imprisoned in a jail of our own making, when the key to the door is so easily within our reach? The jail of poverty, the jail of ill health, the jail of fear, the jail of ignorance. The desire for freedom of body and mind is a universal desire among all people, but few ever attain it because most who search for it look everywhere except the one and only source from which it may come—*within their own minds.*

The desire for riches is also a universal desire, but most never come within sight of the real riches of life because they do not recognize that all riches begin within their own minds.

The mechanism of the mind is a profound system of organized power which can be released only by one means, and that is by strict self-discipline. The mind that is properly disciplined and directed to definite ends is an irresistible power that recognizes no such reality as permanent defeat. It organizes defeat and converts it into victory, makes stepping stones of stumbling blocks, hitches its wagon to a star, and uses the forces of the universe to carry it within easy grasp of its every desire.

And the person who masters himself through self-discipline never can be mastered by others! Self-discipline is one of the Twelve Riches, but it is much more; it is an important prerequisite for the attainment of all riches, including freedom of body and mind, power and fame, and all the material things that we call wealth.

It is the sole means by which one may focus the mind upon the objective of a *Definite Major Purpose* until the law of Cosmic Habitforce takes over the pattern of that purpose and begins to translate it into its material equivalent.

It is the key to the volitional power of the will and the emotions of the heart, for it is the means by which these two may be mastered and balanced, one against the other, and directed to definite ends in accurate thinking.

It is the directing force in the maintenance of a *Definite Major Purpose.* It is the source of all persistence and the means by which one may develop the habit of carrying through one's plans and purposes. It is the power with which all thought habits are patterned and sustained until they are taken over by the law of Cosmic Habitforce and carried out to their logical climax. It is the means by which one may take full and complete control of one's mind and direct it to whatever ends one may desire. It is indispensable in all leadership.

And it is the power through which one may make of conscience a cooperator and guide instead of a conspirator.

It is the policeman who clears the mind for the expression of Faith, by the mastery of all fears. It clears the mind for the expression of Imagination and of Creative Vision. It does away with indecision and doubt. It helps one to create and to sustain the prosperity consciousness that is essential for the accumulation of material riches, and the health consciousness necessary for the maintenance of sound physical health. Also it operates entirely through the functioning system of the mind. Therefore, let us examine this system so that we may understand the factors of which it consists.

The Ten Factors of the "Mechanism" of Thought

The mind operates through ten factors, some of which operate automatically, while others must be directed through voluntary effort. Self-discipline is the sole means of this direction. These ten factors are:

1. Infinite Intelligence. The source of all power of thought, which operates automatically, but it may be organized and directed to definite ends through *Definiteness of Purpose.*

Infinite Intelligence may be likened to a great reservoir of water that overflows continuously, its branches flowing in small streams in many directions, giving life to all vegetation and all living things. The portion of the stream which gives life to humans supplies us also with the power of thought.

The brain may be likened to the water spigot, while the water flowing through the spigot represents Infinite Intelligence. The brain does not generate the power of thought; it merely receives that power from Infinite Intelligence and applies it to whatever ends the individual desires.

And remember, this privilege of the control and the direction of thought is the only prerogative over which an individual has been given complete control. It may be used to build, or it may be used to destroy. One may give it direction, through *Definiteness of Purpose,* or one may neglect to do so, as one chooses.

The exercise of this great privilege is attained solely by self-discipline.

2. The Conscious Mind. The individual mind functions through two departments. One is known as the conscious section of the mind, the other as the subconscious section. It is the opinion of psychologists that these two sections are comparable to an iceberg, the visible portion above the waterline representing the conscious section, the invisible portion below the waterline representing the subconscious section. Therefore it is obvious that the conscious section of the mind—that portion with which we consciously and voluntarily

468

turn on the power of thought—is but a small portion of the whole, consisting of not more than one-fifth of the available mind power.

The subconscious section of the mind operates automatically. It carries on all the necessary functions in connection with the building and the maintenance of the physical body; keeps the heart beating to circulate the blood; assimilates the food through a perfect system of chemistry, and delivers the food in liquid form throughout the body; removes worn out cells and replaces them with new cells; removes bacteria which are deleterious to health; creates new physical beings by the blending of the cells of protoplasm (the formative material of animal embryos) contributed by the male and female of living organisms.

These and many other essential functions are performed by the subconscious section of the mind, and it also serves as the connecting link between the conscious mind and Infinite Intelligence.

It may be likened to the spigot of the conscious mind, through which (by its control through self-discipline) more thought power may be turned on. Or it may be likened to a rich garden spot wherein may be planted and germinated the seed of any desired idea.

The importance of the subconscious section of the mind may be estimated by recognition of the fact that it is the only means of voluntary approach to Infinite Intelligence. Therefore it is the medium by which all prayers are conveyed and all answers to prayer are received. It is the medium that translates one's *Definite Major Purpose* into its material equivalent, a process which consists entirely of guidance to the individual in the proper use of the natural means of attaining the objects of his desires.

The subconscious section of the mind acts on all impulses of thought, carrying out to their logical conclusion all thoughts which are definitely shaped by the conscious mind, but it gives preference to thoughts inspired by emotional feeling, such as the emotion of fear or the emotion of Faith; hence the necessity for self-discipline as a means of providing the subconscious mind with only those thoughts or desires which lead to the attainment of whatever one wishes.

The subconscious section of the mind gives preference also to the dominating thoughts of the mind—those thoughts which one creates by the repetition of ideas or desires. This fact explains the importance of adopting a *Definite Major Purpose* and the necessity of fixing that purpose (through self-discipline) as a dominating thought of the mind.

3. The Faculty of Willpower. The power of the will is the "boss" of all departments of the mind. It has the power to modify, change, or balance all thinking habits, and its decisions are final and irrevocable except by itself. It is the power that puts the emotions of the heart under control, and it is subject to direction only by self-discipline. In this connection it may be likened to the chairman of a board of directors whose decisions are final. It takes its orders from the conscious mind but recognizes no other authority.

4. The Faculty of Reason. This is the "presiding judge" of the conscious section of the mind, which may pass judgment on all ideas, plans, and desires, and it will do so if it is directed by self-discipline. But its decisions can be set aside by the power of the will, or modified by the power of the emotions when the will does not interfere. Let us here take note of the fact that all accurate thinking requires the cooperation of the faculty of reason, although it is a requirement which not more than one person in every 10,000 respects. This explains why there are so few accurate thinkers.

Most so-called thinking is the work of the emotions without the guiding influence of self-discipline, without relationship to either the power of the will or the faculty of reason.

5. The Faculty of the Emotions. This is the source of most of the actions of the mind, the seat of most of the thoughts released by the conscious section of the mind. The emotions are tricky and undependable and may be very dangerous if they are not modified by the faculty of reason under the direction of the faculty of the will.

The faculty of the emotions is not to be condemned because of its undependability, however, for it is the source of all enthusiasm, imagination, and creative vision, and it may be directed by self-discipline to the development of these essentials of individual achievement. The direction may be given by modification of the emotions through the faculties of the will and the reason.

Accurate thinking is not possible without complete mastery of the emotions. Mastery is attained by placing the emotions under the control of the will, thus preparing them for direction to whatever ends the will may dictate, modifying them when necessary through the faculty of reason.

The accurate thinker has no opinions and makes no decisions which have not been submitted to, and agreed to by, the faculties of the will and the reason. He uses his emotions to inspire the creation of ideas through his imagination, but refines his ideas through his will and reason before their final acceptance.

This is self-discipline of the highest order. The procedure is simple but it is not easy to follow, and it is never followed except by the accurate thinker who moves on his own personal initiative.

The more important of the Twelve Riches—such as (1) a positive mental attitude, (2) harmony in human relationships, (3) freedom from fear, (4) the hope of achievement, (5) the capacity for faith, (6) an open mind on all subjects, and (7) sound physical health—are attainable only by a strict direction and control of all the emotions. This does not mean that the emotions should be suppressed, but they must be controlled and directed to definite ends.

The emotions may be likened to steam in a boiler, the power of which consists in its release and direction through the mechanism of an engine. Uncontrolled steam has no power, and though it may be controlled, it must be released through a governor, which is a mechanical device corresponding to self-discipline in connection with the control and release of emotional power.

The emotions which are most important and most dangerous are (1) the emotion of sex, (2) the emotion of love, and (3) the emotion of fear. These are the emotions which produce the major portion of all human activities. The emotions of love and sex are creative. When controlled and directed, they inspire one with imagination and creative vision of stupendous proportions. If they are not controlled and directed, they may lead one to indulge in destructive follies.

6. The Faculty of Imagination. This is the workshop wherein all desires, ideas, plans, and purposes are shaped and fashioned, together with the means of attaining them. Through organized use and self-discipline, the imagination may be developed to the status of creative vision.

But the faculty of the imagination, like the faculty of the emotions, is tricky and undependable if it is not controlled and directed by self-discipline. Without control, it often dissipates the power of thought in useless, impractical, and destructive activities which need not be here mentioned in detail. Uncontrolled imagination is the stuff that daydreams are made of.

Control of the imagination begins with the adoption of *Definiteness of Purpose* based on definite plans. The control is completed by strict habits of self-discipline, which give definite direction to the faculty of the emotions, for the power of the emotions is the power that inspires the imagination to action.

7. The Faculty of the Conscience. The conscience is the moral guide of the mind, and its major purpose is that of modifying the individual's aims and purposes so that they harmonize with the moral laws of nature and of mankind. The conscience is a twin brother of the faculty of reason in that it gives discrimination and guidance to the reason when reason is in doubt.

The conscience functions as a cooperative guide only so long as it is respected and followed. If it is neglected, or its mandates are rejected, it finally becomes a conspirator instead of a guide, and often volunteers to justify our most destructive habits. Thus the dual nature of the conscience makes it necessary for one to direct it through strict self-discipline.

8. The Sixth Sense. This is the "broadcasting station" of the mind, through which one automatically sends and receives the vibration of thought commonly known as telepathy. It is the medium through which all thought impulses known as "hunches" are received. And it is closely related to, or perhaps it may be a part of, the subconscious section of the mind.

The sixth sense is the medium through which creative vision operates. It is the medium through which all basically new ideas are revealed. And it is the major asset of the minds of all who are recognized as "geniuses."

9. The Memory. This is the "filing cabinet" of the brain, where all thought impulses, all experiences, and all sensations that reach the brain through the five physical senses are stored. And it may be the "filing cabinet" of all impulses of thought which reach the mind through the sixth sense, although all psychologists do not agree with this. The memory is tricky and undependable unless it is organized and directed by self-discipline.

10. The Five Physical Senses. These are the physical "arms" of the brain through which it contacts and acquires information from the external world. The physical senses are not reliable, and therefore they need constant self-discipline. Under any kind of intense emotional activity, the senses become confused and unreliable.

The five physical senses may be deceived by the simplest sort of legerdemain, and they are deceived daily by the common experiences of life. Under the emotion of fear the physical senses often create monstrous "ghosts," which have no existence except in the faculty of the imagination, and there is no fact of life which they will not and do not exaggerate or distort when fear prevails.

Thus we have briefly described the ten factors which enter into all mental activities of humans. But we have supplied enough information concerning the mechanism of the mind to indicate clearly the necessity for self-discipline in their manipulation and use.

Self-discipline is attained by the control of thought habits. And the term "self-discipline" has reference only to the power of thought, because all discipline of self must take place in the mind, although its effects may deal with the functions of the physical body.

The Power of Thought

You are where you are and what you are because of your habits of thought. Let me say that again so that you really absorb this information:

You are where you are and what you are because of your habits of thought.

Your thought habits are the only circumstances of your life over which you have complete control—and this is the most profound of all the facts of your life, because it clearly proves that your Creator recognized the necessity of this great privilege. Otherwise He would not have made it the sole circumstance over which we have been given exclusive control.

Further evidence of the Creator's desire to give humans the unchallengeable right of control over our thought habits has been clearly revealed through the law of Cosmic Habitforce—the medium by which thought habits are fixed and made permanent, so that they become automatic and operate without voluntary effort.

For the present, I am interested only in calling attention to the fact that the Creator of the marvelous mechanism known as a brain ingeniously provided it with a device by which all thought habits are taken over and given automatic expression.

Self-discipline is the principle by which one may voluntarily shape the patterns of thought to harmonize with one's aims and purposes.

This privilege carries with it a heavy responsibility, because it is the one privilege which determines, more than all others, the position in life each person shall occupy. If this privilege is neglected, by one's failure to voluntarily form habits designed to lead to the attainment of definite ends, then the circumstances of life which are beyond one's control will do the job—and what an extremely poor job it often becomes!

Everyone is a bundle of habits. Some are of our own making, while others are involuntary. They are made by fears and doubts, worries and anxieties, greed and superstition, and envy and hatred. Self-discipline is the only means by which one's habits of thought may be controlled and directed until they are taken over and given automatic expression by the law of Cosmic Habitforce. Ponder this thought carefully, for it is the key to your mental, physical, and spiritual destiny.

You can make your thought habits to order and they will carry you to the attainment of any desired goal within your reach. Or you can allow the uncontrollable circumstances of your life to make your thought habits for you and they will carry you irresistibly into failure.

You can keep your mind trained on that which you desire from life and get just that. Or you can feed it on thoughts of that which you do not desire and it will, as unerringly, bring you just that. Your thought habits evolve from the food that your mind dwells upon. That is as certain as night following day.

Turn on the full powers of your will and take complete control of your own mind. It is your mind! It was given to you as a servant to carry out your desires. And no one may enter it or influence it in the slightest degree without your consent and cooperation. What a profound fact this is!

Remember this when the circumstances over which you appear to have no control begin to move in and upset you. Remember it when fear and doubt and worry begin to park themselves in the spare bedroom of your mind. Remember it when the fear of poverty begins to park itself in the space of your mind that should be filled with a prosperity consciousness. And remember, too, that this is self-discipline—the one and only method by which anyone may take full possession of his own mind.

You are not a worm made to crawl in the dust of the earth. If you were, you would have been equipped with the physical means by which you would have crawled on your belly instead of walking on your two legs. Your physical body was designed to enable you to stand and to walk and to think your way to the highest attainment which you are capable of conceiving.

Why be contented with less? Why should you insult your Creator by indifference or neglect in the use of His most priceless gift—the power of your own mind?

The potential powers of the human mind are beyond comprehension. And one of the great mysteries which has endured through the ages consists in our neglect to recognize and to use these powers as a means of shaping our own earthly destiny.

The 20 Great Powers of the Human Mind

The mind has been cleverly provided with a gateway of approach to Infinite Intelligence, through the subconscious section of the mind, and this gateway has been so arranged that it can be opened for voluntary use by preparation through that state of mind known as Faith.

Let me list these powers for you in greater detail:

1. The mind has been provided with a faculty of imagination, wherein may be fashioned ways and means of translating hope and purpose into physical realities. It has been provided with the stimulative capacity of desire and enthusiasm, with which one's plans and purposes may be given action. It has been provided with the power of the will, through which both plan and purpose may be sustained indefinitely.

2. It has been given the capacity for Faith, through which the will and the reasoning faculty may be subdued while the entire machinery of the brain is turned over to the guiding force of Infinite Intelligence. And it has been prepared, through a sixth sense, for direct connection with other minds (under the Master Mind principle), from which it may add to its own power the stimulative forces of other minds which serve effectively to stimulate the imagination.

3. It has been given the capacity to reason, through which facts and theories may be combined into hypotheses, ideas, and plans.

4. It has been given the power to project itself into other minds, through what is known as "telepathy."

5. It has been given the power of deduction, by which it may foretell the future by analysis of the past. This capacity explains why the philosopher looks backward in order to see the future.

6. It has been provided with the means of selection, modification, and control of the nature of its thoughts, thereby giving the privilege of building one's own character to order, to fit any desired pattern, and the power to determine the kind of thoughts which shall dominate the mind.

7. It has been provided with a marvelous filing system for receiving, recording, and re-calling every thought it has expressed, through what is known as a memory, and this marvelous system automatically classifies and files related thoughts in such a manner that the recall of one particular thought leads to the recall of associated thoughts.

8. It has been provided with the power of emotion, through which it can stimulate the body at will for any desired action.

9. It has been given the power to function secretly and silently, thereby ensuring pri-vacy of thought under all circumstances.

10. It has an unlimited capacity to receive, organize, store, and express knowledge on all subjects, in both the fields of physics and metaphysics, the outer world and the inner world.

11. It has the power to aid in the maintenance of sound physical health, and apparently it is the sole source of cure of physical ills, all other sources being merely contribu-tory. And it maintains a perfect repair system for the upkeep of the physical body—a system that works automatically.

12. It maintains and automatically operates a marvelous system of chemistry through which it converts food into suitable combinations for the maintenance and repair of the body.

13. It automatically operates the heart, through which the bloodstream distributes food to every portion of the body and removes all waste materials and worn-out cells of the body.

14. It has the power of self-discipline, through which it can form any desired habit and maintain it until it is taken over by the law of Cosmic Habitforce and is given automatic expression.

15. It is the common meeting ground wherein we may commune with Infinite Intelligence, through prayer (or any form of expressed desire or *Definiteness of Purpose*) by the simple process of opening the gateway of approach through the subconscious section of the mind, by Faith.

16. It is the sole producer of every idea, every tool, every machine, and every mechanical invention created for our convenience in the business of living in a material world.

17. It is the sole source of all happiness and all misery, and of both poverty and riches of every nature whatsoever, and it devotes its energies to the expression of whichever of these that dominates the mind through the power of thought.

18. It is the source of all human relationships, and all forms of intercourse between people; it is the builder of friendships and the creator of enemies, according to the manner in which it is directed.

19. It has the power to resist and defend itself against all external circumstances and conditions, although it cannot always control them.

20. It has no limitations within reason (no limitations except those which conflict with the laws of Nature), save only those the individual accepts through the lack of Faith. Truly, "whatever the mind can conceive and believe, the mind can achieve."

I could continue to give you at least twenty more examples of how amazingly powerful the mind is. And yet, despite all this astounding power of the mind, the great majority of the people make no attempt to take control of their minds, and they suffer themselves to become cowed by fears or difficulties that do not exist save in their own imaginations.

The Folly of Fear

The arch enemy of success is FEAR! We fear poverty in the midst of an overabundance of riches. We fear ill health despite the ingenious system nature has provided with which the physical body is automatically maintained, repaired, and kept in working order.

476

We fear criticism when there are no critics save only those we set up in our own minds through the negative use of our imagination.

We fear the loss of love of friends and relatives, although we know well enough that our own conduct may be sufficient to maintain love through all ordinary circumstances of human relationship.

We fear old age, whereas we should accept it as a medium of greater wisdom and understanding.

We fear the loss of liberty, although we know that liberty is a matter of harmonious relationships with others.

We fear death, when we know it is inevitable, and therefore beyond our control.

We fear failure, not recognizing that every failure carries with it the seed of an equivalent benefit.

And we feared lightning until Franklin and Edison and a few other rare individuals, who dared to take possession of their own minds, proved that lightning is a form of physical energy which can be harnessed and used for the benefit of mankind.

Instead of opening our minds for the guidance of Infinite Intelligence, through Faith, we close our minds tightly with every conceivable shade and degree of self-imposed limitation based upon unnecessary fears.

We know that humans master every other living creature on this earth, yet we fail to look about us and learn from birds of the air and beasts of the jungle that even the dumb animals have been wisely provided with food and all the necessities of their existence through the universal plan which makes all fears groundless and foolish.

We complain of lack of opportunity and cry out against those who dare to take possession of their own minds, not recognizing that everyone who has a sound mind has the right and the power to attain every material thing he needs or can use.

We fear the discomfort of physical pain, not recognizing that pain is a universal language through which we are warned of evils and dangers that need correction.

Because of our fears we go to the Creator with prayers over petty details which we could and should settle for ourselves, then give up and lose Faith (if we had any Faith to begin with) when we do not get the results we ask for, not recognizing our duty to offer prayers of thanks for the bountiful blessings which we have been provided through the power of our minds.

We talk and preach sermons about sin, failing to recognize that the greatest of all sins is the loss of Faith in an all-wise Creator who has provided His children with more blessings than any earthly parent ever thinks of providing for his own children.

We convert the revelations of inventions into the tools of destruction through what we politely call "war," then cry out in protest when the law of compensation pays us off with famines and business depressions.

We abuse the power of the mind in ways too numerous to mention, because we have not recognized that this power can be harnessed through self-discipline and used to serve our needs.

Thus we go all the way through life, eating the husks and throwing away the kernels of plenty!

Some of the Known Facts Concerning the Nature of Thought

Before leaving the analysis of self-discipline, which deals entirely with the mechanism of thought, let me briefly describe some of the known facts and habits of thought in order that we may acquire the art of accurate thinking.

1. All thought (whether it is positive or negative, good or bad, accurate or inaccurate) tends to clothe itself in its physical equivalent, and it does so by inspiring one with ideas, plans, and the means of attaining desired ends, through logical and natural means.

    After thought on any given subject becomes a habit and has been taken over by the law of Cosmic Habitforce, the subconscious section of the mind proceeds to carry it out to its logical conclusion, through the aid of whatever natural media that may be available.

    It may not be literally true that "thoughts are things," but it is true that thoughts create all things, and the things it creates are striking duplicates of the thought patterns from which they are fashioned.

    It is believed by some that every thought one releases starts an unending series of vibrations with which the one who releases the thought will later be compelled to contend; that we are but a physical reflection of thought put into motion and crystallized into physical form by Infinite Intelligence.

    It is also the belief of many that the energy with which we think is but a projected minute portion of Infinite Intelligence, appropriated from the universal supply through the equipment of the brain. No thought contrary to this belief has yet been proved sound.

2. Through the application of self-discipline, thought can be influenced, controlled, and directed through transmutation to a desired end, by the development of voluntary habits suitable for the attainment of any given end.

3. The power of thought (through the aid of the subconscious section of the mind) has control over every cell of the body, carries on all repairs and replacements of injured or dead cells, stimulates their growth, influences the action of all organs of the body and helps them to function by habit and orderliness, and assists in fighting disease through the immune system. These functions are carried on automatically, but many of them may be stimulated by voluntary aid.

4. All achievements begin in the form of thought—organized into plans, aims, and purposes and expressed in terms of physical action. All action is inspired by one or more of the nine basic motives.

5. The entire power of the mind operates through two sections of the mind, the conscious and the subconscious.

   The conscious section is under the control of the individual; the subconscious is controlled by Infinite Intelligence and serves as the medium of communication between Infinite Intelligence and the conscious mind.

   The "sixth sense" is under the control of the subconscious section of the mind and it functions automatically in certain fixed fundamentals, but may be influenced to function in carrying out the instructions of the conscious mind.

6. Both the conscious and the subconscious sections of the mind function in response to fixed habits, adjusting themselves to whatever thought habits the individual may establish, whether the habits are voluntary or involuntary.

7. The majority of all thoughts released by the individual are inaccurate because they are inspired by personal opinions which are arrived at without the examination of facts, or because of bias, prejudice, fear, and the result of emotional excitement in which the faculty of the reason has been given little or no opportunity to modify them rationally.

8. The first step in accurate thinking (a step that is taken by none except those with adequate self-discipline) is that of separating facts from fiction and hearsay evidence. The second step is that of separating facts (after they have been identified as such) into two classes: important and unimportant. An important fact is any fact which can be used to help one attain the object of one's major purpose or any minor purpose leading to one's major purpose.

All other facts are relatively unimportant. The average person spends life dealing with "inferences" based upon unreliable sources of information and unimportant facts. Therefore he or she seldom comes within sight of the form of self-discipline which demands facts and distinguishes the difference between important and unimportant facts.

9. Desire, based on a definite motive, is the beginning of all voluntary thought action associated with individual achievement. The presence in the mind of any intense desire tends to stimulate the faculty of the imagination with the purpose of creating ways and means of attaining the object of the desire. If the desire is continuously held in the mind (through the repetition of thought), it is picked up by the subconscious section of the mind and automatically carried out to its logical conclusion.

These are some of the more important of the known facts concerning the greatest of all mysteries, the mystery of human thought, and they indicate clearly that accurate thinking is attainable only by the strictest habits of self-discipline.

How Self-Discipline May Be Applied

Chart 1 presents a complete description of the ten factors by which the power of thought is expressed. Six of these factors are subject to control through self-discipline:

1. The faculty of the will
2. The faculty of emotions
3. The faculty of reason
4. The faculty of the imagination
5. The faculty of the conscience
6. The faculty of the memory

The remaining four factors act independently, and they are not subject to voluntary control, except that the five physical senses may be influenced and directed by the formation of voluntary habits.

In Chart 2 we have presented a perspective picture which reveals the six departments of the mind over which self-discipline may be easily maintained.

The departments have been numbered in the order of their relative importance, although

Chart No. 1

Chart of the 10 Factors which constitute the "mechanism" of thought. Observe that the subconscious section of the mind has access to all departments of the mind, *but is not under the control of any.*

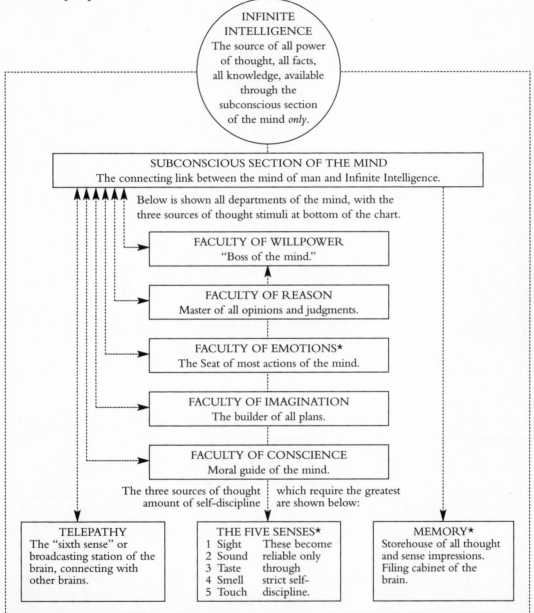

*Not always dependable. Must be under strict discipline at all times.

Chart No. 2

Chart of the Six Departments of the Mind over which self-discipline can be maintained, numbered in the order of their relative importance.

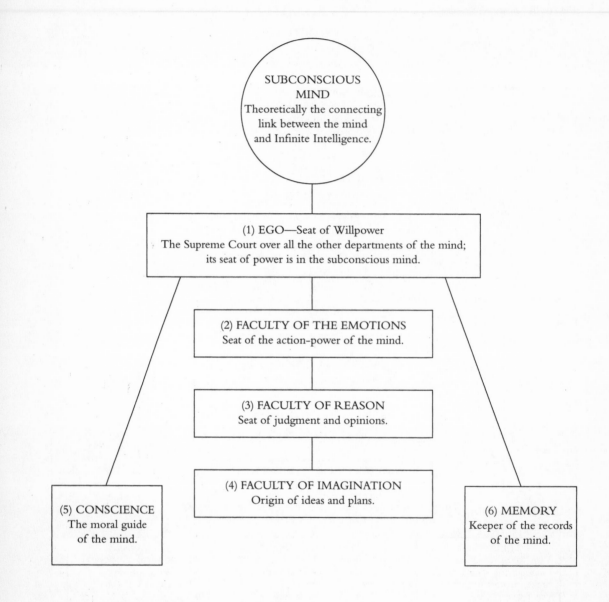

it is impossible for anyone to say definitely which is the more important of these departments, for each is an essential factor in the expression of thought.

We have been given no choice but to place ego, the seat of willpower, in the first position, because the power of the will may control all the other departments of the mind, and it has been properly called the "Supreme Court of the mind," whose decisions are final and not subject to appeal to any higher court.

The faculty of emotions takes second position, since it is well known that most people are ruled by their emotions; therefore, emotions rank next to the "Supreme Court."

The faculty of reason takes third place in importance since it is the modifying influence through which emotional action may be prepared for safe usage. The "well-balanced" mind is the mind which represents a compromise between the faculty of emotions and the faculty of reason. Such a compromise is usually brought about by the power of the "Supreme Court," the faculty of the will.

The faculty of the will sometimes decides with the emotions; at other times it throws its influence on the side of the faculty of reason. But it always has the last word, and whichever side it supports is the winning side of all controversies between reason and the emotions. What an ingenious system this is!

The faculty of the imagination has been given fourth place, since it is the department which creates ideas, plans, and ways and means of attaining desired objectives, all of which are inspired by the faculty of emotions or the faculty of the will.

We might say that the faculty of the imagination serves the mind as a "ways and means committee," but it often acts on its own account and goes off on tours of fantastic exploration in places where it has no legitimate business in connection with the faculty of the will. On these self-inspired tours, the imagination often has the full consent, cooperation, and urge of the emotions, which is the main reason all desires which originate in the faculty of the emotions must be closely scrutinized by the faculty of reason—and countermanded, if need be, by the faculty of the will.

When the emotions and the imagination get out from under the supervision of reason, and the control of the will, they resemble a couple of mischievous schoolboys who have decided to play hooky from school, and wind up at the old swimming hole, or in the neighbor's watermelon patch.

There is no form of mischief which these two may not get into! Therefore, they require more self-discipline than all the other faculties of the mind combined.

The other two departments—the conscience and the memory—are necessary adjuncts of the mind, and while both are important they belong at the end of the list, where they have been assigned.

The subconscious section of the mind has been given the position above all of the other six departments of the mind because it is the connecting link between the conscious mind and Infinite Intelligence, and the medium through which all departments of the mind receive the power of thought.

The subconscious section of the mind is not subject to control, but it is subject to influence, by the means here described. It acts on its own accord, and voluntarily, although its action may be speeded up by intensifying the emotions, or applying the power of the will in a highly concentrated form.

A burning desire behind a *Definite Major Purpose* may stimulate the action of the subconscious section of the mind and speed up its operations.

How the Subconscious Relates to the Parts of the Mind

The relationship between the subconscious section of the mind and the six other departments of the mind, indicated on Chart 2, is similar in many respects to that of the farmer and the laws of Nature through which his crops are grown.

The farmer has certain fixed duties to perform, such as preparing the soil, planting the seed at the right season, and keeping the weeds out, after which his work is finished. From there on out, nature takes over, germinates the seed, develops it to maturity, and yields a crop.

The conscious section of the mind may be compared to the farmer, in that it prepares the way by the formulation of plan and purposes, under the direction of the faculty of the will. If this work is done properly, and a clear picture of that which is desired is created (the picture being the seed of the purpose desired), the subconscious takes over the picture, draws upon the power of Infinite Intelligence for the intelligence needed for the translation of the picture, gets the information necessary, and presents it to the conscious section of the mind in the form of the practical plan of procedure.

Unlike the laws of Nature, which germinate seeds and produce a crop for the farmer within a definite, predetermined length of time, the subconscious takes over the seeds of ideas or purpose submitted to it and fixes its own time for the submission of the plan for their attainment.

Power of will, expressed in terms of a burning desire, is the one medium by which the action of the subconscious may be speeded up. Thus, by taking full possession of one's own mind by exercising the power of the will, one comes into possession of power of stupendous proportions. And the act of mastering the power of the will, so that it may be directed to the attainment of any desired end, is self-discipline of the highest order. Control of the will requires persistence, Faith, and *Definiteness of Purpose.*

In the field of sales, for example, it is a fact well known to all master salespeople that the persistent salesperson heads the list in sales production. In some fields of selling, such as that of life insurance, persistence is the asset of major importance to the salesperson. And persistence, in selling or any other calling, is a matter of strict self-discipline.

In the field of advertising the same rule applies. The most successful advertisers carry on with unyielding persistence, repeating their efforts month after month, year after year, with never-ending regularity; and professional advertising experts have convincing evidence that this is the only policy which will produce satisfactory results.

The pioneers who settled America demonstrated what can be accomplished when willpower is applied with persistence.

At a later period in the history of our country, George Washington and his little army of underfed, half-clothed, underequipped soldiers proved once more that willpower applied with persistence is unbeatable.

And the pioneers of American industry—such greats as Henry Ford, Thomas A. Edison, and Andrew Carnegie—gave us another demonstration of the benefits of willpower, backed by persistence. These pioneers, and all others of their type who have made great contributions to the American way of life, had self-discipline, and they also attained it through the power of the will, backed with persistence.

Andrew Carnegie's entire career provides an excellent example of the benefits which are available through self-discipline. He came to America when he was a very young boy and began work as a laborer. He had only a few friends, none of them wealthy or influential. But he did have an enormous capacity for the expression of his willpower.

By working at manual labor during the day and studying at night, he learned telegraphy, and finally worked his way up to the position of private operator for the division superintendent of the Pennsylvania Railroad Company. In this position he made such effective application of some of the principles of this philosophy, among them the principle of self-discipline, that he attracted the attention of men with money and influence who were in a position to aid him in carrying out the object of his Major Purpose in Life.

At this point in his career, he had precisely the same advantages that hundreds of other telegraph operators enjoyed, but no more. But he did have one asset which the other operators apparently did not possess: the will to win and a definite idea of what he wanted, together with the persistence to carry on until he got it.

This, too, was the outgrowth of self-discipline!

Mr. Carnegie's outstanding qualities were willpower and persistence, plus a strict self-discipline through which these traits were controlled and directed to the attainment of a definite purpose. Beyond these he had no outstanding qualities which are not possessed by someone of average intelligence. By exercising his willpower he adopted a *Definite Major Purpose* and clung to that purpose until it made him America's greatest industrial leader, not to mention the huge personal fortune he accumulated. Out of his willpower, properly self-disciplined and directed to the attainment of a definite purpose, came the great United States Steel Corporation, which revolutionized the steel industry and provided employment for a huge army of skilled and unskilled workers.

Thus we see that a successful person gets started through the application of self-discipline, in pursuit of a definite purpose, and carries on until that purpose is achieved, with the aid of that same principle.

Attaining Personal Power

When Andrew Carnegie said that "the power of will is an irresistible force which recognizes no such reality as failure," he doubtlessly meant that it is irresistible when it is properly organized and directed to a definite end in a spirit of Faith. Obviously, he intended to emphasize three important principles of this philosophy as the basis of all self-acquired self-discipline, such as:

a. Definiteness of Purpose

b. Applied Faith

c. Self-Discipline

It should be remembered, however, that the state of mind which can be developed through these three principles can best be attained, and more quickly, by the application of other principles of this philosophy, among them:

a. The Master Mind
b. A Pleasing Personality
c. The Habit of Going the Extra Mile
d. Personal Initiative
e. Creative Vision

Combine these five principles with Definiteness of Purpose, Applied Faith, and Self-Discipline and you will have an available source of personal power of stupendous proportions.

The beginner in the study of this philosophy may find it difficult to gain control over his or her power of will without approaching that control, step by step, through the mastery and application of these eight principles.

Mastery can be attained in one way only, and that is by constant, persistent application of the principles. They must be woven into one's daily habits and applied in all human relationships, and in the solution of all personal problems. The power of the will responds only to motive persistently pursued. And it becomes strong in the same way that one's arm may become strong—by systematic use.

Those with willpower which has been self-acquired, through self-discipline, do not give up hope or quit when the going becomes hard. Those without willpower do.

A humble general stood in review before an army of tired, discouraged soldiers who had just been badly defeated during the War Between the States. He, too, had a reason to be discouraged, for the war was going against him.

When one of his officers suggested that the outlook seemed discouraging, General Grant lifted his weary head, closed his eyes, clenched his fists, and exclaimed, "We will fight it out along these lines if it takes all summer!" And he did fight it out along the lines he had chosen. Thus it may well be that on this firm decision of one man, backed by an indomitable will, came the final victory which preserved the union of the states.

One school of thought says that "right makes might." Another school of thought says that "might makes right." But those who think accurately know that the power of the will makes might, whether right or wrong, and history backs up this belief.

Study people of great achievement, wherever you find them, and you will find evidence that the power of the will, organized and persistently applied, is the dominating factor in their success. Also, you will find that successful people commit themselves to a stricter system of self-discipline than any which is forced upon them by circumstances beyond their control.

They work when others sleep. They Go the Extra Mile, and if need be another, and still another mile, never stopping until they have contributed the utmost service of which they are capable.

Follow in their footsteps for a single day and you will be convinced that they need no taskmaster to drive them on. They move on their own personal initiative because they direct their efforts by the strictest sort of self-discipline. They may appreciate commendation, but they do not require it to inspire them to action. They listen to condemnation, but they do not fear it, and they are not discouraged by it.

And they sometimes fail, or suffer temporary defeat, just as others do, but failure only spurs them on to greater effort.

They encounter obstacles, as does everyone, but these they convert into benefits through which they carry on toward their chosen goal.

They experience discouragements, the same as others do, but they close the doors of their minds tightly behind unpleasant experiences and transmute their disappointments into renewed energy, with which they struggle ahead to victory.

When death strikes in their families, they bury their dead, but not their indomitable wills.

They seek the counsel of others, extract from it that which they can use, and reject the remainder, although the whole world may criticize them on account of their judgment. They know they cannot control all the circumstances which affect their lives, but they do control their own state of mind and their mental reactions to all circumstances, by keeping their minds positive at all times. They are tested by their own negative emotions, as are all people, but they keep the upper hand over these emotions by making royal servants of them.

Let us keep in mind the fact that through self-discipline one may do two important things, both of which are essential for outstanding achievement: First, one may completely control the negative emotions by transmuting them into constructive effort, using them as an inspiration to greater endeavor. Second, one may stimulate the positive emotions, and direct them to the attainment of any desired end. Thus, if one controls both the positive and the negative emotions, the faculty of reason is left free to function, as is the faculty of the imagination.

Control over the emotions is attained gradually, by the development of habits of thought which are conducive of control. Such habits should be formed in connection with the small, unimportant circumstances of life, for it is true, as Supreme Court Justice Louis Brandeis once said, that "the brain is like the hand. It grows with use."

Controlling the Six Departments of the Mind

One by one, the six departments of the mind which are subject to self-discipline can be brought under complete control, but the start should be made by habits which give one control over the emotions first, since it is true that most people are the victims of their un-controlled emotions throughout their lives. Most people are the servants of their emotions, not the masters, because they have never established definite, systematic habits of control over them.

All who have decided to control the six departments of their minds, through a strict system of self-discipline, should adopt and follow a definite plan to keep this purpose before them.

One student of this philosophy wrote a creed for this purpose, which he followed so closely that it soon enabled him to become thoroughly self-discipline conscious. It worked so successfully that it is here presented for the benefit of other students of the philosophy.

The creed was signed, and repeated orally, twice daily, once upon arising in the morning and once upon retiring at night. This procedure gave the student the benefit of the princi-ple of autosuggestion, through which the purpose of the creed was conveyed clearly to the subconscious section of his mind, where it was picked up and acted upon automatically. I have enclosed a copy of the creed in your orientation packets. To help you get started, I will recite it now. The creed is as follows:

A Creed for Self-Discipline

Willpower. Recognizing that the power of will is the Supreme Court over all other departments of my mind, I will exercise it daily, when I need the urge to action for any purpose; and I will form habits designed to bring the power of my will into action at least once daily.

Emotions. Realizing that my emotions are both positive and negative, I will form daily habits which will encourage the development of the positive emotions, and aid me in converting the negative emotions into some form of useful action.

Reason. Recognizing that both my positive emotions and my negative emotions may be dangerous if they are not controlled and guided to desirable ends, I will submit all my desires, aims and purposes to my faculty of reason, and I will be guided by it in giving expression to these.

Imagination. Recognizing the need for sound plans and ideas for the attainment of my desires, I will develop my imagination by calling upon it daily for help in the formation of my plans.

Conscience. Recognizing that my emotions often err in their over-enthusiasm, and my faculty of reason often is without the warmth of feeling that is necessary to enable me to combine justice with mercy in my judgments, I will encourage my conscience to guide me as to what is right and what is wrong, but I will never set aside the verdicts it renders, no matter what may be the cost of carrying them out.

Memory. Recognizing the value of an alert memory, I will encourage mine to become alert by taking care to impress it clearly with all thoughts I wish to recall, and by associating those thoughts with related subjects which I may call to mind frequently.

Subconscious Mind. Recognizing the influence of my subconscious mind over my power of will, I shall take care to submit to it a clear and definite picture of my Major Purpose in life and all minor purposes leading to my major purpose, and I shall keep this picture constantly before my subconscious mind by repeating it daily.

Discipline over the mind is gained, little by little, by the formation of habits which one may control. Habits begin in the mind; therefore, a daily repetition of this creed will make one habit conscious in connection with the particular kind of habits which are needed to develop and control the six departments of the mind.

The mere act of repeating the names of these departments has an important effect: It makes one conscious that these departments exist, that they are important, that they can be controlled by the formation of thought habits, that the nature of these habits determines one's success or failure in the matter of self-discipline.

It is a great day in any person's life when he or she recognizes the fact that success or failure throughout life is largely a matter of control over emotions.

Before we can recognize this truth, we must recognize the existence and the nature of our emotions, and the power which is available to those who control them—a form of recognition many people never indulge in during their entire lifetime.

Negative Emotions: The Ultimate Enemy

It is a well-known fact that an enemy which has been recognized is an enemy that is half defeated. And this applies to enemies operating within one's own mind as well as to those operating outside it, and especially does it apply to the enemies of negative emotions. Once these enemies have been recognized, one begins, almost unconsciously, to set up habits, through self-discipline, with which to counteract them.

This same reasoning applies also to the benefits of positive emotions, for it is true that a benefit recognized is a benefit easily utilized. The positive emotions are beneficial, for they are a part of the driving force of the mind; but they are helpful only when they are organized and directed to the attainment of definite, constructive ends. If they are not so controlled, they may be as dangerous as any of the negative emotions.

The medium of control is self-discipline, systematically and voluntarily applied through the habits of thought. Take the emotion of Faith, for example: This emotion, the most powerful of all the emotions, may be helpful only when it is expressed through constructive, organized action based on *Definiteness of Purpose*.

Faith without action is useless, because it may resolve itself into mere daydreaming, wishing, and faint hopefulness. Self-discipline is the medium through which one may stimulate the emotion of Faith, through definiteness of purpose persistently applied.

The discipline should begin by establishing habits which stimulate the use of the power of the will, for it is the ego—the seat of the power of the will—in which one's desires originate. Thus, the emotions of desire and Faith are definitely related. Wherever a burning desire exists, there exists also the capacity for Faith, which corresponds precisely with the intensity of the desire. The two are associated always. Stimulate one and you stimulate the other. Control and direct one, through organized habits, and you control and direct the other. This is self-discipline of the highest order.

The Self-Discipline of One of England's Greatest Prime Ministers

Benjamin Disraeli, known to all the history books as one of the greatest prime ministers England has ever known, summarized his great achievements in one sentence: "The secret of success is constancy of purpose."

He began his career as an author but was not highly successful in that field. None of his dozen or so books made a great impression on the public. Then he entered politics, with his mind set on becoming the prime minister of what was then the far-flung British Empire.

He became a member of Parliament from Maidstone, but his first speech to Parliament was widely recognized as a failure.

Fighting on, he became the leader of the House of Commons and later the chancellor of the exchequer. He then realized his Definite Major Purpose by becoming prime minister. Here he met with terrific opposition, enough to make him resign.

But he staged a comeback, and was elected prime minister a second time, after which he became a great builder of empires. His greatest achievement was the building of the Suez Canal. None of this would have happened if Disraeli's career had not been built on self-discipline.

Disraeli succeeded in pushing himself past the greatest of all the danger points of the majority of people: They give up and quit when the going becomes tough; and often they quit when one more step would have carried them triumphantly to victory.

Willpower is needed most when the oppositions of life are the greatest. And self-discipline will provide it for every such emergency, whether it be great or small.

Former American president Theodore Roosevelt was another example of what can happen when a leader is motivated by the will to win despite great handicaps. During his early youth he was seriously handicapped by chronic asthma and weak eyes. His friends despaired of his ever regaining his health, but he did not share their views, thanks to his recognition of the power of self-discipline.

He went West, joined a group of hard-hitting outdoor workers, and placed himself under a definite system of self-discipline, through which he built a strong body and a resolute mind. Some doctors said he could not do it, but he refused to accept their verdict.

In his battle to regain his health, he acquired such perfect discipline over himself that he went back East, entered politics, and kept on driving until his will to win made him president of the United States.

Those who knew him best have said that his outstanding quality was a will which refused to accept defeat as anything more than an urge to greater effort. Beyond this, his ability, his education, his experience were in no way superior to similar qualities possessed by those all around him of whom the public heard little or nothing.

While he was president, some army officials complained of an order he gave them to keep physically fit. To show that he knew what he was talking about, he rode horseback a hundred miles, over rough Virginia roads, with the army officials trailing after him, trying hard to keep pace.

Behind all this physical action was an active mind which was determined not to be handicapped by physical weakness, and that mental activity reflected itself throughout his administration in the White House.

When the mind says "go forward," the physical body responds to its command, thus proving the truth of Andrew Carnegie's statement that "our only limitations are those which we set up in our own minds."

A French expedition had tried to build the Panama Canal, but failed.

Theodore Roosevelt said, "The canal shall be built," and he went to work then and there to express his faith in terms of action. The canal was built! Personal power is wrapped up in the will to win! But it can be released for action only by self-discipline and by no other means.

Perseverance Pays Off

Robert Louis Stevenson was a delicate youth from the day of his birth. His health prevented him from doing any steady work at his studies until he was past seventeen. At twenty-three his health became so bad that his physicians sent him to the South.

There he met the woman of his choice and fell in love. His love for her was so great that it gave him a new lease on life, a new motive for action, and he began to write, although his physical body was scarcely strong enough to carry him around. He kept on writing until he had greatly enriched the world by his writings, now universally accepted as masterpieces.

The same motive, love, has given the wings of thought to many another who, like Robert Louis Stevenson, has made this a richer and a better world. Without the motive of love, Stevenson doubtlessly would have died without having made his contributions to mankind. He transmuted his feeling for the woman he loved into literary works, through habits of self-discipline which placed the six departments of his mind under his control.

In a similar manner Charles Dickens converted a love tragedy into literary works which have enriched the world. Instead of going down under the blow of his disappointment in his first love affair, he drowned his sorrow through the intensity of his action in writing. In that manner he closed the door behind an experience which many another might have used as a door of escape from his duty—an alibi for his failure.

Through self-discipline he converted his greatest sorrow into his greatest asset, for it revealed to him the presence of that "other self" wherein lay the power of genius which he reflected in his literary works.

There is one unbeatable rule for the mastery of sorrows and disappointments, and that is transmutation of those emotional frustrations, through definitely planned work. It is a rule with no equal.

And the secret of its power is self-discipline.

Freedom of body and mind, independence, and economic security are the results of personal initiative expressed through self-discipline. By no other means may these universal desires be assured.

We Near the End of Our Journey

Our journey together is about ended. You must travel the remainder of the distance alone. If you have followed the instructions I have given you, in the right kind of mental attitude, you are now in possession of the great Master-Key, which will unlock the gate to success.

Now I shall reveal to you a great truth of the utmost importance: The Master-Key to Riches consists entirely in the greatest power known to man, the power of thought!

You may take full possession of the Master-Key by taking possession of your own mind, through the strictest of self-discipline.

Through self-discipline you may think yourself into or out of any circumstance of life.

Self-discipline will help you to control your mental attitude. Your mental attitude may help you to master every circumstance of your life, and to convert every adversity, every defeat, every failure into an asset of equivalent scope. That is why a Positive Mental Attitude heads the entire list of the Twelve Riches of Life.

Therefore, it should be obvious to you that the great Master-Key to Riches is nothing more nor less than the self-discipline necessary to help you take full and complete possession of your own mind!

Start right where you stand, and become the master of yourself. Start now! Be done forever with that old self which has kept you in misery and want. Recognize and embrace that "other self" which can give you everything your heart craves. Remember, it is profoundly significant that the only thing over which you have complete control is your own mental attitude!

INDEXES

INDEX TO
YOUR MAGIC POWER TO BE RICH

INDEX TO
THE MAGIC LADDER TO SUCCESS

INDEX TO

THE MASTER-KEY TO RICHES

ABOUT THE AUTHORS

Napoleon Hill was born in 1883 in Virginia and died in 1970 after a long and successful career as a consultant to business leaders, a lecturer, and an author. *Think and Grow Rich* is the all-time bestseller in its field, having sold more than 15 million copies worldwide, and set the standard for today's motivational thinking.

Arthur R. Pell, Ph.D., who revised *Think and Grow Rich,* is the author of numerous articles and books on management, career planning, and human relations. His books include *The Complete Idiot's Guide to Managing People* and *The Complete Idiot's Guide to Team Building.*

Patricia G. Horan, who revised *The Magic Ladder to Success* and *The Master-Key to Riches,* is a thirty-year veteran of New York book and magazine publishing, as well as an award-winning author, editor, copywriter, and playwright. She is the author of *177 Favorite Poems for Children* and is the editorial director of *WisdomHouseBooks.com.*